TEXAS BBQ

THE ART OF LOW AND SLOW

TEXAS BBQ

THE ART OF LOW AND SLOW

 • 13-Digit ISBN: 978-1-40034-039-2 • 10-Digit ISBN: 1-40034-093-X • This book may be ordered by mail from the publisher. Please include $5.99 for postage and handling. Please support your local bookseller first! • Books published by Cider Mill Press Book Publishers are available at special discounts for bulk purchases in the United States by corporations, institutions, and other organizations. For more information, please contact the publisher. • Cider Mill Press Book Publishers • "Where good books are ready for press" • 501 Nelson Place • Nashville, Tennessee 37214, USA • cidermillpress.com • HarperCollins Publishers, Macken House, 39/40 Mayor Street Upper, Dublin 1, D01 C9W8, Ireland (https://www.harpercollins.com) • Typography: Sofia Pro, ITC Quorum Std • Printed in Malaysia • 25 26 27 28 29 PJM 5 4 3 2 1 • First Edition

John Brotherton

December 3, 1974–January 15, 2024

This book is dedicated to John Brotherton, founder of Brother's Black Iron Barbecue, whose passion, generosity, and unmatched sense of humor left an indelible mark on all of us. Revered by his peers, John was not just a friend, but a mentor, cheerleader, and constant source of encouragement for everyone around him. His vibrant personality, unwavering support, and relentless drive to collectively learn and grow have significantly helped shape the industry and promote community over competition, earning him the affectionate title of "the mayor of Texas barbecue." While these pages were being written, we lost a larger-than-life leader, but his legacy and love for the craft live on in every flame stoked, every bite shared, and every person whose life he touched.

CONTENTS

Tootsie Tomanetz, legendary pitmaster at Snow's BBQ

INTRODUCTION

When I moved to Austin two decades ago, I was just emerging from a plant-based collegiate lifestyle, and my East Coast upbringing hadn't educated me on the likes of brisket or ribs. But the scent of oak-kissed meat quickly won my attention, wafting through the air and wrapping around me like a warm embrace. Like many newcomers to Central Texas, some of my first experiences with barbecue took place at Salt Lick BBQ, enjoying endless family-style plates of meat while golden beams of sunlight filtered through the oak grove, and I spent countless hours on the smoke-steeped patio of Ruby's BBQ, a beloved institution for blues and brisket. As my food writing career progressed through the years, I found myself diving deeper into the world of Texas barbecue, uncovering the layers of flavor, tradition, and innovation that make it so unique.

While there have been some excellent books written about the history and traditions of Texas barbecue, none have captured the most recent developments. Barbecue in Texas is constantly changing, and in the past decade, it has undergone somewhat of a renaissance. Ask 10 different people who makes the best barbecue in the state, and you'll get 10 different answers, each one passionately defended. My reply, since researching and writing this book, is now, "Well, that depends what type of barbecue you like." The truth is, the genre encompasses such a range of styles, techniques, and influences that there's no simple answer. But this is to be expected, given the rich tapestry of cultures that have all played a huge role in shaping Texas barbecue over the years.

Native American tribes, like the Caddo, first taught Texans to cook over fire and smoked both fish and meat as a means of preservation. When the Spanish settlers arrived in the seventeenth and eighteenth centuries, they introduced cattle ranching to Texas, which led to beef becoming a major industry and economic driver in the state. The Mexican vaqueros who drove herds of cattle, sheep, and horses brought the tradition of barbacoa—smoking meat in an underground pit—up north into what would become South Texas. In the early nineteenth century, German and Czech settlers opened meat markets, smoked their leftover cuts, and introduced sausage-making techniques that would become integral to Central Texas barbecue. In the latter half of the century, newly freed African American slaves brought with them traditional pit-smoking and cooking techniques as they migrated to Texas from the South, significantly shaping East Texas barbecue.

Long before it became a culinary obsession, Texas barbecue was a practice born of necessity, rooted in sustainability and deeply tied to place. It began as a way to utilize available resources—the wood from drought-stricken trees, remaining cuts from local animals—and turn those humble ingredients into something extraordinary. This zero-waste, "make something from nothing" ethos is still alive today, championed by innovative spots like LeRoy and Lewis Barbecue in Austin. As Bryan Bracewell of Southside Market & Barbeque so eloquently puts it, "That's the beauty of barbecue: it should be an extension of your community and your family and who you are."

Texas barbecue has always been—and continues to be—a melting pot of diverse influences and contributions. The traditions upheld by legendary institutions are crucial to its enduring legacy. Iconic establishments like Louie Mueller Barbecue in Taylor, Cooper's in Llano, City Market in Luling, and Kreuz Market and Smitty's in Lockhart laid the foundational groundwork for Texas barbecue, serving not only as the pillars of the craft, but also as training grounds and inspiration for aspiring pitmasters. When Aaron Franklin (pictured below and profiled on page 233) opened Franklin Barbecue in 2009, his meticulous DIY approach—and unmatched dedication to quality—disrupted the Texas barbecue scene and helped inspire a whole new generation. Franklin's influence bridged the gap between the old school and the new school, pushing the

boundaries of what Texas barbecue could be. Since then, more and more people have taken up the craft, many adding their own unique cultural influences. In this book, you'll learn about pitmasters who have enriched Texas barbecue by incorporating flavors and techniques from Egypt, Vietnam, Pakistan, Italy, Ethiopia, and beyond.

In many parts of the world, the word "barbecue" might conjure up a casual backyard gathering. But in Texas, barbecue is not just a meal. It's a ritual, a craft—some even treat it like a religion. Smoker seekers rise early, sometimes before sunrise, to wait in long lines for the best bites, and make pilgrimages from across the country—and the world—to taste the state's smoked treasures. I have to agree with this statement by John Bates of InterStellar BBQ: "Texas barbecue deserves to be at the top of the conversation when you talk about American food from the South."

From its humble beginnings to its current status as a culinary icon, Texas barbecue remains a reflection of the people and cultures who have shaped it. In working on this book project, I've had the privilege of meeting pitmasters who bootstrapped their way to success by changing careers, taking bold risks, and building something remarkable through sheer grit and passion. It has been an honor to capture their stories here, and I have no doubt you'll find them just as inspiring as I do. Because whether you're a Lone Star native or a first-time visitor, one thing is certain: in Texas, barbecue isn't just food—it's a way of life.

GLOSSARY

Texas barbecue comes with a language all its own, and this glossary is here to help you speak it. From cooking techniques to pit-side slang, these terms will help you navigate the stories, traditions, and flavors that define Texas barbecue.

OFFSET SMOKER/PIT

This style of smoker has become synonymous with Texas barbecue. An offset features a main cooking chamber with a separate firebox attached to the side. Wood is burned in the firebox, and the heat and smoke are drawn into the main chamber, cooking the meat indirectly at low temperatures over the course of many hours. Offset smokers require frequent attention and considerable skill, and are often fueled exclusively with wood, which is why you'll sometimes hear them called "stick burners."

REVERSE FLOW SMOKER/PIT

Unlike a traditional offset smoker, where smoke travels directly from the firebox to the smokestack, a reverse flow pit uses a metal baffle or plate beneath the cooking surface to channel heat and smoke to the far end of the smoker first, then back across the meat toward the smokestack, which is placed on the same side as the firebox. This "reversed" airflow helps reduce hot spots, maintains a more consistent temperature across the cooking chamber, and allows the smoke to flow more evenly over the meat.

FIREBOX

The firebox is the attached chamber on an offset smoker where the fire is built and maintained. Wood is burned here to generate heat and smoke, which then flows into the main cooking chamber to cook the meat indirectly. Managing the firebox—controlling airflow, temperature, and clean smoke—is key to mastering the offset smoker and achieving that signature low-and-slow Texas barbecue flavor.

SMOKESTACK

The smokestack is the vertical pipe responsible for drawing heat and smoke through the smoker. It creates a draft that pulls air from the firebox across the meat, helping regulate temperature and ensuring proper smoke circulation. A well-designed and well-managed smokestack is essential for achieving clean, even burns and that ideal thin, blue smoke prized in Texas barbecue.

DAMPER

The damper is a movable vent that controls airflow into the smoker, typically located in two places: an intake damper on the firebox side and an exhaust damper on the smokestack. By adjusting the dampers, pitmasters can regulate how much oxygen reaches the fire, which in turn affects the temperature and intensity of the burn. Opening the damper allows more oxygen in, fueling a hotter fire, while closing it slows the burn and lowers the heat. Mastering damper control is essential for maintaining steady temperatures and clean smoke during long cooks.

PEACH PAPER

This refers to the pink or peach-colored butcher paper used by pitmasters to wrap meats during the smoking process. This paper is favored over aluminum foil because it allows the meat to breathe, permitting steam to escape and helping maintain a crispy bark while retaining moisture.

BARK

Bark is the dark, flavorful crust formed during smoking as a result of heat, smoke, seasoning, and the Maillard reaction, a chemical reaction between amino acids and reducing sugars that occurs at higher temperatures.

MEAT GRADES

In Texas barbecue, meat grade plays a significant role in the quality of the final product. The grade is essentially a rating given to meat based on factors like marbling (fat content), age, and texture. Pitmasters often favor beef with higher grades like Prime (the highest level) and Choice because of the balance between flavor, tenderness, and fat content.

WOOD SEASONING

Seasoning refers to the process of allowing the wood to dry out and cure over time (around a year is preferred) before it's used for smoking. Freshly cut (green) wood contains a high moisture content, which makes it difficult to burn efficiently and produces a lot of smoke.

BRISKET POINT/DECKLE

A brisket is a large cut of beef that comes from the lower chest area of the cow. The point is the thicker, more marbled section of the brisket. It's often referred to as the "deckle," which is a layer of fat that connects the point to the flat. The point typically takes longer to cook, and is often cooked to a higher internal temperature to break down the fat, resulting in a melt-in-your-mouth texture. This part of the brisket is also referred to as the "moist" cut.

BRISKET FLAT

The flat is the leaner, thinner section of the brisket, located on the bottom side of the cut, and has a thin layer of fat on top called the "fat cap." The fat cap helps to protect the meat during smoking and keeps it moist, but it can be trimmed depending on personal preference. The flat cooks more evenly than the point and is often the first part to reach a desirable level of tenderness.

BURNT ENDS

Crispy, caramelized chunks of meat that come from the brisket point after it has been cubed, re-seasoned, and smoked further until they develop a crispy, caramelized crust and tender, juicy interior.

SMOKE RING

The smoke ring is a pinkish band that forms just below the surface of the brisket, created by a chemical reaction that occurs during the smoking process. The smoke ring is often seen as an indicator of good barbecue, signaling that the meat was cooked properly and exposed to ideal conditions.

BINDER

The binder is a layer of liquid or fat rubbed onto the surface of the meat (typically brisket) before it is seasoned with dry rub. Its main purpose is to help the seasoning adhere to the meat and form a flavorful, textured bark during the smoking process. While using a binder isn't necessary, it is a tool many pitmasters use to improve upon their final product.

BRISKET STALL

The brisket stall is a period of time (up to four hours) where the meat's internal temperature stops rising, usually between 150°F and 170°F. Some pitmasters use the "Texas Crutch," a method of wrapping the brisket in butcher paper or aluminum foil, once it hits the stall. This helps to retain moisture, speed up the cooking process, and push through the stall more quickly.

RESTING

Resting is the period of time meat sits after it has been removed from the smoker or grill and before it's sliced and served. It allows the juices inside the meat to redistribute, ensuring a more tender and flavorful piece of barbecue. After brisket (or any other meat) has finished cooking, it should rest for about 10 to 20 minutes, and larger cuts can rest for even longer, 30 minutes or more.

HOLDING

Holding refers to keeping the meat at a safe, warm temperature after it has been cooked and before it's served. Holding is generally done after resting and often done using cabinets are designed to keep cooked meats at a temperature of between 140°F to 160°F for extended periods of time.

TEXAS TRINITY

This phrase is used for the three essential meats that define traditional Texas barbecue: brisket, sausage, and pork ribs.

HOT LINKS

These spicy sausages are a staple in East Texas barbecue, and typically made from a combination of beef and pork seasoned with chile peppers, garlic, paprika, onions, and black pepper.

HOT GUTS

Hot guts, associated with Central Texas and West Texas barbecue, are primarily made from beef, with pork fat added for moisture, and spiced with garlic, chili powder, and black pepper. Hot guts are typically looser in texture than hot links, with a higher fat content and a more subtle spice.

JUICY LINKS

Also known as "grease balls," these juicy, coarsely ground beef sausages are only found at a handful of establishments in Southeast Texas. They are made with pork fat, heavily seasoned, and hand-tied, then traditionally served by squeezing the sausage out of its casing onto white bread.

NORTH TEXAS

GOLDEE'S BARBECUE

FORT WORTH

Childhood friendships often fade with time, but the founders of Goldee's Barbecue defied the odds. Not only did Jalen Heard, Dylan Taylor, Lane Milne, Jonny White, and Nupohn Inthanousay maintain their bond, but they also transformed it into a thriving barbecue business. After growing up together in Arlington, Texas, the group's journey into barbecue began when they moved to Austin after high school.

"It's something we didn't really grow up eating, so it was kind of different when we got out to Austin, seeing how good barbecue can be," says Heard, whose early idea of barbecue was what fast casual regional chains were serving. "I mean, we were used to Dickey's, Spring Creek—those type of places."

"We got into barbecue because it was a regional cuisine to Texas," adds Milne. "It was intriguing for us to try barbecue spots from all over the map and explore new towns."

After visiting independently owned barbecue joints around Central Texas, they started working at some of the state's most legendary spots. Taylor and White worked together at la Barbecue (see page 249) while Heard and Milne worked at Freedmen's. Then they branched out to work on their own—White at Franklin Barbecue (see page 233 for a profile on founder Aaron Franklin) and Valentina's Tex-Mex BBQ, Taylor at

Truth BBQ (see page 121) and Terry Black's Barbecue (see page 359), Milne at Micklethwait Craft Meats (see page 271), and Heard at Banger's Sausage House & Beer Garden.

These experiences helped them build a strong foundation in the art of smoking meat. After six years of working for others, however, they began identifying elements that they would change if they had their own place, and set the wheels in motion. The group decided it was time to team up and carve out a path of their own, and started seeking out a space for their concept in the Fort Worth area. Milne's mom lived in Kinnedale, a neighborhood southeast of downtown, and knew of an old barbecue joint that had been abandoned for quite some time. Not only was the humble barn-red shack already set up for their purposes, but it came with plenty of parking and a spacious area for a pit room.

"We're as far as you can be from downtown while still being in Fort Worth," says White. "When we found this building, we said if the food was good enough, people would come out for it. So that was our main focus."

After extensive recipe development and countless taste tests, the team came together on meat-smoking techniques and crafted a lineup of sides that could stand on their own, regardless of the protein they sat next to. They opened the doors of their brick-and-mortar location in February 2020, only to face an unforeseen challenge: just five weekends later, the pandemic forced them to shut down. But rather than despair, they used the unexpected downtime to refine their recipes and streamline their processes.

"We'd come in and make all the sides and then bring them to our parents and anybody else to try," remembers Heard. "I would say the sides really improved because of that. COVID was bad, but our food got a lot better because we slowed it down and figured it out. We got our cook schedules better too, and learned that way."

A month later, when Goldee's was able to open for takeout and curbside service, they'd perfected pillowy housemade brioche, in lieu of packaged sliced white bread, and zingy housemade dill pickles. Their sides include jalapeño-kissed cheesy grits, creamy and herbaceous potato salad, tangy Dijon coleslaw made with shredded cabbage and kale, flavorful chili beans simmered with tender strands of brisket, and a unique, savory pork-and-rice hash. Dubbed Kinnebac hash and inspired by their travels to South Carolina, it serves as a vehicle to utilize pork rib trimmings.

The Goldee's team developed two different all-beef sausages made with brisket trim. The house link features pops of flavor from mustard seeds and coarse black pepper, and the jalapeño cheese features pieces of the chile pepper tempered by ribbons of melted cheddar. After tasting Inthanousay's recipe for Lao sausage, they developed it into a Central

Texas-style smoked sausage, served with sticky rice and jeow som, a sweet-and-sour dipping sauce. At first, they offered this as an April special to celebrate the Laotian New Year, but due to its popularity, it began making more regular appearances on the menu, along with other Laotian specials like smoked laab made with ground beef and herbs, gai ping (grilled chicken), sin savanh (a version of beef jerky), and mango sticky rice.

Even while operating as a takeout-only restaurant for the entire first year of its existence, Goldee's drew statewide acclaim, thanks to glowing write-ups in *Texas Monthly*, *The Dallas Morning News*, *D Magazine*, and more. The crew started offering free beer to the lengthening line winding through the parking lot.

By the spring of 2021, Goldee's opened its dining room for the first time and, that fall, *Texas Monthly* awarded them the coveted number 1 spot on its Top 50 barbecue list. Now guests began arriving the night before, armed with umbrellas, camp chairs, coolers—I even spotted a playpen on one visit. Inside, a neighboring table had trays piled high with meat, an entire loaf of housemade bread, and a towering stack of banana puddings. They were shouting exclamations and expletives with full mouths.

"The first hour is hardcore barbecue heads," explains White. "They want to get their wait's worth for sure. Everyone tends to overorder here—but that's what I do when I go to barbecue places too!"

Goldee's approach to smoked meats is as meticulous as it is straightforward, with every detail carefully refined. Their fires are fueled by post oak, aged for at least eight months to achieve optimal burn and flavor. They've crafted their own signature seasoning salt—a housemade twist on Lawry's—made from a blend of paprika, table salt, cayenne, garlic powder, onion powder, celery salt, and sugar. This versatile seasoning is the sole component used on their pork belly, which is smoked to a tender, juicy interior encased in perfectly rendered fat, then finished with a peach sauce infused with oregano, thyme, and turmeric.

"It's our play on a Greek sausage called loukaniko," explains Milne. "What makes barbecue special is the way all of the little details build up and affect the final product."

Their brisket is seasoned with a simple yet precise blend of 16-mesh black pepper, table salt, and that signature seasoning salt, then smoked to perfection on 1,000-gallon Mill Scale offset pits. According to White, fire management is a crucial factor in achieving the exceptional flavor and texture that define their final product.

"We're intense about our fire management," says White. "We build fires that are really chill—not big raging fires—then we trap a lot of heat with the doors closed and the damper closed, and it's a much softer, more humid environment. So we're able to take the brisket all the way until it's done, and then it might be a little crispy, but then we rest it in the foil and it softens all the way back."

Both pork ribs and turkey are rubbed with just the house seasoning salt and black pepper. The Goldee's team designed a backyard pit with M&M BBQ Company, and they use that to smoke up to 18 turkeys at a time. The succulent slices of white meat are deliciously complemented by their Carolina-inspired, mustard-based sauce. Goldee's spareribs are a particular standout. Juicy, flavorful meat pulls off the bone with just the right amount of give and a light, vinegar-based glaze results in the perfect amount of tangy caramelization. An investment in an M&M rotisserie smoker has made smoking their pork ribs much more efficient in recent years, and just as flawless.

Goldee's was originally named after Taylor's golden Ford F-250, which accompanied the team in the early days of their journey. While Taylor has since moved on to working on a regenerative ranch, he remains a partner and an integral part of the Goldee's story.

"Working with friends has been a blast," says Milne. "You become better communicators and closer through the ups and downs."

Heard echoes the sentiment. "It's definitely fun working with your friends. I mean, we obviously fight, but it's fine because we've been friends for years. We all have an end goal for what we want to do, so at the end of the day, it's just business up here."

The team has become quite known for fostering a spirit of collaboration within the barbecue community. The pitmasters behind both Redbird BBQ (see page 204), Barbs B Q, Bar-A-BBQ (see page 139) and Sabar BBQ (see page 60) spent time learning the ropes at Goldee's, and Inthanousay has been developing a Laotian-Texas barbecue pop-up called Dually's when he's not working at Goldee's.

"Being surrounded by like-minded, creative people helps us to continue learning and to stay creative in our techniques, recipe making, and methods," says Milne. "I think trying to keep barbecue processes a secret only hinders yourself and the cuisine from progressing. We feel confident in our abilities and food and truly love doing our part in growing the barbecue community."

They currently offer brisket classes, and plan on offering more classes in the future. In these hands-on workshops, attended by both professionals and passionate hobbyists, they freely share tips and recipes. (Though, as Heard notes, they are constantly tweaking their recipes, always striving to improve.)

"I write recipes down for our classes, and I just tell them, 'Hey, if you want to be original, use this as a base and just add one cool ingredient and then you made it your own!'" says White.

Goldee's ongoing success has garnered numerous accolades, including being named James Beard Award semifinalists in 2023, *Food & Wine* Best New Chefs in 2024, and receiving a prestigious Michelin Bib Gourmand award in late 2024. The team feels awed and humbled by these recognitions, and remains focused on innovating and expanding Texas barbecue's boundaries.

"I like how things are moving from traditional barbecue to traditional dishes with a smoke element to it," says Heard. "It's the new generation. Barbecue's getting a little bit younger now, and I think that's a cool thing."

Though they want to keep Goldee's its own singular location, the crew has some other concept ideas up their sleeve. In 2023, they opened a more fast-casual, rib-focused concept in a former Sonic in central Fort Worth. Ribbee's offers baby back ribs in rotating flavors, a more classic creamy coleslaw, seasoned fries, and housemade honey butter rolls. They also serve Goldee's thick, custardy banana pudding, which is topped with a generous shower of cookie crumble.

"We have an ever-growing list of ideas we would like to do at some point in the future, but just like we did with Goldee's, we want to take our time and do it the way we like best," says Milne. "That's the Goldee's way!"

PANTHER CITY BBQ

FORT WORTH

Panther City BBQ's remarkable rise began from humble roots. That trajectory makes it even more fitting that owners Chris Magallanes and Ernie Morales named the business after their city's own story of resilience and growth.

The nickname "Panther City" dates back to the late 1800s, when a Dallas lawyer wrote a letter to the *Dallas Herald* remarking that Fort Worth was so desolate, he spotted a panther sleeping in the middle of Main Street. His comment was meant to disparage the city, which had taken an economic downturn after the Civil War, but locals instead embraced the panther as a symbol of their strength. Not long after that, the railroad was built and Fort Worth became a trade hub, with cattle beginning to be shipped via rail.

Today, there is a sleeping panther statue in downtown Fort Worth, and many local businesses proudly use the Panther City moniker in their name. Panther City BBQ has the sleek cat emblazoned on a round medallion painted on the front of their building. They too started small, and they're now one of the top-rated barbecue joints in Texas.

Morales's sister and brother-in-law introduced him to their good friend Magallanes, who was a project manager for an audiovisual company at the time.

Magallanes needed some extra hands for a big project out in Lubbock and hired Morales to help with it.

"He ended up being one of my best employees," says Magallanes. "We started hanging out through that and grilling every single weekend. Ernie, my brother, friends—we would all get together and make fajitas, taquitos, burgers."

In 2014, the two decided to enter the competition circuit. And when they entered their first barbecue competition together in Burleson, they ended up being named champions for their brisket, half chicken, and ribs.

"We screwed up a lot of barbecue first," admits Magallanes. "It was very expensive, which is one of the main reasons we started selling it. Because the wife was like, 'You can't keep making three or four or five briskets a week, we're gonna go broke!'"

Before selling their barbecue for the public, though, they had to adapt their style from the over-the-top dishes they'd perfected to win competitions.

"Competition is a completely different thing," explains Magallanes. "You're dressing it up and basting it and injecting it. The way you cut it and trim it—everything's different. It's a one-bite wow for the judge . . . You'd get sick after two or three bites. It would just be too much."

In 2015, the duo started doing Panther City BBQ pop-ups at breweries around town, and quickly became known not only for their velveteen post-oak smoked brisket and tender pork ribs, but for playful offerings like brisket-topped pizza and sides with a Mexican twist—interpretations of the things they'd grown up cooking and eating. Their most popular item became their creamy elotes (which Ernie was known for making at cookouts) topped with juicy chopped brisket, queso fresco, hot sauce, and cilantro.

Heim Barbecue (see page 50) had been the first to bring craft barbecue to Fort Worth, and when they partnered with investors to open their first restaurant, the food truck they'd been using became available. Morales and Magallanes leased it from the owners, who ran a dive bar on the property, and opened in January 2018.

Travis Heim had created and popularized pork belly burnt ends, and Panther City BBQ had been selling those at their pop-ups. But now that they were taking over Heim's former space, they wanted to serve something that bore their own signature. Texas Twinkies, the bacon-wrapped jalapeños stuffed with brisket and cream cheese created by Hutchins Barbeque (see page 69), had also grown in popularity. So Magallanes and Morales came up with a marriage of the two ideas, and created the pork belly burnt end popper: a smoked-and-glazed pork belly burnt end stuffed with cream cheese into a jalapeño, and then wrapped with bacon.

we said, 'Who's gonna hate on bacon wrapped in bacon?'" laughs Magallanes.

By mid-2019, Panther City BBQ had expanded into a small building on the property, where customers could walk up and order at a window, and enjoy their barbecue at picnic tables or inside Republic Street Bar. Magallanes and Morales continued to expand their menu, offering succulent turkey rubbed with cayenne and cumin and two types of snappy house-made sausage (jalapeño cheese and beef garlic).

While much of the brisket trim went into those sausages, they still had even more to use, so Magallanes developed a brisket guisada he still runs as a weekend special. First he makes a slurry of tallow, spices, flour, and water, then he braises cubed brisket scraps in that spicy gravy. It is great on its own, or sprinkled with cheese and folded into a griddled beef tallow flour tortilla. Another weekend special is beef cheek barbacoa, available by the pound or tucked into corn tortillas and topped with onion and cilantro. These street tacos, which Panther City has become known for, can also be filled with brisket or pulled pork, or made into quesadillas.

In 2020, beef birria had made its way from Mexico to California and then on to Texas, where it was trending. Magallanes took inspiration from crispy quesabirria tacos to create his own cheese-griddled taco, stuffed with brisket or barbacoa, asadero cheese, onions, and cilantro. He passed them out for free one day and they were a huge hit, so he rolled them out the next week. Morales's brother, whose nickname is "Flaco," was manning the griddle at the time, so the name—Flaco's Tacos—pretty much wrote itself.

Seeing their success with creative items (and particularly their Mexican-inspired offerings), Morales and Magallanes continued to add on to their menu with sides like a smoked spicy mac and cheese finished on the pit, borracho beans, spicy vinegar slaw, and collards made smoky and spicy with bacon, brisket tallow, and jalapeño. They found potato salad to be polarizing, so they offer two. Flaco's Half-Baked Potato Salad has a sour cream base and is topped with cheese, crumbled bacon, and chives—the cold version of a loaded baked potato. The dill potato salad has a little mayo, a little mustard, and lots of herbaceous notes from fresh dill.

"I think, not just in Texas but everywhere, if your potato salad is not like your grandma's, nobody likes it," says Magallanes. "You know, some hate mustard, some hate mayo. So we offer two different ones."

As Panther City BBQ continued to grow and flourish, Morales and Magallanes established a barbecue brotherhood of sorts. Rookie pitmasters like Brandon Hurtado, Dayne Weaver (of Dayne's Craft Barbecue, see page 64) and Trevor Sales (of Brix Barbecue, see page 57) would visit several times a week to enjoy their food and pick their brains about how they might turn their pop-ups into full-time businesses.

"Heim was the first craft barbecue to come into the area, then we were the second ones to break through, and then the floodgates opened up," says Magallanes. "What people tell us—and this is their words—is that we gave them the courage to try it too."

Rather than gatekeeping information, which was previously common in the industry, Morales and Magallanes encouraged their peers to start their own concepts, and even invited them in to help out behind the scenes.

"They all started out doing backyard barbecue like we did, so we would encourage them," says Magallanes. "Because when we started, there was nobody doing that. Barbecue was still kinda hush-hush—nobody would tell you anything. We would go to these barbecue festivals and go stand in line and wonder how we could get on the other side. So when we got on the other side, the first thing we did was invite these other guys doing pop-ups to come help us."

Panther City's continued success (which includes a spot in the prestigious *Texas Monthly* Top 10 and a Michelin Guide Recommendation), enabled Morales and Magallanes to buy the main building on the lot from their landlords in May 2022. They refurbished the interior of the former dive bar, adding fresh coats of paint, a brick facade, tin tiles behind the bar, and a vibrant mural done by a local tattoo artist, depicting the state of Texas, a panther, a taco-eating Day of the Dead calavera, and a sombrero-wearing pig enjoying elotes. After building out their new bar and kitchen, they were able to move in by that October.

Now with five 500-gallon and two 1,000-gallon Moberg offset smokers, Magallanes and Morales have been able to greatly expand their production. They offer weekend specials like massive juicy beef ribs and pastrami brisket, which they slice and serve on tortas. They also offer daily double brisket smashburgers topped with pickles, onions, and a creamy special sauce. As for desserts, they expanded beyond classic banana pudding and are known for their Nutter Butter cheesecake pudding and a smoked pecan bread pudding Magallanes learned how to make from his mother-in-law.

Next, they greatly expanded their outdoor seating, replacing the previous gravel with Astroturf and adding a stage for live music on the weekends. They also have plenty of space to host their BBQU classes. Once a month, Morales and Magallanes offer a four-hour class where attendees learn the ins and outs of wood selection, fire management, smoker selection, meat selection, knife selection, and best practices for trimming, seasoning, and slicing meat. They also offer a unique, less frequent pro class for just four people at a time. The in-depth 12-hour class, taken by both professionals and passionate home cooks, offers invaluable hands-on experience alongside Morales and Magallanes. Students spend the day learning how to trim, season, and smoke each meat offered at Panther City BBQ, then they return the next day to finish their cooks. Each participant is able to invite four guests, and they present their food, talk about each item and what they learned before sitting down to enjoy it together.

"The class isn't gonna make them a pitmaster overnight, but it may show them some techniques that'll save them some time and frustration, and kind of put them on the right path," says Magallanes. "It's all about repetition and practice. People ask if we're afraid one of them will come set up across from us one day [and sell barbecue]. No, but if they do and they make it—well then more power to 'em because they worked for it! We just want to make sure that Texas barbecue keeps going. And if we don't show it to somebody, who's gonna do it?"

DANIEL VAUGHN

Even before he worked for *Texas Monthly*, Daniel Vaughn used to scour the state of Texas, discovering unknown barbecue joints and broadcasting his detailed reviews across his blog. But social media has certainly changed that dynamic.

"The hidden joints almost don't exist anymore," says Vaughn. "Now, once anybody with an Instagram account figures out that a place is really great, it's pretty much over."

But that doesn't necessarily make Vaughn's job any easier. As the magazine's barbecue editor, his beat is meat—of the smoked variety—and there's enough of it in this massive state to keep him very busy. In just over a decade, he estimates he's visited over 2,300 barbecue joints. He's also undoubtedly one of the most influential people in the world of Texas barbecue.

"I think that certainly having somebody dedicated to the job, just covering Texas barbecue, has certainly heightened the prestige—or maybe just the awareness of—Texas barbecue," says Vaughn. "Just the splash that it made when I was named the barbecue editor was such a big deal. I don't think a lot of the people who wrote about it then, sometimes in snarky terms, ever expected that 10 years later, I would still be doing it. But it's still as relevant as ever, and barbecue's not going away."

Vaughn grew up in Ohio, and got his masters in architecture at Tulane University in New Orleans before moving to Dallas in 2001, where his wife had been offered a job. A lifelong fan of barbecue ("Something that we *called* barbecue was a part of my life growing up" is his snarky take), it didn't take long for him to become totally enamored with the smoked meats of Texas. He was working for an architecture firm when he planned a Hill Country road trip with a friend, using *Texas Monthly*'s 2003 Top 50 BBQ Joints list as a guide.

"I didn't really expect that the barbecue was gonna be all that much different than the barbecue I really enjoyed in Dallas," Vaughn remembers. "Boy, was I wrong!"

The two hit 16 barbecue joints in three days, but it was the peppery bite of brisket from Louie Mueller Barbecue (see page 240) that left the strongest impression on him.

"It was like I was eating a different kind of food," says Vaughn. "It wasn't like any sort of barbecue I had eaten before, and so that was a transformative experience for sure."

He returned from that trip more hooked on 'cue than ever before, and started to make his way around the Dallas–Fort Worth area, determined to try it all. In 2008, he launched a blog called Full Custom Gospel BBQ as a means of keeping track of his travels and research. He found inspiration in Robb Walsh's 2002 book *Legends of Texas Barbecue,* as well as Lolis Eric Elie's 1996 book *Smokestack Lightning: Adventures in the Heart of Barbecue Country*, which takes the reader on an exploration of barbecue culture around the US. Vaughn used the latter as a model for his book *The Prophet of Smoked Meats*, a Texas barbecue travelog he published in 2013.

That same year, the editor-in-chief of *Texas Monthly*, who had been following Vaughn's work closely (as well as his @bbqsnob social media accounts), reached out to offer him the brand-new barbecue editor position. (At the time, it was the first of its kind in the country—and possibly the world—until *Southern Living* and the *Houston Chronicle* followed suit the following year). Without hesitation, Vaughn quit his day job and turned his weekend passion into a new career.

In his role, Vaughn travels all over Texas on research trips to seek out the best barbecue in the state. His typical order is the Texas Trinity: brisket (a slice of both fatty and lean), pork ribs, and sausage (he'll be sure to inquire if it's made in-house), as well as any other signature proteins and sides. He'll usually see about getting a peek behind the scenes too.

"It's one of the few restaurant types where asking for a tour of the kitchen or the pit room is a common thing, so you can always go see what they're working with," says Vaughn. "I like to see what the woodpile looks like, smell what they're cooking with wood."

In addition to writing reviews, Vaughn also publishes pieces on barbecue culture and history, interviews major players, and covers events and festivals. Every four years, he will assemble a tasting team to help him scout for the esteemed Top 50 list. When *Texas Monthly* put out its inaugural Top 50 list in 1997, a group of just five had visited 245 establishments. The magazine very quickly positioned itself as the definitive authority on barbecue in the Lone Star State. In 2015, Vaughn added an interim listing of Top 25 Best New & Improved BBQ Joints. By 2021, a team of 35 visited 411 spots and selected a Top 50, as well as 50 honorable mentions.

"That's just because so many of the new places opening in Texas are doing such a great job, It's really hard to limit it to 50," says Vaughn. "But we don't ever want to change the Top 50 to be any more frequent because I think there's a huge benefit in waiting those four years and just allowing the barbecue scene to change, and then jumping back in, seeing how they're all doing right then and there."

It's safe to say it's every Texas pitmaster's dream to land as close to the top of that list as possible. And if they can accomplish that, life will change virtually overnight for them. Lance Eaker says his revenue doubled when Eaker Barbeque (see page 327) landed on the Top 50 after being open for just four months. Greg Moore says pit builder Sunny Moberg bumped Tejas Chocolate + Barbecue (see page 133) up on the offset smoker waitlist after they placed #6 in 2017 and were turning away throngs of hopeful barbecue enthusiasts because they couldn't keep up with the demand. Similarly, John Bates recalls the late John Brotherton calling him up to lend him another pit after InterStellar BBQ (see page 278) placed #2 on the list in 2021, and Bates is eternally grateful for Brotherton's foresight, as a line has flanked his building ever since then.

In 2010, *Texas Monthly* established an annual barbecue festival to bring the state's best pitmasters together for a big smoky celebration. For the first 11 years it was held in Austin, but in 2022, the festival relocated to Lockhart, the "Barbecue Capital of Texas." On the Saturday of the fest, Lockhart's town square turns into the BBQ World's Fair, an open-to-the-public event filled with tastings from Vaughn's favorite new joints in the state, live music performances, live fire demos, a sprawling marketplace,

and a dedicated Taco Trail. The next day, the top-rated restaurants take over Lockhart City Park for the Top 50 Picnic, and there is no better way to relish in the talent and diversity found in Texas barbecue.

"It's evident in the barbecue list—there's so much new energy," says Vaughn. "I think there's been a massive change in expectations of what you get from a barbecue joint. And I think those expectations have heightened in the last few years, seeing the way the immigrant community has really embraced barbecue and used barbecue as a way to show off their culture and their cuisine and their ingredients paired with barbecue."

In the past couple of years, Vaughn has been expanding his horizons by traveling all around the country to investigate Texas-style barbecue in other regions, from Georgia to Nebraska to California and beyond. But he's always happy to return to his favorite barbecue in Texas (after a cleanse of sushi and Thai food, that is—even pros get barbecue fatigue.)

"As far as just the sheer variety, amount, and quality of barbecue," says Vaughn, "Texas is unmatched anywhere else."

CATTLEACK BARBEQUE

FARMERS BRANCH

Arriving at Cattleack Barbeque on a Saturday morning, you'll have plenty of time to take in the seven beautiful murals depicted on its brick wall while you wait in line, anticipating the moment you'll round the corner and step inside the restaurant. The murals, painted by Dallas-based artist Steve Hunter, portray seven noteworthy pitmasters: Tootsie Tomanetz (Snow's BBQ, see page 308), Wayne Mueller (Louie Mueller Barbecue, see page 240), John Lewis (Lewis Barbecue in South Carolina), Sam Jones (Sam Jones BBQ in North Carolina), Aaron Franklin (Franklin Barbecue, see page 233), Roy Perez (Kreuz Market, see page 295), and the late Mike Mills (17th Street BBQ in Illinois).

When Todd David opened Cattleack Barbeque in 2013, he commissioned these murals to pay homage to the pioneers that paved the way for pitmasters like himself. David was a passionate barbecue hobbyist who owned a disaster restoration company to rescue businesses damaged by fire, water, and smoke. He would regularly host barbecue lunches for his company, cooking for hundreds of clients and employees. So when he retired and sold the company after more than 30 years, he decided to start a barbecue catering operation with his wife in an industrial office park in Farmers Branch, a suburb just north of Dallas. After exclusively catering out of the space for a couple of years, David decided to open the doors one day a week upon customer request. Then one day grew into two.

"You know, some guys go play golf, and some guys travel, but this is what he wanted," says Andrew Castelan, the current owner of Cattleack Barbeque. "It was a retirement project at the end of the day for him. He wasn't trying to create the beast that he created! But as time went on, because he's so obsessive about quality and doing things the right way, he just naturally built this business into something that he might not have expected when he started out."

Castelan also didn't set out to own a barbecue restaurant, but he was bit by a similar bug. Born and raised in Plano, 20 miles northeast of Farmers Branch, Castelan moved down to Austin to attend the University of Texas, right around the time Franklin Barbecue started making headlines.

"I'd gone to Salt Lick and IronWorks and some of these other joints," recalls Castelan. "They were significantly better [than what] I grew up on, which was Dickey's and Spring Creek BBQ [two Dallas-area chains], so I was like—how much better could it be? Around 2011, I finally went to visit Franklin Barbecue, and it was that 'holy shit!' moment that people talk about. You know, that sugar cookie—that *wow* experience. And it really made me realize what barbecue could be."

After earning a graduate degree in accounting from University of Texas Austin, Castelan began working as an auditor for Ernst & Young, a global accounting firm—and cooking on his Weber kettle each weekend as a release from stagnant office life.

"Because, when you're sitting in a windowless cubicle, it's nice to just do something outside," says Castelan. "And eventually I moved up to a Weber Smokey Mountain [a bullet-shaped charcoal smoker], which was a really big deal for me. I remember the day I got it—when it came to the door, I was so excited that I still had my dress clothes on and there I was, putting this Weber Smokey Mountain together."

When Castelan's mother passed away in 2014, he and his wife went out to her family's lakehouse to grieve and spend time together. There, a neighbor gifted him an old Oklahoma Joe offset smoker he'd restored for Castelan.

"It was like this 'Oh my God' moment that changed the course of where I was gonna go forever," says Castelan.

Right around that time, Franklin's first book was published, so Castelan used it as a guide to begin smoking with wood for the first time. The next year, he visited Franklin Barbecue again and ended up meeting Franklin there and talking shop with him.

"We spent 40 minutes talking about smokers, airflow, sausages, sausage casing. It was incredible—he was just a wealth of knowledge. And at the time, no one was really building 500-gallon smokers or 1000-gallon smokers . . . but Aaron Franklin gave me the confidence to just go and build one myself."

Castelan purchased a 500-gallon propane tank and, within six weekends, transformed it into a smoker in his garage.

"The HOA didn't like it very much, so we did the natural thing to do—which is sell the house so that we didn't have to deal with the HOA anymore," he laughs. "It became this crazy obsession where I was just like—this is what I want to do for the rest of my life."

Castelan bought a 1,000-gallon tank and was preparing to build another one when Mill Scale Metalworks (see page 286) emerged on the scene. He purchased one of their pits instead, and began to strategize how he might open his own barbecue place someday. He quit his accounting job and began working full-time at Ten50 BBQ in Richardson. After nine months there, he applied to work at Cattleack, which had just been named the #3 spot in the state by *Texas Monthly*.

"I don't like the term 'craft barbecue'—I just think of it as barbecue where you give a shit," says Castelan. "Well, Cattleack was one of the few in Dallas doing it that way. So that's why I wanted to work there, because I knew they were cooking the way I would want to cook."

Castelan didn't step foot in the pit room for the first six months he was at Cattleack. He started off doing dishes and scrubbing floors before a position opened up and he joined the pit crew, smoking meat on four 1,000-gallon Austin SmokeWorks offsets.

"I just absolutely loved it," he describes. "I loved it so much that I stopped pursuing my own thing. I was like, *I cook the way I want to cook, I do everything the way I would want to do it anyway, so what gain is there for me to leave this place to go open up my own spot?*"

Cattleack was one of the first barbecue joints to source (and still one of the only ones exclusively using) HeartBrand Akaushi Wagyu beef, known for its distinct marbling and buttery texture. They use a mustard binder, thinned down with pickle juice, before seasoning with simply kosher salt and black pepper ground to two different meshes (16 and 32).

"The flavor on that beef is unreal," says Castelan. "It's not like a commodity cow, where it's pumped up with a ton of grain like corn. It's still grain-fed at the end but the grains are a higher quality, so you get this much deeper, richer, better flavor from the fat that we really don't want to mask in any way."

At Cattleack, Castelan reached a new level of obsession with perfecting brisket. Joe Zavala, of Zavala's Barbecue (see page 37), says he's the best brisket trimmer in the business—high praise coming from someone who is just as obsessed with the cut of meat.

"When people compliment my brisket trims, I really appreciate that, and I've kind of become known for it, which is funny," says Castelan, who regularly documents his brisket on his @goodthingsbbq Instagram account. "But to me, it's not just the brisket trim that I take to that ridiculous level—everything I do in cooking I take to that level. How we season the briskets, where they're placed, how we move them, how we wrap them, how tight we wrap them—I'm super OCD about every single aspect of what we do with those briskets. I get that from Todd too—he's the same way. We have this mental image in our mind, both of us, of what a perfect brisket should look like—an absolutely perfect brisket. And we keep pushing that bar a little further."

For trimming, Castelan swears by an eight-inch Victorinox filet knife with a thin blade that he keeps very sharp. It's also flexible, which helps him work around edges and pull through the meat with little resistance.

"I analyze every little aspect of it to get to a point where it's just this beautiful pebblestone—this flawless thing that has no points and no jagged edges," he describes. "Because the real reason you trim briskets is so, when it's in that smoker and the heat and the smoke are coming through it, it's not catching on anything. The air is going up and over. If you have anything that's odd and poking out, it'll start to char up and it just can't last through a 12- to 15-hour cook. So you need these really nice rounded edges and a smooth, sports car effect to it, so that way it doesn't overcook in certain spots."

Castelan says trimming is as important to good brisket as the cook itself, and is one of the reasons modern craft barbecue brisket is superior to the brisket at old-school joints.

"All those barbecue joints' approach was just to cut the flat from the points," says Castelan. "Because they don't trim on the front end, they have to trim on the block, which means they're taking off most of the fat and most of the seasoning along with it. The whole idea of trimming it on the front end is so, when you're on the block, you're giving them the meat with a little bit of fat cap with the seasoning on top. And every slice is presented that way because you've already done the trimming on the front end to be able to present them everything that's good."

Cattleack has also become known for its pastrami brisket, which marinates for two weeks in a brine containing coriander, juniper berry, sugar, allspice, and cinnamon stick before it is seasoned with pepper and smoked with post oak on the offset. When cooking, Castelan goes by look and feel over temperature, which can vary depending on different factors. Once the brisket has developed a nice blackened crust, he wraps it in butcher paper to finish cooking on the rotisserie.

Each week, Castelan rotates between featuring pastrami brisket and pastrami beef ribs as a special, and regular beef ribs are available daily—though there's nothing *regular* about these gargantuan ribs, seasoned with just salt and pepper to showcase their rich beefiness.

"We always cut the center bone out so there's only two ribs on each rack, but they're the monster pound-and-a-half, two-pound beef ribs," describes Catelan. "Which isn't great business for us, because we're losing almost a pound on each rack, just to get thrown in the trash can. But at the end of the day, I want to create something where, when people come, they're like, 'Holy shit—that was incredible.' Money matters, obviously, because that's how you stay in business. But if it comes down to me spending or losing a few extra bucks to put out something that is really going to blow someone's mind, I'm gonna do that all day long."

The seasoning used on the pork ribs is the most involved one he uses, consisting of over 20 ingredients including salt, pepper, different types of chili powder, and cumin. After the ribs are smoked on the rotisserie pit, they are basted with a glaze made from a peach smoothie mix, for a sweet, glossy finish.

The Wagyu brisket trim, pork butt trim, and rib trim all go into sausage that was developed by Jacob Karns, another pitmaster at Cattleack.

"Jacob, in my opinion, is probably one of—if not *the*—best sausage maker in Texas," Castelan says decisively.

Before it was trendy in Texas barbecue to do so, Cattleack was crafting special sausages in flavors like Frito pie, blueberry gouda thyme, and lamb with fig. While those creative sausages will still appear as specials, their three top-sellers are the ones on the daily menu: mild original, hot and spicy Texan, and a medium-spiced Hatch chile and cheese. And because Cattleack yields up to 200 pounds of brisket trim a week, David also developed a beef bologna recipe to utilize it. The value-friendly option, which is not typically found at Texas barbecue joints, has been a huge hit.

Cattleack has continued to draw the masses through the years, and ranked #6 on the 2021 *Texas Monthly* list. Several years into Castelan's tenure at Cattleack, David began hinting at the idea of selling him the restaurant, and now with three kids at home, Castelan was uncertain how much longer he could continue supporting his family in the same role without the prospect of advancement.

"Then one day, we had a really serious conversation about what I wanted for the future and where my head was at," said Castelan, "and within the next 48 hours, we had hammered out what the deal would be for me to buy the restaurant. [Todd] was in a place where he wanted to step back a little bit, and I was in a place where I wanted to step up."

When Castelan and his wife bought Cattleack in August 2023, they decided to open on Wednesdays and the first Saturday of each month (Cattleack had only been operating on Thursdays and Fridays). On the Saturdays they're open, Cattleack usually passes out beer and has live music in the alley for customers in line. Castelan has also preserved the tradition of smoking a whole hog on Saturday, which David learned from North Carolina pitmaster Sam Jones.

Mill Scale Metalworks crafted a massive burn box for them, which Castelan dubbed 'The Beast.' ("It's a burn barrel on steroids," he explains.) Once the wood burns down into coals, they're shoveled under the BQ Grill, where the salted pig cooks over them, fat dripping down onto the coals for a distinctly robust flavor. At the end they flip the pig skin-side down over the fire to create a crunchy, chicharrón layer. Then the hog is chopped and mixed with a chili and vinegar-based sauce and sprinkled with chicharrónes right before it is served.

Beyond extending hours, Castelan has been very reserved in making too many other changes to Cattleack beyond slight tweaks to the menu. ("It's like the expression goes—if it ain't broke, don't fix it," he says. And considering the restaurant was honored with a Michelin Bib Gourmand award in 2024, he's onto something) The Hatch chili mac and cheese is the same luxuriously cheesy dish with a nuanced maltiness from the addition of Lone Star. Creamy grits still swap out seasonally with zesty Mexican street corn. The beans have even bigger chunks of brisket burnt ends in them, and Granny's Cole Slaw is still made using David's grandma's classic recipe. The newest dish is an apple broccoli salad made from chopped broccoli, Granny Smith apples, red onion, red pepper, walnuts, almonds, and raisins dressed in a vinaigrette. The team also makes their own pickled onions, jalapeños, and cucumbers, and bakes fresh cornbread for each day of service.

As for dessert, Cattleack's famous Crack Cake will never leave the menu. It's inspired by the gooey butter vanilla cake famous in David's hometown of St. Louis. The super rich base is sprinkled with powdered sugar before baking, which gives it a sweet, crackly top. For their second dessert offering, Castelan says they're always trying out something new, from Nutter Butter banana pudding to Oreo peanut butter cream pie to banana cream cannolis.

These days, David is back to the part of the barbecue he fell in love with: cooking. He now works at Cattleack, making the rubs, sauces, and chili, plus experimenting with new creations.

"But as far as the day-to-day operations, he doesn't really have anything to do with that part of it, which is what he wanted—and which I'm now getting to stress about," laughs Castelan, whose wife Natalie also helps out in the front of house when she isn't working her full-time job as a nurse. And with their three kids getting older, Castelan says, "I got some dishwashers in my future!"

Zavala's
Barbecue
FARMS

ZAVALA'S BARBECUE

GRAND PRAIRIE

Some people take up pottery as a hobby, or play golf—maybe learn an instrument or volunteer on the weekends. But Joe Zavala? He mastered the art of smoking and runs one of the DFW area's best barbecue joints when he's not working as an IT consultant for Microsoft. He also hosts a podcast called Brisket & Main, throws a monthly BBQ speakeasy event, teaches barbecue classes, and runs a monthly subscription service called Zavala's BBQ Distribution. And when you meet the high-octane Zavala in person, his multi-hyphenate life starts to make more sense.

"I started with an Oklahoma Joe [smoker] in my backyard, named Guadalupe, then we built this 500-gallon, named Henrietta for Henrietta King," he says, introducing all the smoking apparatuses surrounding his restaurant while dressed in his characteristic long shorts, tall socks, dark-rimmed glasses and fitted cap. "Then we got Emily D. West, the original sidepiece of Texas. She was Santa Ana's friend. Then we have Bluebonnet closest to us here, and the El Cucaracho smoker is named Alina Emilia de Zavala after the granddaughter of Lorenzo de Zavala. Is he related to us? I don't know, but it's a cool story. Robot is our burn barrel. And this here is the Ferrari of smokers: our Mill Scale, Selena."

Growing up in Grand Prairie, a suburb of Dallas, Zavala's dad was the pitmaster of the family. Then Joe married his high school sweetheart, Christan, whose father also loved backyard barbecuing. After years of watching and admiring them, he decided to try his hand at a brisket for the first time on July 4, 2015—and that's when his obsession began. He spent a year perfecting his meats for friends and family before starting Zavala's Barbecue out of his backyard, taking orders on social media and hosting pop-ups with the help of his wife and high school best friends CJ Ramirez and Drew Wright. The team set up a table in a nook on Grand Prairie's Main Street, selling barbecue on Saturdays outside a coffee shop called The Brass Bean. Throughout that year, the lines kept getting longer, so he and Wright went in on an 800-square foot space that was built in 1947 to house a Weber Root Beer stand. In early 2019, Zavala's Barbecue opened as a brick and mortar in the unique round building with a stone exterior—located on the corner of Brisket Lane and Main Street.

It's appropriate that his restaurant resides on the only "Brisket Street" in the world ("That was the best $550 application fee I ever paid!" he says with a laugh), because Zavala has mastered the cut. He exclusively uses 44 Farms brisket, made from all-natural Black Angus that is produced without any antibiotics or hormones. His is exquisitely tender, with a consistent pink smoke ring glowing under a peppery bark, made extra thick from the copious amounts of the coarse, 12-mesh pepper used to season it. And he serves it the way he grew up eating it: accompanied by fresh, fluffy flour tortillas, a mound of pico de gallo, and additional housemade salsas.

The green salsa (a blend of poblanos, cilantro, serranos, tomatillos, and garlic) is fresh and vegetal with a nice kick, and perfectly brightens up a mound of Zavala's peppery beef cheek barbacoa. The Sloppy Juan is an homage to Zavala's barbecue mentor Jordan Jackson, who put a Sloppy Joe on the menu when he was the pitmaster at Bodacious Bar-B-Q in Longview. This Texican version is made from chopped brisket and pulled pork mixed with sweet, tangy, and touch-spicy Sloppy Juan sauce, then folded into a tortilla. The Spicy Pizza Pepper Sausage is also a nod to Bodacious, as Zavala created it with Jackson using crushed red pepper as the heat source. In lieu of mac and cheese, Zavala whips up a comforting, cheesy jalapeño hominy. The Hill Country Potato Salad is based on his friend Jordan Eastman's country creation, whereby potatoes tossed in ranch get sprinkled with crunchy bacon. And Pop's Beans, which are studded with brisket and crowned with a burnt end, were indeed born from his dad's pinto bean recipe.

"I use mesquite for direct cooking and fajitas but 90 percent post oak for everything else—and a little pecan," says Zavala. "Does it do anything? Probably not, but it reminds me of my dad."

Zavala's was only open on Saturdays to start—then they expanded hours to Thursday through Saturday to keep up with demand. But in late 2019, Joe was diagnosed with multiple myeloma, a rare cancer of the plasma cell. Zavala underwent chemotherapy and other treatments throughout 2020 while running

TEXAS
ZAVALA'S
BARBECUE
#ZAVALAS

his business from the sidelines. His smokehouse wall is scrawled with monumental dates—like the day he found out he had cancer, and the day a grease fire started at the restaurant while Zavala was in the hospital getting stem cell surgery. But he also uses this space to document his light chains and other cancer metrics that have continued to improve since he went into remission. In 2020, the Zavala Family Foundation was established to provide assistance to those in the restaurant industry who are battling—or have family battling—cancer. Each Labor Day, they throw a big fundraiser called Zavala Bash, where Zavala makes barbecue while musicians perform—last year they raised $18,500.

On Cinco de Mayo weekend, Zavala hosted a free brisket class, and asked that participants donate to the Multiple Myeloma Research Foundation. Normally his classes run from $189 (for public classes) to $450 (for corporate workshops), and people come from as far as Canada and Maine to take them. He's also been the featured celebrity chef for the Dallas Cowboys for four years, and the Mavericks and Stars for two years, holding classes for season ticket holders. Each session is filled with invaluable guidance, but he also steps into the role of your biggest barbecue cheerleader.

"You can't screw up your brisket—you can *always* save it!" he promises the captivated class. "If you ever need help, you can call me, but it's gonna be more of a coaching that you're doing okay!"

He then launches into Fire Management 101, explaining how to build a coal bed, select and stack wood pieces, and use dampers to control the heat and air flow. Next, he covers how to select a brisket (smaller is better, and prime is great insurance, he assures). He demonstrates how to trim the fat off the brisket, then generously season it with his ratio of 4 cups of black pepper to 1 cup of salt. Then his briskets smoke for 10 hours, until their interiors are 178°F to 185°F. At that point, he wraps them in foil and cranks the heat to 275°F to 300°F for the last 2 hours before taking them off to rest in butcher paper.

"Let's be honest, we are in a recession and it's really fucking expensive to go to a barbecue joint," says Zavala. "It's much better to have some friends over, tell them to bring the beer and you'll have the food. And you can look like the hero because people will be saying that's the best barbecue they've ever had!"

After a brisket-cutting demo, the unstoppable Zavala jets down the street to Mas Coffee Co, the coffee shop his wife, Christan, runs in a former 1957 hardware store. He offices out of the back, which is where he and Ramirez record their *Brisket & Main* podcast, and where he's also recently set up a BBQ Speakeasy. Here, he showcases 51 sauces and 39 rubs (and counting) made by *Texas Monthly* Top 50 barbecue joints (Zavala's Barbecue joined that prestigious club in 2021). He's also just launched Zavala's BBQ Distribution (BBQ Distro for short), a monthly subscription service for barbecue enthusiasts to access exclusive content plus gear and products from their favorite joints from across Texas.

"The power of us altogether is so much more impactful than us individually," says Zavala. "My friends work so hard running their barbecue joints," says Zavala. "If I can help tell their stories, we can help people cook better in the backyard and make them want to go to the barbecue joints to see if their food tastes the same.

Each month, Zavala throws a party to celebrate the latest featured pitmasters, using their sauce or rub in a dish and serving it alongside free Lone Star. A local duo of guitarists plucks away outside and Zavala starts documenting the scene for social media as the space fills up with friends, fans, and the intoxicating aroma of 44 Farms fajitas.

"With everything that's happened to me more recently, it made me realize I just need to make the most of life," says Zavala. "Look at all these happy, smiling people. This is what barbecue is all about—happiness."

ROSSLER'S BLUE CORD BBQ

HARKER HEIGHTS

Not many people can say that barbecue saved their life, but Steven Rossler doesn't know where he'd be without it.

Steven and his wife, Kristen, are originally from the Midland area, but he was stationed as an Army staff sergeant at Fort Cavazos (formerly Fort Hood) in 2003. He was deployed to Iraq in 2004, followed by Afghanistan in 2011, where he experienced a traumatic battlefield attack that claimed the lives of three of his fellow soldiers. Sergeant Rossler returned to the base, where he was showered with gratitude from the community, receiving a Bronze Star Medal for his bravery. However, he was also quietly battling the debilitating affects of PTSD, often turning to alcohol to bury the painful memories.

Steven knew he needed something else to focus on, for the sake of his mental health. Barbecue had always been a part of his family life, and something he loved, but he never got a smoker as an adult because he was always moving and stationed in different places. Once back in Texas, he decided to get one and turn his attention to it. He started recalling everything his dad had taught him while he was growing up, and use these practice sessions to cook for friends and family.

"My dad usually smoked chicken or, if he wanted to get fancy, he would cook brisket," remembers Steven. "He used a cylinder-style pit that had a water pan where he would put Olympia beer. Then he would add corn and potatoes in there and, throughout the cook, the smoke, beer, and drippings did something magical to those vegetables."

In 2015, he and Kristen married, then she gave birth to their first child and moved from Midland to Killeen to live on the base. A Navy brat herself, she was no stranger to living on the base, and she also supported Steven's smoking hobby, which had proved to be quite therapeutic. Back in Midland, she not only cut hair, but had various service industry jobs, ranging from working in a busy ice cream shop and deli to managing a restaurant.

Steven connected with Brett Boren from Brett's Backyard Bar-B-Que and the late John Brotherton of Brother's Black Iron Barbecue. He counts these two as his primary mentors for teaching him efficient ways to run the pit, develop recipes, and transform his passion into a successful business. "I consider them family now," says Steven.

In 2016, Steven began offering catering services while he was still stationed at Fort Cavazos. But the late-night hours and solo time tending the fire led to him drinking even more. After Kristen kept finding him passed out with meat on the pit, she gave him an ultimatum.

GOD BLESS
TEXAS

"Facing my demons head on [by] getting help after my wife threatened to leave with our daughter made it easy for me to focus," he remembers. He found a therapist who was also a veteran, and was able to open up about his past and let the healing begin. Meanwhile, Steven laid off the drinking and turned his attention to fine-tuning his cooking, with Kristen by his side.

"This business and my family have gotten me through some tough times," he says. "You could say that barbecue made me a better husband, better dad—a better man."

He taught Kristen how to cook on their Moberg offset smoker, in a style he calls "very Central Texas with a small West Texas twist." They mostly use post oak as their fuel, but they throw a stick of mesquite into the firebox every two hours for added flavor. They use salt, pepper, and garlic as their base rub for brisket, adding a few other ingredients to give a kick to the pork and turkey. They make tomato-based barbecue sauce with a hint of spice and fruit, and a mustard-based sauce with a whisper of chipotle pepper. That same mustard sauce is used to glaze the ribs and mixed in with the pulled pork, enhancing the smokiness of both offerings.

Some of their first sides—old-fashioned, mayo-based potato salad, creamy coleslaw and decadent mac and cheese—came from family recipes, and Kristen has developed some others too. She thought up a

cooling, elote pasta salad for scorching summer days, and she makes a pecan streusel–topped sweet potato casserole inspired by the annual Thanksgiving feast they host. Another favorite is her spiced banana pudding made with Slaton gingersnaps, cinnamon, nutmeg, and other holiday spices.

As the Rosslers' catering business continued to flourish, they decided to open a trailer in Harker Heights, right near the base, in January 2021. Steven named it Rossler's Blue Cord Barbecue to honor the infantry blue cord earned and worn by soldiers after fighting on the front. Shortly after opening, he decided to retire from the military, ushering in a new era.

"I always knew that if we were going to do barbecue full time when I retired, that I wanted to have a piece of family and military service in the name," Steven says. "Being an infantry man wasn't easy at times, but that was some of the best 20-and-a-half years of my life. It's half of who I am, and I wanted to incorporate that."

The Rosslers still dedicate their weekends to catering, so the truck's hours are a bit unorthodox. They operate from 11:30 a.m. to 4 p.m. (or until sold out) on Wednesdays and Thursdays in the parking lot of Smile Doctors Orthodontics. Sometimes they'll take on weekday catering jobs too, during which Kristen will run the truck while Steven heads the catering. And when their kids come to help out, it's an entire family affair: Paisley is the dessert girl, while JuJu is head taste tester.

In addition to their regular menu of proteins and sides, the truck will often feature specials, from smoked brisket lasagna to SR Sliders (made with smoked prime rib, golden onions, creamy horseradish and arugula) named after Steven's dad. Steven Rossler Sr. catered alongside his son until he passed away in 2021.

"I wouldn't be the pitmaster I am today without the knowledge he gave me," says Steven.

The Rosslers get all sorts of catering requests, including vegan orders, which keep them on their toes. And many of their creations will reappear as specials, or even join the menu, which now reads like a culinary scrapbook of their travels and experiences. Steven first tasted Hawaiian mac salad while stationed in Oahu, and Kristen originally created theirs to cater a Tongan menu. And both the cheesy poblano grits and tangy, savory collard greens were inspired by Steven's time spent in Georgia for basic training.

"Harker Heights and Killeen is a melting pot of multiple cultures because of Fort Cavazos," says Steven. "If we can help soldiers and civilians have a little taste of home, that makes it all worth it."

Boss Man
SMOKE-A-
BBQ · FWTX

SMOKE-A-HOLICS BBQ

FORT WORTH

Nestled in Fort Worth's historic Southside, Smoke-A-Holics BBQ is more than a barbecue joint. It's a love letter to smoke, soul food, and community transformation. Derrick Walker, the man behind the pit, has roots deeply entwined in this neighborhood, where he grew up and now runs one of the most celebrated barbecue spots in the city.

"Barbecue has always been a part of my upbringing," says Walker. "I have a love for soul food and I have a love for barbecue, but barbecue always tugged at me a little stronger. Probably because I like being outside and playing with fire."

Walker's passion for barbecue was sparked by his grandfather, who bought a smoker on a trailer when Walker was about 12. His family would congregate at his great-grandparents' land in East Texas for family reunions, birthdays, and holidays, and he remembers barbecue being a big part of those gatherings.

"We'd load the smoker up in Arlington, Texas, and then hit the highway, cooking meat down the road!" remembers Walker. "It's only a two-hour drive, but we would put the briskets on and hit the highway in the morning. And maybe an hour into the drive, he'd pull over at a rest stop, we'd check the meat, throw a log in, and then we'd keep going until we got there."

Walker cooked in a variety of kitchens before working his way up to food service director for the Baylor healthcare system, where he oversaw day-to-day operations in food service at rehab facilities and hospitals throughout the metroplex. As early as 2001, he started connecting with other barbecue enthusiasts on the online forum Barbecue Brethren, and in 2003 he joined the International Barbecue Cooking Association (IBCA) and started competing. Then his professional barbecue journey began in 2006, when he began hosting pop-ups outside his wife Kesha's salon. By 2018, he decided to open a food trailer on the weekends (using Panther City BBQ's previous trailer once they upgraded).

While other barbecue joints around the state were incorporating Tex-Mex flavors and ingredients into their barbecue, Derrick also started to merge the types of food he grew up on. Alongside his smoked meats, he offered Southern comfort classics like collard greens, cornbread, yams, broccoli rice casserole, dirty rice, and baked beans.

"I coined the phrase Tex-Soul because I wanted to include my love, passion, and upbringing with soul food into barbecue," says Derrick.

Business continued to grow, as both Derrick and Kesha hustled on the weekends—with the help of their kids—while working their full-time jobs during the week. They decided to use the nest egg they'd been saving for a house to go all-in on a brick and mortar in Fort Worth's historic Southside, where Derrick's parents still live in the home he grew up in. This section of the city has seen significant transformation in recent years, and will soon be home to a Juneteenth museum, as well as a mixed-use development called the Evans and Rosedale Urban Village.

"Fifteen years ago, I wouldn't open a restaurant over here—the area was so crime riddled," says Derrick. "I was born and raised here, and I moved to get away from trouble. I was a Crip growing up over here and did a lot of bad over here so I wanted to bring a lot of good back to the area."

Walker's vision for Smoke-A-Holics is aligned with the neighborhood's growth, as he has expanded the restaurant to meet increasing demand, and looks forward to continued expansion. In 2019, Derrick quit his day job to open the brick and mortar in a former bakery with just one 1,000-gallon offset smoker. He gradually expanded to two, plus a road pit on a trailer, all crafted by AJ's Custom Cookers. Though pecan is his wood of choice, he got feedback from customers that the meat didn't taste smoked *enough*. So, after experimenting with blending pecan with mesquite, Derrick made a crossover to oak, which imparts a stronger smoke taste he feels customers are more used to.

He keeps his beef rub simple—just kosher salt, cracked black pepper, and garlic powder—for his brisket. Pork gets seasoned with paprika, brown sugar, garlic powder, and black pepper, and both his spareribs and the rib tips he has become known for get a spritz of apple cider vinegar and apple juice before they are wrapped and pulled off the pit. He is opposed to glazing ribs, but he does glaze his turkey with barbecue sauce for added flavor and color. And each Tuesday he smokes turkey legs, and uses that meat in his collards and green beans.

Until he has more space and time, Derrick sources his jalapeño cheddar and beef hotlink locally. He does smoke salami and bologna in-house, and recreates the "bolo sandwiches" he grew up eating—thick-cut bologna on toasted potato bread, an offering he calls a "black staple."

Many of his sides were based on family recipes, like his mom's mustard-based potato salad and broccoli rice casserole, and his aunt's pasta salad made with spaghetti. His method for Cajun-seasoned collard greens is a combination of his grandmother's and aunt's recipes. Instead of the pinto beans often found in Texas barbecue, Derrick bakes his with ground beef, bacon, brown sugar, bell peppers, and onions. He's developed a Cajun creamed corn with a bacon-jalapeño roux, and the creamy mac and cheese is layered with four types of cheese before it's finished in the smoker. And on Soul Food Sundays each offering comes off the pit: hamburger steaks, pork chops, smoked meatloaf, smoked oxtail, and smoked and smothered chicken.

"At one point, everything here was kissed by smoke," says Derrick. "That's really what I like—I like everything to at least touch smoke."

The fittingly named Smoke-A-Holics has also become known for their over-the-top offerings like brisket nachos (tortilla chips topped with brisket, cilantro, jalapeños, and queso with a side of sour cream), loaded cornbread (piled with baked beans, brisket, shredded cheese, sour cream, green onions, and barbecue sauce), and the Big Macc Bowl (a loaded mac and cheese topped with chopped brisket, sausage, green onions, and barbecue sauce).

In addition to housemade banana pudding, Kesha developed a Coca-Cola cake (this one actually came about by accident, and Derrick now counts it as one of their many secret recipes). She also created something they call a Peach Thang, a cross between a cobbler and a cake that comes out both butter-soft and crispy. Something else they're always developing are their sauces. Derrick spent ten years perfecting his original tangy red barbecue sauce—a top-secret recipe featuring lots of different fruits, among other elements—and he has three or four more sauces in the works.

Despite all the attention to detail the Walkers put into their food, Derrick was hesitant to embrace the term "craft barbecue" for quite some time.

"Actually I hated the term *craft barbecue*," admits Derrick. "I'm like—so we're calling ourselves craft barbecue like we elevated something. What does that mean to the guys who taught us how to do it? I originally thought it was a slap in the face to those that came before us, but as I looked at it as a whole, I realized we *did* take what they taught us and we elevated it. And that's what brought us to where we are today."

HEIM BARBECUE

DALLAS & FORT WORTH

These days, Fort Worth is a hotbed of craft barbecue, but that wasn't always the case. Travis and Emma Heim, the husband and wife team who launched Heim Barbecue, are responsible for leveling up the scene with a brand they dubbed "farm to smoker barbecue." The innovation was such a hit that Heim Barbecue quickly grew to four restaurant locations.

Travis grew up cooking family recipes with his grandmother, Jane Tucker, and mother, Robin. At 13, he smoked his first brisket on his grandfather's smoker, and it quickly became an obsession. A couple of years later, he built a smoker out of a trash can and then crafted another out of a Weber grill. He started taking over cooking ribs for the family and, with his brother, developed a tangy, touch-smoky barbecue sauce recipe you'll now find bottled at his restaurants.

"My grandfather would cook barbecue, especially ribs for big family occasions," remembers Travis. "My uncle, Roger Heim, was a welder and would make his own smokers way back in the '70s. So initially it just started out as something I thought was cool and wanted to emulate those guys. Once I started cooking regularly in high school and college, I was really interested in the science behind it and the craft of the whole process."

Travis met Emma in junior high at a church event, and they started dating several years later, then moved to East Texas for college. Barbecue was a constant in their lives. They would eat ramen throughout the week to save money to go to hole-in-the-wall barbecue joints around on weekends, while Travis continued to hone his backyard craft. When they moved back to Fort Worth, Travis got his first catering gig cooking brisket for a lunch at their church. Together, the Heims started a pop-up dinner called T&E MEATClub as a way to test out dishes for their friends and family to enjoy with beer and live music. Travis hoped to open his own barbecue place someday—one focused on high-quality ingredients.

"Our belief was always that we should serve the best food possible, just like if you were having friends over to eat at your house," says Travis.

At the time, starting their own business seemed like a faraway dream for the newlywed couple. But when Travis got laid off in 2013 from his job at an oil-and-gas company, he decided to roll the dice and take his passion to the next level, despite his lack of capital and industry experience. His uncle gave him a big offset smoker he'd built out at the family farm in Marshall, Texas, Travis found a food truck for lease online, and the couple emptied their checking and savings accounts to put down a deposit and buy supplies for Heim Barbecue's first day of service. It was a true gamble, but one that worked out in their favor. They already had some traction in the community

from their MEATClub events, but before long everyone in town was hearing about Travis' tender brisket, juicy pulled pork, savory-savory pork ribs, and a soon-to-be-iconic creation known as bacon burnt ends, all smoked with post oak.

For the bacon burnt ends, Travis wanted to make something similar to Kansas City's famous burnt ends, but he felt like using brisket for them was almost sacrilege in Texas ("That goes against every Texan fiber in my body," he says). So he experimented until he perfected the method using pork belly, which he first turns into bacon with a cure of brown sugar, salt, and pink curing salt. This process, done in the refrigerator for five to six days, draws out the moisture, and then he cold smokes the belly at around 200°F for about three hours. After it cools, he cuts it into cubes, which get tossed and generously coated with his Burnt Ends Rub, a brown sugar–dominant seasoning mixed with pepper and some other spices. The cubes get spread onto a sheet tray and smoked at 250°F for about three hours, until they are candied on the outside and succulently rendered inside.

Emma created the sides, with help from Travis's mom, tweaking recipes from both sides of the family. The menu started out with just a couple of options: a colorful crunchy slaw made from red cabbage and carrots, and an indulgent twice-baked potato salad with pops of flavor from cheddar, bacon, and green onion. They also offered all their meats on sandwiches, including a triple threat of stacked brisket, jalapeño-cheese sausage, and bacon burnt ends called the BBQ Snob Sandwich, named after *Texas Monthly* barbecue editor Daniel Vaughn (see page 26). But Vaughn was already hot on their heels—and when his positive article came out in October of 2015, their already-growing line expanded tenfold.

Emma quit her job and came on full-time, and the couple hired a single employee to help them. They ran a Kickstarter campaign to purchase another smoker, and raised $15,000 within 30 days. Once added to their repertoire, they were able to triple their cooking capacity, but even that was not enough to serve the masses who were now traveling from even further away to visit Heim Barbecue. Six months later, they were approached by Will Churchill and his sister Corrie Watson, twin great-grandchildren of the prominent Fort Worth car dealer Frank Kent. They had a 1921 property off Magnolia Avenue, a beautiful historic entertainment district, and a vision of making it Heim Barbecue's brick and mortar. Thanks to the support of their new business partners, the Heims were able to build their dream restaurant. And thanks to the relationships Travis had forged with meat suppliers, he was able to scale the concept and continue sourcing high-quality proteins.

"When we started buying prime briskets we were the first barbecue joint in town to sell them," recalls Travis. "Niman Ranch didn't even market their prime 123A beef ribs because no one would buy them. Our partnerships with Certified Angus Beef and Niman Ranch specifically have been a key part of our success because, without them, it would be impossible to source high-quality products and still meet the demand we had."

By August 2016, Heim Barbecue's Magnolia restaurant was open for lunch and dinner six days a week thanks to a full team of employees and a whole new fleet of smokers (J&R Oyler rotisseries, M&M BBQ Company rotisseries, and 1,000-gallon Moberg offset smokers). Their goal was to get rid of massive lines and make their food as accessible as possible for everyone. It took some adjusting to figure out a schedule, but soon Heim was smoking all through the day and night to craft multiple batches of barbecue. They also debuted an expanded menu, with gargantuan beef ribs, Heimburgers (made from leftover brisket and 44 Farms ground beef griddled on a flat top) slathered with bacon burnt end jam, hand-cut fries, battered onion rings, plus sides like green chile mac and cheese and smoked bacon collard greens. To Emma's creamy banana pudding, Robin added desserts like her famous fudgy brownies, seasonal handpies, and peach cobbler topped with golden-brown biscuity crumbles.

Heim brought a whole new style of craft barbecue to Fort Worth, so it was fitting that their space reflected that artisan mindset too. The menu is still handwritten on butcher paper, but now it's attached to a seafoam green subway tiled wall. There's an exposed brick wall and the counters boast herringbone wood facades. The white-walled dining room is filled with lots of windows welcoming in natural light, which catches the beaded glass chandelier in the center. Heim also launched a bar program featuring over 40 different types of single-malt Scotch, local craft beer, and a cocktail menu with favorites like Ranch Waters and Bloody Marys.

By the time Heim Barbecue landed on the *Texas Monthly* Top 50 list in 2017, they were hatching plans for a second location. Heim on the River didn't open until April 2019 but the 8,000-square-foot space was well worth the wait. Located in Fort Worth's River District, a shopping and entertainment destination on the banks of the Trinity River, this iteration of Heim features a sprawling covered patio and beer garden for live music and events. By now, the Heim family had grown to three and their River restaurant, with its kid's menu and spacious yard, became known as a family-friendly destination for DFW. In October 2020, the Heims brought their barbecue to Dallas, opening a location on West Mockingbird Lane, and in December 2023, their fourth location opened in Old Town Burleson.

But later that spring, Travis and Emma announced they'd be taking a step back from the day-to-day operations of their North Texas restaurants. Their partner Churchill, who also owns Fort Brewery and Pizza, would be taking over that role so the Heims could spend more time with their two daughters.

"We were fortunate enough to build our business from a food truck with one employee to four locations, food trucks, and a full-service catering business with over 150 employees," says Emma. "That is incredibly rewarding but also can take its toll on you. . . . At the end of the day we love restaurants, and BBQ especially, but it was just the right time for us to move on to other opportunities. It's given us time to focus on our family and mental health, and find our purpose outside of barbecue, which has been incredibly refreshing."

Whenever you see pork belly burnt ends on a barbecue menu in Texas, you can thank the Heims for crafting those smoky, sweet cubes that have spread like wildfire throughout the state. But, as one of the very first barbecue spots to focus on high-quality sourcing, their influence spans well beyond that innovation.

"Our meat supplier recently told me we've purchased over 2 million pounds of meat through them over the years," says Travis. "So I like to think our approach to sourcing has helped shift the industry and now you'd be hard pressed to find a new barbecue joint that isn't following suit. . . . When we opened our food truck in 2015, people were really excited about it because I think it was something familiar to them but we were able to take it to the next level. What's happened since is amazing, Fort Worth has more great barbecue joints per capita than anywhere else in Texas and it's been really cool to see a lot of the places grow and have a ton of success."

BRIX BARBECUE

FORT WORTH

Trevor Sales was born and raised in La Porte, Indiana, but when he found himself in Fort Worth for work—selling steel power poles—he quickly fell in love with Texas barbecue culture. A passion for food was already deeply rooted in his upbringing, thanks to his mother, a cherished home cook known throughout their community.

"My cooking came more so from growing up in the family where everyone came over to eat holiday meals and after-game meals," Sales remembers. "We were always the place where people gathered to hang out, eat and have a good time. Midwestern home-cooked meals, prime rib, great roasted and mashed potatoes, pastas—just hearty, home-cooked meals. I was raised in an old-fashioned, steak-and-potatoes household."

Sales's mother gifted him a pellet smoker when he moved to Texas in 2017, but within a couple of months he was upgrading to an offset pit. A few more months after that, he was hosting pop-ups in a gym parking lot. By 2018, he had branded his business Brix Barbecue, named after his rescued boxer-terrier, and was hosting regular weekend pop-ups while still working full-time during the week. Sales became known not only for his marbled Prime brisket and sweet-and-spicy ribs smoked with a blend of oak and pecan, but for dishes like his Funkytown Hot Chicken Sandwich

(Nashville-style hot chicken fried in smoked beef tallow and served with ranch-inspired "dank sauce") and Brix Balls (cheesy jalapeño brisket and chorizo meatballs deep-fried to order).

As Brix Barbecue's fan base grew, Sales established a fixed location in the same spot where Heim Barbecue (see page 50) and Panther City BBQ (see page 22) got their starts. Sales parked his shiny silver "Smokestream" trailer and his 1,000-gallon offset pit, The Brisket Bomber, in the parking lot across from the HopFusion Ale Works brewery. Several picnic tables, flanked by cactus planters, provided seating, but most customers ordered food to go and took it into the brewery to enjoy alongside beer. On Sunday nights, Sales hosted Brix After Dark events, which featured bar food like smoked and fried wings and LeBrix brisket smashburgers.

One of his biggest fans, Jeremiah Jemente, ended up coming on board to help and quickly became Sales's right-hand man. One of the things Jemente is responsible for is the sausage. There's always a melty, snappy jalapeño cheese link on offer, as well as rotating creative specials, like roasted garlic and fresh basil, or a queso fundido sausage made with pork, Oaxaca cheese, and spices.

Another element that sets Brix Barbecue apart is Sales's incorporation of Italian ingredients and dishes. Italian is his favorite type of cuisine, and the one he prepares most often at home—making his own pasta, curing his own meats, and charring tomatoes on the grill for homemade sauce.

"The thing I admire about Italian cooking in general is they have a knack for making simple things taste really good using good ingredients and techniques," says Sales.

Sales developed a brisket ragù using fire-roasted Campari tomatoes cooked down with chopped smoked brisket, carrot slices, red wine, and Parmesan. He scoops the hearty Bolognese over cavatappi pasta and garnishes it with grated Parmesan and basil. He also offers a classic pasta salad (farfalle with shaved cucumbers, fresh parsley, and finely diced red onion) inspired by one made by his Grandma Sala. He makes an Italian brisket sandwich special topped with spicy giardiniera and inspired by the Italian beef he grew up eating in the Chicago area. And the dish Sales has become the most known for is his Texas Porchetta, a pork belly seasoned with thyme, parsley, lemon zest, and Calabrian chile oil before it is rolled, tied, smoked, and then sliced.

By 2021, Sales and his investors were ready to open a brick-and-mortar location. However, converting an old manufacturing facility into a barbecue joint was no small feat. Construction delays, city permits, and the installation of a fire-sprinkler system added both time and significant cost—$175,000, to be exact.

"It was unfortunately not a small business–friendly

experience," Sales sums up. "Anyone thinking about opening a restaurant in Fort Worth, reach out to me. I can give a lot of advice about what to do and what not to do."

At the end of July 2023, Sales was finally able to open the doors of his first restaurant, which is now open Thursday through Sunday. He'd expanded with a second 1,000-gallon pit (named Black Beauty) as well as an Argentinean-style wood-fired grill for steaks (which he cold smokes on the pit first) and a BQ direct heat pit, where he cooks half-chickens, sausage, and a few whole hogs a year too. He has switched to using all post oak, since the pecan supply has gotten more scarce and doesn't burn nearly as long or as strong.

Alongside his market-style barbecue and signature Italian dishes, Sales now serves a daily lineup featuring smoked beef cheek barbacoa, Mexican street corn, tallow-simmered pinto beans, homemade flour tortillas, and fresh green salsa. Departing from the typical pork belly burnt ends found at many barbecue joints, Sales opts for Wagyu beef belly burnt ends, which he believes offer superior flavor—less sweet and rich, with a more balanced profile. His smoked and fried wings are now on the daily menu, and he offers specials like cowboy cut bone-in ribeye steak frites and smoked and seared fajitas.

Sales features two of his mother's recipes for dessert options: fudgy turtle brownies and the "medium rare" (crisp on the outside and gooey on the inside) chocolate chip cookies that were a staple at his house growing up.

Brix Barbecue now features a big open space, with long community tables and garage doors that open for fresh air and sunshine. The kitchen, visible behind glass windows, is framed by white subway tile and cow-hide panels, and wild game heads are mounted around the perimeter of the dining room. A sign above the bar boasts "Home of the Coldest Lone Star in Texas." The light golden lager may be the only beer they pour on tap, but Sales has built an impressive beverage program featuring world-class whiskey and a well-curated wine list.

"When it comes to beer, I love ice-cold Lone Star—that's why we have it on tap," he says. "Granbazan Albariño pairs awesome with the porchetta. It has a little bit of body, but it's really crisp, and has some saltiness and acidity to it that works well with the fatty pork. Bourbon is always good for dessert—you can't go wrong."

Though Sales sold the Smokestream trailer in 2023, he's not done with pop-ups. Plans are in the works for a more mobile-friendly trailer designed for events. As Brix continues to evolve, it remains rooted in Sales's love for hospitality and feel-good food, crafted with the same love and care his mother instilled in him.

SABAR BBQ

FORT WORTH

Growing up in a Pakistani immigrant family, Zain Shafi remembers barbecue being a big part of every gathering. Except instead of brisket cooked low and slow, it appeared in the form of kebabs and chicken tikka sizzling over live fire. Shafi's father and uncles handled the meats while the aunts prepared an array of sides. But the true "aha" moment that led Shafi down the path to barbecue came while eating at Zavala's Barbecue (see page 37) in Grand Prairie.

"I think the simplicity of using fire, meat, basic seasoning, and time to make delicious food really attracted me," he says.

Working with meat also runs in Shafi's bloodline. His grandparents had actually opened one of the first halal meat markets in the London area in the 1950s and, once his family immigrated to the US in the late 1970s, his father and uncles started selling Western wear in Dallas, eventually transitioning to the furniture business. Though Shafi had dreams of attending culinary school, helping with the family business took precedence.

After taking a class with Dylan Taylor, one of the original co-owners of Goldee's Barbecue (see page 16), Shafi remembers begging the Goldee's crew to let him help out as they prepared to open their soon-to-be-award-winning new restaurant. He came on in

Order Here
Safar
BBQ
SHEA

December 2020, working part-time. When his family decided to sell their furniture business in 2022, he was able to transition to working full-time at Goldee's.

"I learned everything I know from Goldee's—how to cook with fire, and then how to properly develop recipes," says Shafi, who didn't have any prior kitchen experience. But he has the Goldee's boys to thank not only for training him in barbecue, but also for encouraging him to spread his wings and fly. Taylor delivered a 500-gallon Austin Smoke Works pit to Shafi's backyard, where he spent hours practicing and developing his own recipes by blending the barbecue traditions of Texas with the complex flavors of Pakistani cuisine. He named his new concept Sabar BBQ, after the Urdu word for "patience."

Goldee's co-owner Lane Milne suggested he launch in a food truck, and the two hauled Tom Micklethwait's former Taco Bronco truck from Austin up to DFW. Shafi brought on Dallas-based artists Khadeeja Zulqarnain and Safwan Chowdhury to paint the trailer a bright blue with detailed floral details inspired by the art on Pakistanti commercial trucks and Urdu lettering translating to "hot," "fresh," and "delicious."

In November 2023, Shafi opened Sabar BBQ in central Fort Worth with a menu of post-oak smoked proteins and accompanying sides with a distinct Pakistani twist. Brisket, which he sources from Creekstone Farms, is rubbed not only with standard salt and pepper, but also a blend of cloves, cumin, bay leaf, nutmeg, cinnamon, and cardamom. He smokes at a low 225°F (whereas most newer barbecue joints aim for around 275°F), which creates a pronounced and aromatic bark.

While Sabar isn't entirely halal, the menu is pork-free and halal-ish, which is the diet Shafi himself follows. Therefore, he forgoes pork ribs in favor of lamb ribs sourced from Superior Farms, and this robust dish actually pays homage to the Muslims in Xi'An, China, who grill skewered lamb over fire. Shafi seasons his ribs with Sichuan peppercorns, cumin, ginger, garlic, onion, Chinese five-spice powder, white pepper, and sesame seeds before smoking them and finishing with a final dusting of seasoning for robust layers of flavor.

Shafi rubs his turkey with a blend of tandoori seasonings —Kashmiri chili powder, cumin, black pepper, cinnamon, black cardamom, star anise, lemongrass,

cloves, garlic powder, onion powder, and ajwain—then wraps each turkey breast in butcher paper with butter to finish the cook. Then he collects the drippings, and gives the sliced turkey a last, luxurious dip in them in before they are plated.

In Pakistan, kebabs stand in for sausages, so Shafi decided to develop a sausage filled with all the traditional flavors used in a seekh kebab, like Kashmiri pepper, garam masala, cumin, coriander, and turmeric. At Sabar, naan stands in for white bread and Shafi pickles his own onions. In addition to a tangy chili crisp barbecue sauce, he makes a cilantro and mint-brightened raita that serves as a cool complement to his spice-forward dishes.

Shafi's sides draw inspiration from cherished family recipes and memories. Instead of beans, dal chawal (lentil rice made with both yellow and orange moong and masoor lentils) is a comforting staple, reminiscent of weekly family meals. And in place of coleslaw, Shafi offers fruit chaat, a sweet and tangy seasonal fruit salad traditionally enjoyed to break the fast during Ramadan. Kachumber—a fresh salad of tomatoes, cucumbers, tomatoes, and herbs—also adds a fresh, vibrant touch to the plate.

"You could say it's our version of pico de gallo," says Shafi. "I think just finding dishes that mimic the traditional Texas barbecue items makes it work so well. And using Pakistani flavors really brings something different to the tray."

Met with an overwhelmingly positive reaction since opening his truck, Shafi has started to run even more Tex-Pak specials and test out other creative dishes, like burnt end nihari (a take on the national dish of Pakistani, made with a flavorful ginger curry), and biryani boudin (the popular South Asian rice dish put into boudin form). He launched with a warming gajrela (carrot and rice pudding) as his sole dessert, but plans to add two lighter options, kheer rice pudding and mango pudding, to the menu too.

For now, Sabar is only open on Saturdays and Sundays, and Shafi is tweaking and developing things each week, with plans to slowly expand without sacrificing quality. After all, he knows making great barbecue is about more than just excellent ingredients and culinary know-how. It also takes a good amount of patience.

DAYNE'S CRAFT BARBECUE

ALEDO

Dayne Weaver was inspired to pursue barbecue from people like Joe Zavala of Zavala's Barbecue (see page 37) and Andrew and Michelle Muñoz of Moo's Craft Barbecue in LA, who started off selling barbecue out of their yards before slowly building up their businesses.

"I was really most inspired not by big, popular places but more small, grassroots barbecue movements," says Weaver. "These kinds of stories just made it feel like doing something with barbecue was within my reach."

Weaver's earliest barbecue memories are of his dad smoking ribs in their own backyard—and those ribs left such an impression on him that he'd request a rack of them each year for his birthday.

"I've always said that I think that barbecue is a perfect mixture of cooking and camping, which are two of my favorite things, so it just made sense for me to be drawn to it," says Weaver. "The amount of time you have to put into it really makes you appreciate the food more, and there's really no way to recreate that flavor indoors."

Weaver started his own Fort Worth backyard experimentations by watching YouTube videos and then using that information to put his own spin on different techniques. He reached out to Joe Zavala in 2017 and asked if he could come assist with a pop-up. He left even more educated and inspired to create his own underground barbecue operation. After lots more backyard practice, he and his wife Ashley launched a monthly pop-up in January 2018, selling to friends, family, and neighbors for seven months.

Dayne became known for his superlative smoked meats: thick, succulent Creekstone Prime brisket, paprika-rubbed and honey-glazed pork ribs, and juicy, tomato-brightened pulled pork. He established a program to repurpose trim into creative sausages with flavors like Cheesy Bratwurst, Margherita Pizza, Chicken Cordon Bleu, and Berry Gouda. And his equally innovative sides included crisp apple slaw, beans topped with Frito pie fixings, and creamy elotes showered with crumbled Flamin' Hot Cheetos.

"Sides have always been important to us because, a lot of times, that's the deciding factor of where to go eat when kids and wives are involved," says Dayne, who is a father to four of his own.

Once the Weavers obtained an LLC for Dayne's Craft Barbecue, they started hosting pop-ups at breweries once or twice a month before landing a spot at Lola's Trailer Park in September 2019. They sold their barbecue from an outdoor bar that wasn't being used (which they dubbed "The Shack"), selling out every Saturday for about a year. Around this time, Dayne also developed something called bacon brisket. When he found himself with an excess of pork belly that wasn't selling well, he treated it like a brisket by rubbing it with the same seasoning (salt, pepper, double-cut crushed red pepper, and seasoning salt), smoking it and letting it rest. This process yields rich, perfectly rendered slices with a peppery bark that quickly became Dayne's signature item.

In the summer of 2020, the Weavers purchased a food trailer from Helberg Barbecue (see page 419) and served items to go until pandemic restrictions were lifted. And in March 2021, they reopened three days a week from "The Shack" at Lola's Trailer Park & Saloon. That year, Dayne's Craft Barbecue also landed on the *Texas Monthly* Top 50 list. Unfortunately, right when they'd built up momentum, Lola's Trailer Park lost their lease, and the Weavers moved their truck to a property in west Fort Worth. The idea was to build a brick and mortar at that spot, but when they couldn't reach an agreement with the real estate partner, they began to seek out a different location. When another spot became available in nearby Aledo, just 20 miles west of Fort Worth, they visited and knew they'd found their forever home.

Dayne had always hoped to have a spot in a small Texas town one day, and the move especially made sense as Fort Worth continues to become increasingly saturated with barbecue concepts. Their brick and mortar, which opened at the end of 2023, is housed in a 1930s building that once served as the town general store. It's right in the middle of downtown Aledo, which has a population of 3,000 (and rising as people move out of the city), alongside a railroad track with a nearby grain mill visible. With a 2,700-square-foot building and a dedicated pit room, Dayne now has more space than ever before.

"It's been easier in some ways and more difficult in others, but we're doing our best to recreate everything on a larger scale," says Dayne, who has expanded his hours and more than doubled his cooking capacity and production, now using two 1,000-gallon and one 500-gallon offset Cen-Tex smokers.

Now, Dayne is able to make enough food to make it through the day without selling out until the end. He has also streamlined the ordering process and alleviated his lines by adopting a counter-service model using numbers and runners.

He's utilized his experiences from the last seven years to make culinary improvements by simplifying in some ways. For example, Jalapeño Havarti and Beefy Texan sausages are now menu standards, alongside one rotating special. He discovered less is more when making turkey, so he switched to a simple rub of salt, pepper, and sugar, which results in a firmer bark. And though Dayne still uses post oak, he'll occasionally mix in hickory or red oak if that's what's available. ("It doesn't make a huge difference to us as long as the wood is seasoned well," he discloses.)

In addition to the layered cheesecake pudding desserts they'd become known for in their truck (in flavors

like Banana Bourbon Delight and Cookie Butter Bliss), Dayne has revived a recipe for chocolate lasagna that holds a special place for him since Ashley made it for his birthday 12 years ago. His four-layered annual birthday treat is made from crushed Oreos, creamy cheesecake, light chocolate mousse, and whipped cream, then sprinkled with chocolate chips and drizzled with chocolate sauce.

Though he's streamlined the menu in some ways, Dayne maintains a robust schedule of specials. His hugely popular brisket trim smashburger is available Wednesday through Sunday. Weekends bring massive, peppery beef ribs. Saturdays are for barbacoa, while Sundays are for seasonal burnt ends (in flavors like blueberry lemon for the spring/summer and candied apple for the fall/winter). He also launched brunch (starring burritos and kolaches), and has whole hog events and chef collabs coming soon. And now with a deli case in the front, customers can take home vacuum-sealed smoked meats and containers of tallow.

In addition to building a new community and brightening the tapestry of the small town of Aledo, Dayne also sees plenty of his regulars from Fort Worth make the drive out. Dayne insists their success comes not just from the food, but those relationships they formed along the way. When Ashley worked the register every day during their early years, she learned customers' names, favorite orders, birthdays, pet names, and more.

"We used our local resources to network and bump elbows with everyone we could in our culinary community while developing real and lasting relationships along the way, relationships we still have and cherish," says Dayne. "Making genuine, grassroots connections over the past six years in our community is what has led to our success and helped us more than any list or magazine coverage could ever do."

Hutchins
BBQ
Est. 1978

HUTCHINS BARBEQUE

MCKINNEY & FRISCO

When Tim Hutchins (pictured on page 74) says he grew up in the barbecue business, he means it. That's because when his dad, Roy Hutchins, first started the business in 1978, the family lived in a room attached to the restaurant (Tim was also born in that room). In those early years, the restaurant was known as Roy's Smokehouse. Set in a small metal building on the side of the road in Princeton, which is just east of McKinney in North Texas, Roy's quickly grew in popularity. Eventually, the family moved to a bigger location in McKinney, and then rebranded as Hutchins Barbeque in 1991.

"My brothers and I were immersed in the barbecue lifestyle at a young age," says Tim, who started washing dishes at age 14, and then made barbecue sauce and sides before rising to meat cutter at 17 and pitmaster at 19.

In 1994, the Hutchinses expanded again with a location in Frisco, which Tim's older brother Tracy ("Trey") ran. In 2002, Roy collaborated with Randy White, a Dallas Cowboy legend, and changed the name of the Frisco restaurant to Randy White's Hall of Fame BBQ. He opened three more Randy White's locations, but within the first six months, the business began hemorrhaging money, and Roy found himself in some tax trouble. His tax attorney suggested he find a new owner for Hutchins Barbeque in McKinney. So 22-year-old Tim became the owner and president of Hutchins, while his brothers Trey and Wes operated Randy White's. Roy remained a partner, but took a back seat to let his sons handle the businesses.

Upon assuming control of Hutchins, Tim prioritized strengthening the business financially, making changes based on insights fostered during his experience growing up within the restaurant. He opened for more hours and enhanced leadership, then started to make some small recipe changes. Through trial and error, he also found more efficient ways to tweak the meat-smoking process, creating a more consistent product while continuing to uphold some of the traditions Hutchins had established.

"Consistency is key with most things in life, including barbecue," says Tim. "While we made some upgrades, we've kept many beloved aspects of Hutchins the same, including continuing to use pecan wood and wood-burning rotisserie pits."

He also kept Roy's recipes for creamy potato salad and the spicy-sweet barbecue sauce, plus his mother's famous recipe for broccoli salad, made from finely chopped broccoli, shredded cheddar, red onion, and salty bits of bacon tossed in a light, creamy sauce. But Tim also expanded the menu with sides like decadent bacon-infused mac and cheese and creamed corn made with fire-kissed kernels and a hint of spice. While Roy created the original sausage recipe, Tim continued to expand that program with a new brisket hot link and seasonal sausage specials like roasted pepper jack porch and chili cheese Frito pie. Tim has also carried on the tradition of offering free banana pudding, peach cobbler, and soft-serve ice cream for all dine-in guests.

When Franklin Barbecue kick-started the craft barbecue movement, Tim began going on barbecue tours around the state, building relationships within the industry and identifying more changes he could make to improve the quality of Hutchins' food. And in 2012, when a devastating fire caused Hutchins Barbeque to close its doors for five months, Tim used the unexpected break to begin sourcing higher-quality meats, including Prime brisket, which is a sine qua non order at Hutchins. Tim seasons his beef simply with salt, pepper, and garlic powder to let the flavorful meat come through, and smokes it low and slow to juicy perfection, starting with oak and finishing with pecan. He has also become known for brisket burnt ends that taste like a peppery meat candy, dazzling the palate with a burst of flavor, and the massive, tender beef ribs he makes each day. The rib rub Tim developed for the pork ribs is more complex than what goes on the beef, made with about 10 different ingredients, but it still manages to add flavor without overpowering the meat. The resulting pork ribs are well structured but perfectly tender, with a touch of sweetness and spice.

One day at the end of a shift in 2013, Tim was playing around with ingredients with his team, and ended up creating the Texas Twinkie, which has now become

an iconic Texas barbecue dish that is often replicated at other joints. The Texas Twinkie begins with a smoked jalapeño that is filled with brisket and cream cheese, then wrapped in bacon, seasoned with salt and pepper, glazed with secret sauce, and smoked.

All these changes certainly got the attention of *Texas Monthly,* and Hutchins landed on the Top 50 list in 2013. With business booming, Tim sought out a separate space just to fulfill catering orders. He ended up buying out his brother Trey and turning the Frisco location of Randy White's back into a Hutchins Barbeque—and then brought his brother on as a manager, and eventually a partner. At first, that location was only open to the public 12 hours a week, but Tim ended up opening it full-time, as the awards kept piling up and the customers kept coming. Hutchins was continuously landing on Best of DFW lists, and went on to be named a *TM* Top 50 restaurant in 2017 and 2021.

Tim's brother Wes also returned to work at Hutchins again, but he and Tim did not see eye to eye on how the business should grow. Wes and Roy (who was feeling antsy in retirement) thought the restaurant's successful momentum was a sign to start opening other locations, while Trey and Tim wanted to continue to improve upon the existing McKinney and Frisco locations. And when Wes and Roy decided to branch out on their own and use the Hutchins Barbeque name to open more locations, a barbecue family feud unfolded. Tim filed a trademark lawsuit against his father and brother in an attempt to protect the name he'd worked so hard to build up. However, they were eventually able to compromise, and the suit was dropped.

"Through many conversations, we came to an agreement so that both groups could utilize the family name Hutchins in different formats in order to distinguish the two brands," says Tim, who kept the Hutchins Barbeque brand, while Roy and Wes created The Original Roy Hutchins BBQ brand (which they opened in Trophy Club, a planned community about 50 miles southwest of McKinney). "The resolution has restored peace in our family. We all cheer each other on to create the best barbecue in Texas."

In 2023, Tim added a new pit building onto the McKinney location, and at press time he was in the process of adding an 8,000-square-foot expansion to the Frisco location, with 2,500 square feet dedicated to the pit room. In addition to 1,000-gallon offset smokers from M&M BBQ Company (see page 76) Tim also uses J&R and M&M rotisserie smokers, and worked with M&M to design a custom Zeus rotisserie pit that can smoke up to 100 briskets at a time. This pit has reduced wood costs by 30 percent, saves on space, and requires much less manpower to monitor fires. In the past year, Tim has also introduced three 500-gallon trailered pits made by Hutchins Fabrication (owned by Roy and their uncle, Kent Hutchins) for catering jobs.

Despite his continued success, the rise of Hutchins Barbeque has not been without challenges. Tim experienced another big fire in 2020 that required him to close for months during the pandemic for repairs. And in 2021 the legendary John Mueller (of the Louie Mueller Barbecue family, see page 240) joined the team as a pitmaster—but then passed away suddenly just a few months later.

"We've certainly overcome our fair share of challenges!" says Tim. "But we've always seen obstacles as moments to pause, pivot, and rebuild to be even stronger than before. We couldn't be where we are today without God, the support of my wife, and our family, including the team members at both our restaurants."

M&M BBQ
EST. 2003
COMPANY

ROTISSERIE REVIVAL

Though offset smokers have been the pit de rigueur for a few decades now, rotisserie smokers have a long history in Texas—and thanks to M&M BBQ Company, these efficient machines are finding their way back into the limelight.

The first rotisserie barbecue pit is said to have been created by Leonard McNeill, a Houston machinist who won a restaurant in a game of craps in 1949. He changed the Lenox Café to Lenox Bar-B-Q and started picking up catering jobs. McNeill was a popular businessman with connections at different oil companies, and by the 1960s he was picking up huge catering jobs at refineries along the Gulf Coast. The indirect heat brick pits being used at the time couldn't accommodate the amount of meat he needed to smoke for these events, so he brainstormed how he might be able to mechanize a smoker to suit his needs. When he saw that a local bakery used large, rotisserie-style ovens to bake their bread, he purchased one and modified it by attaching a smokestack and a firebox to burn wood.

Right around the same time, in 1967, a Mesquite barbecue restaurant owner and inventor named Herbert Oyler also started experimenting with rotisserie smoker designs. His was a steel barbecue pit with an electric carousel, fueled by wood burned in an attached firebox. Oyler patented his "barbecue cooking oven" in 1968, and built and sold a few of his own, with the help of a welder named Arthur Norman Bewley (who would go onto launch A. N. Bewley Fabricators). It wasn't until 1973 that he decided to meet with local engineers H. E. Finley and Mike Higgins of J&R Manufacturing about commercializing his creation. But immediately after the meeting, Oyler was killed when his pickup truck was struck by a train. By 1974, Oyler's widow negotiated a patent deal with Finley and Higgins, and the two began fabricating Oyler rotisseries.

Throughout the years, J&R Manufacturing added additional features to different models, including temperature gauges and electric heat elements, and convection fans and dampers to control the flow of smoke over the meat. The company, which celebrated 50 years of business in 2024, still produces Oyler rotisseries used by top pitmasters, like Ronnie Killen of Killen's Barbecue (see page 197), Patrick Feges of Feges BBQ (see page 185), and Will Buckman of CorkScrew BBQ (see page 225).

Mike Miller Sr. was the sole repairman for J&R Manufacturing for a number of years. In that time, he traveled all over the country repairing pits, often with his son Mike Miller Jr. in tow. So to say Mike Jr. got an early education in barbecue is an understatement.

"With my dad doing service, I would go on calls with him on the weekends," Miller remembers. "Being able to smell all the meat being cooked is something I'll never forget, not just because I'm still around it, but because it reminds me of all those times with my dad."

In 2003, Mike Sr. decided to branch off and start his own repair and service company, launching M&M Pit Repair about 50 miles southeast of Dallas, in Tool, Texas. After graduating from the University of North Texas with a marketing degree, Mike Jr. joined his dad in the shop and they began to shift their focus from repairing rotisserie smokers to building them from scratch. As Mike Sr. started to think about retiring, Mike Jr. reached out to his childhood friend Matt Sutton to join the team.

Sutton and Miller grew up together in Garland and have been friends since they were 10 years old. Matt cooked at Rudy's BBQ while he also attended the University of North Texas, where he also received a marketing degree. But after college, he moved to Wyoming to attend WyoTech, an automotive technical school, where he completed the Collision and Refinishing Technology program with specialty competitions in chassis fabrication, structural fabrication, refinishing and paint, and trim and upholstery. He had his sights set on building custom cars, and did exactly that in California after graduation.

But in 2017, he decided to change gears and move home to join forces with Miller, forming M&M BBQ Company. The Millers had already made some changes to the rotisserie's design, informed by years of fielding service calls, but once Sutton joined the team, the real innovation started. They started by reaching out to rotisserie users to see what they loved about the smokers, and what they'd like to see changed or added.

"Mike and I began implementing and brainstorming changes to improve current issues and cook performance," describes Sutton. "We constantly communicate with chefs and pitmasters at restaurants to continue to innovate and improve our product, making our customers' lives easier and less stressful while moving to produce a better product."

"We have developed an innovative heat delivery system that allows for virtually even cooking," explains Miller. "The firebox design allows for heat to move smoothly into the cooking chamber, while still allowing plenty of room for a coal bed, which helps with the efficiency of the unit. We made several other changes to protect wiring and other components, based on feedback received from our customers."

In the 1970s, companies like Southern Pride and Ole Hickory further automated barbecue by using gas or electricity to do the cooking. These "gassers," as they've come to be known, gave rotisseries the reputation of being hands-off machines that allowed restaurants to "set it and forget it." However, plenty of rotisseries—including those made by M&M BBQ Company—are fueled solely by wood.

"One of the misconceptions is that you can set it and forget it, but that is not the case," says Miller. "Our rotisseries are [powered by] 100 percent wood, with no fans or convection—just motors controlling the thermostat—and if you forget it, then you have no fire and you are no longer smoking! We are constantly working to show the world that they are as legit as it gets and absolutely true Texas BBQ—wood, fire, and smoke."

By the time Texas craft barbecue was on the rise in the 2010s, rotisserie pits had fallen out of favor for the large offset barrel pits that have now become representative of Texas barbecue. But offsets require the skilled labor of a pit hand to monitor the cooking process for up to 18 hours at a time. With the already-high cost of meat, that's just not a profitable choice for most pitmasters. Plenty of high-volume barbecue restaurants continued to use rotisseries, but kept them out of sight, while proudly displaying their offsets as a perceived symbol of craftsmanship. But now the tables are turning. M&M BBQ Company also builds offset smokers, but they produce about six times as many rotisserie smokers—and they see more and more pitmasters either supplementing their offset pits with an M&M rotisserie, or switching over completely. They've created customized pits for Burnt Bean Co. (see page 436), Hurtado Barbecue, Brett's BBQ Shop (see page 217), Hutchins Barbeque (see page 69), Helberg Barbecue (see page 419), Goldee's Barbecue (see page 16), Heim Barbecue (see page 50)—and other pitmasters all over the country.

"There are many benefits to using a rotisserie versus an offset, as they check virtually every box that offsets check without the extra labor, excessive wood consumption, and higher yield," says Miller.

"The M&M rotisserie is incredibly easy to use, efficient, and can produce incredible volume," says Phillip Helberg, who ordered one to supplement his Moberg offsets and increase capacity, as Helberg Barbecue is about to expand into a much larger space.

Esaul Ramos, who has only ever used offset smokers at his 2M Smokehouse (see page 426), ordered an M&M rotisserie in order to keep up with demand without straining his staff.

"It's hard to hire people nowadays," says Ramos. "And especially hard to hire people to tend the pit in the heat and the cold and the rain, and all that. So that's why I got that M&M—because it alleviates me from having to have somebody there cooking 16-hour days."

Goldee's Barbecue supplemented their two Mill Scale offsets with an M&M rotisserie pit, and loved it so much, they ordered another one to use for their fast casual rib concept, Ribbee's.

"We used to cook overnight, but we don't have to do that anymore," says co-owner Jonny White. "Now that we have this [M&M rotisserie], we have plenty of room to cook everything in a normal timeframe. I love this thing so much. It saved my life because I don't have to be up here all night. It also saved us a ton of money on wood."

Hutchins Barbeque began a relationship with M&M BBQ Company 25 years ago, when they brought the Millers in for pit repairs. Last year, M&M created a custom Zeus pit for Hutchins.

"This giant wood-burning rotisserie pit can smoke up to 100 briskets at one time, reduces wood costs by 30 percent, uses less manpower to monitor the heat, and saves on space. We also have five M&M 1000 Series rotisserie wood-burning pits, with several more on order, and two 1,000-gallon offset pits, with more on the way as well. We look forward to continuing our partnership with M&M for another 25 years!"

While an M&M rotisserie, which can range between $20,000 and $30,000, is certainly an investment, business owners are likely to see a return on that investment, in the money saved on both wood and labor. Dusty Miller of Miller's Smokehouse (see page 339) ordered a pair of M&M rotisseries as his volume was increasing, and he was so pleased with the results, he ended up getting rid of all his offset smokers and ordering two more.

"Our wood consumption has gone down drastically, we are putting our most consistent product out, and we are getting to cook new items due to the efficiency of these pits," says Miller. "This wasn't any easy decision by any means, However, when it came to ordering our second pair of M&M 2000s, it was a no-brainer."

In addition to all the practical reasons for incorporating rotisseries, the pieces M&M BBQ Company are crafting have irresistible hot rod flair thanks to Sutton's custom automotive experience. They're building customized pits and trailers with flashy paint jobs in every color imaginable—gold, hot pink, electric blue, fire-engine red—plus details like gold leaf and custom signage advertising with not only the barbecue joints' logos, but meat brands, sponsors, and sports teams. In other words, these aren't the kind of rotisseries anybody is hiding in the back.

As the Texas barbecue continues to thrive so does M&M BBQ Company. (Their lead time for building a pit is currently nine to 12 months for offsets and four months for rotisseries.) And with more of Miller and Sutton's creations finding their way into pit rooms all over Texas, they are proud to be a part of this growing industry.

"When I was first introduced to BBQ with my dad, everything was very hush-hush," remembers Miller. "No one shared their recipes or invited you into their pitrooms, but now it happens all the time. You constantly see classes, collaborations, and pitmasters supporting each other. One thing we know for sure is that we are here for it and will support it by bringing our brand of functional aesthetics and innovation to the barbecue community!"

LOCKHART SMOKEHOUSE

DALLAS

Despite growing up in Lockhart, the barbecue capital of Texas, Jill Bergus had to move to New York to dig into her roots. She didn't just grow up there—Bergus is descended from barbecue royalty—her grandfather Edgar Schmidt ran the legendary Kreuz Market (see page 295) from the time he purchased it from the Kreuz family in 1948 until he passed it onto his sons in 1984.

Bergus was working in television production and living in New York with her husband, Jeff, in 2007, when Hill Country Barbecue Market opened and took the city by storm. They were the first to offer high-quality barbecue, smoked low and slow, that the city had never before seen—a phenomenon completely inspired by the barbecue traditions laid down by her family.

"We went to visit [Hill Country Barbecue] and photos of my Uncle Ricky and all my family were on the wall," remembers Jill. "I was like, 'Okay, if this can work in New York City, surely we could do this in Dallas, Texas.' Aaron Franklin was picking up a tailwind and the craft barbecue movement was starting up. Pecan Lodge had just opened down in the farmer's market and they were only open for lunch. And then you had your Sonny Bryan's, your Dickey's, your Mike Anderson's—the traditional kind of Dallas institutions at that time—but there wasn't really any Central Texas–style barbecue."

Jill and Jeff relocated to Dallas, and soon partnered with chef Tim McLaughlin to open the first Lockhart Smokehouse in Dallas' hip Bishop Arts district in 2011. McLaughlin trained with Jill's cousin Keith Schmidt and long-time pitmaster Roy Perez at Kreuz Market, then educated the rest of the Dallas team on how to craft the legendary post oak–smoked meats. Israel Rodriguez has now been the pitmaster for over three years, though Jill says, "We try to think of ourselves as Lockhart Smokehouse, as opposed to the cult of one pitmaster."

Lockhart Smokehouse is one of few places with in-door pits, which is a godsend for temperature control during sizzling Texas summers, but rendered them unable to use the same sort of open-brick pits Kreuz used; instead, they opted for a customized Bewley pit. Invented in 1960 and still crafted by A. N. Bewley Fabricators, the thick steel pit is still an offset smoker, but it features a closed design with easy-to-open doors and multiple inner racks. Not only can they smoke even lower and slower than Kreuz's original brick pits (up to 16 hours for brisket), but the Bewley only goes through two cords of wood a month.

Lockhart Smokehouse carries Kreuz Market's regular and jalapeño cheese sausage links, which are made using the family recipe that's been passed down for generations. Their dry-rubbed proteins also mirror the offerings at Kreuz. In addition to brisket, with its main character energy, there's half and whole chickens, turkey, spareribs, and two items you don't see very often in Texas barbecue joints (outside of Lockhart, at least): pork chops and shoulder clod. The former is thick-cut and heavy with flavor and natural moisture, while the latter is leaner than brisket, with a distinct beefy flavor profile. Other proteins—like beef ribs, burnt ends, prime rib, and baby back ribs—show up as weekly or one-off specials.

When it comes to sides, however, Lockhart Smokehouse has created all of their own recipes, and will occasionally add more to the rotation. Brisket makes its way into the potato salad, the smoked baked beans, and the deviled eggs. On the vegetarian end of the spectrum, they offer regular and spicy mac and cheese and newer creations like blue cheese coleslaw and Mexican street corn, which can be topped with your choice of protein. Surprisingly, banana pudding only recently joined the classic peach cobbler as a dessert option.

Initially, Lockhart Smokehouse did adopt one other Kreuz Market tradition: for years, the family business didn't offer any barbecue sauce or forks (though they have since added both). Lockhart-style Central Texas barbecue is distinguished by its use of more subtle post oak and simple dry rubs (just salt and pepper for the beef, though they use a touch of sugar in their chicken and pork rubs), letting the flavor of the meats shine; the goal is to produce barbecue that does not need any sauce. So when Lockhart Smokehouse first opened, they followed in those footsteps, but it was not well received.

"When you tell people they can't have something, they want it a whole lot more." Jill says matter-of-factly. "So for our first review for the *Dallas Morning News*, we got one star. It was awful! So we put up a special that day—it was 'Fork you, Leslie Brenner' Day,'" named after the infamous Dallas food critic.

Despite that unexpectedly rocky start, Lockhart Smokehouse went on to gain great acclaim (they were named one of the Top 50 in both 2013 and 2017, then dropped to an Honorable Mention in 2021). In 2014, they opened a location in a 100-year-old building in Plano's historic district, and in 2018, they partnered with the Texas Rangers to open a third location in the Texas Live! entertainment district in Arlington. All three locations feature a considerable collection of wall decor, from neon beer signs to vintage oil signs, and the original location is particularly collaged with framed signed photos, street signs, and the like. Look closely and you'll even see—hidden right in plain sight—the original Kreuz Market sign suspended from the ceiling, a reminder of where it all really began.

SMOKE'N ASH BBQ

ARLINGTON

Strip malls in the Dallas–Fort Worth area are filled with all sorts of delicious surprises. In fact, one unassuming cluster of storefronts in Arlington is home to what may be the only Tex-Ethiopian barbecue joint in the world. Patrick and Fasicka Hicks opened Smoke'N Ash in 2012, serving Texas barbecue, but it was seven years later, when they began serving Ethiopian food, that they really found their stride.

Fasicka migrated to Arlington from Addis Ababa, Ethiopia, in 1996 to attend school while living with her oldest sister. She met Patrick a year later, and the two began dating, got married, and had two kids. Fasicka cooked for her family, recreating Ethiopian dishes she'd learned from her mother. Meanwhile Patrick, an engineering technician for Siemens Engineering, had grown up watching his family run two barbecue joints (One Stop BBQ in Waco and Dallas). While smoking in his backyard, he daydreamed about carrying on that tradition. Fasicka's Ethiopian family also loved Patrick's barbecue, and encouraged him to pursue his passion.

So in 2012, Patrick and Fasicka opened a weekend-only food truck serving Texas barbecue. They ran it for six years until they'd built up enough momentum to open a brick and mortar in Southeast Arlington. A few months later, Patrick quit his job to go all-in on barbecue. They were seeing success within the community, but Fasicka had become bored and missed cooking her family's dishes. She suggested they experiment with an additional Ethiopian menu to see how their customers responded.

The Hicks named the other concept Cherkose Ethiopian Cuisine, honoring Fasicka's late mother's maiden name, since she inspired each of the recipes. At first, they treated it like a separate restaurant with the same address, but not only did the new menu attract members of DFW's Ethiopian community—it also interested their barbecue regulars, who started to make requests combining the two cuisines. So they took the feedback to heart and, in addition to a Texas menu and an Ethiopian one, they began offering Tex-Ethiopian creations, combining the two cuisines into unique dishes bursting with flavor and soul.

"My family thought it was a brilliant idea [to merge the two cuisines]," says Fasicka.

Patrick fuels his Ole Hickory smoker with both hickory and post oak to smoke Prime brisket, pork ribs, rib tips, pork sausage, beef and lamb sausage, pulled pork, pulled lamb, and chicken. He seasons these meats simply and serves them by the half-pound, sandwich, or plate. Their Tex-Ethiopian barbecue all gets glazed with awaze, a red sauce made with kibe (a mix of cardamom, caraway seeds, nigella, garlic, ginger, and a minty herb called koseret), then mixed with berbere spices and steeped in clarified butter.

Berbere spice blends can vary widely in Ethiopia. Fasicka gets hers straight from the source; her sister ships their family's blend of dried and ground chiles, dried shallots, ginger, garlic, rue leaves, caraway seeds, nigella, clove, cinnamon, and coriander. This magic mix appears all over the menu: in the mac and cheese, brisket stew, smoked chicken stew, barbecue beans, on the rib tips, and accenting the sweet potato pie and Texas sheet cake. Though there are chiles in it, Fasicka uses just enough berbere to these dishes to add complexity and flavor without introducing spicy heat.

Another important spice her family sends her from Ethiopia is shiro powder, a spiced chickpea blend used in a wide variety of wat (stew) like missir wat (slow-simmered lentil stew), shiro wat (chickpea stew), bozena shiro wat (pureed chickpea stew with beef), doro wat (spicy chicken stew), smoked dubba wat (pumpkin stew), key siga wat (spicy beef stew), and alicha yebeg siga wat (lamb stew). Tibs is a popular Ethiopian stir-fry usually made with either lamb or beef, and sauteed with onions, peppers, and spices. At Smoke'N Ash, the tibs are made with smoked beef sirloin, lamb, chicken, mushrooms, or cauliflower.

Out of Smoke'N Ash's 16 different side dishes, most are vegetarian and a good number of them are vegan too. There are classic Texas barbecue sides—creamy potato salad and BBQ beans (but no coleslaw) and there's both classic mac and cheese and a version enhanced with berbere spice. Comfort-food influence comes through in offerings like brisket green beans and fried okra. And then there's an entire listing of vegan Ethiopian sides like gommen (collard greens), tikil gommen (cabbage and carrots), ater kik wat (split yellow pea stew), and key sir wat (beet-and-potato stew). Smoke'N Ash offers a vegan combo plate, with all six sides, as well as an Ethiopian combo plate (three meats and three veggies).

But their signature dish is the Tex-Ethiopian platter, which comes with smoked doro wat, rib tip tibs, awaze brisket, awaze pork ribs, missir wat, and substantial collard greens (with an option to switch lamb for pork, which is forbidden by Ethiopia's two major religions, Islam and Ethiopian Orthodox Christianity.) All combo plates come with a slice of thick Texas toast and either rice pilaf or injera, a spongy, sourdough flatbread that somewhat resembles a large crepe. Fasicka makes her own by fermenting the dough for 24 to 48 hours, then griddling the injera for 1 to 2 minutes on a mitad, or flat-top stove. Ethiopian food is traditionally presented atop this springy crepe, with rolls of it served on the side and used to scoop up the savory stews in lieu of utensils.

Smoke'N Ash also features some fun mash-ups. In addition to the mac and cheese, baked potatoes, and fries loaded with barbecue that have become popular at a lot of spots, they offer injera nachos as a way to utilize any leftover injera. They are cut into triangles and baked until crisp, then loaded with your choice of barbecue meat or shiro wat, barbecue sauce, both shredded cheese and ayib (fresh crumbled cheese), pico de gallo, and jalapeños. In Ethiopia, leftover injera is simmered with tomatoes, onions, and garlic for a dish called firfir. Smoke'N Ash makes a creation called firfir migas, where the injera pieces are cooked with eggs, your choice of barbecue meat, shredded cheese, ayib, jalapeños, and pico de gallo. And every dish can benefit from a heavy dash of barely sweet barbecue sauce, which Fasicka makes with bebere, jalapeños, onions, and carrots.

The desserts at Smoke'N Ash follow a similar model. Banana cream pudding and peach cobble remain traditional and are offered alongside a subtly spiced berbere sweet potato pie and a Texas sheet cake with berbere fudge frosting and berbere-dusted pecans. And no visit to Smoke'N Ash would be complete without an Ethiopian coffee ceremony, which Fasicka performs upon request. She roasts the coffee beans in a traditional coffee roasting pan and brings them out to the dining room for the guests to experience the aroma. Popcorn is a traditional snack served in an Ethiopian coffee ceremony, and at Smoke'N Ash, they season it and smoke it before serving.

The response to Fasicka and Patrick's unique Tex-Ethiopian concept has been so great, they moved to a bigger space (two miles down the road) in 2023. They were honored with a prized Recommendation from the Michelin Guide in 2024, and they're currently working on publishing their first cookbook. While the Hickses are thrilled with their continuing success, they are unsurprised that the community is drawn to the marriage of Ethiopian and Texas cuisines, which pair well both culinarily and culturally.

"My husband says all time," explains Fasicka, "that not only do the Ethiopian spices blend so well when used to smoke meat, but also the Ethiopian concept of communal dining and hospitality is very similar to Texas barbecue traditions."

EAST TEXAS

STANLEY'S FAMOUS PIT BARBECUE

TYLER

Visit Stanley's Famous Pit Barbecue at lunchtime, and a long line will undoubtedly stretch from the entrance to the black-painted brick building around the open-air patio. Visitors in denim and cowboy hats will be largely outnumbered by the scrub-donning colleagues who walk over from one of two nearby hospitals in midtown Tyler. But visit Stanley's at night and you'll encounter a very different scene. If there's a show happening, the patio will have transformed into a venue, with bands playing on a stage built from wooden pallets and decorated with license plates arranged in the shape of Texas. Even when there's not live music, there's a lively bar scene, with friends congregating inside and out while a killer soundtrack sets the scene.

This is the world Nick Pencis has created, but Stanley's Famous Pit Barbecue started back in 1953 as Sam's Barbecue Spot. It later changed hands and become Watson's Famous Pit-Bar-B-Q until Bill Watson sold the place to J. D. Stanley, a former oil field worker, in 1961. Stanley then ran the business for decades, building a loyal following of East Texas barbecue enthusiasts. Once Stanley passed away, Chris and Samia Smith bought the business for a period of time. Meanwhile Pencis, a drummer who'd been touring with a band called Greyhounds, had returned to Tyler to pursue a business degree while bartending

BE KIND HAVE

on the side. He began working at Stanley's and soon dropped out of school to run the restaurant full-time. He also tapped into his contacts to book BYOB shows on the uncovered deck outside.

"Initially, live music was just a way to get younger folks in the know about Stanley's," says Pencis. "When I took over, it was very much an old-timer place on the side of town where there was not a lot happening, and so folks my age didn't really know about it. It was just kind of the spot where all the old men went and drank coffee in the morning and talked about politics."

In 2006, he took over the business and his wife, Jen, quit her job as a pilates instructor and personal trainer to come run it with him. The closest thing to barbecue experience Pencis had under his belt was some casual backyard grilling, and a few dreamy memories of visiting his grandmother in a barbecue joint where she worked in Buda. Stanley's originally had flat brick pits but, after the previous change of hands, the health department had come through and insisted they be removed. So when Pencis took the reins, the only smoker on site was an Ole Hickory rotisserie.

"I felt like the legacy of this place was important, so when I took over one of the first things I did was take a trip to Lockhart to go see some of the legendary places down there," says Pencis. "And from that moment on I was like, 'OK, we have to get back to the roots of this place and we have to start cooking [barbecue] the right way and have a legitimate process.'"

Pencis made some kitchen upgrades and built a pit room to house Dutch, an 18-foot offset smoker with double stacks built by Clint Shockey at East Texas Smoker Company. He built up a solid team and kept developing and expanding the menu, which features meat by the pound and classic-leaning sides: a creamy, scoopable potato salad, robust cowboy beans, and bright, citrusy slaw. The brisket, beef ribs, and pork butts are all rubbed with just salt and pepper, and the juicy turkey gets a blend of salt, pepper, garlic, and basil (and is further enriched by a beautifully smoky tomatillo sauce they make in-house). The rub for their Duroc pork baby back ribs is one of J. D. Stanley's original recipes, as are both their original and spicy barbecue sauces, which Pencis found recorded on handwritten recipe cards.

"Our rib rub is a pretty in-depth dry rub that incorporates a Memphis style with white sugar and brown sugar and then some elements that are really prevalent in Texas cuisine [due to] our proximity and brotherhood with Mexico: chili powder, cumin—some things that most people might not normally associate with rib rub, but that's how we roll," says Pencis.

Stanley's is known for its heaping sandwiches, a tradition that began with The Shrove, a stack of sliced pit ham and chopped brisket held together by melted American cheese and invented by Watson back in the 1950s. Most of the other sandwich offerings were created or inspired by customers through the years, such as the Brother-in-Law (a grilled hot link with cheese and chopped brisket or pulled pork) and the Ex-Wife (pulled pork and sliced brisket).

Former pit crew member Jordan Jackson (who went on to work at Bodacious Bar-B-Q, page 143, but returned in 2024 to consult and refine cooking procedures) invented The Mother Clucker, a smoked chicken thigh topped with spicy barbecue mayo, cheddar cheese, and an over-easy fried egg, all nestled in a jalapeño-cheese sourdough roll. Opt for "Super Deluxe" to upgrade any of these sandwiches from a soft white bun to that superior roll, and ask for anything "Yankee-style" to add slaw.

By 2008, just two years after Pencis took over the business, Stanley's was named one of *Texas Monthly*'s Top 50 barbecue spots. Their ribs have twice won the title of Best Pork Ribs in Texas at the magazine's all-star barbecue competitions, and in 2014 they named The Mother Clucker one of the best barbecue sandwiches in the state. As you can imagine, all the attention has allowed Pencis to expand operations even more. He currently has two 1,000-galloon offset smokers, and brought in two Oyler 1700 rotisseries, which the team uses very intentionally.

"We treat those apparatus like they are an offset, where we are not using the automatic controls for fire control," explains Pencis. "We're manually controlling the fires and doing our best to maintain the temperature and the air flow in the machine. It's just that we cook so many damn ribs, and the racks are just a lifesaver when you're moving that many racks of ribs around. You can get a good cook on there when you are involved through its process, instead of how a lot of people use them, [which is] just 'set it and forget it.'"

But with more business come some sacrifices too. Pencis used to use a blend of post oak and pecan, but is now using primarily post oak because he's had a hard time finding a reliable pecan source. And while he used to exclusively source 44 Farms' coveted grass-fed, naturally certified Black Angus beef, he now has to supplement with Upper 2/3rds Choice Black Angus brisket from other packers—they use this for the chopped brisket, which requires a higher fat content. But they still use 44 Farms for all the sliced brisket, as well as the specials like tri-tip, beef cheek barbacoa on Wednesdays, and burgers on Thursdays.

Pencis has made gradual upgrades to the restaurant through the years but in 2013 he significantly expanded the indoor seating capacity, covered the patio, and built a full-sized stage with lighting and a house PA system. To date, their stage has welcomed nationally touring artists from Charlie Crockett and Paul Cauthen to Deerhunter and The Old 97s. "Don [Stanley] comes in quite regularly now and says that his dad would be really proud and excited about what we're doing," says Pencis. "He said that J. D. always wanted to have bands play there."

Pencis also launched a bar program—a major development in a city that was dry until 2012. In 2018, he expanded further, into the space next door, which allowed him to include frozen drinks in the bar program (the Painkiller with a rum floater, one result of this evolution, is a must-try), craft beer, and over 100 different whiskies—the largest selection in East Texas.

"Bourbon is definitely something that I love and it just so happens that folks also share that passion," says Pencis. "I love the process and the history—and obviously the liquid itself is one of my favorite things, and another reason to get people to pay attention to what we're doing here. I just happen to think that bourbon, barbecue, and live music are things that bring people together."

CHIEF FIREWOOD
A WOOD EXPERT COMPANY

FUEL TO THE FIRE

Pitmasters across the state hold strong (and differing) beliefs on the best rubs, binders, and brines for different proteins. But there is one thing they can all agree on: wood, and the fire that results, is the number one most important ingredient to crafting barbecue.

Historically, pitmasters would connect with a local supplier (usually just an individual with a pick-up truck and a wood source) to deliver stacks as needed. But as Texas barbecue started to soar in popularity, it became increasingly difficult to lock in a consistent supply of quality firewood. Over the last decade, more suppliers have been surfacing to keep up with the constant demand to add fuel to the fires all across Texas.

Spend time in enough Top 50 pit rooms and you'll encounter one name over and over again. Chief Firewood's logo can be seen branding wheeled racks of neatly stacked firewood behind the scenes at Franklin Barbecue (see page 233 for a profile on founder Aaron Franklin), InterStellar BBQ (see page 278), la Barbecue (see page 249), Louie Mueller Barbecue (see page 240), Stiles Switch BBQ and Brew (see page 385), Truth BBQ (see page 121), LeRoy and Lewis Barbecue (see page 258), and many more.

Chief Firewood began servicing Central Texas with firewood in 1990, but the story actually begins in Tamaulipas, Mexico, where 13-year-old Joel Sanchez had a job merchandising and stocking in a grocery store. The owner began sending Sanchez to Monterrey to buy produce from larger warehouses at a better price, and encouraged him to bring back extra to resell around town.

"I always liked business, always liked making money—buying and selling," recalls Sanchez.

At 17, Sanchez moved to the US to work in the oil fields of West Texas alongside his older brother, where he quickly identified another lucrative side hustle. He noticed scrap metal scattered everywhere and worked out a deal where he would clean up all the locations in exchange for the scrap, which he would then cash in.

One of the neighboring landowners admired Sanchez's 1984 Ford pickup truck and asked if he would trade him the truck and $500 in exchange for one of his 18-wheelers. The other part of the agreement was that Sanchez would take on a part-time gig hauling wood to his yard in Houston.

"People in Houston started seeing my truck loaded with wood and they'd flag me down because they wanted to buy it, so I started selling," recounts Sanchez. "I ended up having 17 woodyards in Houston I was wholesaling."

In 1990, he quit the oil field and decided to sell wood full-time. When his sons were 12 and 16, they began helping him out, loading and unloading the 18-wheeler full of wood. One of Sanchez's friends supplied wood to Ninfa's, the famous Tex-Mex chain that started in Houston, when Austin-based restaurant group Serrano's acquired it. Suddenly there was a need for wood delivery at a dozen Serrano's. They started Sanchez out with four restaurants and, after a few months, asked if he wanted to take on more. By 1999, he was delivering mesquite to a dozen Serrano's, where the wood was used to grill fajitas. Next, Sanchez picked up Carrabba's, delivering post oak and pecan for the Italian chain to craft their wood-fired pizza.

Joel's son Javier began helping out more with the business as he got older, though it wasn't until he was 30 that he decided to leave his construction job to partner with his dad full-time.

"It took a while for me to finally get my head screwed on right because I didn't have a vision for the business, I didn't have a plan to grow it," explains Javier. "My father is the brains of everything. He always said, 'If we're going to sell wood, we need restaurants—we need barbecue houses.' So that's what I went after when I started picking up accounts."

In 2014, they gained their first barbecue account when Southside Market & Barbeque (see page 346) signed on for wood delivery, and then Franklin Barbecue followed shortly after.

"Franklin was buying from three different suppliers so they could have enough wood," says Javier. "And Aaron said once they started buying wood from us, they never had to worry about whether they'd have enough. Before that, they couldn't sleep at night, because they didn't know if they were going to have wood to cook the next day. But once we start supplying them, no worries."

It was around this time that they designed customized wheeled racks so they could more efficiently make deliveries to their growing barbecue accounts. A cord is a stack of wood eight feet long by four feet tall by four feet wide, and can run anywhere from $400 to $700, depending on the type of wood, level of seasoning, distance of the delivery, and other factors. Franklin goes through about four to five cords of post oak a week. Terry Black's Barbecue (see page 359), another one of Chief Firewood's big clients, burns through about seven cords a week at just one of their locations. Joel and Javier's weekly haul ranges from 80 to 100 cords a week, across Houston, Austin, San Antonio, and parts of Dallas.

Chief Firewood's headquarters is based on 20 acres in Smithville, a town located 47 miles southeast of Austin. Four crews (with two men per crew) bring wood in from a 40- to 60-mile radius. Joel and Javier network with farmers, ranchers, land developers, and tree trimmers to find sources, which are often areas that have been affected by weather extremes—namely drought.

"We've been losing post oaks for over 10 years now because of drought," explains Javier. "The majority of our wood comes from dead trees. We do ranchers a favor by going out there, removing their dead trees, and we can use the product versus just piling it up and burning it. Instead, barbecue places and restaurants can use the wood."

Other times, their harvest is a result of landowners clearing trees either for agricultural purposes or development.

"Post oaks have a really sensitive root system," says Javier. "So let's say somebody buys 100 acres and they want to build a home on it. So they get a 'dozer in there and clean everything up. That usually disturbs the root systems and the trees die. Then we go in and cut them."

Once the logs come in from the fields on trucks, the crew off-loads them using a grapple and boom. They use a 60-inch circular saw blade to cut each log into 18-inch-long pieces, and a splitting chamber to split the wood into variables of 8 to 16 splits per log. The wood then travels via conveyer belt into 20-foot-tall piles, where it will season for at least a year, and for up to 18 months.

"Oak is such a tight-grained wood that it takes longer for it to season than other trees," says Javier. "For instance, a pecan tree would season in half the time that it takes oak wood to season."

Seasoning refers to the process of leaving the wood out in the elements to dry before it is used. Seasoned wood is easier to ignite and keep lit, and it burns hotter and cleaner, producing less smoke and less damage to the environment. The longer the wood seasons, it also releases phenols like vanillin and Isoeugenol, by-products of lignin combustion that produce notes of cinnamon, sugar, and vanilla.

As the most prevalent wood found throughout the region, post oak is most commonly used for Central Texas barbecue. It's preferred for the gentle smoke flavor it imparts, enhancing the meat without overpowering it. It also maintains a high heat for a long time, making it ideal for the long cooks required for brisket, and is known to produce a deep smoke ring and dark, thick bark.

"Aaron Franklin made it popular," says Javier. "But truth be told, post oak burns a lot cleaner and it's easier to work with—it lights a lot easier and gives that clear blue smoke. The live oak is a harder wood, so it's harder to light, harder to work with, and doesn't burn as clean."

There are typically a couple of thousand cords of wood stacked up in their yard, with a section dedicated to mixed hardwood for residential customers.

"All this live oak goes to residential," says Javier, gesturing toward one pile. "We used to sell them post oak, but not anymore. Now we need it all for barbecue!"

Post oak makes up 90 percent of Chief Firewood's inventory. Massive piles of it cure until they are well-seasoned enough to be stacked and packed for delivery. A pile of mesquite logs, unmistakably reddish toned, also toasts nearby under the Texas sun. Mesquite burns much hotter, so it isn't ideal for low-and-slow cooking, and it produces a much more prevalent spicy, smoky taste. However, once the wood burns down to coals, that harsh smoke mellows out, making it ideal for direct-fire cooking.

"A lot of people in South Texas have used mesquite forever, because that's what they have down there," says Javier. "But once they try post oak for barbecue, they're like—'Ok, post oak is where it's at.'"

"We do have some guys that ask for mesquite and then they mix it into the oak for flavor," adds Joel. "Or we have some guys who mix together the pecan and the oak. When you start mixing the wood, then you get different flavors."

Next, they want to venture into the pellet market, which will serve as a great way to process their wood scraps and eliminate waste, while fueling a majority of backyard smokers. Next, they are bringing firewood to the masses by packaging foot-long logs and chunks into boxes that are sold to consumers on their website.

"We want to reach the weekend warriors that don't have room to buy a whole pallet of wood," says Javier. "They just want enough wood for one or two cooks."

It was only after 31 years of doing business entirely by word-of-mouth that the father-son team finally branded the company. (The name Chief Firewood comes from Joel's nickname "Chief," when he was a foreman in the oil fields.) In 2022, they started printing merch, launched a website, and started utilizing social media. Videographer Derek Clerk creates high-quality videos of their clients giving pit room tours, sharing barbecue tips, and talking about their experiences as pitmasters. The account quickly gained thousands of followers and continues to grow organically, with its shareable content attracting even more customers.

"It took me a long time to really come to the realization of how important wood is," Javier admits. "To me, it was just wood, you know? I never thought it would be a big craze. In the early years, I'd say it was just a big fad—but it's only gotten bigger and bigger."

WOOD TYPES

With the rise in popularity of Central Texas–style barbecue, post oak has become one of the most well-known and well-loved wood types for smoking, in high demand by pitmasters (and home cooks) across the state. But historically, pit cooks used what was locally available to them, making barbecue an inherently regional and sustainable cuisine. Now, thanks to companies like Chief Firewood, Sierrah Wood, and ButlerWood, barbecue operations can have seasoned cords of their preferred wood delivered straight to their backyard.

OAK (Post, Red, Live)

- Widely available throughout Central Texas
- Gives off an even and predictable heat, great for maintaining a low-and-slow fire
- Post oak produces a gentle smoke flavor without overpowering the meat
- Produces a nice smoke ring and dark bark on brisket
- Can produce nice vanilla and cinnamon notes if seasoned correctly
- Red oak and live oak burn a little slower and produce a stronger smoke flavor

PECAN

- A member of the hickory family, widely available in North and East Texas
- Cures much more quickly than oak
- Makes for a good fire starter
- Gives off a mild smoke flavor and adds a hint of sweetness
- Good for adding color to ribs
- Turns to ash quickly without making coals, and thus is best for short cooks

HICKORY

- Widely available in North and East Texas
- Should be aged for up to a year
- Cures much more quickly than oak
- Burns hot and fast
- Produces a nice sparkless flame
- Gives off a bold smoky-sweet flavor and an aroma reminiscent of bacon (since most bacon is smoked with hickory)

MESQUITE

- Widely available in South and West Texas
- Should be aged for at least a year to let the flavor mellow
- Burns hot and fast
- Can be challenging to work with and keep lit
- Very robust smoky flavor can be overpowering
- Good for cooking with direct heat, especially once it's turned to coals

1701 BARBECUE

BEAUMONT

James "Blue" Broussard (pronounced "BROO-sard") is producing some of the best barbecue in Beaumont at 1701 Barbecue. And, though he comes from a long line of entrepreneurs, Broussard was born into a very different industry; his family has been in East Texas for seven generations now, and five of those generations have worked as funeral service providers.

In 1889, Broussard's great-great-grandfather Alex Broussard turned his livery stable into an undertaking business, opening the first funeral parlor in Southeast Texas. Today, Broussard's Mortuary has six locations around the Golden Triangle. Blue's father, Jim, is the president, his sister Jayme is the CEO, and Blue acts as Director of Special Projects.

"I've just always been one of those guys that's always doing a lot of different things," says Blue. "I like to stay busy, and then I've got a good support system with my family to allow me to be able to do that."

Blue's first special project involved turning one of the original mortuaries into an events center called Broussard's Centre. After that, he converted a historic dancehall on his family's ranch into a wedding venue called Sevenne Hall. Broussard Farm is a working cattle ranch and hay operation located just outside of Beaumont in Fannett, where Blue grew up, and his dad continues to operate the ranch.

"I was always around agriculture, so that's another aspect of my life too," Blue says with an East Texas drawl, through his signature salt-and-pepper handlebar mustache. "I was country when country wasn't cool."

After graduating from Sam Houston State with a degree in agricultural business, Blue toured with his country act, The Blue Broussard Band, for several years, and spent a lot of time in Nashville, playing the guitar, singing, and writing songs.

"I had my fun doing that, then got into barbecue, got married, and got a family," he says. "So now I've traded music for barbecue."

Barbecue was certainly nothing new for Blue; in fact, you could say it's in his blood. Blue's Acadian ancestors settled in Louisiana, where they worked as cattle raisers, making their way further west into Texas in the 1800s, in search of better grazing land. And in the Broussard family's long history of ranching, their Cajun-Creole gatherings were always centered around food, from pork ribs to gumbo.

In 2015, Blue partnered with his friend David Thompson on a trailer called Blue Dave's Barbecue, but Blue—who had become a licensed funeral director and was working full-time in the family's business—never felt like he could give the business the time needed to get it off the ground. They sold the trailer in 2019, but Blue soon realized he could not shake the barbecue bug.

"If I'm into something, I dive headfirst into it," says Blue. "So I've probably read every book there is about barbecue, watched every YouTube video. Whatever I'm into, that's what I'm doing."

Blue and his sister Jayme had been talking about introducing some new concepts into the family business, and barbecue seemed like the next logical step. Beaumont, which is located just 30 miles west of Louisiana, has its own distinct barbecue tradition of beef links (see the profile on Patillo's Barbeque on page 212 for more on this tradition), but there was no Central Texas–style barbecue being made in the area at the time. They also already had the space for a barbecue business, in a building on the same property as their event space.

Some of the family was understandably hesitant about breaking into a brand-new industry (albeit just a different type of service industry), but they got behind Blue's passion and talent. Though they were planning on opening by August 2020, the pandemic threw them a curveball. However, they kept moving forward with the project, opening 1701 Barbecue on December 1, 2020.

The restaurant—which is named after its street address—is housed in a former service station built in 1942, and both the walls and floor show its long history. Blue's renovations provide a perfectly rustic backdrop for his homestyle but elevated barbecue menu. The attached pit room features four locally crafted pits (all 750-gallon and smaller)—one was even a wedding gift—which Blue uses to smoke the high-quality meats he sources.

He's cracked the code on flawless, melt-in-your-mouth 1855 Black Angus Prime brisket, which is hugged by a dark, soft bark. The trimmings from that brisket go into flavorful boudin and the all-beef sausage, the latter of which is made with a coarse, rustic grind, and both are stuffed into a snug pork casing for a satisfying snap. Rich beef ribs from 44 Farms are available daily, and the pork ribs have the perfect balance of black pepper and sweetness, merged through patiently obtained caramelization. The pork is rubbed with Cajun seasoning, then mixed with their barbecue sauce (which is more like a thin, tangy mop sauce) once it is pulled. And the turkey is simply rubbed with black pepper and coated in butter, resulting in a crisp crust and moist interior.

Blue's wife, Rachel, developed most of the sides, like the fresh and crunchy fish taco–inspired cilantro coleslaw and savory collards simmered with bacon. The pinto beans are spiked with chunks of sausage and brisket, and then smoked on the pit, and potato salad gets jazzed up with sweet jalapeño relish for briny pops of flavor. In two more nods to the Broussard family roots, maque choux makes an appearance on the menu (corn and peppers are bathed in a Cajun cream sauce) and Cajun cracklins' are often on offer to top the creamy pepper jack mac and cheese.

In addition to making their own bread and butter pickles, 1701 also bakes their own yeast rolls and buns for sandwiches, and are about to start baking all their sliceable white loaves in-house too. And in the realm of the desserts, 1701 has a passionate baker on staff who crafts delightful creations like banana bread pudding, pumpkin whoopie pies, chocolate espresso cake made with local coffee, bundt cakes drizzled with Steen's syrup, and seasonal fruit cobblers.

When 1701 first launched, it was open for lunch Monday through Friday only, since the part of downtown Beaumont it resides in is more of a daytime business district. But, after prodding from his customers, Blue decided to shift the schedule to Tuesday through Saturday, and now Saturday is his busiest day. Not one to get too far from his loves, Blue has also established music programming at the restaurant. He'll invite local musicians in to perform during Saturday service, and he also has an NPR Tiny Desk–inspired series, where he records local bands in the space when it's closed.

When 1701 first opened, Blue was manning the pits every day. Now that he's built up such a strong team ("a group of passionate, talented, and hardworking people," he says), Blue has been able to step into more of an operations role, for both the restaurant and the funeral home, while still managing events at the venues and finding time to book live music and host occasional barbecue classes.

"My phone's always ringing and I never know what it's for!" he says. "It's a crazy life, but it's our life and we have fun with it. You're not here for that long, so we've tried to make the most of it, you know?"

BLOOD

BLOOD BROS BBQ

HOUSTON

Houston is a true melting pot of cultures—and that rich ethnic diversity is celebrated in the city's vibrant culinary scene. The southwestern neighborhood of Bellaire is a microcosm of this cultural mosaic, offering a wealth of dining experiences that reflect the city's many global influences. Here, you'll find everything from Korean barbecue and Mexican street tacos to traditional dim sum and the city's famed Viet-Cajun fusion cuisine, all served by mom-and-pop eateries tucked into bustling shopping centers. At Blood Bros. BBQ, all of these flavors (and more) come together in a uniquely Houston twist on Texas barbecue.

Quy Hoang was born in Vietnam and then spent most of his childhood growing up alongside brothers Robin and Terry Wong in Alief, just west of Bellaire.

"Now they call it the International District because you can get all kinds of food," says Hoang. "We had friends from all over [the world], and you'd go to their house and get to try their food."

After graduating from high school, Hoang got into the aquarium business with his uncle, while the Wong brothers opened Glitter Karaoke together. They would throw customer appreciation parties periodically, and Hoang offered to grill steaks for one of them.

"Growing up, I always did a lot of backyard grilling, like a lot of Super Bowl parties and quick stuff like chicken," says Hoang. "I laugh now because I used to say, 'I don't have 10 hours of my life to waste cooking.'"

They started to throw steak night events regularly, and by 2013 Hoang had graduated to cooking pork shoulder and ribs on his Weber grill. Then a karaoke customer offered to sell them an offset smoker—the trio went in on it together, and Hoang set to work tackling brisket for the first time.

"I'm somewhat of a perfectionist when it comes to things," he says. "When I do something, I'm always all in. I don't do it halfway. So I wanted to perfect [brisket]—and it just kind of grew from there."

They started putting on pop-ups regularly under the name Blood Bros. BBQ ("They are real brothers and I'm the 'blood brother,'" explains Hoang). Hoang produced proteins, Robin created sides, and Terry acted as their "hype man slash promoter." After about a year, Chris Shepherd, the influential and esteemed Houston chef, reached out to invite them to cook for his Off the Wall dinner series, where they cooked alongside Gatlin's BBQ (see page 171) and Feges BBQ (see page 185). This, their first big event put on by a well-known Houston chef, really launched Blood Bros. BBQ into the public eye. For the next several years, they continued to make a name for themselves by hosting pop-ups at different bars and breweries around town, including a series they called Beats + BBQ + Brews, which combined their love of craft beer, barbecue, and hip-hop (Robin is also a DJ). They made appearances at barbecue festivals, where they featured head-turning and flavor-packed dishes like gochujang beef belly burnt ends, char siu pork belly bao buns, and Thai green curry boudin—long before Texas barbecue was as cross-cultural as it is now.

"I don't want to just cook brisket for the rest of my life—even though I *am* cooking brisket for the rest of my life," says Hoang with a laugh. "We just want to have fun. Our influences are from the stuff we grew up eating in Houston. We're all Asian guys so the first thing people think is—OK, Asian barbecue. But we're more than that. We just eat what we love, we cook what we love, and we want to have fun doing it."

Blood Bros. BBQ's popularity was surging so the trio decided to start seeking out a location for a storefront. They found a space that was formerly a Blockbuster, and then a Smoothie King, in a Bellaire strip mall, painted the walls bright orange, and hung them with framed photos and paintings created by their artist friends. No one in the group had any restaurant experience (the Wong brothers had some experience running bars), but they didn't let that phase them. With all hands on deck, they managed to turn their pop-ups into a full-fledged operation, and opened their doors in December 2018.

"We're blessed—all the chefs that we hired on [had] worked in plenty of restaurants, so they really helped us, even in laying this place out," remembers Hoang. "But since we never ran a restaurant, it was a big learning curve!"

To start, Hoang added in a vault-style smoker that functioned like a reverse-flow offset to burn the blend of post oak and pecan he uses. He now uses two J&R Oyler rotisserie pits, which not only cut down on the amount of time needed to tend the fires, but drastically reduce the amount of wood he uses, by about half.

For their pop-ups, Robin had developed a few sides—jalapeño coleslaw, rich jalapeño creamed corn, and a mac and cheese with Gruyère. Now that they had a brick and mortar with a kitchen, he began to greatly expand their repertoire to include a honey mustard potato salad, traditional charro beans, brothy collards, and an evolved, ultra creamy mac and cheese with smoked Gouda.

"My mom was a really good cook and when I moved out, I didn't have a lot of money, so I cooked a lot at home," says Robin. "[She] was one of those mothers that could make anything taste good. You know, whatever was in the fridge. So I think that's how I got that skill to wing it and not really follow a recipe."

Hoang started off with a menu of Texas barbecue staples: perfectly rendered 44 Farms brisket, tender pork ribs with a touch of cumin, snappy jalapeño cheddar sausage, and pulled pork tossed in honey mustard. He took the heat way down from what it had been during their pop-up days and created three different rubs, which the restaurant now bottles and sells. The beef rub is made with garlic, onion, paprika, and cayenne. The pork rub shares that base and has coriander and cumin added, and the poultry rub is a sweetened version of the beef rub. After salting and peppering each protein, they then get rubbed with the respective seasoning. In the early days of Blood Bros. BBQ, they started off with a couple of specials a week, typically based off the dishes they personally like to eat.

"We like to tell people we use traditional cuts of meat and traditional cooking methods, but the flavors we love—not just growing up, but that we *love*," says Hoang. "It blends well together."

They created a brisket fried rice with kimchi as a delicious way to use up brisket trim, and added it to the sides menu, where it has become a bestseller. Then one day they made brisket and gai lan chow fun for a staff meal, and served it for the *Texas Monthly* BBQ Festival that same year. The dish—made with wide rice noodles stir-fried with brisket, Chinese broccoli, bean sprouts, garlic, soy, hoisin, oyster sauce, sesame oil, and fried shallots—continues to be a huge hit.

"Barbecue's at a very exciting time right now, because for so long, people were more scared to do something different," says Robin. "People would look at us like, 'What the hell are they doing to our barbecue?' But now it's like people are really excited!

They're like 'Yeah, I had the brisket, it's great, but I want to try all this other crazy stuff you're doing!' And it's like that all across Texas."

When Hoang and the Wong brothers started to notice that their specials were becoming more popular than the staples, they started to feature them more prominently. Each day, they run a daily menu as well as an entire menu of features only available on that particular day. Favorites include their tri-tip pastrami sandwich, gochujang glazed pork ribs, sweet and sour fried ribs, pho-rubbed beef belly, and char siu pork banh mi, togarashi split chickens, brisket loco moco, Thai red curry sausage, and more. They've also become quite known for pork belly burnt end specials in flavors like peach habanero, al pastor, and a Vietnamese lemongrass-and-garlic marinade called thịt nướng. And each Sunday, the specials menu reads "Hermanos de Sangre" and offers barbacoa and Tex-Mex creations like cheesy suadero tortas, sloppy Joe tacos, brisket nachos, and more.

"If we ran our restaurant in a traditional sense, with the same menu every day, a lot of those ideas would never see the light," says Robin. "So we're like, 'Why don't we do different things every day?' And now we see we have the same customers that come in different times a week, to get all different things. So that's another way to keep your customers from getting bored."

They also added more nontraditional sides to the daily menu, like seasonal watermelon salad with feta and fresh mint, and an equally refreshing cucumber salad. When the weather cools off, they switch to a kale salad topped with orange, grapefruit, or strawberry. And yes—that is *that* ambrosia salad on the sides menu. The notorious blend of pineapple, coconut, marshmallow, and maraschino cherries is a favorite in Robin's family.

"Some people love it," says Robin. "They're like, 'It tastes just like my grandma made, or just like my mom made.' And I'm like—'That's awesome.' That's what we want. We want to create that nostalgia."

"Also, we both love Luby's!" adds Hoang with a grin, referencing the beloved Texas-based, cafeteria-style chain restaurant known for its own ambrosia salad.

You'll notice that sort of playful nostalgia in other parts of the menu. Blood Bros. offers a MacRib, a deboned rib topped with a scoop of mac and cheese on a sesame seed hoagie bun. The Terry O'Toole (maple-jalapeño bacon, smoked turkey, Creole mustard, house pickles, and melted Swiss on a pretzel hoagie roll) is a riff on a Bennigan's sandwich called the Turkey O'Toole. And Blood Bros. sauces are all packaged in little foil-sealed cups you'd be more likely to see at a fast-food joint.

The S.W.A.T. sauce (which stands for (South West Alief Texas) is their ketchup and vinegar-based original sauce with a spicy kick, while Houston 34, a sweeter sauce enhanced with mustard and ginger, pays homage to the three Houston legends (Earl Campell, Hakeem "The Dream" Olajuwon, and Nolan Ryan) who all wore 34 on their jerseys.

In 2023, Hoang and the Wong brothers opened a second spot in Garden Oaks. LuLoo's Day & Night is a sandwich shop and bakery. The only barbecue you'll find here is the brisket and sausage they put in the kolaches, but LuLoo's handles all the baking for Blood Bros., crafting marbled rye, hoagie rolls, pretzel rolls, and milk bread for them to use for their sandwiches and specials. Meanwhile, Blood Bros. makes a variety of different pickled veggies (dill pickles, pickled red onions, jalapeños, and carrots and daikon for bánh mi) plus a spicy Thai chile sauerkraut, which they sell in jars at LuLoo's.

Despite the extensive and ever-changing savory menu, Blood Bros. BBQ keeps the dessert offerings simple with a blueberry peach cobbler and a banana pudding. But you could also opt for a liquid dessert at their full bar, where a bartender is always pouring a great selection of local craft beer plus specialty cocktails (including two frozen drinks). The wall behind the bar is splashed with a graffiti-inspired Alief mural, a reminder of the vibrant community that inspired the whole operation, which earned a Michelin Bib Gourmand award in 2024.

"We always say [we're] Texas barbecue," says Robin. "But I really think it'll transition into Houston barbecue for us because Houston is so diverse compared to other places. But I definitely think Texas is open to it, so you're gonna see a lot more diverse flavors in Texas barbecue."

"I think a lot of it is that more barbecue guys aren't afraid anymore because they see it working," adds Hoang. "I tell the young guys—'Just do it man, don't be afraid! Make good food!' So I think a lot of people are embracing their culture. They're not scared to put their culture with the term 'Texas barbecue' because more people are open to it."

BBQ CONFESSIONAL

As barbecue culture continues to flourish across the state, a number of photographers have established themselves as documentarians of the smoky scene by photographing pitmasters, their tools, and the fruits of their labor.

Wyatt McSpadden and Jody Horton (@jodyhorton) have filled many coffee table books with their beautiful images over the years. Robert Lerma (@robertjacoblerma) captures pit life by playing with light and smoke, while Joe McGregor's Ministers of Smoke project (@ministersofsmoke) features documentary-style portraits of pitmasters in their sacred spaces. Jeremy Brand (@bbqandbacksquats) and Ben Yanto (@benyantovisuals) have captured vibrant meat trays and sizzling action shots for companies like Mill Scale Metalworks (see page 286), Nomad Grills, and YETI. And influencers like Jason Wilson (@meat.therapy) and Jimmy Ho (@thesmokingho) have built Instagram followings and earned brand sponsorships from their mouth-watering barbecue shots.

Another photographer whose work I have been absolutely captivated by is Ben Sassani. His Instagram account (@bensassani) features a blend of breathtaking landscapes and cinematic portraits, all exuding great depth and emotion, plus crisp, textured food photos you can practically smell and taste. From there, you can link over to his BBQ Confessional (@bbqconfessional) page: a collection of black-and-white photos and video footage of pitmasters from all over the country telling stories that range from poignant to scandalous to hilarious.

Sassani's photography career started at the end of 2007, when he and his wife were expecting their first child. His original goal was to make sure his kids had great pictures growing up, so he bought a Nikon D80 and a kit lens to start documenting. Just a few months later, after he'd bought a couple more lenses, a friend who had started a photography business of his own invited him to come act as an assistant shooter at a wedding to see how he liked it.

"I was very nervous because shooting on the fly at an important event like a wedding was absolutely terrifying to me," he remembers. "What if I missed an important moment? What if I screwed up something that only happens once? Lots of what-ifs, but after shooting that [first] wedding, I realized it was a lot easier than I actually thought it would be."

At the time, Sassani had a job managing automotive repair shops in Austin, Phoenix, and Houston. In 2009, he got recruited to do regional sales for a private oil and gas company, and the job was flexible enough for him to take on photo gigs simultaneously. After getting a few smaller weddings under his belt in 2008, he booked a few bigger ones in 2009. By 2011, he had raised his prices and was focusing on bigger budget weddings, including two large-scale Indian weddings.

"Indian weddings are mostly over-the-top and very detail oriented—not to mention long," Sassani explains. "Most Indian wedding couples—or parents—don't want to hire just anyone to shoot them, so most of them are by referrals and word of mouth. So if you do one and the guests like you, you're basically in the community and will be asked to do more. And that's exactly what happened."

As Sassani began to shoot increasingly bigger weddings around the country, his eyes were also opened to Texas barbecue. Growing up in the Austin area, his memories of barbecue were limited to chains like Rudy's and Bill Miller's. His barbecue awakening happened when he first started going to pop-ups put on by pitmasters like Patrick Feges and Ronnie Killen around 2013.

And then at the end of 2014, during the weekend of Sassani's brother's wedding, when their cousin Shawn Matian was in town from LA, he had his first taste of Franklin Barbecue (see page 233 for a profile on founder Aaron Franklin) and la Barbecue (see page 249). After that, Matian started coming to Houston several times a year for visits with his longtime friend Burt Bakman (before Bakman went on to open Slab BBQ in LA) The trio began to travel all over Central Texas, getting to know pitmasters from Lockhart to Lexington to Brenham.

"Most of the pitmasters I meet are not about fame and notoriety," Sassani says. "Everyone is welcoming and they all make you feel as if they've known you for a long time. They don't mind their pictures being taken and it makes it more appealing to me [to take] pictures of them in their work environment, doing what they do and wearing the very clothes they've been working in for hours. There's nothing fancy about it."

As Sassani began documenting their barbecue trips, he found himself hearing a lot of intimate and captivating stories behind the scenes. He decided to register a couple of different domains—"BBQ Confessional" and "BBQ Confidental"—with the goal of eventually compiling a book.

"The BBQ Confessional name was perfect for it because barbecue is a religious experience for a lot of folks," he muses, "and these stories are going to be told to one person—me—before they make it to the public."

When Sassani interviews his subjects, he prompts them to tell a personal story—one that's meaningful to them and not one they've told very often. He began posting these first-person stories to the BBQ Confessional Instagram account in 2019. The first few interviews started out pretty brief, and he was thinking they'd all be like that, but the stories people shared kept getting longer and longer, eventually causing him to exceed Instagram's 2,200-character limit on posts. So he began to present the pitmaster stories in video format, with the black and white portraits serving as the cover of the post.

By 2021, the long hours and workload involved with wedding photography was wearing on Sassani, so in his professional photography life, he now focuses on headshots, corporate events, and various food shoots around the Houston area. But his extracurricular documentation of the barbecue world is still some of his favorite work to date.

"To me, the inspiration comes from seeing what really goes on behind the scenes," he describes. "The long hours, the heat, smoke, and labor put into making the food so many eat and enjoy."

GARLIC
SPICY LINK
PRICED
POUND

TRUTH BBQ

BRENHAM & HOUSTON

Pitmasters throughout Texas speak with reverence about Leonard Botello IV, the owner of the acclaimed Truth Barbeque. Yet, sit down and chat with the humble Botello, and he mirrors that same profound admiration when discussing the figures who inspired his own barbecue journey.

Botello grew up in the Gulf Coast town of Lake Jackson, where his parents owned a restaurant that kept them busy working late nights and weekends. Determined to avoid a similar path, Botello went to college and studied biology. But visits to Franklin Barbecue and la Barbecue on the same day in 2013 completely shifted his perspective, leaving him in awe of the craft.

"That was basically my 'holy shit' moment when I had barbecue for the first time—like *barbecue* barbecue for the first time," he remembers. "I thought, 'If this is barbecue, I don't know what the hell I was eating growing up as a child!'"

In addition to John Lewis (who was the pitmaster at la Barbecue at the time) and Aaron Franklin, Botello counts Wayne Mueller, the owner of Louie Mueller Barbecue, as another legend who put wind in his sails.

"I always tell people you can go in there with a friend that's deaf and blind and they can feel it," says Botello. "You can just *feel* that eeriness and that barbecue

aura around there in the smoke. I love that about Louie Mueller."

After Botello graduated in 2013, his father's health took a turn, and he found himself managing the family restaurant and its 50 employees—until the family decided to sell Cafe Annice, get out of the restaurant business, and move out to Brenham. Not long after that, Botello found a barely used Klose offset pit for sale on Craigslist ("A $25,000 pit for like $2,000 bucks!" he marvels) and drove up to Ohio to pick it up.

This was before Instagram and YouTube became treasure troves of barbecue knowledge, a time when pitmasters were far more guarded about their techniques. Undeterred, Botello immersed himself in every barbecue book he could find and honed his skills by experimenting with select briskets purchased from H-E-B and Kroger, using each one as an opportunity to refine his craft.

"[At first], you don't realize that all the books are basically just guidelines," says Botello. "Once you start to get the feel for it and understand that every piece of wood is going to be different, every brisket is going to be different, and the cook is always going to be different—then it kind of opens up your mind. And that's what I love about barbecue . . . it is technically the same thing over and over again, but it's basically a new challenge every day."

One day, while visiting Louie Mueller Barbecue, Botello recalls Mueller sitting down to talk shop with him. During that conversation—"probably one of the more important conversations that I've had with special people," says Botello—Mueller gave him detailed barbecue advice. At first, Botello didn't understand why he would share this valuable information.

"Wayne basically said it doesn't do him any good to keep all this information locked down and keep it secret," remembers Botello. "He'd much rather help other people to keep this thing going and make it more unique and more special. At that point, I realized that I shouldn't be chasing what somebody else is doing. The only way to make it special is being true to myself, and true to the things that I love. So that's always stuck with me, because Wayne is basically the Dumbledore of Hogwarts for barbecue. Like he's a genius. He's a wizard. He knows everything about barbecue."

In 2015, Botello purchased an old shack in Brenham—on Highway 290, between Austin and Houston—and decided to open up a barbecue joint in it. His parents had barely gotten a taste of retirement before diving back in to help with the new business, which Botello named Truth Barbeque. He and his dad, Leonard III, ran the pits, while his mother, Janel, baked the massive cakes, cut into towering slices, she'd become known for at Cafe Annice.

The little roadside building exudes rustic charm with its limestone brick facade, weathered corrugated tin roof, and aged wooden paneling adorned with vintage signs. A couple of mismatched wooden tables and chairs provide the only indoor seating, and guests scan the chalkboard menu and then place their order at a counter where Janel's sky-high cakes balance on cake stands. Outside, shaded picnic tables provide the majority of the restaurant's seating, and neatly stacked post oak, seasoned for 12 to 14 months, reflects Botello's commitment to traditional Central Texas smoking methods. He constructed a screened-in pit room to house his Klose smoker, firmly believing that barbecue pits perform best when exposed to the natural Texas climate.

"Every time that I travel, I'll take my pit, my wood, my briskets, my seasoned salt—everything from the restaurant, ready to go—but nothing cooks the same as [it does in] Texas," he says. "Because, no matter how much we complain about the humidity and the heat, the barbecue comes out better with all of that."

Ethical and sustainable sourcing is central to Truth BBQ's philosophy. From the beginning, Botello prioritized high-quality ingredients, sourcing Angus beef from 44 Farms, Creekstone Farms, and Double R Ranch beef from Snake River Farms. He also selects Duroc pork ribs and shoulders to ensure exceptional flavor and responsible practices.

"We always like to work with smaller farms because those farmers get their asses kicked day after day at the big farms—they just churn and burn," says Botello.

"But with the smaller ones, the farmers are paying attention to genetics, they're taking care of the cows, and the cows are living a good life."

Botello places a strong emphasis on trimming, a crucial step he believes is often underestimated in its impact on achieving the perfect brisket.

"The shape of the trim is very important, to keep everything uniform and cooked properly, breaking down at the same rate," he explains. "You want something that's very aerodynamic because that heat's gonna go straight into whatever is sticking out. So it keeps it from drying out, keeps it a lot more uniform and the fat over the top is trimmed down to where we know each piece of the brisket is gonna be a good bite."

When it comes to seasoning, Botello keeps it simple—a principle he adopted from renowned pitmaster Tuffy Stone. Every cut of meat is seasoned with the same straightforward blend of salt, pepper, garlic, and onion, allowing the quality of the protein to shine.

"You want to be able to taste your protein, so you need to use smoke the same way you would use salt," says Botello. "So we use the same seasoning for all the proteins, just to enhance the flavor of what they're truly supposed to taste like—so you can taste the fats, the meats, and all that stuff. It just needs to be like a good steak. Like when you go to a steak house, they're just putting salt and pepper on there, and you're just tasting the sear on each side. That's it. So that's what we try to do here—just enhance it in its purest form."

Mueller guided Botello in developing a brisket rotation system inspired by the methods at Louie Mueller Barbecue. To ensure consistent smoking, Botello rotates all of the meats every hour, achieving even heat and flavor throughout the long 16- to 18-hour cook.

"You don't want them touching because they'll have bald marks on there," explains Botello. "You don't want them too close to the walls and the doors, because that's where the most radiant parts of the pit are, with all that heat coming off the metal. The ones on the outside go to the inside and the ones on the inside go to the outside, so they're all getting cooked at the same rate. It's one big game of Tetris!"

This thoughtful attention to detail given to high-quality ingredients quickly earned Truth BBQ a reputation for having some of the best smoked meat around. It didn't take long for locals to begin arriving before opening to line up for juicy slices of brisket, glistening with rendered fat and held together by a peppery, thin but sturdy bark, tender and caramelized pork ribs, moist and flavorful turkey, and succulent pulled pork with a peppery profile.

Truth was one of the first outfits in Texas to use brisket trimmings to create in-house craft sausage.

After extensive trial and error, experimenting in five-pound batches, Botello perfected a lineup that includes garlic, jalapeño-cheddar, and pepper jack sausage. Ground, stuffed, and smoked fresh each day, these sausages feature a fine, smooth grind encased in a delicate, snappy casing. Prior to serving, they are sliced into thin rounds, showcasing their impeccable texture and flavor.

Truth BBQ has also set itself apart with its homestyle, Southern-inspired sides, elevating the barbecue experience beyond the usual fare. Botello drew on family traditions, including his grandmother's cherished corn pudding recipe—a dish she prepared every Thanksgiving and Christmas. This sweet, rich casserole is creamy and indulgent, with a crunchy, golden-brown topping that adds the perfect texture. Another standout is the now-iconic tater tot casserole. A Christmas morning favorite in Botello's home, it was originally served with over easy eggs and bacon on top. At Truth, the bacon is diced and folded into the casserole, adding savory bursts to the sweet mushroom cream base, and then the dish is crowned with crispy fried onions—a nostalgic twist reminiscent of green bean casserole.

Botello crafted the rest of the recipes with his parents, drawing on their many years of restaurant experience, and discerning input from his wife, Abbie. The decadent mac and cheese is elevated with a rich alfredo sauce, while the coleslaw offers a fresh, crunchy bite with a subtle cayenne heat.

TRUTH

Departing from the traditional pinto beans common in Texas barbecue, Truth serves baked beans perfectly balanced with caramelized brown sugar and tender chunks of pork. Classic Southern vegetable sides like collard greens and green beans are joined by a standout: made-to-order Brussels sprouts. These are tossed in a bold mix of honey, lime juice, sriracha, and soy sauce, flash-fried for a crispy finish, and topped with Fresno chile slices for a spicy kick.

At a time when Mrs. Baird's was the standard for buns and loaves at barbecue joints, Botello turned to Kraftsmen Baking in Houston for a more distinctive option. He also bypassed the typical Best Maid pickle slices, and instead established his own house fermentation program, crafting pickled red onions, dill pickles, and a spicy-sweet escabeche mix made with cauliflower, carrots, onions, jalapeños, and fresno chiles. For sauce, he offers a tangy Gold Sauce, made with whole mustard grains, and a sweet and peppery, but well-balanced, tomato-based OG Sauce.

Botello's meticulous commitment to craft barbecue certainly paid off. By 2017, Truth BBQ was #10 on *Texas Monthly*'s Top 50 list. They eventually expanded from three days of business to four (Thursday through Sunday), and in 2019, they expanded with a sprawling brick and mortar in Houston's Greater Heights area. This 4,800-square-foot space can accommodate seating for 200 diners and a bar featuring house cocktails and an incredible selection of whiskey. Guests sitting at the bar can also order from a menu of bites like brisket Phillies, smashburgers, and South Carolina–inspired hot gut-and-collard green egg rolls.

Botello's mother single-handedly made all the cakes for the first five years, but because of the volume and demand, Truth now has a dedicated pastry chef recreate her recipes. And with the added space in the Houston location, guests can choose from a huge variety of different cakes, from banana caramel and red velvet to coconut cream and German chocolate, plus homemade banana pudding, brownies, and apple cobbler.

Botello had his Houston pits built to the exact same measurements and specs as his pits up in Brenham. He also commissioned Mill Scale Metalworks (see page 286) to build a pit for him, and he notes that's his present favorite.

"But they're all evolutions of the one before, and I already have ideas for the next one," says Botello. "You start to realize different things you can change . . . to evolve barbecue and make it better time after time, because even little tweaks here and there can affect it."

Now with five 1,000-gallon pits, Botello can run weekend specials like beef ribs on Saturdays and smoked and fried half chickens on Sundays. He's also become known for his Cajun burnt end boudin, which started as a special but is now offered daily and served with housemade hot sauce. Each Saturday, Botello and his team cook a whole hog, Carolina style over direct heat. After sawing open and salting the 120- to 140-pound pig, smoldering coals are transferred under the BQ grill, where the pig will cook for 12 hours before it's flipped at the end to crisp up the skin and achieve a chicharron-level crunch.

"You have to understand how radiant the heat is from the coals, and you have to know how many coals to put under what area of the pig—it's very strategic," says Botello. "You can hear the crackling of the fire and then the fat dripping on the coals, sizzling. And you become very in tune with these things, and it just starts to become a sixth sense. Some people pick it up very fast and some people never get it. I've been fortunate enough to have a handful of guys that pick up a shovel, and I teach them how to do it, and they coast. But it took me years to do it myself."

Having gained invaluable knowledge from others early on, Botello places a strong emphasis on education and believes in its potential to drive progress in the industry. Many of his staff came to him with no barbecue knowledge, and some transitioned over from the fine-dining world. Once they're ready, he empowers them to take the lead on cooks and step into public-facing roles, like giving pit tours.

"I make the guys do it, because I didn't realize how much knowledge I had locked in my head over the years until I actually started talking about it in classes," he says. "These guys think that they're just cooking barbecue until you get them talking about barbecue and they know so much."

Botello hosts a barbecue class for 10 participants, held one Sunday each month. During the four-hour session, each attendee receives hands-on instruction and leaves with a whole brisket, a trimming knife, a meat thermometer, and a Truth Barbeque swag bag.

"Barbecue has been around for forever, but it's our job to educate the community on how to cook, why we cook the way we do, why we source the meats we do, and how pricing affects everything," Botello says. "I also like to encourage working with smaller farms and not wasting your product. After going out to farms and seeing how much work, from start to finish, actually goes into that [meat] before it gets to you, we use everything. I know that animals were put on the earth to feed us, but it's also very important not to waste. So we try to educate people on how to do that."

When the *Texas Monthly* Top 50 was released in 2021, Truth BBQ climbed to the #3 spot, and at the end of 2024, the restaurant was honored with a prestigious Michelin Bib Gourmand award. As business continues to boom, Botello has expanded Truth to include dinner service at the Houston location. After inevitably selling out during the day, the restaurant closes for a few hours before reopening at 5 p.m. This is made possible by adding an extra cook to ensure fresh meat is coming off the pits in the afternoon, along with adjusting staffing to meet the demand.

"Our margins in barbecue are so slim," says Botello. "We don't do it for money. We do it because we get instant gratification from serving somebody and seeing their smile. That's our form of currency."

Botello says he doesn't plan to open another Truth BBQ location in Texas, as he wants to keep the existing ones special. However, in 2023, he unexpectedly took on another restaurant concept when his close friend, restaurateur Lee Merritt Ellis, unexpectedly passed away. With the encouragement of Lee's wife, Melissa, Botello stepped in to operate Merritt Meat Company in Round Top, where he honors the legacy of his bold, trailblazing friend by preserving the barbecue restaurant exactly as Ellis had envisioned it.

"He was the first person to tell me, 'It's okay to be yourself, be true to yourself,' remembers Botello with tears in his eyes. "He didn't care what people thought about him. He just wanted to make people happy with this food . . . But the people that didn't like him, didn't like him because he drew outside of the lines and it made them uncomfortable. He was basically the person who told me it's okay to draw outside the lines."

Botello remembers the first time he met Ellis, who walked into Truth BBQ with buns in hand, ready to assemble his own sandwich.

"I couldn't believe the nerve on this guy!" laughs Botello. "But he left them that day and I made a sandwich and realized it was better than the bread we had. They were Martin's potato rolls—before people were using Martin's potato rolls. He was always one step ahead of everybody else."

Just like he switched to Martin's potato rolls back then, Botello is constantly evaluating his processes and cooking techniques to find areas for improvement. For instance, he learned that different forms of wood are better suited for specific proteins, depending on how quickly they burn and the distinct smoke they produce. As a result, they now use stumps cut into splits for brisket, while round branches are reserved for ribs.

"Once you get stuck in your ways and think, 'I cook the best brisket ever,' there's somebody in your rear view—you can't just get comfortable with it,' says Botello. "It's important to always evolve. I tell people the barbecue we cooked six years ago is not the same as we cook today and it won't be the same six years from now. I always think it could be improved somehow or another. You've just got to pay attention, and that's it. These days, there's no secrets in barbecue—it's just hard, tedious work."

THE CUTTING EDGE

For chefs and pitmasters, knives are more than just tools: they're as crucial to their craft as a painter's brush or a musician's instrument. A blade's balance, weight, and sharpness significantly affect the way it cuts meat, drastically impacting both texture and appearance. So it is no wonder some of the industry's top talent swear by the high-alloy steel knives crafted by Dr. Stephen Pustilnik, a man whose eye for detail isn't limited to the kitchen. Pustilnik works full-time as a forensic pathologist and the chief medical examiner for Fort Bend County, where he uses razor-sharp knives daily to perform autopsies.

"I examine organs in such a way that, if photography is needed for presentation in court or for educational purposes, I want smooth surfaces with no chatter on the surface," explains Pustilnik.

Pulstinik got into cooking while he was in medical school, acquiring a huge collection of cookbooks during his kitchen experiments. But he continuously felt limited by the knives he was using at home, and decided to craft culinary knives that were as high quality as the autopsy knives he used at work during the day. He reached out to local bladesmith Russell Montgomery of Serenity Knives and began apprenticing with him.

"After the knifemaker showed me how to use the equipment and the basic techniques, I began studying culinary blades from different regions around the world," says Pustilnik, who prefers the design of sleek Japanese cutlery, followed by the sturdy German and aesthetically pleasing French blades. "I design my blade profiles on large graph paper and each has to appeal to my own sense of the classical aesthetic of length, heel height, spine configuration, and tip geometry. . . . As I profile out the blade in a piece of metal and hold it in my hand, I assess and reassess and make final changes to the profile and handle length and configuration."

Pustilnik found that he preferred working with high-alloy steel, which has high percentages of vanadium, tungsten, and niobium alloying elements. He uses a method called stock removal, whereby he profiles blades on a grinder starting with sheets of steel in defined thickness.

"My niche is using ultra high–alloy steels that most other knifemakers shy away from [because they are] harder to machine, but give a super-high performance in edge maintenance and sharpness," Pustilnik explains. "I do not forge steel because that requires low-alloy steels . . . I admire the knifemakers who produce those artistic pieces. However, at the end of the day, beautiful Damascus low-alloy carbon steel blades are still low-alloy steel that rust easily and have less longevity in sharpness and edge holding."

In 2013, Pustilnik founded Houston Edge Works, a side business that allows him to craft knives for both passionate home cooks and professionals. He first began by reaching out to local Houston chefs, like Chris Shepherd and Kelly Boyd, with offers to build them custom knives. After that, word spread quickly about the quality of Pustilnik's work, and he has since made knives for celebrity chefs like Jet Tila, Andrew Zimmern, Michael Solomonov, Thomas Keller, and Michael Voltaggio. He's also crafted brisket slicers, chef knives, cleavers, and filet knives for top Texas pitmasters like Leonard Botello IV of Truth BBQ (see page 121), Ara Malekian of Harlem Road Texas BBQ (see page 166), and Joey Victorian of Victorian's Barbecue (see page 410).

When a pitmaster asked for a custom brisket slicer, I realized that a full-size brisket is approximately the width of an adult human liver," says Pustilnik. "The presentation of a competition brisket slice to the judges is supposed to be clean and without chatter on the cut surface, same as examining an organ in the morgue. Therefore, I designed my brisket slicer to be the same length as my autopsy organ examination blade for that same single draw cut for the cleanest cut surface; brisket for presentation to judges, organs for diagnosis and photography."

Once Pustilnik finds steel he likes for chef knives, he'll make a blade to use in the morgue to test edge retention and sharpenability. He also measures his customers' palms and examines their joints and knuckles in order to design ergonomic handles that can still be used comfortably by those who have arthritis or hand injuries—and securely by the always-greasy hands of a pitmaster. He has a wide variety of rare and unique materials his customers can choose from for their custom handle, including abalone, buffalo horn, exotic burls, stabilized woods—and even 40,000-year-old mammoth teeth.

Pustilnik prices his knives based not only on the handle material, but also on the type of steel used, length of the blade, and any other add-ons. They generally range from about $375 to around $2,000, and the current lead time is up to a whopping 7 to 10 years for one of his custom-made knives. That's because Pustilnik is running a one-man operation, and he likes to take his time, focusing on just one knife at a time.

"I like being hands-on for each knife," says Pustilnik. "Perhaps at some undetermined time in the future, I'll get a bigger space for knife-making classes or [take on] an apprentice."

In the meantime, hopeful customers should waste no time joining that lengthy waitlist. Because, if some of the country's leading chefs are to be trusted, then a knife from Houston Edge Works is absolutely worth the wait.

TEJAS CHOCOLATE + BARBECUE

TOMBALL

The Moore brothers' path to award-winning barbecue unexpectedly started with a passion for chocolate.

By day, Scott Moore Jr. sold railcar equipment. But on nights and weekends his culinary pursuits had him mastering backyard barbecuing and studying agave spirits. Then, he was bit by the chocolate bug. And, inspired by the Mast Brothers and Chocolate Alchemy, Scott set out to create premium, bean-to-bar chocolate out of his home kitchen.

His brother Greg Moore, a professional chef, was running a French-Italian restaurant at the time, and became fascinated with his brother's latest obsession. Greg came on board and together, along with Scott's partner, Michelle Holland, they began producing chocolate bars for wholesale accounts using premium cacao beans sourced from boutique farms in Madagascar, Bolivia, Mexico, Belize, and beyond. With bars flying off the shelves of Whole Foods, Spec's, and Central Market, the group decided to seek out a retail space to sell even more confections.

And that's how they came across the 1907 home in the historic Old Town district of Tomball, Texas. The brothers had grown up in the area, and knew the charming town (located 30 miles northwest of Houston) was a popular destination, particularly on weekends. The farmers market, constant street fairs and festivals, and the town's shop-lined streets drew a steady stream of visitors, and a chocolate shop would be a perfect addition.

In 2015, they opened Tejas Chocolate Craftory ("Tejas" being derived from the Caddo Indians' word for "friends and allies"), but as they weren't selling enough chocolate to pay rent on the oldest house in Tomball, they decided to bring in an additional stream of income. Since Scott was already known among friends and family for his backyard cooking skills—and there was nowhere in town to get high-quality barbecue—it was a no-brainer for the fifth-generation Texans to purchase a smoker. Pretty soon, Greg left the fine-dining world to work with his brother at Tejas full-time.

"We really started this to fund our chocolate-making addiction," Greg says frankly. "And brisket takes a long time to cook, so it gives us something to do while we're eating chocolate, making chocolate, and putting out chocolate."

In 2017, *Texas Monthly* named Tejas the sixth best barbecue in the state, and they immediately had a consistent line wrapped around the front of the building. Black October, the converted propane tank they'd purchased from a competition team, could only fit a dozen briskets, so they were quickly selling out. Sunny Moberg of Moberg Smokers crafted a customized 1,000-gallon offset smoker for them, and they named it Dude Abides after the protagonist in *The Big Lebowski*. Soon afterward, they ordered two more 1,000-gallons and named them Walter and Donny.

Now running a hybrid business, they renamed to Tejas Chocolate + Barbecue. Scott had been roasting his cocoa beans in an oven inside, but realized he could take the operation outside, alongside the barbecue pits. A friend built him a customized roaster out of a rotisserie retrofitted with red bricks (they have since upgraded to a handmade clay brick oven.) The month-long process of making chocolate starts with roasting the beans, followed by winnowing, cracking, and stone-grinding them.

"Every little step is important, and barbecue's the same way," says Greg. "I think that was part of the attraction for us: both of them are a long process and no two days are the same. There's a lot of variables going on, particularly relating to weather conditions and temperature. . . . My mentor, my original chef, told me in the first couple of days at work—if you're not learning something new every day, you're not paying attention. I think that can definitely be said for barbecue."

The Moore brothers continued honing their craft of meat smoking, just as they had perfected their chocolate making. They learned how to use different sizes and cures of post oak (along with the pit's gauge and damper) to maintain a clean and consistent fire

producing thin blue smoke. They trim their briskets aggressively because they feel a more aerodynamic shape yields an even cook. They season simply, with salt and pepper, to let the quality of the Creekstone Farms all-natural Prime brisket speak for itself. They wrap the brisket in butcher paper during the stall (a period of up to four hours where the brisket's internal temperature stops rising) to maintain moisture and a subtle smoke flavor.

The resulting brisket is tender and juicy, with perfectly rendered fat and a sturdy bark. Enjoy it by the pound or on a sandwich, in a taco, piled on a loaded baked potato, or draped across a salad dotted with blue cheese (Tejas is among a select group of barbecue spots that feature leafy green options on their menu).

Other protein highlights include toothsome pork ribs, perfectly peppered beef ribs and burnt ends (featured on Fridays and Saturdays), and moist and flavorful turkey (also available on a salad or in a sandwich with bacon, avocado, and a fried egg). To make pulled pork, Tejas breaks down the pork shoulder into smaller pieces for a faster cook and more bark, giving it more texture and flavor than most.

Tejas has an impressive house sausage program as well. Kielbasa, made from pork shoulder and brisket trimmings, is a staple, as is an all-beef chile relleno sausage stuffed with poblano peppers, pepper jack cheese, paprika, and cumin, a nod to the Tex-Mex the brothers grew up eating. Boudin is featured three times a week, and both bratwurst and chorizo also make regular appearances on the menu.

In order to utilize brisket trimmings, Tejas began running burger specials, perfecting both a smashburger and a smoked burger finished on the flat top. Brisket tallow is used to make fries, and also to toast the buns on the griddle. The response to these burger nights was so great that, when a nearby space became available in 2019, they opened Tejas Burger Joint on Main Street in Tomball. They also opened Tejas To Go Market, a storefront right next to the restaurant where they vacuum seal smoked meats and sell grab-and-go sandwiches and sides.

"Most of the sides came from things that we grew up with or shared with family," says Greg. "This is our house, and our families welcome you to have food with us. It's our little slice of cultural cuisine. This is what we grew up on."

They use their grandmother and great aunt's recipe for creamy, classic potato salad with boiled eggs, green onions, and just a hint of mustard. The pudding-like cornbread casserole is their mother's recipe, and one she'd use to stuff the bird on Thanksgiving each year. Michelle, who used to work at a gourmet food shop, developed recipes for both the comforting broccoli-and-cheese casserole and a velvety, savory-sweet carrot souffle that has become their most buzzed-about side.

The historic home's rustic, welcoming interior is the perfect setting to enjoy such homestyle offerings. (And for fans of the paranormal, this spot—which has been featured on the Travel Channel's *Trending Fear*—is well worth digging into.) The walls are a patchwork of original wood paneling and lids from vintage shipping containers and wine boxes. Hung from them are a variety of flags—representing both Texas and the US—plus a neon outline of the state and railroad signage (the tracks are located just across the street from the restaurant).

Before settling into a dark wooden table inside the sunlit dining room or slipping into a picnic table on the side porch, you'll place an order at the front counter, where a chalkboard lists the day's barbecue offerings as well as drinks, from lemonade and Mexican cola to local craft beer. Tejas also offers Texas-grown wine by the glass and bottle, made by Newsom Vineyards (their Tomball tasting room, The Empty Glass, is located just across the street).

Once your food is ready, you'll pick it up from a small room in the back of the house, where there's a bar of condiments for the taking. Tejas makes their own dill pickles and pickled red onions, as well as four unique sauces. The Original sauce is a red barbecue sauce with Southwest flavoring and a vinegar twang, great on any of the meats. The Spicy Chili-Lime sauce is best with pork belly burnt ends and pork ribs, and the Spicy Honey-Lime sauce was developed specifically to be drizzled on their barbecue banh mi sandwiches. Lastly, the Verde Q is a green barbecue sauce made with tomatillo and cilantro with a vinegary twang, best on the smoked turkey and pork belly. Of course, the best practice is to try all four sauces and figure out your own favorite combinations.

Unsurprisingly, their staple desserts—bread pudding and panna cotta—both feature the chocolate they craft in-house. And of course, there's no leaving until you peruse the case of truffles at the entrance, which is always stocked with around two dozen rotating flavors, from boozy options like Mojito and Manhattan to signature creations like Tejas Float (dark chocolate with Dr. Pepper syrup and a Coca-Cola gummy on top), Key to Happiness (key lime pie), and Campfire (s'mores). These Texas-sized truffles might seem daunting after a filling barbecue feast, so take a box home to truly appreciate the complexity of each handcrafted piece.

After all, Greg says, "We just wanted to make barbecue to get enough people to come in the room and buy chocolate."

As the positive reviews and accolades continue to roll in year after year—including a Michelin Bib Gourmand award in 2024—they've proven that barbecue and chocolate can, in fact, share the spotlight.

SOLO
PL200N

BAR-A-BBQ

MONTGOMERY

Even the best pitmasters made mistakes at the beginning of their careers. For Cooper Abercombie, those moments were exactly what motivated him to master the craft.

"Making really bad barbecue drove me to get better at it," he says. "I hate being unable to do something, and when I saw the people that spend a lifetime chasing something unattainable, [barbecue] attracted me and drug me in."

Cooper has fond memories of visiting Hinze's in Wharton, Texas, when his family would head out there to visit his grandpa each weekend. He didn't try to cook it for himself, though, until he bought his first home with his wife, Shelby, in their hometown of Montgomery, Texas, located just over 50 miles north of Houston. His first experiments happened on a Traeger in his new backyard, and resulted in some overcooked and undercooked brisket. That was enough to inspire him to dive into the YouTube teachings of Meat Church and Malcolm Reed, which in turn prompted him to upgrade to a Backline Fabrication 500-gallon offset smoker.

"Most of my inspiration comes from those at the top of the game in the barbecue world within Texas: Goldee's, Feges, Burnt Bean, 2M . . ." says Cooper. "And trial and error a thousand times over. We played with ingredients and salt levels for months."

He reached out to the Goldee's Barbecue boys for advice via Instagram, took a class with co-owner Jonny White, and later drove up Goldee's on different occasions to help the team out and soak up all the knowledge he could. They taught him how to render beef fat into tallow, develop a sauce (Abercrombie's is an homage to Goldee's mustardy Golden Sauce), trim his proteins, and make sausage in-house using that trim. Cooper developed his flavorful Beefy Texan sausage using trimmings from brisket, pork ribs, and pork shoulder, the South Texan link adds pepper jack and dried chiles, and the Cheesy Texan snaps open to reveal melty Monterey Jack and fresh jalapeños.

For the rest of his proteins, Cooper's motto is "keep it simple." He starts with the high-quality meat from Creekstone Farms, and then seasons the brisket, turkey, and beef ribs first with Fiesta brand 16-mesh pepper, followed by Fiesta Season-It-All (a seasoning salt). Turkey gets a garlic butter bath before it's wrapped post-cook. Pork ribs are seasoned with the same pepper and Diamond Crystal kosher salt, then glazed after the cook with a sweet, tangy sauce (brown sugar, ketchup, honey, Worcestershire, apple cider vinegar, cumin, garlic, and onion) before they're wrapped.

Though Cooper is using post oak as a fuel source, his brisket and beef ribs have a more robust smoke flavor than oak typically lends. That's because he cold smokes them overnight (at about 150°F to 200°F) with the damper and doors tightly shut. When he arrives at 3 a.m., both proteins have already developed a lot of color. He feeds the fire, getting it up to around 250°F to 280°F and finishes them with a hot smoke, rendering all that marbled fat into perfectly melty ribbons.

As Cooper continued to refine his meat smoking, Shelby helped him develop sides and desserts. Both Cooper and Shelby's grandparents owned restaurants, so many of their creations are inspired by family recipes.

"We have tweaked them to maybe balance them out or add our flair to them, but they are 95 percent the OG recipes," says Cooper.

They've elevated comforting hash brown casserole into their Cheesy Taters with fresh potatoes and a cheesy bechamel. Their green bean casserole subs fresh beans and fried onions for the canned stuff and gets a little kick from chile pepper. The Cowboy Pinto Beans are made creamy and flavorful with Monterey Jack and deseeded jalapeños. There's also a savory, flavor-packed brisket dirty rice and a cool cucumber salad inspired by the now-shuttered Brett's Family BBQ.

For desserts, Shelby took a family recipe for oatmeal chocolate chip cookies and swapped shortening for beef tallow to create a sweet and just-a-touch-of savory sensation that sells out daily. The Cornbread Puddin' (which is made with Jiffy mix, the one thing Cooper says comes from a box) is a take on the honey cornbread pudding topped with warm milk his grandma used to make. And their smooth, creamy banana pudding takes inspiration from Goldee's recipe, but the Abercrombies' oldest son, Palmer, added spicy gingersnaps to it—hence the name, Palmer's Pudding.

"Palmer loves to help momma bake," says Cooper. "And Duke likes to hang out with me at the pits."

Cooper ended up meeting James McFarland of Nomad Barbecue at his local H-E-B and the two formed a friendship. McFarland offered advice and mentorship as Cooper transitioned from backyard cooking to cooking for the public. In 2019, Cooper started hosting pop-ups around Montgomery with the help of Shelby and his younger brother, Caleb. Caleb had been selling farm and ranch equipment and had a show cattle operation called Bar-A Cattle. They took on the name, at first temporarily for the pop-ups, but when Caleb ended up learning the pits and working alongside his brother, Bar-A-BBQ stuck.

Over the next couple of years, their barbecue operation continued to grow in popularity. Cooper and Shelby renovated a vintage ice cream truck and parked it at a space called Meadow to Market to sell barbecue alongside a coffee trailer. At this time, Cooper was still working in residential and commercial fencing and Shelby was a high school special education teacher, but they knew they'd need to go all in and quit their day jobs when they opened a brick and mortar.

They sought out a space for the scaling operation and, in March 2023, they moved Bar-A-BBQ into a 70-year-old farmhouse in the middle of Montgomery. The Abercrombies painted the exterior a deep blue, stained the hardwood floors a dark mahogany, and outfitted the interior with aluminum trim against white walls hung with mounted buck heads. They've now sold their previous truck and upgraded to a more road-friendly one, which they send out weekly for caterings and events.

Cooper has also upgraded his pit setup. He now uses a 1,000-gallon Cen-Tex offset smoker and a 500-gallon Mill Scale offset. He's expanded his menu to include pork steak, pulled pork, and any number of specials, from half chickens to tri-tip. Thursdays are for cheesy double smashburgers, made from brisket trimmings, and juicy beef ribs are reserved for Saturdays.

And now the tables have turned, with Cooper becoming the one teaching classes. He's always allowed people to come and assist in exchange for learning, but the requests started to get out of hand once a couple of barbecue influencers' interviews with him went viral on YouTube. Now he offers master classes with hands-on, one-on-one instruction, where he teaches participants how to craft handmade sausage and how to trim, season, and smoke brisket.

"Neither of those are secrets we learned from anyone—just us making bad barbecue for so long," says Cooper.

Columbia

BODACIOUS BAR-B-Q

LONGVIEW & OTHER LOCATIONS

Bodacious Bar-B-Q starts with the kind of humble origin story that is perfectly suited to becoming a legacy. In the 1950s, Roland Lindsey was working at his family's restaurant—Lindsey Café in Duncanville—and proposed they start making barbecue to bring in extra money. Roland, all of 15 at the time, crafted a smoker using found bricks and a manual damper made from an old metal gas station sign.

Back then, the Lindseys sliced up beef clod and then doused it in a sauce they called "Arkansas gravy" (made from water, sugar, salt, Worcestershire, and tomato sauce). These beef plates were served with sliced white bread, and the restaurant also offered sausage made by Rudolph's, a Dallas-based butcher shop. When Roland wasn't at the pit, he could be found pursuing one of two other loves—football (he played first for Duncanville High School, and then for Kilgore College) or drag racing, making quite a name for himself at the latter.

Roland was drafted to Vietnam but, when his father unexpectedly passed away, he became the main provider for his family. He was sent back home, where he found success selling burgers and barbecue out of a little A-frame building under the name Little Roland's (after his childhood nickname). After marrying his wife, Nancy, in 1964, he sold the building, and the two moved to Commerce to be closer to

Nancy's family. Roland had intentions of returning to school to pursue teaching, but he'd already been bit by the barbecue bug. He ended up renting a space from one of his professors and started his first barbecue-specific concept, Little Roland's BBQ.

His barbecue was a hit—but Roland longed to be back among the pine trees of East Texas. So in 1967, he and Nancy found a building in Longview where he could start anew, and that's how Little Roland's Bodacious Bar-B-Q was born, with Nancy (a professional ballroom dancer) working right alongside her husband. By the next year, the name had been shortened to Bodacious Bar-B-Q, and a loyal customer base had formed around Roland's brisket and the Rudolph's sausage links smoked on Oyler pits. (Roland later befriended and sourced pits from A. N. Bewley, who had worked with Herbert Oyler to build his wood-fired steel rotisserie pits, then went on to manufacture his own Bewley Pits with the addition of an electronic damper.)

From there, Roland began expanding his barbecue menu, first adding on pork ribs—smoking them with hickory for a slightly sweeter finish. He used a blend of oak and mesquite for the briskets, turkey, pork, chicken, and sausage. He also tweaked and perfected his barbecue sauce during these early years, achieving a perfect balance of sweet, spice, and tang with ingredients like ketchup, Worcestershire, tamarind, anchovies, clove, mustard, brown sugar, and orange juice. He modified his sides through the years but always kept them classic: a creamy potato salad seasoned with salt, pepper, celery seed, and vinegar; toothsome, smoky pinto beans with a kick of chili; and a simple, but fresh and crunchy, coleslaw.

Roland developed a rub for brisket, pork shoulder, and poultry made with salt, white and black pepper, garlic, and onion; another paprika-heavy barbecue spice for ribs and pork belly, a seasoning salt used in many of the sides, and a chile pepper–dominant spice blend for the beans. When he decided to franchise the company in 1978, he would train the staff personally at each new location and blend the sauces, spices, and sides on-site. But by the mid-90s, when they had grown to six locations, he built a central kitchen to make and distribute those items to guarantee consistency and provide quality control. Nancy's sister and brother-in-law, Jan and John McKinnon, came on to help with this program and still manage sauce production today.

This dedication to barbecue was unmatched," says his granddaughter Madilynne Lindsey-Halling, the Director of Operations for Bodacious Bar-B-Q. "He was generous with his time and resources and wanted to ensure that anyone wanting to learn and provide for their families had access to the same knowledge and network he did. This led to many Bodacious franchises coming to be and, in fact, many barbecue places in the state of Texas and around the country first began with the help, employment, and instruction of Roland."

In 2014, Roland received a cancer diagnosis that forced him to slow down for the first time in his life. After a temporary closure of the flagship location, Jordan Jackson stepped up to the plate. Jackson had graduated from Le Cordon Bleu College of Culinary Arts in Austin and moved back home to East Texas, where he was working at Stanley's Famous Pit Barbecue (see page 92) in Tyler. In 2012, he married Roland's daughter Paige and, in 2015, he took over the pits with Roland's blessing. Under the mentorship of Roland, Jackson mastered his methods of smoking meat. And with the help of another culinary school grad, Scott Turner, Jackson began leveling up the business in new ways—like using hormone-free Angus briskets from 44 Farms and developing an in-house sausage program.

In 2017, Bodacious Bar-B-Q was named the #4 barbecue joint by *Texas Monthly,* which really put the mini-chain on the map. They brought on Bryan Bingham to help with increased business at the original location, and for a while it was smooth sailing. Then, in 2018, Roland passed away and the family business was rocked by both the loss of its patriarch and the many changes to follow. Jackson ran Bodacious for another year before leaving town (he now works as a barbecue consultant), Bingham stepped up to the helm for several years, but also eventually left, to open his own venture, Sunbird Barbecue (see page 147).

Nancy, who remains the CEO and President, shuttered the Mobberly location temporarily until the company could settle on the best fit for pitmaster: Spencer Halling. Spencer, who is married to Madilynne, had started working part-time at the Gladewater location while he was in college. But when there was a sudden need for a pitmaster, Spencer stepped up, taking and acing a crash course in fire management and meat smoking through books, YouTube, and hands-on experience.

"It has been fun to learn as I go and to now feel confident in the food I produce every day," says Halling of the literal trial by fire. "Despite how crazy the barbecue industry is—long hours, meat prices, etc.—there is an ease to what I do now. It's also really cool to be a part of the Bodacious legacy."

And how the Bodacious legacy lives on. The Mel-Man is a special created by a pitmaster named Mel in the 1990s, and the classic duo of chopped brisket and hot links on a bun is still the #1 bestseller (and will show up as an honorary offering on menus at other barbecue spots too). The Sloppy Joe—a mix of chopped beef and pork doused in sauce and served on a bun—was originally created to use up scraps, and remains an inexpensive favorite of regulars and college students alike. Halling has also maintained the housemade sausage program and continues to run innovative specials like apple pie pork belly and Dr. Pepper burnt ends, keeping up the flagship location's tradition of ingenuity.

"Mobberly has been the starting place for many pitmasters," says Madilynne. "It has been a place where people get to experiment and test their skills and interests. For that reason, the menu has fluctuated with the trends over the decades from old-school to craft BBQ, but we pride ourselves in always keeping it simple and classic for our lifelong customers too."

At its peak, Bodacious boasted over 20 locations—many run by siblings, nieces, and nephews of Nancy and Roland—and 15 of those are still in operation today: Arlington, Gilmer, Gladewater, Hallsville, Henderson, Kilgore, Lufkin, Marshall, Tatum, Tyler, San Angelo, Sulphur Springs, and three restaurants in Longview (Loop 281, Mobberly Avenue, and Sixth Street). The Mobberly Avenue location stands out as the flagship, with its wood-paneled interior, vintage soda crates and signs, a daily menu written out on butcher paper, and a shelf of Bodacious Bar-B-Q sauce for sale by the half gallon. Framed photos of the Lindsey family create a visual timeline of the many achievements and memories they've shared through the years.

"Being amongst the oldest barbecue places in Texas means there is a rich history shared by both family and pitmasters alike," says Madilynne. "There is a shared community of people who this place means so much to. Families who have had birthday parties here, pitmasters who once had their first high school job here, and for our own family, which has both grown in size and lost loved ones. This place blends work and family for us, and that is a really special gift."

SUNBIRD BARBECUE

LONGVIEW

When Bryan Bingham was ousted from the Christian metal band A Bullet for Pretty Boy in 2010, he never imagined his next stage would be barbecue. But after being dismissed for occasionally drinking beer, he found himself at a crossroads. Bingham, a Rowlett native who'd moved east to pursue a record deal with the band, began exploring life beyond music, enrolling in Kilgore College's culinary arts program at 28.

Bingham's wife, Kimmy, played a pivotal role in expanding his culinary horizons. A fan of cooking shows and an experienced home cook, she inspired Bryan to explore new flavors and techniques. After a series of backyard grilling experiments—many of which ended disastrously—Bryan became obsessed with perfecting the craft of barbecue, and began religiously studying Aaron Franklin's YouTube videos. In 2017, he joined the team at Bodacious Bar-B-Q's original location in Longview, a pivotal chapter in his barbecue journey.

"When I first started working, they had just been named number four in the state by *Texas Monthly*, so it really caused me to learn quick and grow at a rapid pace," remembers Bryan. "I took my backyard knowledge and honed my skills by doing it professionally every day."

In 2018, Bodacious Bar-B-Q's founder, Roland Lindsey, passed away, and the next year Bingham's

mentor, pitmaster Jordan Jackson, stepped away, leaving Bryan unexpectedly at the helm right before the pandemic unfolded.

"When I started running [Bodacious], I learned even more from the business side, and then COVID happened and I had to navigate running a restaurant in a pandemic when I was still learning how to be a boss," Bryan recalls. "It showed me what I was capable of and I think that has helped me immensely to never give up, despite how hard this line of work can be."

Kimmy, who had always dreamed of working in kitchens as a child, eventually left her hospital administration job to join the team at Bodacious, where she began making all the sides and desserts. And while searching for help in the pit room, Bryan found David Segovia.

"David came by one afternoon and we talked for a while and I immediately knew I wanted to work with him," says Bryan. "He started out like I did, as a backyard cook and actually wanted to get more into the competition side of cooking. I think the job was meant to be a stepping stone for him . . . but thankfully he stayed on."

Kimmy, Bryan, and Segovia found that they made a great team. So when Bryan began to feel increasingly frustrated with aspects of the business, and limited in his role as a manager, Segovia suggested they team up to open their own business together.

In May 2021, Bryan, Kimmy, and David launched Sunbird Barbecue as a food truck parked at a Longview gas station, using a trailer and reverse-flow pit borrowed from Arnis Robbins of Evie Mae's Pit Barbeque (see page 482). The name "Sunbird," another term for a phoenix, symbolized their rebirth from the ashes of previous challenges. However, their journey was far from smooth.

After a falling out with their investors, their trailer and smoker disappeared in the middle of the night. And yet they persevered, returning to two backyard pits Bryan had started out using (one built by his dad and the other built by Kimmy's father). As they began the legal process of buying out their former partners, they decamped to nearby Shreveport, Louisiana, and popped up in different locations as Fulbright BBQ (named after Bryan's grandparents), with Bryan and Kimmy's two boys helping out as well. Once the dispute was settled, the Binghams and Segovia returned to Longview and endured a couple of location changes while searching for a building. Finally, in December 2023, after nearly a year of battling city bureaucracy to secure permitting and working at local barbecue joints to pay rent on a building they couldn't yet use, Sunbird Barbecue opened its brick-and-mortar location in Longview.

"It's really hard to believe, after everything we went through, that we're all still standing and are in our building now," says Bryan. "When we started Sunbird, we didn't have a plan really, but our passion and love for serving people pushed us to make it. Everything we've been through has taught us a lesson on what we're capable of and what we can do together."

Once settled in their location, the trio was able to focus on what they do best: create delicious food. Bryan and Segovia are now using a 1,000-gallon offset smoker built by Cen-Tex offset, and we are in the process of adding a second identical one. They use a blend of mesquite and oak for a more robust smoke flavor, and they've developed their own spice blends, starting with a brisket rub and a Tex-Mex seasoning, followed by a rib rub and poultry seasoning.

"Our style constantly evolves and changes, which is the best part of us owning our own business," says Bryan. "David and I are always tweaking things to make them better and never settle. [We're] working on the way we trim, season, and smoke constantly."

While Sunbird has perfected classic barbecue offerings like exquisitely rendered brisket, succulent glazed baby back ribs, moist, pepper-crusted turkey, and exceptionally flavorful pulled pork, they've also become known for craveable creations you won't find at other barbecue joints. Segovia infuses Sunbird with the rich flavors and cherished recipes passed down through his family, blending tradition with innovation to create specials like smoked brisket guisada, chicken tinga, and brisket enchiladas. His family's green salsa enhances Sunbird's tacos, which they serve daily on locally made tortillas.

In addition to the house sausage made with brisket trim, Bryan has worked hard to develop specials like a poblano taco link with quesillo cheese and a variety of unique boudin links, like a cumin-laced Tex-Mex boudin (with brisket, Spanish rice, cilantro, green onions, and Tex-Mex seasoning) a chicken-and-sausage gumbo link, a holiday boudin stuffed with turkey and cranberry, and a broccoli casserole–inspired link filled with tallow-fried broccoli and cheesy rice. Pork belly burnt ends, glazed in flavors like strawberry-jalapeño and mangonada, are another one of their regular specials, and they've also created many different varieties of Armadillo Eggs, an over-the-top offering composed of a cream cheese–stuffed jalapeño inside a sausage ball and wrapped in bacon.

"We know anyone can get barbecue from multiple places either locally or in other cities, so we try our hardest to make things that are different or that have our own unique twist to bring people in," says Bryan.

Kimmy has taken great care to make sure all the sides are just as exciting. Each day, they offer charro beans, made flavorful with onions, peppers, and spices, as well as a creamy street corn, which can be loaded with meat and features cotija cheese, cilantro, a wedge of lime, and fresh jalapeños. She also makes a bright and refreshing cilantro poblano slaw and a decadent bacon ranch hash brown casserole. And Kimmy's smoked mac and cheese, which took her years to perfect, is so special, she only makes it on Fridays and Saturdays.

"We also are limited on how much we can offer every day just because, with us having a small crew, we all have a ton to do every day so we have to maximize what we're able to accomplish," says Bryan.

When she's not in the kitchen, Kimmy acts as the expo and runs food, and Sunbird hired a cashier shortly after opening. David's wife, Kay, manages the accounting, completing their small yet powerful team—a team poised to grow alongside their thriving business. Their success keeps them so busy that they have little time for promotion, not that they need it.

"I'd say one of the biggest things that got us through each challenge was our commitment to what we built, our families who helped us financially and supported us, but most definitely the community and our customers," says Bryan. "Every move, every pop-up, every closed door—they were always there for us and, without them, we wouldn't be here. I'm very thankful for all we've accomplished and how hard we've worked. Most of what we've been through would cause most people to walk away, but we never considered that."

MIMSY'S CRAFT BARBECUE & STEAKHOUSE

CROCKETT

Who doesn't love a good barbecue love story? Wade and Kathy Elkins grew up as high school sweethearts in the small town of Magnolia before relocating to Houston together to kick-start their individual culinary careers. Kathy, who is classically trained, was a chef at restaurants all over the greater Houston area—Giacomo's Cibo e Vino, Harold's, Hunky Dory, Better Luck Tomorrow, Hubble, and Hudson (now TRIS) in The Woodlands and the Woodforest Golf Club in Montgomery.

Wade's passion for barbecue started in the backyard with his dad using the family's old stand-up smoker. He then started using that smoker for his own experimentation, and he began taking on catering gigs, eventually quitting his job with a Houston-based imported foods distributor to focus on smoking full-time. Next, he went on to work at Feges BBQ in Houston, and then came on as a partner at Reveille Barbecue. That is, until an opportunity to open their own spot brought Wade and Kathy out of the city and into the small town of Crockett.

The structure housing Mimsy's was built in the early 1980s as an electric supply company, then sold to Crockett ISD as their maintenance barn before Wade's mom and stepdad turned the building into a manufactured ice company. Wade and Kathy transformed the space into Mimsy's (named after Wade's great-grandmother) in November 2020, using old-school bleachers as their customer service counters. ("Love notes and all!" says Kathy).

The duo commissioned Arnis Robbins of Evie Mae's Pit Barbeque (see page 482) in Lubbock to build them a 1,000-gallon reverse-flow pit, which they use for cold smoking bacon, lamb chops, salmon, and other specialty items, primarily using fragrant applewood smoke. Everything else is smoked with post oak in their second pit, a 1,000-gallon offset which Kathy describes as their workhorse. "Her name is Kimber, and she's always burning!" she says.

The former warehouse has high, sweeping ceilings, with rustic touches like wood paneling and a cattle trough sink. ("Wash your hands and say your prayers 'cause Jesus and germs are everywhere," reads a sign on the wall.) There's also some mounted deer heads, an American flag, Texas memorabilia, and an entire wall of encased guitars from Troubadour Fest. The decor fits right into rural East Texas, but the menu offers much more than that.

The brisket tends to steal the show at most Texas barbecue joints, and Mimsy's is phenomenal: juicy HeartBrand Akaushi Wagyu brisket boasting a sizable stripe of perfectly rendered fat and a rosy smoke ring right under the coarse pepper bark. The smoked turkey is also exceptionally moist and flavorful, and the half chicken is unbeatable. They submerge the bird in a brine of salt, sugar, and white and black tea for two days, then coat it with their Cowbery Jerk rub (allspice, cinnamon, cumin, nutmeg, black pepper, and cayenne pepper) before smoking it to an internal temperature of 160°F. The bird is then held in a warmer until an order comes in, when it is dropped into a fryer for two minutes, then brushed with a blend of pureed cilantro, garlic, jalapeños, oil, toasted chile flakes, and vinegar. Served with their super-herbal jerk sauce, it is absolute perfection. Depending on the day, you might encounter any number of specials on the menu, from their notorious brisket boudin and smoked short ribs with beef demi-glace to a smoked bone-in pork chop and the Ranch House, a brisket smashburger layered with pimento cheese, a crispy chicken tender, and buttermilk ranch on a brioche bun.

Meanwhile, Kathy flaunts her culinary prowess with sides like coconut-based cream curry corn and smoked maple Brussels sprouts (which were perfectly crispy and the right amount of sweet). Ridged cavatappi is the ideal pasta shape for catching cheese sauce, as exhibited by the smoked queso poblano mac and cheese. Mimsy's also offers a seasonal selection of salads, which are a great balance to the rich meats, and they make a staggering amount of different housemade pickles (which also fluctuate with the harvest): bread and butter cauliflower, cabbage marmalade, pickled red onions, pickled green tomatoes, pickled carrots, and jalapeños. (The cabbage marmalade is a delicious enhancement to the tender pulled pork).

Don't even think about leaving without trying Kathy's cheesecake. Other flavors make appearances, but banana pudding is a mainstay. She manages to capture the essence of the classic dessert throughout the entire creamy cheesecake base, set on a sturdy golden graham crust, and topped with a caramelized top layer, a dollop of whipped cream, and a crown of Nilla wafers.

There's a market attached to the smokehouse where you can find both packaged cuts of fresh meat and house-smoked deli meats and sausages, plus prepared foods and a curation of cheeses and snacks fit for the finest picnic. They also sell a variety of condiments, like local honey and hot sauce, and Mimsy's own line of rubs, from Cowboy Jerk to East Texas Rib Rub. They don't yet bottle their expertly developed sauces, so you'll need to keep visiting to taste those. And let me tell you: the sweet chile sauce and herb-rich jerk sauce are both worth the drive.

MARTIN'S PLACE

BRYAN

There are a number of historical barbecue joints still operating in Texas, but some of the oldest businesses have changed hands, and typically locations, through the years. Martin's Place is the only one with a Texas Historical Commission marker at the entrance, and in 2025, the Kapchinskie family celebrates 100 years of business on that very same plot of land in Bryan.

Martin Kapchinskie was a butcher who moved to Bryan in 1925 and purchased land once owned by Stephen F. Austin. Martin built a little wooden, shiplap structure with a brick barbecue pit built into the floor inside. That same year, he opened it as a convenience store for travelers, where he offered groceries, a public telephone, gasoline, and barbecue. Located midway between Bryan and College Station, Martin's Place was an ideal stop for farmers heading back to their ranches after making the trip into Bryan to get their goods for the week.

Martin sold some of the land to keep afloat during the Great Depression and, as his business continued to grow, he tore down the old building in 1939 to build a bigger brick building in its place. At the same time, he constructed a flat brick pit, where he would indirectly smoke meat over oak coals using salt as the only seasoning. He turned Martin's Place into a full-fledged diner, serving breakfast and lunch items like

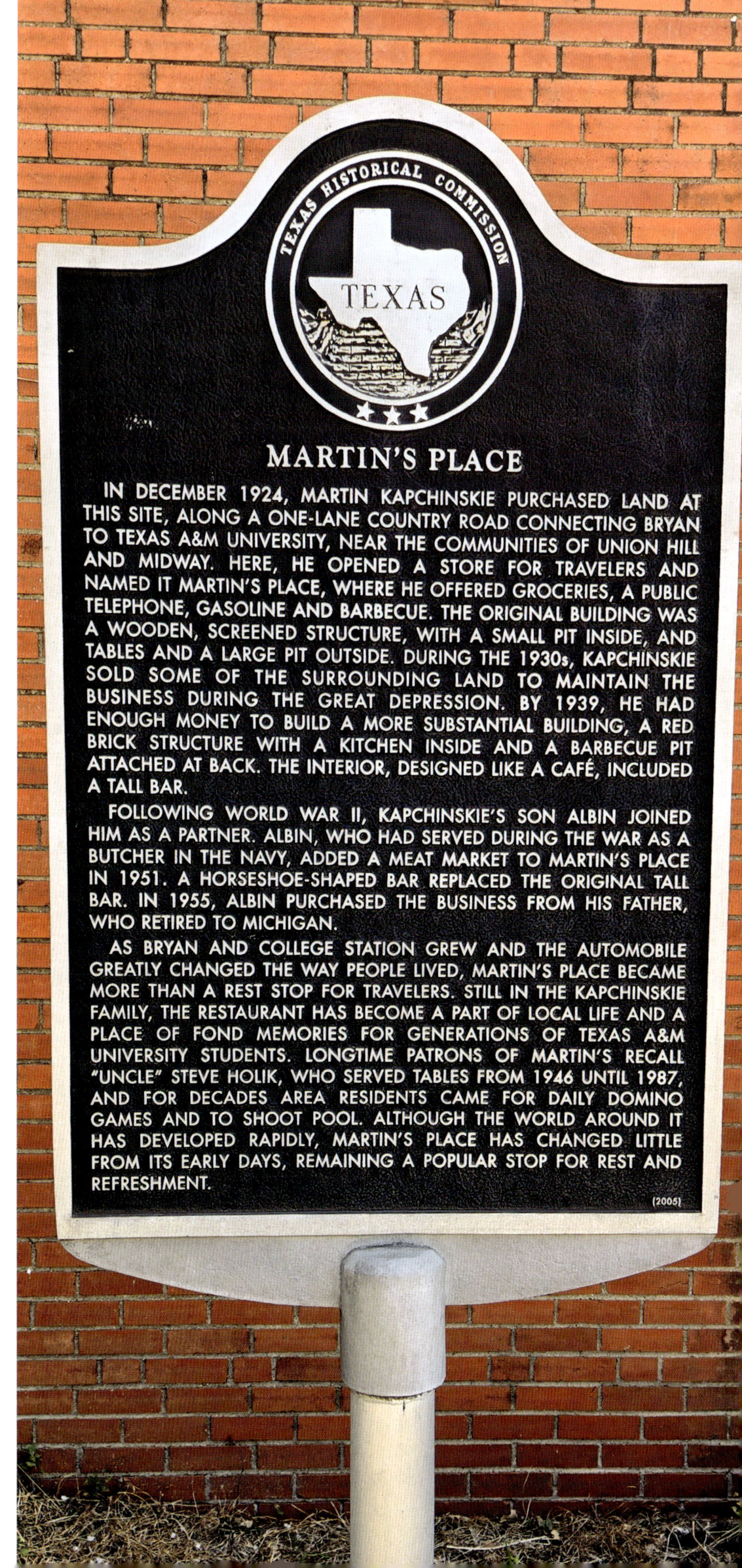

goose liver on toast for $0.15 and steak sandwiches for $0.25. He butchered whole cows and served cuts like T-bone and round steaks, and the only "barbecue" on offer was a chopped mélange of whatever pieces remained—served by the plate or as "opened faced" or "closed" sandwiches.

After serving in World War II, Martin's son Albin joined on as a partner. Albin, who had served as a butcher in the army, suggested they add a meat market component, so in 1946 they added a walk-in cooler and started selling raw cuts. This continued until sometime in the 1960s, when regulations changed and would have required replacing everything with stainless steel. With business still booming, they also added a second brick pit in 1949.

In the late 1950s, Martin retired and Albin took over. He ran Martin's Place with the help of his wife's uncle, Steve Holik, in the front of house. (Holik, who customers affectionately called "Uncle Steve," remembered everyone's go-to order and worked at Martin's Place from 1946 until he died in 1987.) Albin's son Steve (who was named after Holik) also helped out at the restaurant starting at the age of 12.

Steve Kapchinskie remembers a time, after they began using boxed meat from packing companies in the 1970s, when they started serving brisket and regulars lingered for hours, playing dominoes and pool, and drinking beer. Albin developed throat cancer right when Steve graduated from high school, so he took over the restaurant in 1976, when he was just 20, while his dad underwent treatment. And when Albin passed away five years later, Steve became the owner.

"I grew up with [barbecue]," says Steve. "I've been around it all my life and started helping my dad when I was 12. I sort of knew what was going on, so [taking over so young] wasn't so bad."

Over the years, Steve made some changes. His dad and grandfather had been staunchly opposed to using anything but salt on the meat, but Steve wanted to incorporate black pepper and garlic on his brisket,

pork shoulder, and pork ribs. He still uses those same soot-blackened brick pits to smoke all the proteins over oak coals, just as he's been doing for the last 50 years. He knows those pits like the back of his hand and he has a system of rotating meats through the hot and cold spots.

"The pit I use every day was built when the building was built," says Steve. "It's a brick pit, no electronics, no thermometer. I gotta do it all with my know-how, and I cook over the coals the way my grandfather did. A lot of places put the wood on one side and smoke the meat, but I cook directly over the coals. It brings that extra bit of flavor up through the meat—something about that meat dripping down on those coals makes a big difference in flavor."

In 1985, Steve added air-conditioning inside the restaurant and removed the pool table to add more seating. In addition to their brisket and beef-pork sausage made for them by Ruffino Meats, Steve smokes pork ribs and pork butt, which he slices in lieu of pulling.

"We never got into that pulled pork," he says with a laugh. "We leave that to the East Coast. We keep ours sliced."

The pinto beans and creamy potato salad created by Steve's uncle have remained the same, and so has his ketchup-based barbecue sauce, which is seasoned with salt, pepper, and paprika. Steve expanded the sides offered at Martin's by adding green beans and his version of German potatoes: mashed potatoes with bacon, onion, and butter. ("It's a dressed up baked potato without the skin!" he says.) In the 1990s, he also incorporated some fried items like curly fries and corn nuggets, which are similar to a corn fritter.

Located on South College Avenue, Martin's Place is a stone's throw from Texas A&M University, and Aggie maroon is found throughout the dining room, from the blinds and chairs to the horseshoe-shaped bar. The wood-paneled walls are hung with beer signs and old framed photos of the Kapchinskies through the years. Steve's wife, Betty, began working the front counter in 1999, and still uses an old-fashioned pad of guest checks to take orders. During COVID, Steve and Betty started closing on weekends, and they decided to keep it that way. Now, the restaurant is open Tuesday through Friday only.

"We're semi-retired, so we decided to take the weekend off to do things that we missed out on for 50 years," says Steve.

In 2004, Steve's daughter Mandy started working in the kitchen right out of high school. She'll eventually take over the restaurant, but hasn't learned the pits just yet. Steve is still manning those for up to 13 hours a day.

"I don't know if she can handle the pit yet," he says. "You've got to be pretty tough to stand that heat, to stick your face in that pit. Sometimes when it's real hot, it gets around 130. I go by the window and sit and spray myself down with a water bottle. When you cook like I do, you gotta watch it constantly. Other places just set a thermometer and walk away, but not us. This is the way we've always done it and the way I'm going to keep doing it as long as I can."

KHÓI BARBECUE

HOUSTON

There may be a line winding through the yard of Khói Barbecue's future location in Houston's Northside Village, but the vibe is so congenial, it feels like a friend's backyard party. On this sunny winter day, Don Nguyen is pulling apart tender smoked whole hog at the pit and stuffing fresh-baked baguettes that he's slathered with tallow aioli and shingled with housemade pickles.

"We cook with fire a lot in Vietnam, but it's mostly grilling over direct heat," Don says. "So you go around Saigon and you'll see a lot of people grilling on a Weber-type grill on the street, selling food. Char-grilled pork bánh mì is probably one of the most popular Vietnamese items in any restaurant or bánh mi shop. We love flavor, we love textures—and we love cooking outdoors."

After the Vietnam War, Don's family was separated by political upheaval. His father's side, who fought with South Vietnam, were part of the refugee wave relocated to Texas, while Don's mother's side of the family stayed in Vietnam. Don was born in Saigon and lived in Da Nang for the first five years of his life, before he and his mom were able to emigrate to Houston to reunite with his dad in 1991.

"It was a Vietnamese Romeo and Juliet sort of deal," Don says.

Houston was a key resettlement area after the Vietnam War, largely due to its similarly warm, tropical climate and proximity to the ocean. Today, the city is home to over 140,000 Vietnamese Americans, making it one of the largest Vietnamese diasporas in the country. Growing up in Alief, located in southwest Houston, Nguyen was not only immersed in Little Saigon's vibrant Vietnamese food scene, but highly influenced by his own family's cooking. He and his brother Theo (nine years his junior) also fondly recall marking special occasions with all-you-can-eat ribs at Luther's BBQ and visiting their cousin when he worked at Salt Lick BBQ in Dripping Springs. These flavors and memories are what laid the foundation for the Viet-Tex dishes Don and Theo craft at Khói Barbecue.

Don spent two years at the United States Military Academy West Point before transferring to the University of Texas at Austin, where he studied economics and math. While there, he had a mind-opening experience at Franklin Barbecue (see page 233 for a profile on founder Aaron Franklin). But his own hands-on experience didn't come for several more years. After returning from Taipei, where he studied Mandarin, Don started watching Franklin's PBS series. Then, during one fateful trip to Costco for a rotisserie chicken, Don instead returned with a ceramic Kamado Joe, which he began experimenting with. It didn't take him long to scour Craigslist for a small backyard offset smoker, followed by a trailer.

When Hurricane Harvey hit Houston in 2017. Don and Theo found themselves, much like Lance and Boo Eaker (see page 327), feeding a group of their friends as they emptied out their freezer and congregated in solidarity.

"I thought, 'This is cool—barbecue really brings people together,'" says Don. "And that was how it all started."

Just one week after Harvey, Don and Theo hosted their first pop-up and donated the proceeds to those affected by the hurricane. They then connected with local brewery Baileson Brewing and began popping up there once or twice a month. As Don further refined his Central Texas barbecue, he started thinking about how he could incorporate the flavors of their childhood into their newly named concept, Khói Barbecue (khói translates to "smoke"). He started seasoning his 44 Farms brisket with salt, black pepper, and highly prized aromatic green pepper from Phú Quốc island. He adds palm sugar to the rub for his Compart Duroc pork ribs, and glazes them halfway through to create a caramelized crust. And he enhances the pulled pork with lemongrass, adding a floral touch as well as zing to the finished product.

"Barbecue has really helped me connect with and appreciate my motherland's cuisine in ways I never imagined," says Don.

Don had already begun a project to start documenting his mother Tiffany's Vietnamese recipes. He discovered her recipe for pho paired well with umami-rich slices of brisket. He started cooking the chicken broth with a beef rib bone to add even more richness while it simmers with traditional spices like star anise, cardamom, and coriander. Another dish their mom made was a poached chicken and rice dish, which starts with raw rice toasted with chicken fat, chicken bouillon, and garlic in a wok. The Nguyen brothers make theirs using brined, spatchcocked, and smoked skin-on chicken seasoned simply with salt and then finished with yuzu kosho, a fermented citrus chile paste that lends spice, acid, and complexity to the dish. This creation won them their first barbecue competition at the Houston BBQ Throwdown in 2019, and it's now one of their signature items.

"It was just intoxicating, just doing something with my hands," says Don, who had begun working full-time trading renewable energy when his foray into barbecue started. "My job is sitting in front of a computer, looking at spreadsheets all day. So to have a craft where you can make something with your hands and share it with people and see their positive reaction to it—it's really cool . . . I was also intrigued by the precision of it—but also the lack of precision sometimes. Cooking with fire, there's a certain exact temperature you try to keep, but there's also a band that you can waver in between. And no brisket's the same shape, so the temperatures will never be the same. The wood you get will always be different. It's about how you react to it, and then make it work."

After a glowing profile on Khói Barbecue ran in the *Houston Chronicle*, the Cooking Channel's *Man, Fire, Food* reached out to film an episode with the Nguyen brothers that aired in May 2019. Khói has since been featured in publications like *Texas Monthly, CNTraveler*, and *The Local Palate,* and in 2022 Don was invited to compete on *BBQ Brawl*, where he cooked a whole hog for the first time on-air, impressing judges Bobby Flay, Brooke Williamson, and James Beard Award–winning South Carolina pitmaster Rodney Scott, who Don went on to learn from and collaborate with in Charleston.

"Rodney Scott is a huge inspiration to me," says Don. "It's an honor to know him and to get to learn the whole hog traditions of that region, because pork is such an important part of Vietnamese cuisine."

Don likes to treat the hog like Chinese crispy pork belly, applying a salt crust which pulls out moisture and crisps up the skin. He typically cooks it for 10 to 12 hours on a BQ direct heat pit at 200°F. He then serves the pulled hog a number of ways: simply dipped into fish sauce, tossed into mì Quảng, a Central Vietnamese turmeric noodle dish, steamed in rice rolls to make bánh cuốn, or folded into turmeric crepes to make bánh xèo, which is then served with fish sauce, chile jam, perilla, mint, and cilantro. The elements of bright herbs, briny fish sauce, and punchy spice perfectly round out the richness of the savory smoked pork.

Thanks to his love of whole-hog cooking and time spent in Charleston, Don also befriended pitmaster Hector Garate, who combines Texas and Carolina barbecue techniques with flavors and ingredients from his native Puerto Rico at his restaurant Palmira Barbecue. The two have collaborated multiple times now, conceptualizing dishes like broken rice hash, which often appears on Khói's pop-up menus now.

"The idea was—hash is a very poor person food, and super traditional in the Carolinas," explains Don. "But for me, broken rice is the poor people's food. It's the leftover rice in the milling process nobody wanted. That is a story we can tell of humble foods that are extremely delicious but come out of necessity."

Just about every Khói Barbecue pop-up features new dishes connecting the Nguyen brothers' Texas upbringing with their Vietnamese roots. Don makes a few different types of sausages based on Vietnamese dishes or ingredients. The Spicy Sapa is made with peppers from the Lào Cai region. Don and Tiffany developed a Laughing Cow Birdseye Chili link to honor his grandfather's favorite cheese with a spicy Viet-Tex spin on a jalapeño cheese link. And the Bò Lúc Lắc sausage is crafted with lemongrass, honey, fish sauce, palm sugar, and the lolot leaf (piper sarmentosum) used in traditional Vietnamese shaking beef.

"The [sausage-making] techniques are almost the same, just the ingredients are different," explains Don. "We mix it, we stuff it, and we cold smoke to get that snap. So the whole thought process is, just like

Khói itself, to really dive deep into tradition on both sides and then marry traditional bò lúc lắc ingredients with a really traditional Czech-German sausage-making technique."

Another dish Khói has become known for is the beef rib curry. Pepper-barked beef rib, rosy with a post oak smoke ring, is sliced and then served over garlic rice in a fragrant coconut-based curry made with galangal, makrut lime, and Vietnamese fish sauce.

"We love curries," says Don. "Vietnamese curry is more turmeric-based . . . and Southern Vietnam uses a lot of coconut milk, so a lot of curries we ate were coconut-based. And when I think of a curry that would pair well with barbecue, to mellow out some of the spices, the peppers, the fat—a coconut-based curry was the one. I think what makes our curry different is just the viscosity. You want that mouthfeel—it has to have some kind of silkiness to it. So we use coconut milk and coconut cream to get that ratio."

The curry became so popular, the Nguyen brothers began bottling and selling it, with the help of M. Brady Clark (see page 322), who also designs their line of merch like shirts, hats, stickers, and patches. These are for sale, along with their food, at the pop-ups they host regularly both on and off-site—now with the addition of two 1,000-gallon Moberg offset smokers—one is named Bé Bu, which means "thick baby mama" or "big baby" in Vietnamese, while the other, Một, Hai, Ba, Dzô, translates to "One, two, three, cheers!"

These days, Don is still trading energy full-time and Theo, who used to take the late-night pit shifts in between seasons of Fortnite, is now in more of a front-of-house position with Khói, and manages a restaurant as his full-time job. Each time the brothers host a pop-up in the yard, they have a group of close friends who help make it happen.

"We're super lucky to have a group of friends that believe in what we do," says Don.

Since closing on a 1970s bungalow in early 2022, the Nguyen brothers have been gradually transforming it into the permanent dining space of their dreams.

"I want it to be traditional barbecue, but it'll be things that inspire me—wabi sabi, Japanese philosophy, West Texas, lots of ocotillos, and some bamboo," says Don. "Just a place I wanna enjoy being because we're gonna be here a lot, I guess."

The brick-and-mortar Khói Barbecue will serve trays of barbecue by the pound, alongside a rotating roster of Viet-Tex dishes they've been honing since 2017.

"I love the market style you see at Smitty's, or City Market in Luling," says Don. "I've got to do by-the-pound barbecue because I want that lineage to continue. But we'll do specials the way my mom cooked, the way I grew up eating."

HARLEM ROAD TEXAS BBQ

RICHMOND

Ara Malekian's culinary path is nothing short of remarkable.

Malekian's family is Armenian, but he spent his early years in Iran, where his father was working for the Shah. When a period of political unrest began, his parents sent him to live with his grandmother in Switzerland and attend Catholic boarding school. He spent much time in the kitchen learning from his grandmother before taking cooking and restaurant management as an elective in school. By the time he was 12, Malekian was apprenticing at a Michelin-starred French restaurant in the city of Lugano, where he started off doing dishes and prep work before honing skills like sausage making and cheesemaking.

By the late 1980s, Malekian's family had relocated to California and settled in Glendale, a city known for its Armenian population. After finishing high school and college in the States, Malekian resumed working in restaurants, moving into bigger roles. He worked as a consultant and a chef-operator, opening high-end Italian and French restaurants across the country. And then, in a career milestone, chef Wolfgang Puck brought Malekian on as his corporate executive chef. During the three years he worked for him, Malekian was in charge of all Puck's existing restaurants in the US, helped open new ones, and catered the Academy Awards dinner each year.

"My first Texas barbecue experience was in California, at a place called Dr. Hogly Wogly's Tyler Texas Barbecue in the Valley," says Malekian. "Arnold Schwarzenegger actually told me about it."

It was during this time that Malekian visited his brother, who had moved to Sugar Land with his family. That trip convinced him to relocate in 2006 to be closer to his young nephews. Malekian found that there was plenty of consulting work available in the Houston area, as well as opportunities for catering multicourse fine-dining dinners. He found a storage unit in Richmond, located 30 miles southwest of Houston, which he used to store all his equipment, including a full mobile kitchen he would tow to cater events. The owners of the storage facility also owned 1,000 acres of nearby grassland, and wanted to open a barbecue joint on that parcel.

"My landlord asked me if I wanted to build a barbecue restaurant and there was nothing like that out here," recalls Malekian. "I said, 'Yeah, totally—that's a great idea!' So that's how it all came to be."

Malekian built the barn-like structure in four mouths, using oil well drilling pipes as structural beams to reinforce the cedar walls. But it took another year and a half (and $200,000) to establish water and sewage infrastructure on the undeveloped land, and then get city permits sorted out. He opened Harlem Road Texas BBQ, named after the street it's on, at the start of 2018.

"I built this place from the ground up," says Malekian. "I designed it so that when you come inside, you feel like you're somewhere else. There's no low windows—all the windows are high so all you see is Texas sky. I didn't want you to feel like you were in Richmond."

The restaurant's dining room is as curated as Malekian's unique signature look (he is typically dressed all in black, donning a cowboy hat, with a lit cigar resting under his silver mustache and framed by a coiled two-pronged goatee). The rustic wood walls are hung with items and relics Malekian has collected through the years: an elk he hunted in Colorado and a kudu he hunted in Africa, a 100-year-old British milk cart he acquired, a guitar custom-made for him by a friend from a Texas license plate with the letters "HRB" on it (for Harlem Road Barbecue). Malekian designed and built all the wooden picnic tables, and there are a few old wine barrels made from the same French oak staves he uses to smoke his meat.

"The wine is stained inside of the barrels, so you get some of that sweetness and aroma in the smoke that comes off of that wine as it burns off," explains Malekian, who buys 100 retired barrels a year and keeps them in his nearby storage unit and chops them into pieces as needed. "And even though you can taste the smoke, it's not overpowering. After you eat a heavy, heavily smoked meat with just regular oak, you're constantly feeling that heartburn, for several hours. But with my barbecue, you don't get that. It's a lot cleaner."

Malekian uses three cabinet-style vault smokers by Pitmaker, which he finds much more efficient due to their heavy insulation. He says it takes him about 40 percent less time to smoke the the same brisket than it would with an offset smoker.

"With offset smokers, you have the round pit which is usually made from old propane tanks, and then the firebox is on that side and those are not insulated at all," explains Malekian. "And every time you open up the door, you lose a lot of heat and you have to constantly rotate the briskets because the firebox is on one side so there's a hot spot and a cold spot."

Malekian gets all his Prime-grade beef from Snake River Farms' Double R Ranch and, while he keeps it simple to showcase this high-quality beef, he does have a few tricks up his sleeve. He always salts his meat first, to be sure to evenly distribute it, and then he adds pepper (whereas many pitmasters season with a blend of the two). He also uses both 16-mesh and 30-mesh peppercorn, to vary texture, and he incorporates sumac for a citrusy note as well. And he does all his seasoning the night before to help build the bark.

"Most people don't realize that what develops bark is the pH level on top of the meat," says Malekian. "So the longer you leave the salt and pepper on the meat, the better bark you get."

Harlem Road Texas BBQ is one of few restaurants who feature daily beef ribs on the menu, as well as pork ribs. In addition to that salt, pepper, and sumac blend, all his pork (Duroc ribs, shoulder, and shank) gets seasoned overnight with apple cider vinegar and molasses, and both pork and chicken are rubbed with a seasoning made from smoked paprika, granulated onion, and granulated garlic. Using his beef and pork trim, Malekian makes two sausages in-house. Both are 80 percent beef and 20 percent pork, and one has heat from the addition of chipotle.

Each Sunday, Malekian runs a pork shank special that he's become known for. The pork is smoked for three hours and then tenderized in a foil-covered pan for four more, until the meat is falling off the bone. He blends the drippings with hot butter to create the base of a flavorful curry sauce enriched with fenugreek, turmeric, paprika, star anise, dried ginger, garlic powder, and cayenne, and thickened slightly with potato starch. In other uniquely delicious specials, he offers smoked lamb chops each Friday that draw customers from all over the state. He'll also occasionally smoke an octopus after cooking it sous vide in red wine, and then serve it with a pomegranate balsamic reduction. When he was on the Food Network's *BBQ Brawl* in 2021, he came in second place thanks to this recipe.

Malekian offers traditional sides, but all bear the undeniable mark of a top-flight chef's attention to detail. The pinto beans are finished under the brisket, so they catch drippings that add rich flavor, and he then adds brisket burnt ends to the beans, as well as

chopped raw onions for sweetness and crunch. Mac and cheese is made ultra creamy with béchamel and three types of cheese. Malekian's version of German potato salad features baked Texas red potatoes mixed with apple cider vinegar, julienned onions, mayo, and mustard, and is then served cold. And the coleslaw is fresh and light, with sunflower microgreens and local Fulton County honey. Devoid of mayo, it's more like a little side salad on your tray.

To make pickles, Malekian cures small Persian cucumbers with juniper berries, árbol chile peppers, and a bit of sugar for 72 hours. And his barbecue sauce was inspired by a US Army recipe from the 1930s. He adapted it by switching out the canned and dried ingredients for fresh, and lowered the ketchup and sugar components, instead adding molasses and apple cider vinegar for increased tang and minerality. Malekian also replaced the water in the recipe with Armenian coffee, which is a specialty of his.

Katz Coffee roasts a custom light blend for Harlem Road Texas BBQ, using single origin beans from Laos. Bags of this blend are available for purchase at the counter, either as whole beans or in the Armenian grind, which is so fine it requires a special copper pot because it's too delicate to brew any other way. Malekian directs his guests to an instructional YouTube video where he explains exactly how to brew a cup of Armenian coffee the traditional way in under two minutes.

"When we do barbecue festivals, I end up making 100 and 120 of these [demitasse cups] because all the pitmasters come to me to make coffee for them. I spend more time making coffee than I do smoking meat!"

The lighter roast beans make for a highly caffeinated coffee with less acidity and more aromatics—perfect for pairing with one of Malekian's desserts. He makes a chocolate bread pudding using semisweet Belgian chocolate, Armenian coffee, and butter croissants. And his pecan pie is classic but extraordinary: he presses his own sugar cane juice in lieu of corn syrup, which results in a silky, lightly sweet pie. Malekian even carries a portable burner and pot in his truck so he can brew Armenian coffee on the go.

"When I want coffee, I just drop the tailgate and make myself a cup of coffee," he says. "That's part of the eccentric personality of being a chef. We're very particular about everything that we do and we eat and we drink. I'm not willing to sacrifice for lesser quality."

This ethos carries through to the rest of his tools and equipment. He uses chopsticks in the kitchen, and always carries a set with him while traveling. One set of his knives was crafted by Hattori, a renowned sword maker, in Japan. Another set (a brisket knife, chef knife, and trimming knife) was made for him by Stephen Pustilnik of Houston Edge Works (see page 130), a knifemaker who now has a nearly decade-long waiting list for his high-alloy steel blades.

And right outside the entrance of the restaurant is Malekian's pride and joy: a live fire pit he designed, inspired by a Viking-style grill he experienced in Denmark (where he used to sail Viking-style ships as a hobby). He uses the pit on weekends and for special events to cook everything from whole lambs and tomahawk chops to king salmon on cedar boards.

"It's very primal, cooking with fire and smoke, and every culture in the world has a form of doing barbecue and cooking with live fire," says Malekian. "What I like about Texas barbecue is that it's very clean—you can actually taste the meat."

This globe-trotting chef, who speaks seven languages and has worked all over the world, has chosen the Lone Star state as his home and embraced its barbecue as his own. We'll consider that a victory for Texas.

GATLIN'S BBQ

HOUSTON

Greg Gatlin brought craft barbecue to Houston in 2010, and his pioneering efforts featured a soulful twist, inspired by the dishes he grew up cooking and eating with his family. Gatlin's earliest barbecue memories actually trace back to Louisiana, where his family congregated and his uncle owned a barbecue joint just outside of Shreveport.

"Uncle John had brick pits and used to do the whole hind leg quarters for pulled pork," remembers Gatlin. "And he'd be mopping that big pork over direct heat. I remember he'd always be like, 'Hey, make sure y'all don't get over there by that hot coal!'"

During their family gatherings, his dad and uncles would handle the cooking, and as they got older, Gatlin and his cousins started taking an interest too. Even while attending Rice University, Gatlin returned home whenever he could, finding that smoking meat with his family provided the break he needed from football and academics. After graduating, Gatlin took on roles as a benefits consultant and then as a commercial real estate appraiser. Barbecue remained a cherished hobby until a friendly rivalry with a former teammate uncovered a deeper passion.

"There was a buddy of mine that I played football with, and we used to compete all the time," remembers Gatlin with a grin. "And he always used to talk about his honey ribs. I was like, 'Dude, I got your honey ribs beat!'"

The two teamed up and started barbecuing for alumni behind the Rice football stadium every home game. Before long, catering requests started pouring in, and Gatlin began to see a future in barbecue. Although he had some front-of-house experience from waiting tables in college, he wanted to build his management skills. Leaving the corporate world behind, he joined Pappadeaux Seafood Kitchen as a

manager to gain hands-on industry experience—all while continuing to cater on the side.

In 2009, Gatlin stopped for a po'boy on the way to a catering, but the shop was shuttered. There was a For Rent sign and a phone number on the door, and Gatlin called the number and inquired about the possibility of putting a barbecue concept in the space. The landlord not only welcomed the idea, but completed the buildout entirely for free. Gatlin signed a lease on the little Shady Acres cottage and turned it into a 30-seat restaurant. When they opened their doors in 2010, it was just Greg's dad, Henry, on the pits, his mom, Mary, in the kitchen and front-of-house, and Greg taking turns working alongside both parents. In 2019, Greg's brother Kevin decided to take a break from teaching and coaching to come join the team, and now helps in both the kitchen and the pit.

"[My dad and I] would come back every four hours to make sure the pits stayed lit," remembers Gatlin, who rolled his trailer-mounted offset behind the small building. "So he would do the first four hours and then he would go home, and I would come back and do the second, and then by that time, it was time for him to come back. So yeah, it was insane; there wasn't a whole lot of sleep."

Greg and Henry season their briskets in salt, pepper, garlic, and cayenne overnight before beginning the smoking process using a blend of hickory and oak. Once they've formed a nice crust, they spritz them with a solution of apple juice, apple cider vinegar, cayenne, and hot sauce, then wrap them in butcher paper and put them back in the pit to tenderize.

The pulled pork, spare ribs, and baby back ribs are all rubbed with a house rib seasoning before they're smoked. The chicken is brined, then seasoned with that same rib rub and sprayed in the pit with a blend of herb-infused water, vinegar, and lemon. The turkey also gets the rib rub, as well as some fresh herbs, and it gets basted with a spice butter as it's cooking, then coated in butter and wrapped in foil to finish out the cook. Not only were the Gatlins the first in Houston to take such care in each detail of the smoking process, but they offered a much bigger variety of sides than any other existing barbecue joint at the time.

"When we had [family] barbecues, we had a lot of sides," says Greg. "So we didn't want to be pegged into just potato salad, baked beans, coleslaw."

In addition to those classic sides, Greg created flavorful pinto beans, savory green beans, and a unique cabbage dish—first grilled for added flavor and color, then sautéed to perfection. Gatlin's quickly became known for its dirty rice, a Louisiana recipe passed down from Greg's great-aunt. True to tradition, they prepare it by cooking down chicken livers and gizzards, then adding sautéed onions, red and green bell peppers, and fresh parsley. This mixture is thickened into a rich gravy, blended with rice, and baked, creating a comforting and flavorful side dish.

Candied yams are another family recipe they serve. The sweet potatoes are peeled and glazed with sugar, brown sugar, vanilla extract, orange juice, and salt, then baked in the oven and finished on the stovetop until tender and caramelized.

Gatlin developed his barbecue sauce when he began catering, and strived for a balanced condiment that isn't overly spicy, sweet, or tangy. However, Greg won't hesitate to run back to the kitchen and blend in some honey or sugar, if a customer likes a sweeter sauce, or chile de árbol for added spice upon request.

"I always say that, if I can be a close second to your grandpa or your dad, I think I got you, because it touches that thought of what barbecue is in your mind," says Greg.

Within the first year Gatlin's was open, it had drawn considerable attention thanks to positive reviews from one-time *Houston Chronicle* restaurant critic Alison Cook, and then *Texas Monthly* barbecue editor Daniel Vaughn (see page 26).

"So it just consistently started to grow, and that wasn't even my intention," says Greg. "It was just—'Hey, this is what we do.' I'd seen barbecue places here in Houston get really big and commercial, like Luther's, and then you had some smaller guys that were really good, but at that point in time, people weren't really writing about barbecue like that. The only barbecue people talked about was up Austin way, or Central Texas, because that was the zeal of Texas barbecue at that point in time."

Gatlin's had already long outgrown its original dining space and, as developers started to buy up all the land around it, the Gatlins no longer had enough parking either. So in 2015, Greg relocated the business to a much bigger, newer space in Oak Forest. Since he was unable to bring offsets into the space, he switched to using Old Hickory wood-fired rotisseries, which cut down on both the amount of wood used and the time spent tending the pits through the night.

"Now it's not the barbecue that's making me not sleep—it's my kids," says Greg, shaking his head.

After their move, the accolades continued to roll in, from placing on the *Texas Monthly* Top 50 in 2017 to Greg's selection as a semifinalist for a James Beard Foundation award for Best Chef: Texas in 2023. Also instrumental in Gatlin's growth, acclaimed Houston chef Michelle Wallace spent six years at the restaurant before competing on *Top Chef: Wisconsin* and departing to open her own concept.

A now-spacious kitchen has allowed the Gatlins to greatly expand on the menu, with offerings like beef ribs, pastrami brisket, and oxtails, made in either a jerk or traditional Southern-style gravy. Greg offers several different specialty burgers (either smashed on the flat top or smoked) with different toppings, and a number of other sandwich offerings, from smoked chicken salad to a smokehouse Cuban. Smoked wings can be tossed in buffalo, Thai chili, raspberry, or jerk sauce. The sides have also grown to include even more soulful dishes, from a melty mac and cheese and brothy collards to smoked corn spiced up with red onions, jalapeño, red bell pepper, and Cajun seasonings. There's also loaded fries, baked potatoes, fried okra, and chili. At one point, Greg served catfish and gumbo, but those dishes have since moved over to Gatlin's Fin & Feathers, his Southern seafood–focused sister concept, which opened in 2022.

Gatlin's also features an expansive dessert menu, including his Aunt Merc's 7UP cake and German chocolate cake, both made by Greg's cousin Lonnie. Greg bakes chocolate chip cookies and snickerdoodles, and his mom still comes on weekends to make her famous peach cobbler. Since she went through cancer treatment some years ago, Greg insisted she pull back from working in the kitchen and just enjoy her visits instead.

"She became my official taster, so she'll always be included," says Greg. "And my dad was supposed to get out after two years. We laugh all the time like, 'I thought you were retired, man.' He's like, 'Hell, I work harder now than when I was working my corporate job!' But he wouldn't know what to do with himself if he didn't come up here every day. It's become such a part of him. I think he enjoys the time with his sons and just seeing us grow from kids into men now."

BBQ U

Many of the top pitmasters in Texas offer classes to share their tips and techniques with backyard enthusiasts. While many of these classes are in-depth and even provide hands-on opportunities, none can compare to the educational opportunities available at Camp Brisket and Barbecue Summer Camp. Held annually at Texas A&M University's Department of Animal Science in partnership with Foodways Texas, these programs are uniquely immersive and comprehensive.

Foodways Texas, established in 2010 by a dedicated group of chefs, journalists, ranchers, and farmers, is a nonprofit organization committed to preserving and celebrating Texas's distinct culinary traditions. Food writer and cookbook author Robb Walsh, one of the founding members, was already connected to Texas A&M University's renowned meat science program.

At Texas A&M, Rosenthal Meat Center manager Ray Riley and professor Jeff Savell (pronounced SAY-vull) were already teaching a freshman Barbecue 101 course. They had invited Walsh, the author of the *Legends of Texas Barbecue* cookbook, to come speak on regional barbecue styles.

"I was sort of an interface between the Austin food folks and the A&M meat science folks, who were focused on meat judging competitions and serving their function as extension agents, helping cattle farmers and so forth," says Walsh.

At the same time Foodways Texas began considering fundraising ideas to support its mission, the A&M professors were discussing with Walsh how to expand their barbecue programming and incorporate more food-focused experiences. So they partnered with Foodways Texas in 2011 to create Barbecue Summer Camp, a three-day event focused on in-depth barbecue training for both passionate enthusiasts and professionals.

"[We host] men and women from all over the world," says Marvin Bendele, who has served as executive director of Foodways Texas since its founding. "We see beginners to accomplished backyard cooks to restaurant owners all attend as campers."

"I really think our camps are best because of the Aggie hospitality," adds Riley. "Our camps are taught in a very comfortable environment so that everyone feels at home, and we use pitmasters to discuss the art of barbecue [while] we provide the science of barbecue."

Barbecue Summer Camp encompasses a wide range of barbecue topics, featuring classes on meat processing and fabrication and preparation of beef, pork, and poultry. Attendees engage in practical butchery demos, lectures from meat scientists, and interactive tasting experiences, gaining insights from some of Texas's top pitmasters, pit builders, and more.

"The Texas A&M meat science center is constructed with rails in the ceiling so, when they talk about beef, they wheel a side of beef into the lecture room and cut it open to show you how to grade [it]," explains Walsh. "There's also a cow skeleton so they can hold each piece of meat up to the skeleton and show you where it came from. There's no place else that's doing that . . . this is a completely different level."

The success of Barbecue Summer Camp inspired Camp Brisket, which launched in 2013 as a two-day workshop dedicated to Texas's most iconic cut. Campers learn about different types and grades of meat, and grad students will cook cuts of Choice, Select, Prime, Top Choice, and Wagyu for participants to blind taste and score. A similarly structured trial is used to compare wood types, as they blind taste and score brisket smoked with oak, pecan, hickory, and mesquite.

"Grade of meat is a greater indicator of preference than is the type of wood used to smoke," says Savell. "It is not perfect nor is it linear, but the top barbecue places in Texas use higher graded briskets. . . . There is no clear preference for woods over time. One year, oak may be preferred, the next year, it may be pecan."

During Camp Brisket, pitmasters will also go into detail about knife style and selection, fire maintenance, pit design, and seasoning. Meanwhile, professors tap into the science behind techniques like the low and slow method of cooking, which is crucial for transforming tough brisket into tender barbecue.

"Most barbecue cuts have high levels of connective tissue," explains Savell. "The collagen in connective tissue is converted to gelatin at a certain temperature, and the low and slow method is the best way to achieve this elevated temperature without getting the exterior of the cut too done."

Camp Brisket always concludes with Savell interviewing a panel of well-known pitmasters, and many will cook throughout the program as well. Past participating pitmasters include Tom Perini, Aaron Franklin, Wayne Mueller, Kent Black, Russel Roegels, Greg Gatlin, Tootsie Tomanetz, Kerry Bexley, Jess Pryles, Arnis Robbins, Lance Eaker, and many more. Bryan Bracewell, owner of Southside Market & Barbeque and a founding member of Foodways Texas, is a regular attendee who looks forward to returning to his alma mater to share his expertise at the camps.

"It's held by the same professors that I studied under when I was at A&M and in the same facilities, so it feels like going back home," says Bracewell. "I get to work alongside my mentors, people I respect very much in the industry, and who are now my friends. And it's a good opportunity for me to get away from the four walls of Southside because it reminds me that this is pretty cool, what we get to do. I'm thankful for that and it kind of reinvigorates my barbecue soul, because day in and day out, it can turn into a job. And that is when it gets to be not as fun as other days. I go down to Camp Brisket or Barbecue Summer Camp and surround myself with 100 other barbecue geeks, and we get to talk about barbecue and realize that what we get to do is a privilege."

In a state where barbecue is practically a religion, Camp Brisket and Barbecue Summer Camp at Texas A&M offer an experience unlike any other. These programs give attendees rare access to the knowledge, techniques, and science behind Texas's most iconic cuisine, with industry legends as their guides. Both camps have become so popular that Foodways Texas utilizes a members-only lottery system to allocate tickets, prioritizing long-time members. Ticket prices have steadily increased as well, currently averaging around $500. Through Camp Brisket and Barbecue Summer Camp, Foodways Texas is ensuring that Texas barbecue—an art and an institution—remains a vital part of the state's cultural landscape for generations to come.

PIZZITOLA'S BAR-B-CUE

HOUSTON

In its 90 years of operation, Pizzitola's Bar-B-Cue has aged gracefully by embracing change while honoring its deep roots. This iconic Houston restaurant, originally called Shepherd Drive BBQ, was opened in 1935 by John and Leila Davis. At first, Leila cooked and served barbecue out of a small shop in the back of their home while John was away working for a rail scale company, and then he began helping too.

"Mr. Davis was working for the railroads and Mrs. Davis was a stay-at-home mother," explains Pizzitola's general manager Tim Taylor. "As the story goes, she wanted him home more as opposed to being on the railroad, and she had an uncle that barbecued out in Jasper, Texas, so John learned how to barbecue from him."

The Davises became known for their brisket, pork ribs, and juicy links, all seasoned simply with salt and pepper, and cooked with hickory smoke in two offset brick pits. They would use their home kitchen to boil potatoes for potato salad and partially cook their beans. Then they'd simmer the thin, tangy tomato-based barbecue sauce and finish the beans off on the pit, their only source of fire in the original restaurant.

For over 50 years, Shepherd Drive BBQ remained a Black-owned business frequented by a diverse customer base. During Jim Crow–mandated segregation, the Davises welcomed their Black customers in the dining room for sit-down service, while white customers were served from a window in the back, where they could sit at a few picnic tables or take their food to go.

"It was a Black-owned business and segregation was the law, so they kept the business segregated as per the law—they just did it in their own way!" says Taylor.

Jerry Pizzitola grew up dining at Shepherd Drive BBQ with his father and grandfather, and remembers that those who wanted takeout knew to bring a vessel to carry it out in. When Pizzitola ended up taking over the business in the 1980s, he was surprised that some customers still kept up this tradition. In fact, some long-standing older patrons have been known to bring their own pots in more recent years, just for old time's sake.

As Houston continued to grow, so did business. While the original location was torn down for I-10 to be built in 1959, the Davises purchased a lumber yard a few blocks away, and built a bigger structure on it. John had a bricklayer tear down his two brick pits and rebuild them in the new kitchen, where they still stand today, grandfathered in as two of the last remaining indoor brick pits in Houston.

The Davises continued to run Shepherd Drive Bar-B-Cue together for the next two decades. When Leila died in 1979, followed by John in 1981, their daughter

Lois ran the business for a period of time. At the time, Pizzitola was president of his family's business Regal Food Service, which pioneered the food truck concept and commercial employee food services. Not only had Pizzitola grown up going to Shepherd Drive, but he'd continued to foster his love of live-fire cooking with his dad and then by grilling for his own family. He asked Lois if she would let him run the business, but she declined several times over the course of a year and a half. Then, on Memorial Day in 1983, Pizzitola invited Lois, her brother Lynwood, and their families to his backyard for a barbecue to prove to them that he could cook. A few months later, she agreed to let him take over operations of the business and lease the building from her.

Despite his lack of restaurant experience, Pizzitola was thrilled to leave his other career and take over the business. He brought on some employees with barbecue experience, and he changed the name to Pizzitola's Bar-B-Cue. As for the interior, Pizzitola kept the same burgundy booths, wooden and chrome dinette tables, and low-back chairs. He did have a wall constructed, to separate the kitchen from the dining room, and he decorated it with fishing and sports memorabilia.

Pizzitola was able to eventually coax the barbecue sauce recipe from the Davis family, and he continued to rub the brisket and pork ribs with salt and pepper, then smoke them using hickory. He also sourced the same juicy pork links from V&V Sausage Company, a family-owned business in Flatonia. Pizzitola did switch out the potato salad with his own mother's recipe, which he grew up with, and added chicken, green beans, and coleslaw to the menu. His mother, Marguerite "Sugar" Raley, also began making fresh desserts, like banana pudding and coconut pineapple cake, each day in the restaurant.

Pizzitola added table service to the dining room, as well as cloth napkins to each table, and provided warm towels for guests to wipe their hands off after their meal. The Davises had only used white bread, but Pizzitola introduced buns for sandwiches upon customer request. He also began serving each order with warm barbecue sauce presented in a small pitcher. In 2003, he hired Tim Taylor as general manager, who brought with him a wealth of restaurant experience and helped to modernize operations, extend the hours of operation into the evening, and establish off-site catering.

Pizzitola ran his eponymous barbecue joint until 2019, when he decided to retire and sell his majority interest to his friend and restaurateur Willie Madden (who had operated five locations of Texadelphia before this). Just a couple of months later, COVID hit. Taylor had left to pursue other opportunities just a couple of years prior to that, but Madden called him back in to navigate operations during the pandemic and lend his expertise to energize the restaurant.

"This crazy little thing known as craft barbecue had blossomed and we were clearly not a craft barbecue business model," says Taylor. "so we've had to redo some things to try to compete at some level with craft barbecue. That is an all-encompassing change because it meant bringing in people who could function to help facilitate that, it meant menu changes, new vendors—and it was somewhat like walking a tightrope because you have to be respectful to the tradition, but also embrace what is new in order to stay relevant."

Madden had already brought in a steel offset smoker to supplement the two historic brick pits, and they began to use that to smoke brisket and pork shoulder. They also hired a new pitmaster, Eudel Hernandez, and started experimenting with different types of wood. After much trial and error, the team decided to phase out hickory and instead use post oak for some cuts of meat, and a blend of mesquite and post oak for others.

"Certain things we kept the same, they were sort of sacred, which is mainly the way we cook ribs, chicken, and our sausage," says Taylor. "We implemented

PIZZITOLA'S
JOHN & LELA DAVIS - PITMASTERS 1935-1983

ston's Home for
Spareribs
PIT-STYLE BAR B CUE
Since 1934
ORIGINAL SHEPHERD DRIVE BAR-B-CUE
OPEN
PARKING ONLY

a new method for smoking brisket—we started experimenting with new cuts of meat, we changed some recipes, and we became more of a scratch kitchen than we were in the past."

To modernize the menu, Hernandez and Taylor brought on new proteins and cuts like turkey, pork butt, and beef shanks. They kept Pizzitola's core menu, but doubled it with the addition of new items like Texas caviar, brisket mac and cheese, smoked cabbage with sausage, pit-roasted street corn, nachos, brisket enchiladas, barbecue fajitas, and more. They also created three new signature sandwiches: a brisket burger, a chunky chicken salad, and a new take on a BLT, stacked with brisket, a link, and turkey. They also started making their own salad dressings and pickles from scratch. Still, there is one recipe of the Davises that remains, and will never change: the barbecue sauce.

"I keep the original recipe in my wallet on an old padded piece of paper," says Taylor. "That was Mr. Davis's recipe and we're not changing it!"

Of course, Pizzitola's still has plenty of old-timer customers who are steadfast about sticking to their regular order—but even they come around to the new offerings every once in a while.

"It's like when you go to feed your kids something new and then they like it after they fought you over it," laughs Taylor. "We still have traditionalists who won't change—they don't want to look at a menu, they just want their brisket and their ribs and that's it. And then every once in a while you'll get an old guy who will see a plate go by and say, 'I didn't know you had that!' And we'll say, 'Well, you never want to look at the menu!'"

When Madden passed away suddenly of a heart attack just two years after taking over the business, his business partner James Maida took over ownership. Taylor continues to run operations, and John and Leila Davis's grandchildren still own the property. In 2024, Pizzitola passed away at the age of 81, but not before he got to celebrate the restaurant being named a Texas Treasure Business by the Texas Historical Commission and the city declaring July 23 Pizzitola's Bar-B-Cue Day. The restaurant walls now display a timeline of photos and articles throughout the years, all honoring the oldest barbecue joint and the second oldest operating restaurant in Houston.

"No one who's around today [in Houston] has been doing it longer than we have," says Taylor. "We're the only table service barbecue restaurant that operates now, where a waitress actually comes to your table and takes your order and serves you. We pride ourselves in holding on to a specific tradition. We feel like we're old-school with some new techniques. In the city of Houston, we're the granddaddy and we struggle hard and fight hard to keep that position."

FEGES BBQ

HOUSTON & SPRING BRANCH

When Erin Smith and Patrick Feges (pronounced FEE-jiss) opened Feges BBQ, they didn't just create a standout spot with fresh, innovative ideas—they crafted a heartfelt tribute to their hometown of Houston.

Smith grew up in Houston before attending Texas Tech University to study biology. However, her career path took a twist in her senior year, when she chose to pursue culinary arts over medicine.

"It turns out that the pH scale and acids and bases and a lot of things you learn in biology and chemistry pertain to the skills you need to have for cooking, so it paid off," says Smith.

Smith honed her craft at the California Culinary Academy in San Francisco and then moved to New York, where she worked at renowned restaurants like Thomas Keller's Per Se and Mario Batali's Babbo. But Houston's culinary scene was stirring, and Smith felt drawn back to her hometown in 2010.

"There was a lot of really great energy to the city," Smith remembers. "Everybody was hopeful and felt like anything was possible."

"We think the food here is amazing, but Houston had always been overlooked," adds Feges. "Then suddenly

DER

[the city] was finally getting the attention that we felt like we always deserved."

Feges grew up in Sugar Land, a southwestern suburb of Houston, eating barbecue with his family. He joined the army right out of high school and trained as a cook before being deployed to Korea, followed by Iraq. But after surviving a severe shrapnel injury, Feges was honored with a Purple Heart and medically discharged. During his rehabilitation, he began experimenting on a fellow soldier's Brinkman smoker, and discovered his passion for smoking. When he had healed and was released from the hospital, he enrolled in Texas Culinary Academy's program in Austin before returning home to Houston.

There, Feges worked for a couple of different restaurants before landing at fine-dining icon Brennan's, where he worked under chef Chris Shepherd. And when Shepherd left to take on the role of executive chef at Underbelly, Feges followed. That's where he met Smith, who was the culinary director of the Clumsy Butcher culinary group, and the two hit it off. It was also while cooking at Underbelly that Feges kicked off Feges BBQ pop-ups, selling his smoked meats at bars like Grand Prize and Anvil.

"I've always been the meat cook, I've always ran the grill everywhere I've worked, so dealing with meat is just kind of what I did anyways," says Feges. "There's just something about sittin' around playing with fire, drinking beer, and cooking meat. I tend to be more rustic with my food anyway. When I was at Underbelly, the dishes I put on the menu had three or four components, just all done really well. And barbecue lends itself to that too—with brisket, there's nothing hiding it. Just salt, pepper, a couple of other seasonings, and smoke. So it's a fun challenge and it's something I love to eat."

"I have some theories about why Patrick likes barbecue," says Smith with a smile. "I feel like he likes to do things the hard way . . . that's kind of the way he likes to operate—adding more challenge, not ever really taking the easy way out."

Barbecue wasn't a big part of Smith's life before she met Patrick, but once they began dating, they were constantly driving around the state together for barbecue when she wasn't helping him with pop-ups. During this crash course in smoking meat, Smith recognized an opportunity for them to leverage their culinary expertise and bring innovation to the barbecue world.

"I noticed that there was not a ton of variety," she recalls. "The meats were the clear focus, and it just seemed like there was this big opportunity. I like to [include] foods that I would want to eat. I really kind of thought of it selfishly—like what would *I* want to eat at a barbecue restaurant? I thought it was fun to take things that existed and ask, 'How can we do this differently?'"

At the time, creamed corn was on just about every barbecue menu, so Smith had the idea of making elotes. In addition to charro beans, they offered chana masala—curried chickpeas. (And though that did eventually come off the menu, it had some staunch fans during its tenure). And instead of the standard collard greens that often make an appearance at barbecue restaurants, Smith created a spicy Korean braised greens dish using kale, stock, burnt end bark and other delicious meat scraps, plus their Hot Red BBQ Sauce.

Feges created Hot Red one day by mixing his sweet barbecue sauce with the gochujang sauce that came with Underbelly's famous goat dumplings. After he realized how well those flavors married, he started playing with adding the Korean red chili paste and other ingredients to his barbecue sauce until he achieved Hot Red. Then he used that sauce in a take on Money Cat Potatoes, an iconic Houston dish that has appeared on different restaurant menus through the years. The dish was originally made by their friend and fellow chef Justin Yu, for pop-ups before he opened Oxheart restaurant, and features roasted and fried potatoes tossed in Hot Red gochujang sauce, then topped with Japanese mayo and green onions.

Feges wanted to open his own brick and mortar, but knew he still had a lot to learn. So when decorated Houston chef Ronnie Killen opened his first barbecue concept, Killen's Barbecue (see page 197), in 2014, Feges left Underbelly to work as his pitmaster. Though both restaurants utilized high-quality ingredients and classic culinary techniques, working at Killen's Barbecue gave Feges the opportunity to craft barbecue for the masses (they served between 1,500 and 2,000 pounds of meat each weekend). Next, Feges joined the team at Southern Goods, a new Southern restaurant where he led the barbecue program and dove deep into the art of Carolina whole hog smoking.

In 2016, Smith won the Food Network's *Chopped*, and they used her prize money to at last open the restaurant they'd been working toward. In 2018, Feges BBQ opened in Greenway Plaza, a food court set inside a sprawling office complex in central Houston. Because of the setting, Feges was unable to use an offset smoker, so he switched to a rotisserie fueled by post oak.

"At the time, the only one that I could put in that wasn't gas-assist was an Oyler," says Feges. "It's more contained and a little bit safer than a traditional offset—and there's more real estate [available] because it's a rotisserie."

Feges had plenty of experience using Oylers at Killen's Barbecue, so he was able to easily adapt his own meat-smoking methods. He utilizes three different base rubs: beef gets salt, pepper, onion, garlic, and MSG; the poultry seasoning adds turbinado sugar, paprika, and lemon to the previous mix; and the pork rub has less salt and pepper to make room for a host of other flavors, including brown sugar, paprika, cayenne, cumin, cinnamon, coriander, and more.

"When it comes to sauces and rubs, I don't keep it simple for those!" jokes a laughing Feges.

Pork ribs are wrapped when they come off the smoker, then glazed with a blend of Mae Ploy sweet chili sauce, white vinegar, and Feges Sweet Red (original) barbecue sauce for a punchy finish. Chicken and turkey are rubbed with both poultry rub and a little beef rub. And for brisket (which they mainly source from Creekstone Farms), Feges swears by the "foil boat" method developed by Evan LeRoy of LeRoy and Lewis Barbecue (see page 258).

"For me, it's the best of both worlds," says Feges. "You're keeping that bottom, the leaner part, more protected from drying out and still get that nice super-crispy bark on top. We let it rest in that boat to soak up those juices a little bit more."

Feges developed three types of sausages (a spicy all-beef hot link, a mild beef-and-pork link, and an all-pork paprika link). Smith developed a number of sides, separating them on the menu into traditional and signature offerings, like sweet and spicy Brussels sprouts, Moroccan spiced carrots, and roasted beet salad. Feges BBQ was also one of the first spots to offer healthy dishes like Tex-Mex salad, kale salad, and the Feges Bowl, which features a base of rice, lettuce, or both, plus poblano crema, pico de gallo, sour cream, elote, green onions, and cracklins.

The chef duo's friend and esteemed pastry chef, Jill Bartolome, developed desserts for Feges, which also venture far beyond the typical sweets you'd find in a barbecue joint. The PB&J chocolate cake is made from four fudgy levels of cake separated by thin layers of peanut butter icing and raspberry jam, and a golden brown rum raisin bread pudding features rum-soaked raisins stirred into a rich pudding batter and drizzled with caramel. The banana cream pie is made from a flaky tart crust coated with salted caramel, then filled with banana pudding and a cloud of whipped cream.

In 2021, after landing on the *Texas Monthly* Top 50 list, they opened a second location in a much bigger space in Spring Branch, the northwest Houston neighborhood where Feges and Smith reside. The 5,000-square-foot space is bright and airy, with pendant lights, succulents in concrete planters, contemporary interpretations of vintage cowboy motifs, black-and-white Westerns projected on the walls, and bright orange-and-blue chairs lending pops of color. A picture window offers a view into the pit room, where an Oyler rotisserie does the heavy lifting for the restaurant.

"When we opened here, if we used the same smoker it would be easier to train, but it would also be less of a fight with the city," explains Feges. "Because if I had an offset, I'd have to put hood vents over everything."

Once opening this much bigger space, Feges was able to bring his whole hog dreams to life. On a research trip to South Carolina, Feges visited Scott's Bar-B-Que, led by lauded pitmaster Rodney Scott. He went on to study Scott's methods and techniques through the years and has connected with the legend at festivals like Southern Smoke and Windy City Smokeout. While Feges has built his own pit for use at festivals, at the restaurant he uses a burn barrel to burn post oak down to coals and then shovels the coals underneath a BQ Grill. He uses the direct heat pit to cook the hog, then flip it and pull it, folding pork rub in as a last step. Feges is one of the few places in the state to smoke a whole hog each week, offering pulled hog on the daily menu, and they also sell crunchy pork cracklins made fresh daily and savory-sweet hog fat cornbread with cinnamon butter.

Spring Branch has a dedicated space for selling Feges BBQ merch, as well as their lines of rubs and sauces. Beyond the Hot Red and Sweet Red, Feges and Smith have developed three other sauces to accompany the diverse menu. The mustard-based Texas Gold and the sweet-and-tangy Mop Sauce both go well with the pork and whole hog. And they are one of the first (and still only) barbecue joints in Texas to offer an Alabama white sauce. The mayo-based sauce with horseradish and apple cider pairs well with the smoked turkey, ribs, and wings.

And in addition to all of the smoked meat by the pound, sandwiches, and salads available at Greenway, they offer additional items like smoked chicken wings, a smashburger, chicken and sausage gumbo, fried chicken, and a smoked turkey BLT. They also have an entire kid's menu, and kids eat for free on Wednesdays (while veterans eat free on Fridays). One of the main reasons Smith and Feges, themselves parents, wanted to open in this neighborhood is because they saw a need for family-friendly restaurants.

Smith, who spent a year as a sommelier at beloved Houston wine bar Camerata before opening Feges, created a 16-bottle wine list of selections that pair well with the menu, from Lambrusco to Chilean País. Smith leans toward small producers using sustainable farming practices, and always offers some Texas-grown options. They also offer beers from Houston breweries like Eureka Heights, 8th Wonder, No Label, and more.

With their innovative menu and welcoming atmosphere, Smith and Feges have created a place that's rooted in regional barbecue traditions while pushing boundaries with unexpected offerings and global flavors—a true expression of Houston's vibrant, evolving culinary identity.

FEGES
BBQ
ALABAMA
WHITE
16

KILLEN'S BARBECUE

PEARLAND, CYPRESS, & SHENANDOAH

While there are some Texas pitmasters who come from a background in fine dining, few boast restaurant careers as illustrious as Ronnie Killen's. Killen started cooking with his grandmother when he was just eight years old, and was making meals for the whole family by the time he was 14.

"My grandma was the person who inspired me to be a chef," says Killen. "She didn't really like people, she was quiet and shy like I am, but she loved to cook for them. That was her love language, her way of expressing herself to them—and I'm the same way."

While growing up in Pearland, Ronnie also watched his dad and uncle smoke meat, and in his early 20s he helped his dad open a barbecue-and-beer joint called Killen Time. About six months into its opening, a customer offered Ronnie his own space in a nearby strip center. He maxed out his credit cards to buy equipment, and opened Killen's Country Barbecue when he was just 23. Five years later, he opened an even bigger bar and grill—Killen's Sports Café—but found he was in over his head after construction costs.

"I learned a lot about what to do and what not to do and how to deal with contractors," says Killen. "To me, if you don't have failure you can't be truly successful because you don't know what it's like to lose everything."

Little did the young Killen know the best was yet to come. He sold both restaurants and took on a sous chef position at The Brownstone, a fine-dining institution in Houston. By the next year, he'd decided to enroll in culinary school at Le Cordon Bleu Culinary Institute in London, which had schooled greats like Julia Child, Martha Stewart, and Ming Tsai.

"If I was going to culinary school, I wanted to go to the best one there is," says Killen. "And I used to watch Julia Child when I was younger, so it really meant something to me to go there."

But Killen accomplished something none of his predecessors had: he achieved perfect scores across all his disciplines and graduated first in his class with a prestigious Honor of Distinction. After graduation, he went on to work for several four-star hotels—such as Big Cedar Lodge in Ridgedale, Missouri, and The Ritz Carlton in Rancho Mirage, California—but in 2003 he returned to Texas to take on the role of executive chef at Brenner's Steakhouse. During that time, he was selected as a finalist to be a White House Executive Chef and named a Certified Executive Chef by the American Culinary Federation, an honor held by a select group of chefs across the country.

In 2006, Killen returned home to Pearland to open Killen's Steakhouse, a high-end steakhouse concept, to rave reviews. He won many accolades through the years, and garnered editorial praise, first in the *Houston Chronicle* and *Texas Monthly,* and then

nationally, as he was recognized by publications like *Food & Wine* and *Travel & Leisure.*

But Killen was already plotting his next concept. He was watching from Pearland as Aaron Franklin (see page 233) had kicked off a craft barbecue movement in Austin, and he wanted to bring a high-quality smokehouse to his own region. So he started hosting pop-ups, first at the steakhouse, and then on the grounds of Pearland's former school cafeteria, which he was renovating into a barbecue restaurant. He made T-shirts with the tagline "The Best Barbecue, Period." and he stirred up a little friendly competition with Franklin, announcing his plans to overthrow him as "king of barbecue."

Like Franklin, Killen was focused on sourcing quality meat, like briskets from Snake River Farms' Double R Ranch, Duroc pork from Compart Family Farms, and Bell & Evans chickens. He also brought extensive chef experience to the field. For example, he found the molecular sous vide he studied at culinary school extremely beneficial to his understanding of cooking and resting meat.

"Pitmasters are not chefs," says Killen. "They can't make a souffle or a mother sauce. And being both, for me, was eye-opening. We were trained classically, and know the technical things."

It's that culinary knowledge, and attention to detail, that gives Killen's a leg up on the competition. For instance, Ronnie uses just salt and pepper as the rub on all his meats—but he uses three different meshes (12, 16, and 22) of Malabar, a black pepper that becomes more aromatic the more it is ground. So the finer mesh adds a little heat, while the coarser mesh builds bark with texture and crunch.

"I've had so many people go, 'There's no way this is salt and pepper,'" says Killen. "But the chef in me understands there's a thousand different types of peppercorns, just like grapes."

Through extensive research and development, Killen pinpointed the best type of wood to use for each protein. Brisket, pork butt, and beef ribs are all smoked with a 4:1 ratio of post oak to pecan in an Oyler rotisserie.

"When I was real young and used to barbecue with my uncle, he would put pecan shells on regular coal and post oak," remembers Killen. "That's how he would cook his briskets, just adding a little bit at a time. The shells give it a nice, sweet taste, with a little smoke."

Killen uses a similar ratio of post oak to hickory to cold smoke his sausage on an offset smoker. When it has a good color on it, he adds wood and gets the fire going to add pork ribs and turkey. Then he uses mesquite to cook his chicken over direct heat on a BQ smoker. The chicken drippings hit the mesquite coals, giving it that charred, grilled note and creating steam to lock in moisture.

"Good barbecue is a by-product of managing a fire," says Killen. "If you manage it correctly, it's going to be good."

In 2013, Killen's Barbecue was the only barbecue place in the area offering six different proteins and, besides Gatlin's BBQ (see page 171) up in Houston proper, the only one making high-quality craft barbecue. Ronnie immediately had lines wrapped around the block, as people flocked to the site for his offerings. Franklin Barbecue had normalized (and even, to an extent, glamorized) the notion of waiting in a huge line for barbecue, but Killen set to work figuring out how to alleviate those lines.

"With lines like that, you can only capture the people who have traveled here, the barbecue enthusiasts," he points out. "But the people who are here just once a year don't pay your bills. The locals do and if there's a huge line, they'll just go somewhere else that's not that busy."

So by the time Killen's Barbecue's brick and mortar was open, Killen had purchased more pits (not to mention recovered his original reverse-flow pit, which had been stolen), extended the restaurant's hours and implemented a ticket system so guests could return rather than stand out in the elements for hours. He also calculated the ideal amount of time for each protein to rest and formulated a schedule of cooking around the clock with different shifts of pit teams.

"We cook all through the day and night because we want to make sure people are getting fresh food all the time rather than food that's been sitting in the warming cabinet for 10 to 12 hours," says Killen. "Who wants to stand in line for barbecue and then have something that's been sitting in the warming box? We went from a 3-million-dollar-a-year restaurant to a 7-million-dollar restaurant, and we were serving better food."

Killen started out serving staple sides like an ultra-creamy mustard-based potato salad, savory pinto beans cooked with leftover pork rib ends, and a fresh coleslaw with ramen noodles adding extra crunch. But he quickly started adding to those sides with cheffed-up creations made with multistep processes using classic culinary techniques. For his baked beans, Killen uses navy beans cooked with bacon, brown sugar, and molasses on the pit for six hours. His creamed corn is inspired by his grandma's recipe ("but mine's better," he notes), and made with fresh sweet corn shaved off the cob and corn gravy made from cob-infused cream, all baked with parmesan for added umami.

Mac and cheese was the very first dish Killen made as a kid, but he's of course developed the dish through the years. He's famous for the version served at his Killen's Barbecue, made melty with both yellow and white American cheese, then topped with Gouda and panko before it is baked. Killen was certainly one of the first to add Brussels sprouts to a barbecue menu. After quickly flash-frying them, he tosses them with bacon pieces and a sweet-and-tangy red wine vinaigrette. And once cooler weather returns, his broccoli rice casserole reappears on the menu. The comforting dish is rich with béchamel, onions, and mushrooms, then topped with a cheesy golden-brown cap. Killen says he aims to hit "the five Ss" when he cooks: sweet, sour, salty/savory, smoky, and spicy.

"It hits the roof of the mouth, when you get it right," he describes. "And when all these things are going on, it almost makes you high."

Killen grew up working in a watermelon patch and would deliver the melons to Luling and sell them in the market square. So most of his favorite early barbecue memories came from City Market (see page 397). He developed his tangy barbecue sauce (with ketchup, mustard, butter, brown sugar, and Lone Star) to mimic City Market's famous golden barbecue sauce. The sweet version has less mustard and more brown sugar. And the coffee sauce, developed to pair with the beef rib, is made with balsamic vinegar and coffee.

Killen says he is a "pastry chef at heart," and that shows in his incredible dessert offerings. His bread pudding is legendary in Houston and has appeared in a slightly different form on each of his restaurant menus. At Killen's Barbecue, it is made with croissants and comes topped with a scoop of tres leches, which melts like ice cream over the hot pudding. In addition to thick homemade banana pudding, there's also a New York–style banana pudding cheesecake made from a creamy banana base, topped with whipped cream, vanilla wafers, and pieces of banana. The Godiva chocolate cheesecake starts with an Oreo cookie base and is topped with chocolate-spiked cream cheese and a smooth, rich chocolate ganache. Killen has also developed a torched, crackly-topped crème brulée cheesecake inspired by one he experienced at the restaurant on Chateau Mouton Rothschild's Bordeaux vineyard.

Due to the success of Killen's Barbecue, Killen has expanded to three locations— the original in Pearland, as well as one in Cypress and Shenandoah (The Woodlands). Each location has its own vibe but all remain elegantly minimal, with white walls and dark wood tables, lit by pendant lights and the glowing red neon outlines of chickens, cows, and pigs. His restaurant empire also currently includes Killen's Steakhouse, Killen's Burger (opened in 2016 on the site of his dad's original Killen Time restaurant), and Killen's, a Southern concept dedicated to the foods he grew up with. And with all these years of experience running restaurants, Killen maintains that barbecue is the hardest of all.

"It's such hard work because there's so much manual labor that goes into it," he says. "You're working in a noncontrolled environment, in the heat, and it drains you very quickly. So I respect all the people that do barbecue because it is very difficult to do."

In 2023, Killen broke his back while transporting a barbecue pit. Not realizing the damage that had been done, he kept working through the pain and didn't see a doctor for six months. By early 2024, he had a spinal fusion performed and has been recovering from that. His team of 350 employees keeps all his concepts flourishing (and earned Killen's Barbecue a Michelin Bib Gourmand award in 2024) and he visits to put out proverbial fires. However, you can't keep the chef out of the kitchen for long. These days, he cooks most often on the six barbecue pits in his backyard (Pitts & Spitts offset, Mill Scale Metal Works offset, barrel pit, pellet smoker, Weber kettle grill, and Gateway drum smoker). Most recently, he was experimenting with adding dehydrated beef stock to brisket to see how that enhanced its flavor.

"The chef in me doesn't want to settle on what we have been doing," says Killen. "If we can make something taste better for the guest, that's what it's all about."

REDBIRD BBQ

PORT NECHES

Redbird BBQ is not only turning out some of the best barbecue in the state—it's also a shining example of the power of community and family.

Food was always a big part of Amir Jalali's upbringing in Port Neches, so he and his then fiancée (and now wife), DeLani, would often toy with the idea of opening their own restaurant. After college, the two were living and working in Houston, where Amir was the sales director at a workforce solutions company. Under the fluorescent lights of his office job, he daydreamed about cooking instead. He took on a part-time job working for Patrick Feges and Erin Smith at Feges BBQ (see page 185), and during his time there, helped them open the Spring Branch location. He knew right then that barbecue was in his future.

In 2021, Amir decided to quit his day job and move back home with DeLani to open a concept in their hometown, which was devoid of quality barbecue. He was already in touch with Jonny White, one of the owners of Goldee's Barbecue (see page 16), for guidance, and the crew invited him up to Fort Worth to get some more hands-on experience. He made the 300-mile drive just in time to work a midnight rib shift the night before Goldee's was announced as the #1 barbecue joint in the state by *Texas Monthly*.

SIDES
SANDWICHES
CHOPPED BEEF $12
TURKEY $12
DESSERTS
POTATO SALAD
DOMESTIC-$5
IMPORTED-$6

"I would have to give the Goldee's guys up in Fort Worth mostly all of the credit for what I know about barbecue," says Amir. "Each owner at Goldee's spent countless hours teaching me and helping me learn as much as I could, without any hesitations."

For 18 months, Amir made the trek back and forth across the state, working for a stretch at Goldee's before returning to spend time with DeLani. In that time, he got to experience just about every aspect of the business, from running the register and trimming brisket to smoking meats and cleaning the pits.

"Working up there gave me so much insight and knowledge on how to barbecue and run a restaurant at such a high level," says Amir. "The volume they are doing in three days (a week) showed me that anything was possible, and Redbird wouldn't be the restaurant it is now without them."

Back in Port Neches, he sought out a space, landing on a vacant building downtown, right next to Neches Brewing Company. He got to work building out the interior, with the help of friends and family, and he ordered a customized 1,000-gallon offset pit from Cen-Tex Smokers (and has since added another one). He named the pit Koko after his brother Kody, who passed away unexpectedly in 2018. Cardinals, or redbirds, are thought to be spiritual messengers sent by departed loved ones, and Amir started seeing them frequently after Kody's passing. When one landed near him while he was practicing smoking a brisket in his dad's backyard, he decided to name the restaurant in his brother's honor too.

"The name Redbird resonates with many people that have lost loved ones—we have people tell us this all the time," says Amir. "I think that's a big reason why the name is so special. It's a name that's bigger than just me or our small little barbecue joint."

Since the first day they opened in September 2023, Amir and DeLani have been met with enthusiastic support from their hometown, in addition to hands-on help from their friends and family. Their moms join them behind the counter during service, and friends have driven in from Houston to help them out too. Family is the inspiration for many of the recipes as well. Amir says his dad Hamid is "a doctor by day and a chef by night." One of his favorite dishes to make regularly is homemade Caesar salad, which made its way onto Redbird's menu in the form of a slaw, made with kale and cabbage (in lieu of romaine) tossed in creamy housemade dressing and sprinkled with housemade croutons.

Hamid, who emigrated to Texas from Iran as a child, also helped Amir develop a recipe for the Persian Koobideh sausage his family grew up eating. The Redbird version is an adaptation of a Central Texas all-beef sausage with the addition of turmeric, sumac, saffron, mint, basil, parsley, and green onion. It's served with fluffy housemade pita and whipped feta dip.

In lieu of mac and cheese, Amir drew inspiration from the scalloped potatoes he enjoyed as a child during family visits to steakhouses. He's created an absolutely perfect version, made with thick slices of potato shingled with Gruyère and cheddar and bathed in a fragrant garlic cream sauce, then cooked until bubbly and brown on top.

Red beans and rice, another East Texas staple, appropriately takes the place of pinto or baked beans on the menu, and it took Amir countless hours of recipe testing and adjustment to perfect it. He starts with a slow-stewed stock made from roasted pork bones and the house Cajun rub, then adds cold-smoked pork trimmings to the rice and beans.

That same Cajun rub plays an important role in the smoked meat as well. Amir studied existing blends and experimented until he dialed in the perfect ratio of onion powder, garlic powder, cayenne, white pepper, black pepper, granulated garlic, granulated onion, celery salt, paprika, sugar, rosemary, thyme, and oregano. The turkeys get rubbed down with this blend overnight, then slathered with butter and wrapped in butcher paper after smoking, resulting in an impossibly juicy bird.

The brisket, beef ribs, and pork ribs are all rubbed down with a Cajun-seasoned salt made from a blend of that same house Cajun rub, Diamond Crystal kosher salt, and garlic and onion from TexJoy (a local Beaumont spice company). All of the meats

but turkey get a binder of mustard, Worcestershire sauce, and water, and the briskets sit in the walk-in overnight after seasoning, a detail which contributes to their substantial bark and buttery interiors. The pork ribs get a hot honey-vinegar glaze at the end of the cook, which adds a spicy-sweet caramelization to each tender piece.

Amir spent more than a year developing the brioche yeast rolls he serves with his barbecue trays. The light and pillowy little buns are perfect on their own, but can be leveled up with cinnamon honey butter, which is made in-house with beef tallow. He goes through close to 1,000 rolls each weekend and, if any happen to survive the rush, they'll appear on the Sunday menu in the form of chocolate chip bread pudding.

His commitment to making everything from scratch trickles right down to the tangy honey mustard barbecue sauce, and the mayonnaise used in Redbird's classic potato salad and coleslaw. Amir also makes a spicy pickled veggie mix (jalapeños, cauliflower, red onion, carrots, and garlic) and tangy garlic dill pickles (cucumbers, vinegar, fresh dill, fresh garlic, black peppercorns, red pepper flakes, mustard seeds, salt, and sugar), which he sells by the jar. For Amir, all of these details are just as important as mastering the meat itself.

"After working at Goldee's, I want [*Texas Monthly*] top five," he says with a grin. "That's what I'm going for!"

POTATOES
MUSTARD GREENS
DRINKS
WATER $1
SODA/TEA $3
COKE $4
HOUSE
BRISKET
Barbs
ALTO-SHAAM
Fabri-Kal

PATILLO'S BARBEQUE

BEAUMONT

It may come as a surprise that one of the oldest barbecue joints in Texas doesn't sell brisket. But what should be even more surprising is that you've likely never heard of it.

Patillo's Barbeque was opened in 1912 by Jackson ("Jack") Patillo in Beaumont, and it has been run by his great-grandson, Robert Patillo, since 1981. That makes Patillo's the oldest barbecue joint in Texas still owned by the same family *and* the oldest Black-owned restaurant in the state—yet it has flown primarily under the radar. Perhaps that is partially because Robert doesn't devote much time or money toward marketing. He's been too busy carrying on his family's legacy for over four decades. And, at 77, he still comes into work every day.

"And I'll be here when I'm 80, God-willing," says Robert with a sunny smile.

By 1900, Robert's great-grandfather Jack was a successful real estate magnate with a love of cooking on an open pit. Jack (who was of French-Creole, Native American, African, and Spanish Caribbean descent) became known within his church and the community at large for his gumbo, jambalaya and Creole-Cajun barbecue—including the "juicy links" now emblematic of the region. During Beaumont's oil boom of 1901, Jack and his wife, Roxie, began serving hot meals from their home to the newcomers drawn to the region, and catered meals for the city's more affluent families.

After building momentum over the next decade, Jack opened a brick and mortar in 1912 and ran it until his passing in 1932, when his youngest son Frank Patillo Sr. (also known as "Little Jack") took over. During his tenure, he expanded the business to two locations—one of them being the restaurant's current location, which opened in 1950.

The brown building, recognizable by the white chicken on its rooftop, is where Robert Patillo began working for his grandfather when he was 12—washing dishes, mopping the floor, peeling potatoes, and stuffing sausage. As he got older, his father, Frank Patillo Jr., taught him how to smoke the meats and shared the family's secret recipes for seasoning and sauce. Robert worked with both his father and grandfather for some years before branching off on his own to pursue a medical career. He was working full-time as an ER tech when his father was diagnosed with terminal cancer. Robert came back to work at the restaurant in between hospital shifts and, when his father passed away in 1981, he returned to Patillo's full-time to carry the family torch.

"I felt like taking over the business was a tribute to him and his father, and my siblings weren't interested in it," explains Robert, pointing to a nearby table. "But my brother Frank is in here every day for lunch. He sits right there and annoys me!"

Patillo's Barbeque
2775 Washi
(409)83
Orders To-Go
Beef, Pork, Ribs or Ham (1/2lb) $7.50
Chicken Only (1/2lb) $7.50
Mixed order (Any 2 meats only) $11.50
Whole Chicken $13.50
Lb's $13.50
— ALL Plates —
Beef, Pork, Ribs, Link, Chicken(1/2 lb) or Ham $9.50
2 Sliced Meats (Only 2) $13.50
Sandwiches
Beef, Pork, Ham or Links $6.00
Ribs $6.50
Boudain $6.00
Drinks
Soda or Tea (Small) $1.50
Soda or Tea (Large) $2.00
Side Orders
Beans, Potato, Salad, Cole Slaw, Rice
1/2 Pt.
Pt.
Qt.
Others
Extra Sauce
Sweet Potato Pies
Apple and Pecan Pie
Jalapeno Peppers
Pecan Candy Sm $3.5
Hog Head Cheese 1 lbs $6.
Banana Pudding

TexJoy
100th
ANNIVERSARY
SEAPORT
100th
CLOSED

The dark wood paneled interior of Patillo's feels like a time capsule from the 1950s. Vintage ads for Budweiser and TexJoy (a Beaumont-based spice company) adorn the walls. Red-and-white checkered tablecloths cover the square tables, and red diner stools line the red counter, where you place your order. Tickets are written by hand and then clipped with wooden clothespins to a wire hanging in the window, where pitmaster Quincy Akers can be seen manning the original 1950 steel-and-brick pits. At Patillo's, they smoke with pecan, hickory, and red oak, in a ratio Robert says his family perfected through the years. "Hickory burns real hot, and too much pecan can make it bitter," he explains. "And I like red oak because it puts a real nice brown color on the meat."

Patillo's most famous menu item, and by far the best seller, is the all-beef sausage link now synonymous with the region. To Robert's knowledge, Patillo's was the first to serve them, and the recipe originally came from his great-great-grandmother (Roxie Patillo's mother, Martha McFaddin). The links are made with ground brisket and shoulder clod trimmings, plus a heavy dose of garlic, as well as black pepper, paprika, chili powder, salt, and a few other undisclosed spices. They make anywhere from 500 to 1,000 links a day, individually stuffing each link into beef casing by hand, then tying the ends with twine to form a ring shape that hangs in the smoker.

And locals don't affectionately call these beef links "grease balls" and "juicy links" for nothing: snap one open and red oil should leak out onto your plate. Since the chewy beef casing is harder to chew than more typically used pork casings, most diners like to squeeze the innards of the robustly spiced sausage out onto a slice of white bread, which they will also use to sop up the leaked red oil.

Those beef links are the only place on the menu where brisket appears—an anomaly in most of Texas. Ribs and chicken are the next top sellers, followed by pork (sliced shoulder), and beef (sliced shoulder clod), all rubbed with their signature Texacajun seasoning, smoked and offered by the pound or plate. The barbecue sauce, also developed by Robert's great-great-grandmother, is unique to Texas barbecue too, a dark savory sauce that is more like a thin gravy with a Cajun kick, made to coat any meat it is poured over. As far as sides go, Patillo's offers sweet, scoopable potato salad, pork-studded pinto beans, and creamy chopped coleslaw, as well as a jambalaya rice made with spiced beef stock.

Akers has been handling the pit since 2007, and most of the front-of-house staff have worked at Patillo's for anywhere from 20 to 50 years, so Robert's role is mainly a supervisory one these days. Plus, his longtime customers are some of his best friends—so you can bet he'll be here bright and early in the morning.

"I've got to," he says matter-of-factly. "That's my name out there on the sign!"

BRETT'S BBQ SHOP

KATY

Brett Jackson may have started his culinary journey at Auguste Escoffier School of Culinary Arts in Austin, but his true barbecue education took shape during two formative years at the legendary Louie Mueller Barbecue in Taylor (see page 240).

"The lessons I learned between those smoke-scarred walls laid the foundation for everything today," muses Jackson. "While I've developed my own techniques and methods over time, the core principles and teachings I absorbed at Louie Mueller continue to shape the philosophy and culture in the smokehouse."

Chief among those lessons were mastering the art of fire management by utilizing scientific principles, trusting the senses—not relying on instruments like thermometers and gauges—and pursuing the unwavering standard of perfection set by owner Wayne Mueller.

"Wayne was not just a mentor in barbecue—he was a mentor in life and work philosophies," says Jackson. "Two lessons I carry with me every day are: compete against myself and never settle for 'good enough.'"

Jackson returned to his hometown of Katy with the dream of opening his own place after getting some more experience. He began working with his friend Rolando Garcia at the now-shuttered Midtown BBQ, while also doing some catering on the side. It was while catering that he met Jacqueline Herrera, a hospitality veteran who was running a wedding venue. Herrera had worked in restaurants since she was 19, making her way up the ranks to front-of-house management. After overseeing fine-dining establishments in Boston, Miami, and Washington, DC, she'd ended up in the area because she thought her son would attend the University of Texas.

"I believe everything happens for a reason," Herrera says. "My son chose a different path, and the rest, as they say, is history."

Herrera and Jackson clicked right away and realized what a good team they would make: he had the barbecue knowledge and she the restaurant operations knowledge.

"We began collaborating on events, then opened a restaurant together—for someone else," says Herrera. "We knew from there we had what it took together to do our own thing."

The duo started popping up at events around town under the name Freedom Barbecue, quickly building their reputation around the Houston area. A search for a physical location led them to the restaurant formerly occupied by Nonmacher's Bar-B-Que, a legendary joint that had served Katy for 40 years. The tiny 500-square-foot space was tucked in a strip mall, between a tailor and a tire shop, with enough room for just three tables. So when Brett's BBQ Shop opened its doors in October 2018, it quickly became known as the "Cheers of Katy" because strangers would often sit down to eat together and leave as friends.

"There would be police officers in full uniform sitting next to landscapers sitting next to the superintendent of Katy ISD," remembers Herrera with a laugh. "And then the homeless guy from the median trip would come in and sit down and I'd give him a sandwich too. The place was nuts, it was crazy!"

When Jackson and Herrera moved into the old Nonmacher's, they also inherited a 38-year-old smoker known as the Beast. The massive barrel smoker is the length of a 1,000-gallon barrel, but considerably wider and incredibly heavy. Nevertheless, Jackson was thrilled to fall heir to this relic of barbecue history.

"While the Beast may not compare to the high-end pits being built today, there's no denying its character," he says. "For us, getting a pit with the new location felt like striking gold. It took some time to figure out the quirks and give it the TLC it deserved, but once we got it dialed in, it's been running like a champ ever since."

Jackson fuels the Beast with oak and keeps his primary seasoning simple with a slight twist. His "universal rub" (used on brisket, turkey, beef ribs, and lamb) is made of kosher salt, granulated garlic, and two different meshes of black pepper, which help yield a crispier bark. The rubs for pork and chicken are a bit more complex. Jackson's pork rub uses ancho chile, paprika, celery seed, brown sugar, and a few others, while his chicken rub includes coriander, cumin, chili powder, and sugar ("But really it's our chicken brine that makes our chicken stand out, and keeps it juicy and flavorful," says Jackson.)

As you'd expect from any disciple of Wayne Mueller, Jackson's finely tuned brisket is a sine qua non when visiting Brett's BBQ Shop. He became known for serving Snake River Farms Wagyu on weekends and high-quality Prime cuts during the week. These days, he opts for Double R Ranch Upper ⅓, prized for its perfect balance of marbling. Beef ribs often make a weekend appearance on his menu, showcasing the same rich, tender meat and peppery bark that has become synonymous with Louie Mueller Barbecue. While the closely guarded recipe for the Mueller family's iconic beef sausage eluded him, Jackson has diligently developed his own. After extensive experimentation and fine-tuning, he's achieved a recipe that delivers the perfect balance of texture and seasoning in his signature all-beef links.

Jackson brought on his friend and former colleague Rolando Garcia to help in the pit room, as well as Anna Garcia who, while not related to Rolando, also worked at Midtown BBQ with them. Anna makes all the sides: pinto beans enhanced with pork rib bits, lush mac and cheese, eggy red potato salad, and uniquely salad-like red cabbage slaw, tossed with jalapeño, carrots, cilantro, red bell pepper, and red onion in a bright vinaigrette.

In 2021, Brett's BBQ Shop was named one of *Texas Monthly*'s Top 50 BBQ Joints and placed on *Houston Chronicle*'s Top 100 Restaurants list, distinctions that propelled them to new heights. They'd already more than outgrown the tiny space, and now moving to a bigger location was a nonnegotiable. After months of searching for the right fit for their new location, Brett's BBQ moved to a shopping center in the Katy Boardwalk District.

They closed the first location in July 2022 and spent the next six months transforming the new space, developing a bar program, and growing the team. When they launched in January 2023, the gleaming new restaurant featured a spacious dining room with a full bar and patio. And they'd even brought along The Beast, which had then hit 40 years of age!

"Moving it to the new place was expected to be a dicey operation possibly ending in disaster, but we got it done!" remembers Jackson. He knew they'd need another pit to keep up with the demand they'd grown, so he collaborated with M&M BBQ Company (see page 76) to commission a custom rotisserie pit. "Beauty, as we call her, arrived in the summer of 2022, and she's been a reliable workhorse ever since, turning out perfect smoked meats day after day. Beauty & the Beast. Epic tale as old as time."

After working out of their first Lilliputian restaurant, at first the team felt spoiled in the new location.

"I refer to the new place as The BBQ Palace, compared to where we came from," says Herrera. "There's a lot we can do in the new place that we couldn't do in the old place and finding that balance is very tricky."

Once they found their rhythm with regular service, Jackson and Herrera realized they could finally pursue all the creative ideas they had envisioned from the start.

"From Day 1, one of the core ideas behind our restaurant was to keep things fresh, innovative, and ever-evolving," says Herrera. "Brett and I both get bored easily, so we knew we wanted to constantly change things up. We've spent countless hours exploring the vibrant culinary scene in Houston, sampling everything the city has to offer—from the high-end to the hole-in-the-wall spots. And through those experiences, we realized we wanted to bring a fusion of different cuisines and cooking techniques into a traditional BBQ menu."

The OMG 9-Napkin Brisket Burger—piled high on a challah bun with melted American cheese, housemade Thousand Island dressing, and a generous mound of caramelized onions—became such a hit that it earned a permanent spot on the daily menu. Each year from Memorial Day to Labor Day, Jackson rolls out the Summer of Sandwich, spotlighting a different smoke-infused regional American sandwich each week, from muffulettas to Kentucky Hot Browns to roast pork with broccoli rabe and provolone. On Taco Tuesdays, the restaurant transforms into a pop-up taqueria, serving tacos, quesadillas, and nachos stuffed with smoky, flavorful meats. And Jackson's brisket enchiladas, crafted with a top-secret sauce he perfected over 20 years, just might be the dish he's most proud of.

"Our menu is constantly evolving," says Herrera. "You'll never know what you might find on any given day. One day, you could be sinking your teeth into bao buns—the next, it might be a hearty lasagna. And then, out of nowhere, we might surprise you with soft-shell crab po'boys. The only constant is that we're always pushing the boundaries and keeping things interesting."

ROEGELS BBQ CO.

HOUSTON & KATY

For Russell Roegels, a part-time job in high school unexpectedly set him on a career path. Roegels (pronounced Ray-gulls) grew up in Kilgore and began working at Bodacious Bar-B-Q (see page 143) in Longview when he was just 15, helping out with catering jobs and cleaning up afterward.

"I can't think of a certain thing that originally attracted me to barbecue," muses Roegels. "I was young and the restaurant paid me to help cater. I guess that would mean money attracted me to barbecue!"

After graduation, he entered the Air Force and was stationed at the Barksdale Air Force Base. As the base was located about an hour from Longview, he started working at Bodacious on weekends again. After getting out of the Air Force five years later, in 1995, he began working at Bodacious full-time, starting off as a cashier. One day, a hungover manager let him take over at the pits, and he was able to apply everything he'd picked up while quietly watching for years.

Roegels also met his wife, Misty, through Bodacious. Russell invited her to do a catering job with him, which led them to eventually start dating and get married. Russell went on to work at several different locations of Bodacious through the years until he was presented with an opportunity to start managing a location of the Baker's Ribs franchise. In 2001, the

couple moved to Houston, sight unseen, with their 13-month-old. After about a year and a half, they bought that location, and he and Misty worked side by side running it for the next 12 years. But things changed in 2014, when he was invited to participate in the Houston Barbecue Festival.

"I had never been one to go out and eat other people's barbecue before," explains Russell, who started to visit his peers once his eyes were opened to the world of craft barbecue. "That event changed everything for me. I saw how other people were doing things and I liked their ways better."

Since their contract with Baker's Ribs was up, Russell and Misty decided to leave the franchise, but remain in the same building, on Voss Road in West Houston. Intent on doing things their way and getting their own name on the sign (in fact, they were so eager to change that sign, the transition happened during lunch one day!), the two overhauled the menu, changing recipes and methods for both proteins and sides, and Roegels Barbecue Co. was born in December 2014.

At Baker's Ribs, brisket was smoked unseasoned, and the fat and bark were scraped off before serving. The bark at Roegels Barbecue Co., by contrast, forms a thick, sturdy (and pepper-forward) stabilization for the moist, supple meat beneath it. A blend of salt, pepper, garlic, and chili pepper gives the oak-smoked proteins subtle heat, and the pork ribs get their layers of flavor from an eight-ingredient rub and a light, sweet glaze. Initially, Russell collaborated with Ruffino Meats to create a house sausage, but when he saw how much trim he was throwing away, he made the financial decision to start making his own in-house and realized how much he enjoyed the process.

"I love making sausage," says Russell. "I'd love to open a true sausage production facility where I could sell to restaurants and grocery stores."

The Roegels kept just one Baker's item on the menu—the marinated tomato and cucumber salad—and Misty revamped the rest of the sides, putting her own twist on the coleslaw, potato salad, pinto beans, and mac and cheese. She developed savory, homestyle recipes for collard greens and cornbread casserole, and added more brightness to the menu with a Texas caviar dish made with black-eyed peas and housemade pickled cucumbers and jalapeños. She also gussied up her aunt's recipe for banana pudding with a kick of bourbon, creating the signature Boozy Banana Pudding.

Though they experienced a brief lag in business when they rebranded, it didn't take more than a few months for a rave review from Alison Cook (former restaurant critic for the *Houston Chronicle*) to fill the restaurant back up again. Russell started running specials to keep customers coming back for more: double cut pork chops, lamb chops, pork belly. He developed a brine, and a pepper-and-coriander rub, to create a pastrami beef rib inspired by one he'd experienced at New York's Hometown Barbecue.

He then used that same rub and brine to create brisket pastrami, which he cut into thick slices and served in a Reuben, with housemade sauerkraut and housemade Russian dressing. Next, Russell developed a house-cured ham and Misty perfected a whole-grain mustard for a BarbeCuban sandwich made with pulled pork, Swiss cheese, and pickles on baguette. As one of the first Texas barbecue joints to start experimenting with pastrami, Roegels Barbecue Co. drew much attention from Houston-area foodies for their sandwiches, which also gained praise from Daniel Vaughn. In 2017, Roegels was counted in *Texas Monthly*'s Top 50 list, and they earned the same honor in 2021. And in February 2022, Roegels Barbecue Co. opened a second location in Katy.

In more recent years, Russell started smoking whole hogs North Carolina–style once a month. He pulls the succulent meat and serves it with sweet chopped slaw and a side of hot vinegar, and in dishes like Brunswick stew and whole hog hash. A customized whole hog pit has now joined the arsenal of nine other pits he's accumulated through the years, from offsets and rotisseries to cabinet-style and vertical flow pits.

"Certain proteins do better with certain airflows, in my opinion," says Russell. "I'd have to say my favorite overall pit to cook on is my Moberg 500-gallon. It does all of the proteins great. I'll always be a Bewley guy though. The 800 and 1,100 both do great also."

Back when Russell participated in that first Houston Barbecue Festival in 2014, he connected with the meat scientists behind Camp Brisket and BBQ Summer Camp (see page 175), two seminars held at Texas A&M University. He has been an active participant in their annual programming for the last decade: sitting on panels, cooking for students, and giving barbecue advice. And even after 30 years in the barbecue industry, Russell finds himself learning new things too.

"Camp Brisket and BBQ Summer Camp have been a great thing for me and my barbecue career," he says. "The knowledge and skills that I have learned there over the past 10 years have been great . . . It's always nice to find a better way to do the cook."

CORKSCREW BBQ

SPRING

CorkScrew BBQ in Spring is a great intersection of Texas barbecue tradition with innovation. As you wait in the ever-present line that winds through the covered porch, you'll have time to take in all the vintage street signs and license plates nailed to the side of the house. But once you step inside, the interior is modernized with pink and black walls, magenta accent lighting and mason jar lighting fixtures suspended from a rustic reclaimed wood ceiling. The menu features all the usual suspects you'd expect from a Texas barbecue joint, but you can also order your smoked meat atop one of three different salads. And alongside ubiquitous beer options, they offer canned margaritas and wine.

"We try to incorporate both a male and female perspective," explains Nichole Buckman, who owns CorkScrew with her husband, Will. "We debate on a lot of things to figure it out, but we compromise a lot too. And it's been 13 years, so we've compromised on a lot of things!"

Nichole and Will were high school sweethearts who settled down together in their hometown of Spring, located 20 miles north of Houston. He was a lineman for AT&T and she a stay-at-home mom who had worked in corporate leasing. Barbecue started off as a hobby for Will, who'd worked at a barbecue joint during high school. But his education really started while smoking barbecue in their driveway with an Oklahoma Joe smoker only big enough for one brisket.

"Barbecue is a tradition in Texas," says Will. "I really had no choice but to embrace it."

Soon, he was cooking for friends and co-workers, using up his vacation time at work to take on catering jobs. So in 2010, Will and Nichole built a website, secured a DBA designation, and turned their home kitchen into a commercial kitchen so they could start taking on catering jobs for big companies. By the next year, Will had quit his job to open a black-and-magenta trailer in The Woodlands, where CorkScrew BBQ was quickly gaining a following. Nichole naturally took on the roles of managing the front and back of house, bookkeeping, and handling marketing and social media.

"The hot pink was actually Will's idea," says Nichole, whose best friend designed their cartoon pig mascot with a curly corkscrew tail. "He wanted something that stood out. So even if people couldn't remember the name, they remembered the colors."

They were soon selling out by lunchtime, as word spread about their juicy slices of Prime Creekstone brisket (smoked for up to 18 hours), chile-flecked Compart Farms Duroc pork ribs, and pulled pork with added zing with a peppery vinegar sauce. Nichole, who was inspired by watching her mom cook full Southern dinners every night, developed the sides, though she insists, "I would never in a million years call myself a chef. I'm a home cook, and I'm good with that. That's what we stick with here."

Though her sides are more homestyle than gourmet, the devil is in the details, and she has perfected the methods for each one. She's developed a sauce or dressing for each of them. Potatoes are cooked, cooled, and seasoned, then sauced and rested to soak up all the flavor overnight. The coleslaw dressing sits overnight on its own to come together before it is tossed with fresh cabbage in the morning. Beans are a two-day process: they're sauced, seasoned, and rested overnight, then cooked on the pits underneath the pork ribs and rested another night so they can absorb the pork fat.

The Buckmans had never intended on opening a brick and mortar, but it became clear, after a few years, that they had outgrown their trailer. They began seeking out a location, and landed on a spot in Old Town Spring, a historic section of town known for its annual Crawfish Festival and other events. One handshake deal with the owner on a porch swing later, and it was theirs in 2015.

The brick and mortar allowed them to come closer to meeting the demand of their many devotees, who travel from all over the greater Houston area for their barbecue. Will upgraded to two J&R Oyler wood-fired rotisserie pits, each with the capability of cooking 90 briskets at a time and giving him the ability to cook overnight and get some much-needed rest. He also uses a lesser-known type of Texas oak as his fuel.

"Red oak is prevalent in our area and offers a nice mild smoke flavor," explains Will. "The mildness of red oak allows the natural flavors of our supreme cuts of meat to stand out."

With more capacity for cooking, Nichole and Will started to get more experimental with decadent specials. They had already developed a queso to top the Beefy Cheesy, a brisket sandwich they made for The Woodlands Barbecue Festival, and Nichole had created a green chile ranch for their family. She began adding those creamy, Texas-loved elements to barbecue creations like the deceivingly named Stuffed Potato Salad (warm potato salad topped with queso, your choice of meat, green onions, and green chile ranch) and the Primus-inspired Sailing the Seas of Cheese (mac and cheese drenched in queso, then layered with chopped jalapeño cheese sausage, chopped brisket, and shredded cheddar, then "booped" with a jalapeño).

If that all sounds a bit too over the top for you, remember that they also balance the menu with greens, a hard-to-come-by option at Texas barbecue joints. Any of their meats can be ordered on a house salad or taco salad, and the TRIS-ket Caesar salad (or sandwich) features brisket and creamy dressing made by their friend Austin Simmons, a chef who previously helmed The Woodlands' fine-dining restaurant TRIS.

Another thing that sets CorkScrew apart is their kids menu (also for the "young at heart," the menu reads). Each of these smaller portions comes with a juice box, or add the Kids Piggy Pack for a mere $4 and you'll get Goldfish, a juice box, four mini toys, two activity pages, crayons, and a sticker. They've even catered a good number of birthday parties, often at the request of the kids themselves.

"I think Will and I always tried to look at the restaurant from a customer's point of view versus an owner's point of view," says Nichole, speaking from her experience raising two of her own. "And if the kids don't like the food, a lot of times you will choose to go somewhere else, because you don't want to listen to the crap, especially when they're little. And so I wanted to make sure that the kids enjoyed the food as much as the parents and wanted to go back."

CorkScrew's cobbler has become a local favorite with a bit of a cult following. The many-textured dessert features silky fruit tossed in a doughy crumble, then baked until the crumbs on top caramelize. Nichole says she rotates between canned apples, cherries, and peaches, but won't divulge any other details.

"It's a love secret," she says with a knowing smile. "We have a lot of secrets! We're not open books when it comes to our recipes because we want people to come here to eat them."

And it's those delicious secrets that helped earn them a spot on *Texas Monthly*'s Top 50 list in 2021, amid an ever-growing Texas barbecue landscape. But the Buckmans aren't worried about the competition. In fact, they hold a "rising tide lifts all boats" mindset.

"There's a lot more places, but I think that's given light to Texas barbecue and all the different ways to do it," says Nichole. "I don't know that any one person can be the best at something—at anything. So I always just like to say I think our barbecue's awesome, but I don't want to put us above anybody else, because I know how hard everybody works and I really want to see everybody be successful. And we all have our different ways of doing it."

CENTRAL TEXAS

AARON FRANKLIN

Aaron Franklin has been so instrumental to the progression of Texas barbecue, chronology could really be designated as B.F. (Before Franklin) and A.F. (After Franklin). Before Franklin, there was a rich history of market-style barbecue in Central Texas at places like Kreuz Market (see page 295) and Smitty's (see page 391) in Lockhart, Luling's City Market (see page 397), and Louie Mueller Barbecue in Taylor (see page 240). Franklin remembers the first life-changing bite of beef from Louie Mueller that inspired him to visit and study these temples of smoke long before Austin had a barbecue scene to speak of.

But these were not, however, Franklin's first experiences with Texas barbecue. His parents actually owned a barbecue joint in Bryan when he was about 11 years old. His dad slow-cooked meats on a brick pit from the 1920s, his mom worked the front of house, and Franklin's first kitchen gig involved cutting lemons and onions, and grilling Texas toast on the flat top.

"It was a real mom-and-pop kind of spot with this East Texas lilt to it," he remembers. "That's kind of how I visualized Franklin Barbecue, when Stacie and I first started—I was like, 'Oh, it'll just be us and maybe a couple other people, one day. You know, it'll be suuuuuper lazy, super chill.' I thought that, if we could do 12 briskets a day, we could sustain it and actually, like pay our bills and stuff."

(The irony is not lost on Franklin, who flashes a toothy grin at the thought of his own naivete. These days, he's smoking the maximum space and time will allow: 120 briskets a day.)

But back in the 1980s in East Texas, young Franklin had no plans to pursue barbecue. In fact, he was more interested in music, which also ran in his family (he had a guitar-picking dad and a grandpa who played pedal steel for Bob Wills). He got his first guitar for Christmas in eighth grade and taught himself how to play drums in high school. After his parents closed the barbecue joint, he worked in his grandparents' music store, where he did a little bit of everything—selling instruments, giving guitar lessons, repairing guitars and amps, setting up PA systems. (That penchant for taking things apart and fixing them would end up being incredibly useful to his barbecue career.)

He moved to Austin from College Station in 1996, when he was 18, and played in a number of bands, including the high-energy punk rock band Those Peabodys and psych-rockabilly outfit The Transgressors. His early 20s were a whirlwind of shows (both home in Austin and on the road), with odd jobs keeping him afloat in between.

"That kind of kept me out of kitchens because you gotta kinda pick one—are you gonna stay up late in the kitchen or stay up late in a rock club?" says Franklin. "I definitely went the rock club route."

It was during this period that he met his future wife, Stacy, and began to really appreciate the time he spent at home when he wasn't touring. He bought a lightweight New Braunfels Hondo Classic offset smoker for $99 at Academy Sports, then picked up a brisket on sale for $0.99/pound at H-E-B, and began experimenting in his backyard. (After all, there were no barbecue guides or YouTube channels for him to consult in the early aughts.)

"Barbecue was fun because I had an excessive amount of time on my hands, but not much money," he remembers. "Instead of having good ingredients or a fancy skillet or a nice knife or whatever, you just get a cheap hunk of meat and *fire*—super primitive and fun, and it struck the nostalgia chord. I love the layered flavors of slow foods—pot roast, brisket, a pot of chili that took days, a mole—any of that kind of stuff."

As Franklin's cookouts began getting bigger over the years, he started to think more seriously about turning his passion into a career. He developed and tweaked his recipes for sides—creamy potato salad with a pickly punch, crisp and tangy coleslaw, and perfectly seasoned, brisket-studded pinto beans—and had his friends assist in a big barbecue sauce taste test. He

got a part-time job working for the late John Mueller (grandson of Louie Mueller, one of the forefathers of Texas barbecue)—not cooking, but cutting meat and talking to customers—to see if he liked working in barbecue (spoiler alert: he did). He then upgraded to a bigger, sturdier smoker purchased off Craigslist—a pit made from a 500-gallon tank and filled with layers of grease and ash, requiring a full restoration.

Next, he and Stacy scored a $300 trailer (a 1971 Aristocrat Lo-Liner) on Craigslist, then continued to scavenge every other piece of equipment they needed. Franklin had been helping friends with construction and renovation projects for the last several years, and all those skills (and scraps!) came in handier than he'd ever predicted they would, building shelves and cabinets to utilize every bit of trailer space. By December 2009, Aaron and Stacy were ready to open in a lot on the access road of Interstate 35, where a friend renovating an old gas station into a coffee roastery had invited them to park.

The rest, as they say, is history. Franklin Barbecue was an immediate success, and they quickly outgrew that first pit. Franklin welded his first offset smoker, which he named Number Two, from a 500-gallon propane tank.

"I love cars and working on engines and stuff like that, so I kind of went about barbecue pit design loosely inspired by an internal combustion engine—and that's just airflow and fluid dynamics, essentially," explains Franklin. "Air doesn't like to hit a right angle and move. So square pits are out, and square smokestacks aren't great because air doesn't move in a linear fashion—it spins and oscillates and stuff. So I thought about how a flame just wants to move in this natural curve, and that's really how I designed the barbecue pits from the inside out."

Number Two, with its insulated firebox and 8 inch stack, is still Franklin's favorite, and the prototype all his subsequent 1,000-gallon pits have been based on, each successive one tweaked through trial and error.

"I didn't want them to be consistent because not every piece of meat is consistent," explains Franklin. "So you have to have gradients, and it's not just heat—it's convection and different types of heat that convert throughout the cooker. If you've got a big flat brisket that's super lean, or you've got a small one that's kind of tall but well marbled, they're gonna go in different spots because different fats render at different times. And then whatever you thought you knew is completely different on every cooker, so you have to learn them all individually."

Beyond customizing and fine-tuning the most essential tools to his craft, Franklin also prioritized the quality of his ingredients. Sourcing meat locally was par for the course in the historic meat markets of Central Texas, but as the invention of refrigerated trucks and subsequent rise of factory farming significantly altered the meat packing industry, boxed meat became the new norm. Before Franklin Barbecue launched, the quality and geographical origin of meat was not exactly a hot topic in Texas barbecue, and very few barbecue joints were still making their own sausage in-house. Of course, A.F. (After Franklin), all that has changed.

Franklin established a relationship with Creekstone Ranch in Kansas, and still sources ethically and sustainably raised Prime Black Angus beef from them. For pork ribs and butts, he works with three farms in Iowa who raise all-natural pigs without the use of growth promotants, and he partnered with a couple of farms in Michigan to source all-natural, never-brined turkey made exclusively for him.

After less than a year in the trailer (and being named one of the *Texas Monthly* Top 50 Barbecue Joints in 2009), it had become clear that Franklin Barbecue needed more space to accommodate the customers that were multiplying each week. Franklin already had his eye on an old barbecue place that had just gone out of business on East 11th Street, and a real estate friend got them in touch with the owner. Aaron and Stacy signed a lease and spent the next several months gutting and renovating it, building the counters and cabinets and tables by hand before adding glittery red vinyl chairs and vintage pastel patio furniture. When they opened on the first day of South by Southwest in March 2011, superfans had camped out the day before to become the very first customers in Franklin's soon-to-be-world-famous line.

Meatheads from all over the world began flocking to Franklin Barbecue to wait in line for hours, inspiring a 13-year-old to start a line-sitting service called BBQ Fast Pass. And Barack Obama's visit in 2014 made headlines not only because he was the president, but also because he got to cut Franklin's notoriously democratic line. In an A.F. world, it's not uncommon for people to show up with camp chairs, stocked coolers, and umbrellas to wait in line for top-rated Texas barbecue. But those traditions started here, and that line (though it's mellowed out a little over the years) still attracts early-morning waiters and stretches on until Franklin sells out (typically around 2:30 or 3:00 p.m.).

There is one way to avoid the long line: if you're ordering at least five pounds of meat, you can pre-order online, then pull up to easily pick up your to-go order without having to wait. Franklin says about half the food they cook goes through that to-go trailer, which means the line has been cut down to half of what it used to be. The little turquoise-and-white, 1960s-era restaurant is maxed out, with five 1,000-gallon offset smokers (Muchacho, Rusty Shackleford, Nikki Six, Mork, and Mindy) allowing them to make 120 briskets and 70-something racks of ribs a day. And while Franklin has found ways of streamlining and simplifying service through the years, he has no plans for expansion.

"We would never move and we'll never open another one," he states matter-of-factly. "It'll kill the magic."

Franklin says his biggest challenge these days is simply keeping up with maintenance ("because this building was not built for this kind of punishment," he says). Each year, they close for 10 days to do things like redo the plumbing and re-epoxy the floors. In 2017, a flying ember started a fire in the smokehouse that resulted in a big six-month remodel. (A framed photo of the ashy aftermath is hanging on the wall of the dining room.)

Franklin is always refining his recipes and procedures too, though his menu has remained virtually the same since opening. And sometimes changes come about due to forces beyond his control. When Morton Salt stopped making kosher salt due to a shortage, they phased in a new salt, and when their pepper manufacturer changed screens, they had to start grinding their pepper differently. And he'll make such changes gradually, over the course of a year, slightly tweaking recipes every month or two.

"Looking at what we do now versus what we did then—internally, there's just a world of difference in how we cook things, because we've worked a lot and gotten better at it," says Franklin. "I never considered staying the same, because that's boring . . . I'm also very much in the habit of not looking back and only looking forward. I just like to keep plowing through and trying to make things better."

Then there's the weather, which steadily supplies a set of ever-changing variables for a pitmaster. And Franklin's attention to detail in managing such curveballs is undoubtedly a big part of what makes his barbecue exceptional. He and 14 cooks are on a group text together, and they send overhead shots of brisket slices on the cutting board throughout the cook, adjusting the fire and temperature accordingly. He also has each day's cutters take detailed feedback notes and, if Franklin isn't there in person, they'll FaceTime him to check on the fires throughout the day.

"[The weather] affects everything," he stresses. "It affects how the smoke tastes. It affects how the air flows. It affects how we cook, what temperatures, how fast our fires are. It affects what time we go on, it affects what time we get off, it affects how we rest. It affects how fat renders—allll that stuff."

In 2015, Franklin published his first book, *Franklin Barbecue: A Meat Smoking Manifesto,* co-authored with wine writer Jordan Mackay, with incredible photos by Wyatt McSpadden. In it, Franklin gives detailed instructions for building a customized offset smoker, guidelines for sourcing and seasoning wood, tips for building and managing fires, and then selecting, trimming, seasoning, and smoking meats. A book like this had never existed before, and it became a trusty handbook for home cook hobbyists and aspiring professionals alike. (An incredible number of pitmasters featured in this book credited Franklin for educating and inspiring them to start their careers.) That very same year, Franklin took home the title of Best Chef: Southwest at the James Beard Foundation awards.

The years to follow were filled with a myriad of other awards, recognitions, and milestones, including induction into the American Royal Barbecue Hall of Fame, a PBS special (*BBQ with Franklin*), a Michelin Bib Gourmand award, a line of rubs and barbecue sauces, a MasterClass series and two more books (*Franklin Steak: Dry-Aged. Live-Fired. Pure Beef.* in 2019 and *Franklin Smoke: Wood. Fire. Food.* in 2023). In 2018, he partnered with fellow Austin culinary powerhouse Tyson Cole on an Asian smokehouse concept called Loro, which has now expanded to Houston and Dallas. And he also designed and released a Franklin Barbecue backyard pit, which is crafted from hand-rolled steel and can be purchased online or in show rooms in Tulsa, Oklahoma and Lexington, North Carolina.

All of this, and yet Franklin remains humble and down-to-earth as can be.

"When I started cooking barbecue, I didn't really have a game plan to get creative with it," he remembers matter-of-factly. "It was just fun and I enjoyed doing it. In hindsight, that *was* my creative spin on it. I didn't want to make a plate of barbecue that tasted just like some other restaurant, I wanted it to be Franklin Barbecue . . . The restaurant's been open for 14 years now, but I don't think we're different from anyone else really. The standards are just different now."

Easy to spot with his signature sideburns, bright smile, and dark-framed glasses, he's never too busy to stop and chat with his many friends and fans . . . which is incredible, because the man is *busy*. In 2017, Franklin founded a food and music festival called Hot Luck with Mike Thelin (the founder of food festival Feast Portland) and James Moody (the owner of iconic Austin venue The Mohawk). Now, he finds himself working on that Memorial Day weekend event for most of the year, bringing in top chefs from all over North America, sourcing their ingredients, and making sure everything is completely set up for them, from flights and hotels to their on-site kitchen setups. Not only is Hot Luck the best food festival in Austin, but it's a festival made *for* chefs, so a big part of his focus is their experience.

"I've actually been describing Hot Luck as this," says Franklin. "Imagine hanging out in your best friend's backyard, but your best friend happened to be the best chef in the world, and you guys were just grilling badass hotdogs and drinking a Coors Banquet. It's the best!"

In 2023, Franklin and Moody collaborated again, reviving a long-abandoned historic bar on East Sixth Street into Uptown Sports Club, a New Orleans–inspired bar and restaurant. Whispers of Franklin Barbecue show up on the menu: in slices of sausage drenched in the dark roux of the gumbo and brisket debris gravy drizzled on the hot roast beef po'boy.

"Uptown is my other Franklin, I just kind of bounce in between the two," says Franklin, who is headed there as we speak. "And I'm not looking to do aaaanything else," he emphasizes before pausing for a beat and then admitting, "I do say that a lot, but then I start something else. I really need to stop creating more work for myself. It's time to just enjoy things!"

And with that, he hops into his trusty brown GMC pickup with a signature "Check ya later!" (in the style of Slater from *Dazed and Confused*). Franklin is undoubtedly on his way to tackle the day's next challenges with heavy dashes of humor and wit, two essential ingredients in his recipe for success.

LOUIE MUELLER BARBECUE

TAYLOR

There are a number of highly respected Texas barbecue joints founded by pioneers of the craft, but only one place so revered that it is referred to as the "Cathedral of Smoke." Located 30 miles northeast of Austin in Taylor, Louie Mueller Barbecue is one of the oldest barbecue joints in the state and has been a source of inspiration for countless pitmasters and enthusiasts, who describe their first visit in terms typically reserved for higher realms. Counted among them are Aaron Franklin (see page 233), John Lewis, and Daniel Vaughn (see page 26).

"Michael Fulmer, co-founder of the Houston Barbecue Festival, gets full credit for [the term] 'Cathedral of Smoke,'" says owner Wayne Mueller. "But we've always used a sort of religious motif in talking about what we do. There's something sacred and sanctimonious to some degree about the high priest, or the pitmaster. He's a culinary alchemist, turning this tough piece of lead into gold. But really, we take as much symbolism as we can from the place. As you can see, it has that old Gothic sort of feel to it—high ceilings, dimly lit, dark around the edges and a sense of reverence in some way."

The walls of Louie Mueller Barbecue are layered with an amber patina formed by over 60 years of smoke stains, but the family business began even earlier than that, in the alleyway across the street. Wayne's grandfather Louie Mueller (pronounced "Miller") came to Taylor in 1936 from Illinois to work for the Safeway Corporation. He managed a grocery store in town for a decade before opening his own, Louie Mueller Complete Food Store, just 100 feet away. There was a meat market within the grocery store, but no refrigeration, so he hired a couple of locals to cook leftovers in the alleyway in order to eliminate waste.

When the two quit without warning one day, Louie quickly promoted a stockboy named Fred Fontaine. The Canadian transplant, who'd never used a pit before, experienced a literal trial by fire that day, but over time, he ended up mastering the art of meat smoking. In 1949, Louie Mueller Barbecue was established as a separate entity from the grocery store, and it continued to attract a following for its ever-changing menu that often featured beef clod (taken from the shoulder region of the cow) and beef ribs.

When Louie's son Bobby returned to Taylor from serving in the Korean War, he went to work as a butcher in the grocery store. After two years of apprenticing under his dad's lead butcher, Bobby developed the recipe for "hot guts" that is still in use at Louie Mueller today: an all-beef, German-style sausage coarsely ground with tallow and spices, then stuffed into hog casing. By 1959, Louie Mueller had outgrown the space and moved across the street to the turn-of-the-century building with basketweave brick facade that housed a textile facility and then a gymnasium for a number of years.

JOINTS IN TEXAS
BBQ ROAD TRIP
Barbecue
SOUTH'S BARBECUE JOINTS
2018
Have Fun or Cut Bait
LOUIE MUELLER BARBECUE
HOT SAUCE

"When my grandfather moved in, it was just an empty shell—everything was retrofitted," explains Wayne. "The brick pit was built specifically for brisket so that we could have a horizontal convection flow pit. And that [vertical] steel pit to the left—that was built in 1946. It was the first thing we started cooking on, and we still use it today."

It was on those very pits that Fred Fontaine taught Bobby everything he'd learned about crafting barbecue in the Central Texas tradition—simply seasoned and smoked over the post oak wood native to the region. It was only after moving into the new space that Louie switched from breaking down whole animals in the meat market to buying cases of the same cut and offering a set daily menu. He also decided to start selling beef brisket in lieu of clod, which was a choice Fontaine did not agree with.

"My grandfather had to strong-arm him and say, 'We're doing this because it makes the most sense economically,'" says Wayne. "You can serve a lot of people—maybe 15 or 20 people—with a one-by-one square foot of real estate on the grill. All the beef was still being bought locally, so it was highly abundant and cheap. And he didn't really like clod because it wasn't very fat; it was big and had too many muscles. So brisket became our mainstay from that point on."

Not only is brisket still their mainstay, but they have perfected their method for cooking it through the years. However, one thing has stayed the same from the start: all their beef (brisket and beef ribs) is seasoned with nine parts of coarse black pepper to one part kosher salt, and nothing more.

"A lot of people will use different adhesions for the rub, but we use water," says Wayne. "So we're as base as it comes: salt, pepper, smoke, meat, water, person. I mean, there's really not much else that goes into it. Everybody says that, but very few people actually follow that. But anybody who's ever worked here can absolutely attest, under sworn affidavit, that's all we use."

Bobby and Fontaine mastered smoking brisket by look and feel, without using thermometers at first, but learned that managing their fires to maintain a temperature of between 250°F and 325°F was ideal. They smoked each brisket for about an hour a pound (in trimmed weight), which typically ends up being between 12 and 14 hours of cook time. They also developed a system of rotating the briskets every 30 minutes to protect the leaner, flatter end of the brisket (the flat) from the aggressive heat of the brick pit.

"We have to actually treat our briskets as if they are in classical military formation, meaning they work in rank and file," Wayne philosophizes. "If the heat is the opposition and the briskets are your army, they clash on the front line. They can only stay there for a short period of time before you start doing too much damage to the exterior, the bark and surrounding protein, because there's too much hot air hitting one end and nothing really affecting what's happening on the fat in the back end [known as the point of the brisket]."

As he continued to refine his methods, Bobby revolutionized another important step to brisket smoking—and he did it entirely by accident. In those days before YETIs, Cambros, or any other highly insulated boxes like the ones we have today, Bobby needed a way to keep his briskets warm without drying them out. He used the same white butcher paper they'd brought over from the meat market (and still use today) to wrap the briskets and place them at the back of the pit (because he didn't have anywhere else to put them). He discovered that the waxed paper acted as a seal when it got hot, held water vapor in, and had a braising effect that resulted in a super-tender interior and supple texture.

"It wasn't an intentional rest for the rest's sake; it was out of necessity, an essential sort of move," says Wayne. "But he found out that the briskets coming off at two o'clock, three o'clock in the afternoon that he was resting were better than the ones that he was serving at the start of the day. Sometimes it's better to be lucky than good and, in this case, it was great to be lucky, because he discovered that he could increase the quality value of his brisket, probably a whole letter grade, just through that resting process."

Wayne likes to let his wrapped briskets rest for at least a couple of hours or longer, which helps the meat settle into a gelatinous stage, offering a desirable jiggle

EXIT

when probed. The resulting brisket boasts a thick, dark bark coating a pink sunrise smoke ring with caramelized ribbons of rendered fat running through it. Bobby started handing out a juicy little brisket chunk amuse-bouche to each customer waiting in line, a tradition they still carry on, and one that many others—like la Barbecue (see page 249)—have also adopted.

In 1974, Louie retired and Bobby took over operations. Up until that point, pinto beans were the only side offered. When Bobby took the reins, he introduced Louie's creamy coleslaw to the menu, as well as his mother-in-law's recipe for classic, scoopable potato salad. He added simply seasoned half chickens and turkey to the menu, as well as spare ribs rubbed with garlic, onion, salt, pepper, and paprika, then basted in a tomato-based sauce. Bobby's kids—LeAnn, John, and Wayne—all began working in the restaurant at very young ages, first wiping down tables and doing dishes before serving on the line and eventually prepping food. By the mid-eighties, Louie Mueller Barbecue had been written up by *Texas Monthly, The Atlantic Monthly*, and the *New York Times*. In 1987, Fontaine left Louie Mueller Barbecue just short of his fortieth anniversary, and in 1992, Louie succumbed to a heart attack at age 86.

The restaurant was busier than ever by then. John partnered with his dad for those years, while Wayne was at A&M studying civil engineering and architecture, then at Texas State studying finance. John decided to leave town and branch off on his own, so Wayne bought his brother out in 2001, but remained in Houston, where he was running an ad agency. It was then that Lance Kirkpatrick started working with Bobby, gleaning as much barbecue wisdom as he could from him in eight years before going on to open Stiles Switch BBQ and Brew (see page 385) with Shane Stiles in the early aughts.

In 2006, Bobby got a call that Louie Mueller Barbecue had been selected for a prestigious James Beard Foundation America's Classics Award (making it the first Texas barbecue joint to be recognized by the James Beard Foundation Awards). After returning from the award ceremony in New York, Bobby called Wayne and told him he was getting ready to retire. They hatched a plan for Wayne to return home the next year and work alongside Bobby with the intention of taking over soon afterward.

"Spending those hours in the morning—two o'clock, three o'clock in the morning—with dad was a big part of the reason I wanted to come back," remembers Wayne. "I had things I wanted to ask him, I wanted to have an adult relationship with him. He'd always been the provider, the disciplinarian, and the boss, and I wanted to know this other side. Incredible man, I have to say. He held nothing back and I feel very blessed that I had 18 months to work by his side and that I didn't waste any time saying the things that I wanted to say, and asking him the things that I wanted to know. I really saw the human side of him."

In 2008, Bobby passed away suddenly in his sleep at the age of 69—but not before asking Wayne to promise him he'd keep the restaurant going. And at that point, Louie Mueller Barbecue had reached a whole other echelon of traffic. The restaurant was featured on *Diners, Drive-Ins and Dives* in 2007, which had increased business nearly two-fold. Then it appeared on *Texas Monthly*'s venerable Top 50 BBQ list in 2008. While there was almost always a line stretching from the counter to the door, competition magnified when Aaron Franklin opened Franklin Barbecue in 2009.

"At the time, Aaron was meteoric with brisket," remembers Wayne. "It didn't matter how long we'd been around and it really didn't matter what our brisket tasted like. There was a media momentum pushing [Aaron] and his brisket, and it was the mechanical rabbit you could never catch. So the only way to distinguish yourself was to highlight a cut that was equal or better in quality and value, but it was distinguishably *you*."

Wayne immediately knew the best move was to promote the beef ribs his family had been making from the beginning. However, in the meat market days, they had removed the caps almost entirely and then cut the bone in three pieces, leaving behind a little wafer of meat. This time, Wayne started smoking the entire rib with a substantial chunk of meat on the bone (also known as "dino ribs" for their gargantuan Flintstones appeal). Not many people were making beef ribs at the time, and the ones that did appear

were often undercooked and chewy. Wayne developed a method of air braising and slow cooking the ribs, then wrapping them in plastic wrap and butcher paper to rest in a passive environment before getting cut. The resulting rib was an impossibly juicy, heavily peppered meat chunk that quickly became Louie Mueller Barbecue's most coveted cut.

"When they're on, I don't think there's really much of anything that's better," says Wayne.

With great respect to the history of his family's restaurant, Wayne is very careful and calculating about what he adds to the menu. In 2010, he added dessert, using a Dutch oven peach cobbler recipe from his Boy Scout days, as well as a mousse-like banana pudding recipe created by his catering manager's grandmother. Up until 2011, the only "sauce" on offer was a jus made simply from beef stock, tomato, onion, salt, and pepper. This dip was meant to complement the beef (though Wayne says some drink it like soup or pour it over their slaw and potato salad). But enough people were asking for real barbecue sauce that Wayne finally developed two tomato-based sauces: Divine Swine—a sweet sauce made with brown sugar and honey—to complement the pork and chicken, and House Original— a savory one made with black pepper, onion, and Worcestershire—to accompany brisket.

Aside from those few additions, very little has changed about the restaurant—except that, instead of farmers and ranchers, the locals lined up for lunch are now construction workers and badged employees from nearby Dell and Samsung offices. The smoke-darkened dining room is like a time capsule, filled with artifacts like vintage beer boxes, an old scale, a jukebox whose LPs warped long ago from the radiant heat, and original wooden tables and chairs from the 1940s and '50s (which Wayne rebuilds at home as needed).

The walls are hung with framed photos and articles documenting the restaurant's many recognitions and accomplishments through the years, and two Christmas trees remain lit year-round in an homage to Trish Mueller, Wayne's Christmas-loving mom. Wayne didn't add heat to the restaurant until 2014 or air-conditioning until 2017, in a climate-controlled dining room adjacent to the serving room. In it, Bobby's 110-year-old sausage stuffer stands against one wall, and on it is a black-and-white photo of Bobby using it to crank out his now-famous hot guts.

"In essence, I'm a curator of sorts of this museum," sums up Wayne. "We're operating in a twentieth-century barbecue world, and this is a true footprint still in the past. Modernity sometimes pushes back pretty hard against us, but we're still a meat market at heart. Now it's just cooked meat instead of raw meat."

la BARBECUE

AUSTIN

There's a certain aesthetic associated with Texas barbecue, and it usually involves rustic wood paneling, old Texas license plates, vintage beer signs, antlered trophies, and state flags aplenty. But when you pull up to la Barbecue, it's immediately clear you won't find anything like that at this top-rated Austin spot.

Our Lady of Barbecue, a cleaver-wielding saint depicted in neon, watches over the line that typically wraps around the building. Inside, there's a backsplash of white subway tile behind the wooden counter, and colorful artwork brightens the shiplap walls—most famously a photo of a well-endowed model in a red bra, sausage jammed between her cleavage and yellow mustard splattered across her décolletage.

"I wanted to feel like you're in our backyard, like you're hanging out, living how we like to live: good drinks, good food, good environment, great music, and artwork," said co-owner LeAnn Mueller. "I don't want it to feel like barbecue; I don't want to see anything written on butcher paper with a Sharpie."

This perspective is even more significant once you know the context: LeAnn has been called "barbecue royalty" (by just about every media outlet) due to her family's lineage as some of the earliest pioneers of Texas barbecue. Her grandfather, Louie Mueller (pronounced "Miller"), settled in the community of Taylor (about 30 miles northeast of Austin) and opened a grocery store with a meat market in 1946. He began smoking meat simply to prevent spoilage and further monetize his store, but after his creations skyrocketed in popularity, he moved into a new building and rebranded as Louie Mueller Barbecue (see page 240) in 1949.

"If you do the research, LeAnn's family started the Central Texas cooking process for brisket—first a bone-in brisket and then it evolved to a boneless brisket," said Ali Clem, LeAnn's wife and co-owner of la Barbecue. "And I mean, look how it spread through not just Texas, but the entire world really."

LeAnn's father, Bobby, took over the operation in 1974, and she and her brothers, John and Wayne, grew up in the family business, working the front and back of house through middle and high school. But LeAnn never intended to follow her family's path; her passion was photography. So she saved up her paychecks and sold everything she owned to attend photography school in California in 2000. After a stint back in Taylor, she was living in New York and working as a photographer when Bobby passed away suddenly in 2008. And just like that, she found herself back in Texas.

LeAnn had always had a tumultuous relationship with her brother John, who had moved to Austin and already opened and closed his own barbecue concept. In debt to a number of people, he asked her to help him open another concept in 2011. At the same time, LeAnn had recently met Ali, who was bartending downtown, and the two had hit it off. Ali already had over a decade of food industry experience, so Leanne brought her on to help open the new JMueller BBQ trailer.

"I learned how to cook barbecue from John and LeAnn both," Ali remembers. "Their standards were high, and I had to learn fast or my ass was grass!"

A year in, LeAnn found out the bills weren't being paid and the books weren't balanced. So she let her brother John go, in a very public feud, and took over operations of the South 1st Street trailer. She and Ali reworked the recipes to make them their own, and brought on John Lewis, a former Franklin Barbecue employee, to help run the pits. To complete the overhaul, LeAnn also changed the name to la Barbecue in 2012.

"I wanted to show my brothers that I could do barbecue better than they could and I didn't have to use my parents' names to do it," she explained. "My name is LeAnn with a capital A in it, and then we lowercased the L and the A, to mean 'the barbecue,' and also represent the feminization of barbecue."

In 2013, la Barbecue placed on the *Texas Monthly* Top 50 list, and as the positive reviews continued to roll in, the lines grew longer. The staff would hand out free beer to help alleviate the excruciating hours-long wait for perfectly rendered brisket and tender, peppery beef ribs. Next, they moved la Barbecue to East Austin, which became its forever home. First, the trailer lived on Sixth and Waller, followed by the Good Life Food Trailer Park at the corner of I-35 and Cesar Chavez, and then a few blocks further east on Cesar Chavez to the Aztec Food Trailer Park.

"We call it our Oregon Trail," said LeAnn, and Ali added, with a laugh, "but without the dysentery."

In the beginning, the two kept their relationship out of the public eye, only referring to their business partnership in interviews. But after they married in 2014, they opened up some more. As the food truck flourished, LeAnn continued to balance it with her photography career, which had her shooting portraits of celebrities and public figures—from Willie Nelson to Joel Osteen—for magazines like *Texas Monthly* and *Rolling Stone* (including 13 covers). Ali accompanied LeAnn on shoots as an assistant and the two dove into culinary exploration all over the globe. They tasted their way from Mexico to Portugal to Japan, gathering flavors and dish ideas the way they accumulated tattoos.

Back in Austin, John Lewis had departed to open his own barbecue concept in South Carolina, and the opportunity arose for la Barbecue to move operations into a brick and mortar, sharing space with a convenience store called Quickie Pickie (located just another block east from their final trailer location.) Now with more kitchen space, Ali and LeAnn began further expanding the menu and tweaking their processes based on their experiences and preferences.

They continued to prioritize high quality, all-natural meat (sourced from Hartley Ranch, outside of Dallas), but they stopped using a mustard-and-pickle juice binder and seasoning salt on their brisket, and instead switched to just salt, pepper, and garlic to let the flavor of the meat really shine. They returned to John Mueller's method of cooking their prime brisket hotter and faster and using a heavier mesh pepper to retain a sturdier bark. ("You want to pick the pepper out of your teeth!" LeAnn preached.) They also revamped their sausage program and started making a variation of the all-beef hot gut recipe LeAnn's dad Bobby was known for, as well as the jalapeño and chipotle versions LeAnn had formulated back when she was working with her dad.

"We adapted it though, and used heart to give it that unctuous flavor, while my dad used bull meat for an iron-y flavor," said LeAnn. "Sausage really needs some kind of organ in it, I think, to make it an authentic German sausage."

The Bobby Dog, named in Bobby Mueller's honor, features a jalapeño sausage topped with beans, cheese, chopped or pulled pork, chopped onion, mustard, and jalapeño. It joins a menu of other over-the-top specialty sandwiches, like the El Sancho Loco

(sausage, pulled pork, and chopped brisket topped with pickled onions), La Frito Loco (pulled pork, chopped brisket, chipotle slaw, black beans, Fritos, cheese, and jalapeños), and many more they'd been serving since their trailer days.

Most of la Barbecue's sides are influenced by LeAnn and Ali's travels. This is one of few Texas barbecue joints where you'll find black beans, just like the ones they enjoyed in Oaxaca. The top-secret brisket chili is inspired by their time in Japan, and they developed a fish sauce–based barbecue sauce (as well as a sweet classic sauce, a tangy mustard one, and a serrano-and-vinegar option). In addition to pickling their own cucumbers, red onions, and jalapeños, they started making a heavily gingered sweet pepper kimchi based on their favorites in Korea. The potato salad began with LeAnn's mom's scoopable classic recipe, but a visit to Cassell's Hamburgers in Los Angeles prompted them to give it a kick of horseradish. Bold flavors are favored here, from the chipotle coleslaw and jalapeño and poblano–studded shells and cheese to the notoriously salt-and-peppered proteins.

"The joke around here is like nine handies of pepper and four handies of salt on everything," said Ali and LeAnn added: "You either like our food or you don't."

But a consistent spot on the *Texas Monthly* Top 50 list—and a near-continuous line—indicates that many more people *do* than *don't*. Plenty of celebrities

have also made it a point to visit la Barbecue—Jimmy Kimmel gave it a rave review, Jay-Z had takeout delivered to his private jet, Dua Lipa stopped in for a protein boost when in town for Austin City Limits, and la Barbecue even received a royal visit, from Prince Harry and Meghan Markle.

LeAnn and Ali used their time during the pandemic to flex their culinary muscles even more. Since they had friends who couldn't open their bars unless they sold food, the duo perfected a hot dog recipe (based on the famous red-hued wieners of Taylor) and started doing Red Rocket Wiener Wagon pop-ups at local bars. They also started making their own charcuterie in-house: summer sausage, deli-sliced tri-tip, and chorizo snack sticks using Ethiopian spices. At home, LeAnn cooked more than ever and developed recipe upon recipe, to be used as one-off specials or for special dinners.

"I like to bring different concepts into barbecue besides just brisket, sausage, and ribs," said LeAnn. "My mom Trish loved to cook so much and she inspired me. [She] was obsessed with Julia Child and would throw all these elaborate dinner parties in Taylor, Texas, and would make escargot and homemade cannelloni."

"We like food, just in general, so this is what we do—this is our life," said Ali. "We look past barbecue and incorporate a lot of other different flavors from different places."

In May of 2021, la Barbecue moved into its current home, just another several blocks east on Cesar Chavez, a renovated bungalow that had previously housed a seafood restaurant. In their own brick and mortar for the first time (which came with a liquor license), Ali and LeAnn were able to develop a bar program with a cocktail menu and rotating frozen drinks. They also became known for a pickleback shot that begins with local Still Austin whiskey, followed by a shot of la Barbecue pickle juice, and a finishing bite of juicy brisket.

The beer program features mostly local, craft offerings—like la Beer, a pilsner created for them by nearby Zilker Brewing Co.—but there's also always Budweiser available, an homage to Bobby's brew of choice. A natural wine program offers rotating white, rosé, orange, and red selections by the glass or bottle, and there's even a large selection of high-end Champagne (2012 Dom Perignon!). The Champagne is priced to move and sold alongside caviar and tinned fish, all very unexpected offerings for a barbecue joint.

But then again, this is no typical barbecue joint.

La Barbecue's art-filled, inclusive community space is the embodiment of two women who forged their own path in a male-dominated industry. Choose whichever bathroom you want to go into. ("Whatever: Just Please Wash Your Hands" reads a gender-neutral sign with an alien outlined on it.) The Disco Bathroom,

Y'all Come Back Now Ya Hear

created by trans activist and artist Xavier Schipani, is splashed with gold-chained, martini-drinking revelers, lit by a spinning disco ball and the word "Fantasy" in neon, and always has a Studio 54–styled soundtrack playing. The adjacent bathroom blasts hip-hop and features large-format photographic portraits taken by Mueller that have been embellished with a kaleidoscope of paint and pastel designs by muralist Zuzu.

In June 2023, LeAnn and Ali posted an American Gothic–style photo to Instagram as a kickoff to Pride Month. LeAnn is holding an upturned pitchfork crowned with a whole brisket, while Ali dangles a rope of smoked sausage. With their free hands, they cradle their canine sidekicks, Bobby Dingle and Mr. Pickles. The caption reads: "We are proud to be the *first-ever women AND lesbian-owned BBQ restaurant in all of Texas*! Since November 2012, we have busted our asses to deliver the best BBQ in the game and keep the legend of Bobby & Trish Mueller alive."

Only a few days after that post, Ali and LeAnn were cooking together in preparation for an event when LeAnn suffered a sudden and unexpected medical event. She was rushed to the hospital, but, tragically, did not survive, instead passing peacefully and surrounded by loved ones, at the age of just 51—and just 18 months after her brother John passed away at 52. Her untimely death rocked not only the barbecue world, but Austin as a whole.

There's now a neon cleaver with "L + A = <3" glowing behind the counter. The piece was gifted to la Barbecue by iconic Austin neon artist Todd Sanders, who also created the Lady of Barbecue sign outside, and it matches a tattoo design many of LeAnn's loved ones have gotten inked in her honor. During LeAnn's celebration of life at the restaurant, a mariachi band played in front of Schipani's mural depicting fellow trailblazers Loretta Lynn, Dolly Parton, and Patsy Cline and the words "Y'all Come Back Now Ya Hear."

"Since LeAnn has passed there has been an increased sense of comradery amongst the crew," says Ali. "I'm so grateful to have the staff that I have, who have circled around me to keep me going and to help keep the day to day flowing smoothly."

The two were never keen on the word "pitmaster" because it indicates that one person is more important than the others, ignoring the reality that barbecue is really a team sport. And the team has truly stepped up so that Ali can take on responsibilities that were previously handled by LeAnn. One particularly indispensable crew member, Francisco Saucedo, has been with la Barbecue from the very beginning, and his wife, two nephews, and niece are also on the team.

"Frankie has been a huge part of this company and I consider him family, whether he likes it or not!" says Ali. Saucedo is also responsible for la Barbecue's tender, sweet and tangy ribs—and for a long time wouldn't share his recipe or technique with anyone. "I have only cooked his ribs a couple of times: when he finally took a vacation and the other time because of a family emergency," she remembers. "He calls it job security, like he would ever get fired from here. *I'm* more replaceable than he is!"

Though she has four Austin SmokeWorks offset pits (three 1,000-gallon and one 500-gallon), Ali is still holding onto that first pit she learned to smoke on, alongside John and LeAnn. It's mainly used as an overflow pit for sausage these days, and otherwise stands in the backyard, a smoke-stained monument to Texas barbecue history. These days, Ali honors LeAnn's legacy with new culinary creations that appear as specials in the restaurant—like her award-winning smashburgers (named best in the city at *Austin Monthly*'s Burger Bash), whole smoked chickens, loaded smoked potatoes, and hand-cut ribeyes that she smokes and then sears. She also brings to life the occasional recipe from LeAnn's extensive collection when the time is right. Like the rest of the Mueller family, LeAnn lives on in the exceptional flavors she's gifted us with—and was surely watching with pride when la Barbecue was awarded a Michelin star in 2024.

"We have kept all her recipes intact," says Ali, "and take pride in making them in her honor."

LEROY AND LEWIS BARBECUE

AUSTIN

There are plenty of people producing excellent Texas barbecue by following established formulas—thanks in great part to readily available, step-by-step meat-smoking methods all over the web—but true innovation in the craft is increasingly rare. Evan LeRoy, however, stands out as a trailblazer. By prioritizing locally and sustainably sourced ingredients, experimenting with lesser-known cuts of meat, drawing inspiration from a number of different cultures, and developing his own unique techniques, he has forged a distinctive path.

Evan grew up in Austin, backyard smoking with his dad and surrounded by local barbecue. On weekends, he was nourished by the comforting Mexican food of his maternal grandmother, and captivated by the Food Network programming that had just started to take off. He started working in kitchens while attending Florida State University, where he majored in English and met his wife, Lindsey.

"In the beginning, I thought I wanted to be a food writer because my ultimate goal was to just not have a boss, not to have anybody tell me what to do," says Evan. "But then I realized that I was actually good at doing *the thing*. Better at doing the thing than writing about the thing that was happening."

Evan returned to Austin, where he attended culinary school at Le Cordon Bleu while working at Hudson's on the Bend, a fine-dining, wild game–focused establishment that was one of the first in town to adopt ranch-to-table ideals.

"Hudson's on the Bend is still the place I've worked that has influenced me the most as far as sourcing and creativity," says Evan, remembering that it was also where he encountered barbecue in a way he'll never forget. "That smokehouse was a corrugated tin shack with a Metro rack on one side and a fire in the corner on the other side. But you had to walk into it to put stuff in or take stuff out. So it was kind of crazy and super dangerous! It was a wild experience, but I definitely learned a lot there."

When Lindsey moved to New York for an internship, he decided to continue his culinary career up there. He started off in the kitchen of Tom Colicchio's Craft, but decided "that sort of militant, fine-dining kitchen culture" was not for him. Next, he worked at a steakhouse concept called Hillstone, where he learned how to roll sushi and bake bread, before landing in his first barbecue role at Hill Country Barbecue Market. There, he started off working the counter, and then carved meat before quickly advancing to the pit.

"I started working there because I was homesick and I just wanted to be closer to Texas," he remembers. "And then I saw things happening in barbecue with

LEROY AND LEWIS
NEW SCHOOL
BBQ
OLD SCHOOL
SERVICE
AUSTIN

Aaron Franklin and John Mueller, and we decided it was time to move back here."

When they moved back to Austin in 2012, Evan worked for a stint at the original Torchy's trailer on South 1st, eating often at the late John Mueller's JMueller BBQ trailer across the street. He was hatching a plan to open a barbecue-taqueria concept when he heard about an executive chef job opening. Evan was hired to launch a new barbecue-bar concept, called Freedmen's Bar, in a 150-year-old building near UT Austin's campus. It was here that he got to flaunt his technical barbecue skills, putting out flawless smoked meats, while also drawing on the knowledge he'd gained working in a variety of kitchens.

Freedmen's quickly became known not only for its barbecue, but for standout sides like roasted beets with herbed chèvre served in a cast-iron pan and smoky, tangy German potato salad served in a Mason jar. Evan started making his own pickles and baking focaccia in-house. He also hired on a roster of colleagues that would go on to become Texas barbecue all-stars: Christopher McGhee of Briscuits, Brad Robinson of Chuds BBQ (see page 267), Joel Garcia of Teddy's Barbecue (see page 447), and Jalen Heard and Lane Milne of Goldee's Barbecue (see page 16).

"That was the best barbecue staff, other than [mine] right now, that I think I've ever been a part of," says Evan, "because we really believed in what we were doing, and we were working hard for each other. Everybody was just there to cook really good barbecue."

He also hired Ben Hollander, who now runs an Austin-area deli and bakery called Casper Fermentables. Hollander taught him how to make kimchi, which was something Evan had fallen in love with in New York, after one of his co-workers at Hill Country Barbecue brought a bucket of his mom's kimchi into work one day.

"We put it on this chopped brisket sandwich and it was just a lightbulb moment for me," remembers Evan. "And I was like—this just needs to be alongside every barbecue tray for all time."

Evan also adopted a "foil boat" technique for cooking brisket at Freedmen's— which began with an error. He used to wrap his briskets with foil and then crank up the heat of the smoker for the end of the cook. One day, a sous chef forgot to rewrap one brisket after checking for doneness, leaving the top exposed to the high heat blowing through the smoker. But it actually had produced a wonderfully crunchy bark on top, while the bottom of the brisket remained juicy. Evan has made his briskets this way ever since, and other top pitmasters now swear by the "foil boat" technique as well.

After four years running Freedmen's, Evan decided it was time to take the leap and start his own concept where he could prioritize sourcing his ingredients locally and sustainably.

"At Freedmen's, there were stacks and stacks of cases of meat coming in, and I'd be like—'Where does it come from?'" he remembers. "Even if I go to the website of this place, they don't tell me where it's from, where it's raised, where it's being slaughtered, what it's eating, any of that stuff. ... So that, to me, was the most important thing, the driving force behind opening this place."

Inspired by Aaron Franklin's step-by-step guide to pit building, Evan procured a propane tank and a trailer on Craigslist, then built his own 500-gallon pit in his driveway. Meanwhile, he worked for a spell at Salt & Time, a now-shuttered local butcher shop, to further advance his butcher skills. Then he partnered with Sawyer Lewis, who he had connected with through mutual friends when he moved back to Austin. Lewis brought a wealth of hospitality and management experience to the table, as well as a shared passion for farm-to-table cuisine and sustainability. LeRoy and Lewis was born.

Evan purchased a truck from Smokey Denmark's, a local sausage company, painted it a deep indigo, and dubbed it "Big Blue." As luck would have it, a contact from New York was seeking food trucks for a new South Austin concept called Cosmic Coffee + Beer Garden. LeRoy and Lewis launched out of a food truck on the site in March 2017, and started making immediate headlines for its deliciously inventive approach to barbecue, which Evan dubbed "new school barbecue."

"We try to look at barbecue as a cuisine in general," Evan explains. "We think about its history and how Texas barbecue became a thing. So the influences there are Mexico, Germany, and the Southern US via the Caribbean, Africa, and that whole journey that Southern American barbecue took. That migrated West, combined with the cattle drives and vaqueros coming north and south. And then there was also a large influx of German immigrants in the mid 1800s to Texas. All those things combined to create market-style Central Texas barbecue. On our menu, we try to pull from those influences principally, but also just things that are happening in the culinary landscape."

Though his inspirations are global, Evan only partners with Texas farms and ranches who raise their livestock ethically and sustainably. He sources whole steers from Lorene Farm in Schulenburg, whole hogs from Peaceful Pork in Dinero, lamb from Sloan Dennis in Fredericksburg, chicken from True Bird Farm in Driftwood, and beef from HeartBrand Ranch in Harwood, 44 Farms in Cameron, and Dean & Peeler in Floresville.

"We're the only barbecue [joint] in Texas that is on a first-name basis with all the people who raised the meat," says Evan.

Evan's commitment to sustainability also means his menu isn't structured like most Texas barbecue joints, which lean brisket-heavy and feature market-style

meats by the pound. Considering each cow only has two briskets, and it is in incredible demand these days, it is one of the least sustainable—and least profitable—cuts of beef.

"I'm annoyed by brisket more than anything else," Evan says frankly. "There's so much more of the animal to use! We've been exploring the shoulder a lot lately, trimming out a lot of flat irons and clods and beef chuck rolls—all different things that can be that next impressive sliced barbecue cut that's not brisket. . . . Everybody thinks that [brisket sales are] a measure of how busy you are, like it's a dick-measuring contest. But we figured out a way to make our menu varied and variable enough to where brisket is just a special. It's just one of literally nine or 10 different things on our menu."

Evan's initial move away from brisket came out of necessity. Immediately after opening, he had booked a number of catering gigs for South by Southwest, Austin's massive music and media festival, only to find there were no briskets available from his local, sustainable sources. Rather than straying from their mission, Evan got creative and ordered beef cheeks instead. He seasons them with Diamond Crystal kosher salt and 16-mesh black pepper (a blend he calls Dalmation rub and uses on all his beef), smokes them for four hours, and then confits them with beef tallow for another four hours in the smoker. The resulting beef cheeks are rich, tender, and peppery, and he uses the trim to make barbacoa on Sundays. In a bold move for a Texas barbecue joint, Evan started offering brisket as a weekend special (and now he only offers it on Saturdays), and now beef cheeks are offered Wednesday through Friday.

Another standout on LeRoy and Lewis' menu is whole hog, a style of barbecue that's common in the Carolinas but rarely seen in Texas. Evan cooks 250-pound hogs on a ChudBox, a direct-heat pit designed by Robinson (who ran Freedmen's when Evan left, but eventually came to work for him at LeRoy and Lewis for several years). He simply seasons it with kosher salt, then cooks it directly over post oak coals he harvests from the firebox of his offset smoker.

"Our offset pit does not have an insulated firebox," Evan adds. "A lot of people think an insulated firebox is the best because it saves you on wood, but the more wood we put into our offset, that's more smoky flavor going onto our barbecue and we get to produce energy and coals for the other pit as well."

After the hog cooks for 8 to 10 hours, Evan picks out all the juiciest pieces for the pulled hog he serves on a sandwich or by the plate. The ham of the hog gets ground and stuffed into a pork sausage he makes with Citra hops, and the rest of the pig goes into a savory, saucy pork hash and rice, which is offered as a side. And since he only deals with whole and half hogs, Evan doesn't offer pork ribs on the regular menu, but rather creates coveted bacon ribs with just two to four whole racks of ribs each week. He cures each rack of belly-on pork spare ribs like a slab of bacon, then cuts them into individual ribs, reseasons and double smokes them to divine tenderness before they get drowned in maple syrup.

Evan applies the same nose-to-tail sensibility across the entire menu, making the restaurant effectively zero waste. Scraps of the beef chorizo become a choripapas side dish inspired by his grandmother. He uses tallow to fry beef fat potato chips and bread butts to make croutons for the fresh and crunchy kale Caesar slaw. A robust fermentation program produces housemade pickles, as well as that ubiquitous kimchi. In fact, the only things that get thrown out are spare bones and stock. Not only is this zero-waste practice sustainable, but it helps mitigate their food costs.

"Because all the proteins that we buy are local and sustainable and responsibly raised, they're all probably at least twice as expensive as any other thing that other people buy," says Evan. So he transitioned the menu, from offering meats by the pound and sides listed separately, to a model where customers can order plates with one or two meats and two sides. (Meats can still be ordered by the pound if you ask though.) "It makes it easier for people, and it makes it more profitable for us. It just works a lot better."

Evan has also monetized (and marketed) the business through an organically grown social media following. After getting requests from people all over the world wanting to come work and learn at LeRoy and Lewis, he started a class series called New School Barbecue University. During the pandemic, he converted the trailer into a drive-through and turned the classes into a subscription-based model on Patreon. Next he began posting videos to YouTube (accruing over 22,000 subscribers), and created a Discord channel as well.

"All of that stuff creates super fans of LeRoy and Lewis who know all about us—our staff and our food—who've never even been to Texas before," says Evan. "And they come visit Austin specifically for us, which is incredible. . . . We've taught people from Finland, Hungary, Russia, China, Australia, UK, Germany, Ireland, everywhere!"

LeRoy and Lewis has been written up through the years in publications like *The New York Times, Food & Wine, Southern Living*, and *GQ*, and appeared on The Food Network, The Travel Channel, and the Cooking Channel. When *Texas Monthly* crowned LeRoy and Lewis with the #5 spot in the state in 2021, the team knew they'd really outgrown Big Blue. Evan and Sawyer (as well as Evan's wife, Lindsey, and Sawyer's husband, Nathan—all partners in the business) started to step up their search for a brick-and-mortar location.

Their quest ended with the perfect spot: a new building being finished out as a restaurant in a residential South Austin neighborhood very close to where Evan grew up. Before opening the restaurant in February 2023, Evan designed a 1,000-gallon smoker, which he had fabricated by Backline Creations, and installed a wood grill by Aztec Grills in the kitchen, which also boasts a full hot line, an oven, and a deep fryer. He now has much more space for whole animal butchery, plus 5,000 square feet of dining space.

The expansion has allowed him to build out the meat program even more, offering both flat iron and tri-tip daily in lieu of sliced brisket. There is some education involved, as the staff steers those wanting brisket to the flat iron, while those who want something more akin to a steak should order tri-tip. Evan has also expanded his vegetarian offerings (another anomaly in the barbecue world); after the cauliflower burnt ends saw such popularity at the truck, he added miso-glazed carrots and a new grain-bowl salad made with arugula, wheat berries, and onion rings.

LeRoy and Lewis' smoked brisket burger (topped with melted American cheese, grilled onions, pickles, and special sauce) had garnered widespread love at the trailer, especially after being featured on the Netflix show *Somebody Feed Phil*. Now LeRoy and Lewis has rolled out an entire Anytime Eats menu, featuring that beloved burger, along with items like a pork smashburger, chopped cheese, smoked Italian beef sandwich, hog fat cornbread, and tacos made on housemade flour tortillas. (Pro tip: skip the lengthy barbecue line and go straight to the bar to order off this menu.)

The bar itself offers, in true LeRoy and Lewis form, a well-curated selection of local craft beer and cider, plus Texas wine, lower-ABV cocktails made with wine, sake, and amaro (including a frozen Big Red sangria). Evan's wildly popular cheddar cheesecake with apple butter has been joined by two creative new dessert options: German chocolate cobbler with buttermilk ice cream and banana pudding tiramisu with Nilla streusel.

The restaurant also has a retail shop featuring LeRoy and Lewis merch and bottles of Evan's signature beet barbecue sauce—created as a throwback to his smoked beets at Freedmen's—and the tangy, viscous, mustard-based sauce he modeled after the one he grew up eating at Salt Lick BBQ. You can also take home seasonings like Lawroy's Sizzling Salt (a spicy seasoned salt) and his versatile Dalmation Rub. With these essentials, and Evan's many instructional videos (plus an upcoming cookbook he is working on), you could theoretically recreate LeRoy and Lewis' menu at home—or at least try your best!

"One of the goals of this business was not to be better than anybody else or to be the best at anything," says Evan. "The goal is to just be influential and to try to get other people to look at barbecue in a different way—the way we look at it."

Apparently, the world has taken notice. Less than a year after opening, LeRoy and Lewis earned a coveted Michelin star, cementing its place as one of the most innovative and influential barbecue spots in Texas—and beyond.

CHUDS BBQ

Bradley Robinson ended up in Austin the way many young people do: to pursue a career in the music industry. Born and raised in New Hampshire, he grew up playing in a local band before getting a degree in audio engineering and seeking out a city with a good music scene. He tried his first bite of barbecue from la Barbecue not long after arriving, and it was quite literally life changing.

"Up until this point food was not a big part of my life and I was a notoriously terrible cook," he remembers. "Cooking never interested me much because I knew so little and it seemed like a daunting task. but that first day at la Barbecue I was talking to John Lewis and he showed me the old, repurposed propane tank cooker and talked about the simplicity of meat, salt, and pepper. I was blown away that you could get that much flavor and tenderness from essentially nothing. I always assumed you needed filet mignon and shiny high-end kitchen gear to produce good food, so to see cuisine stripped down to a homemade cooker and the cheapest cut of meat really intrigued me, and seemed approachable . . . I never knew meat could be cooked that way or taste like that. I wanted to keep eating it, but couldn't afford it, so I figured I'd have to learn how to make it myself."

At the time, the only options for offset smokers were cheap, low-quality offerings or extremely expensive professional-grade ones, so he decided to build

one himself. He dedicated six months to watching YouTube videos and dissecting every detail of how to build a barbecue pit. He gathered materials, borrowed a welder and, within three weeks, built the same cooker he's now been using for the last six years. YouTube also taught him how to smoke in his backyard, and his hobby quickly became an obsession, which led him to seek out a job at a barbecue joint. He began working at the now-shuttered Freedmen's Bar under Evan LeRoy in 2015, starting out as a prep cook and moving up to sous chef. Once LeRoy left to work on opening up his own concept, Robinson took over as head chef at Freedmen's. He then worked briefly at Micklethwait Craft Meats (see page 271) before rejoining LeRoy once again to help open up LeRoy and Lewis Barbecue (see page 258) in its original form as a food truck.

"I worked hard for four years [and] wore a lot of hats at that job: breaking down animals, butchering meat, working the pits, as well as building the cookers and smokehouse," says Robinson. "I learned a lot during that time and really improved as a cook, but I always knew I wanted to do my own thing."

Opening his own spot seemed daunting, if not impossible, but he figured out how to apply his barbecue knowledge and skills in another capacity: creating content. Since YouTube was where he first learned to cook, he'd always toyed with the idea of starting his own channel, but was intimidated by the technical side of it. So he began collecting camera gear and spent a year learning to use it before launching the Chuds BBQ channel on YouTube in 2020. Meanwhile, he was getting more and more requests for custom-built ChudPits.

The name Chuds came about as a joke among friends when he was coming up with an Instagram handle. "I didn't want to call it something cliché like Brad's Barbecue so we started throwing funny names out there," Robinson recalls. "Chud was one of those no-meaning words that we would throw around—'I gotta clean the Chud out of the smoker' and so on. 'Chuds BBQ sounds like a dirty shack on the side of the road,' we said. Back then I had no intention of ever using the name seriously, but as the account grew, the name stuck."

"I did a lot of trial runs and put a lot of thought into my online persona and how to create watchable content that is both educational and entertaining," says Robinson. "Back then I would watch barbecue content and always felt that there was something missing: there was no one who actually cooks barbecue professionally sharing their knowledge on the platform. There was a gap in the market that I knew I could fill."

After making a video a week for a year, Chuds BBQ had grown to the point where Robinson needed to step away from working in kitchens to focus on building the brand, which was now earning revenue. His side hustle of building backyard smokers had also taken off. He helped LeRoy and Lewis for another year, working events, training staff, and shooting content for them, and in 2023, stepped away entirely to focus on his own thing.

Robinson's good friend Nick Gambone, who he'd grown up with in New Hampshire, came on to help with the business side of the company, and Robinson calls him "the true backbone of Chuds BBQ." Now the brand features a full line of metalworks that ship nationwide and to the UK: the original ChudBox direct heat cooker, a fully welded charcoal chimney starter called the ChudChimney, a carbon steel ChudPress perfect for smashburgers and tortillas, and the ChudTable, which features an oversized walnut butcher block and a pull-out steel shelf.

A robust merch section on the website features everything from a leather knife roll to branded thermometers, trivets, aprons, meat mitts, and well-designed T-shirts, hats, bandannas, and more. There's also a line of seasonings, which started with the original ChudRub all-purpose blend, and a line of sausage mixes. Next on the agenda is a line of sauces.

As of now, the Chuds BBQ YouTube channel features 400 videos and has 360,000 subscribers and counting, who tune in to watch Robinson teach them how to cook a number of delicious dishes on an arsenal of different devices in his ever-approachable-but-informative, laid-back style. And his website has a huge collection of very clear and detailed recipes he's developed.

While all of this makes it sound like he's become an authority in the barbecue space, Robinson insists he's always still learning himself.

"I'm a carnivore all day long, [and] cooking different cuts of meat and trying to achieve perfection using a variety of techniques will keep me entertained for years," says Robinson. "The challenge of trying to achieve a perfect medium-rare on a steak or the perfect texture and tenderness of a brisket takes skill that I am constantly working on. There is no set method for these things, and there are so many variables it's difficult to obtain the same results twice, which makes barbecue constantly interesting."

MICKLETHWAIT CRAFT MEATS

AUSTIN

Growing up in Austin, Tom Micklethwait always had a love for the historic butcher shops and meat markets peppered throughout Central Texas. One of his favorites was Prause Meat Market, the La Grange institution that shuttered in 2020.

"It was such a time capsule," he remembers. "They had all the refrigerated displays from the '40s and '50s, original Hobart band saws, sawdust on the floor, and an island butcher block in the middle that you could tell had been there for 70 years. It was a legit meat market. And then if you walked around to the backside, they had barbecue—just meat, bread, and a couple sides."

Micklethwait (the "th" is silent, by the way) was working as a technician for Texas Coffee Traders in his late 20s when he really started to obsess over smoked meat. He played guitar in a number of punk bands—The Kodiaks, This Damn Town, and Hex Dispensers, to name a few—and would host backyard barbecues for his friends on Sundays. When he saw sausage casings for sale at Fiesta one day, he decided to up the ante by making his own sausage.

"I would buy casings, and piping bags, and then I added in grinders and started getting more into stuffing it at home," Micklethwait remembers. "I just started replicating market-style barbecue at home for fun—listening to the Punk Melody show on KOOP and making sausage at 7 in the morning on Sunday. What else do you do in Austin?"

He started going to culinary school at night while working as a baker at Vespaio, a long-standing (but now-shuttered) Italian restaurant on South Congress. There, he learned butchery and the art of making pasta and bread. During this time, Micklethwait acquired a mid-century Comet camper trailer, outfitted the interior and painted the exterior a bright daffodil yellow, with acorns and foliage around the order window. A musician friend who welded helped him build his first offset smoker on a different trailer, and he set up a Kickstarter campaign to raise money for equipment, permits, and licensing. By December 2012, Micklethwait Craft Meats was open for business under an oak grove on Rosewood Avenue, a stone's throw from the building where Franklin Barbecue had relocated just the year before.

Initially, Micklethwait focused on making specialty sausages, often offering several varieties a day, flavors like duck and cherry or lamb and fig. He eventually pared things down to a more traditional Tex-Czech sausage (a coarsely ground blend of pork and beef with lots of garlic, black pepper, and chili flake), though his unique creations will still make special appearances. In the beginning, he also only served brisket for dinner, a choice that created quite an uproar.

"The one phrase I heard the most was, 'Don't you know this is Texas?'" says Micklethwait with a laugh. He eventually gave in and rearranged his cook cycles. At Micklethwait, the briskets are cooked low and slow through the night (anywhere from 7 to 10 hours), then wrapped at 195°F and stored in a hotbox at 160°F to continue breaking down slowly overnight. Each of his proteins gets the same master rub, a blend of salt, pepper, garlic, onion, mustard, coriander, and celery salt. Pork ribs and pork shoulder also get Lawry's seasoning salt, and the ribs are mopped with a tangy vinegar-mustard glaze before they're wrapped and rested.

At first, Micklethwait ground all his spices by hand with a coffee grinder and made signature blends. But as business ramped up, he started having Southern Style spice company do his grinding and blending. "We are able to get two or three different meshes that simulate having it go through a coffee grinder, where you get really big chunks and really small chunks," he says.

Micklethwait quickly became known for his sides, which are all made from scratch and feature refreshingly fresh options like lemon poppy slaw and beet salad, plus fluffy jalapeño-and-cheese grits made with polenta, alongside more classic offerings like chili beans and country potato salad. Micklethwait was also one of the first (if not *the* first) pitmasters in the Texas craft barbecue movement to make his own bread, and he did it all in that same 6½ by 13–foot trailer.

"[Making bread] was a tricky one because it was all so very weather dependent," he says. "We didn't have a proof box, so in the wintertime the trailer would be really cold at night and in the summertime it'd be really hot."

Micklethwait used a 20-quart mixer to whip up his pain au lait dough, shaping loaves and rolls at 2 a.m. so they could ferment slowly overnight, then baking

them off right before service. In the early years, Micklethwait handled all the prep himself, but eventually brought in help, including Ren Garcia, who had been the kitchen manager at Vespaio. Garcia came on as a partner and pitmaster in 2017, bringing his own wealth of restaurant experience along with him.

Micklethwait's barbecue sauce is inspired by Cooper's classic golden sauce: a tangy blend of ketchup, mustard, Worcestershire, brown sugar, and vinegar. Garcia also makes a popular lacto-fermented hot sauce that the restaurant sells by the bottle. The team brine cures dill pickles and escabeche (with a hint of curry in the latter, which helps to complement the Frito pie, which began as a special and is now a menu staple). The end of each week brings specials galore, from massive beef ribs and thick slices of prime rib to a Reuben made with pit-smoked pastrami and topped with lacto-fermented sauerkraut and a muffuletta made from house-cured and -smoked deli meats (salami, bresaola, and tasso ham) and slathered with tapenade.

In 2022, Micklethwait took over the former bungalow his trailer had been sitting behind (which had been a number of businesses through the years). Dubbed Saddle Up, it served as a bar, cafe, and bodega with wine and beer for sale. The patio and beer garden became the site of constant parties and events, with Micklethwait's many musician friends providing the soundtrack. It also afforded the space to grow the bakery program and hold regular bake sales. When Micklethwait's trailer first opened, they featured homemade moon pies for dessert. With the opening of Saddle Up, they started offering throwbacks like oatmeal cream pies and "twonkys" (their version of Twinkies), homemade ice cream and sorbet and kolaches stuffed with brisket and sausage, as well as seasonal fruit fillings like blackberry, roasted apricot, roasted strawberry with cream cheese, and candied orange with jalapeño.

Over the years, Micklethwait has refined his operation, and is now using two 1,000-gallon and one 500-gallon offset smokers, all crafted with the help of friends. He continues to source post oak from the same dependable Smithville rancher he discovered on Craigslist back in 2012—a partnership built on perfectly seasoned wood, aged for a year before arriving in neatly stacked cords. By 2023, after repairing and rebuilding his original trailer three times, Micklethwait upgraded to a new model with double the usable space and an extra foot and a half of height. That same year, he also leased a historic East Austin church—originally built as a 1920s general store—providing the team with ample room to tackle the growing demand for catering and expand their operation.

"We're definitely doing a lot more catering and festivals—stuff I never thought about when I just wanted to open a trailer and make barbecue every day!" he says with a chuckle. "I feel like we're now kind of the old guard. When we opened, if you thought about older places, you're thinking of the small town,

market-style spots. Back then, we were the babies of the barbecue world. I feel like we're a little bit more seasoned now."

Micklethwait's modest reflection speaks volumes. As renovations on the church wrapped up, Micklethwait Craft Meats earned a coveted Michelin Bib Gourmand award—a fitting tribute to the closing of one chapter and the opening of another. In early 2025, Micklethwait and his team welcomed guests to their first-ever brick-and-mortar restaurant, a retro-chic space bathed in dark wood and earth tones, where diners can now quite literally worship at the church of barbecue.

MICKLETHWAIT
CRAFT
M
MEATS

INTERSTELLAR BBQ

AUSTIN

Sometimes the process of obtaining top-rated Texas barbecue feels more like waiting in line for an amusement park ride than for a meal. And when you're steps away from entering InterStellar, that excitement is only amplified.

By 10 a.m. on a Friday, the line for InterStellar BBQ stretches down the sidewalk, and it's getting longer by the minute. Anticipation builds as smoke from the pits, stationed right in the parking lot, curls through the crowd. The guy in front of me turns around every few minutes to pose a question. *Is this place better than Terry Black's?* (Entirely different, I reply, assuring him he's in for a treat.) *Are we in Cedar Park or Austin?* (The latter.) *How do we know about today's specials?* As if on cue, someone emerges to announce them: smoked duck with cherry barbecue sauce, Frito pie sausage, and lamb picadillo tostada with chimichurri. At exactly 11 a.m., the doors open and we shuffle in excitedly. The line is now all the way down to the hair salon at the end of the business center. If you arrive after opening, you can expect to wait two to three hours minimum to make it inside.

"And that's the power of *Texas Monthly*," says pitmaster John Bates. The lines have increased tenfold since October 2021, when barbecue editor Daniel Vaughn released the venerable Top 50 list with InterStellar BBQ at number two, and they show no sign of slowing down— especially after the restaurant was awarded a Michelin star in 2024. "When we made the list, John Brotherton [the late founder of Brotherton's Black Iron Barbecue] called me, congratulated me and then the very next thing out of his mouth was, 'You need to borrow a barbecue pit.' And he was right."

But Bates, a chef with over 30 years of experience, is no stranger to fans lining up for his food. When he started The Noble Pig (which later became Noble Sandwich Co.), the line for his duck pastrami and beef tongue sandwiches would wrap around the corner—this very same corner, in fact. But at the end of 2018, he decided to shut down Noble operations and rebrand.

"The sandwich shop had gotten far too complex and overwrought," he says. "Every sandwich was a unique build. We had five or six different types of pickles. We had like seven types of bread, all from scratch, and we were curing all of our meats in-house. Trying to grow that restaurant was really, really hard and just required so much commitment. I was ready for a change, and I just wanted to simplify my life."

Bates, an eighth-generation Texan who grew up in Corpus Christi, had always followed the Texas barbecue world closely, making it his business to visit the top places when *Texas Monthly*'s list would emerge. And, though most people certainly don't get into barbecue because it's *easy* by any means, Bates calculated that making this culinary shift would allow him to function with a smaller team and fewer recipes, while putting just as much love and passion into his food.

After a series of barbecue pop-ups, he decided the last day of service at Noble would be Christmas Eve 2018 and, the day after Christmas, he picked up his first pit, which was crafted on a tight budget by a family friend who welded part-time.

"He'd never done an offset, so we did some research together online," remembers Bates. "I told him what I wanted, we found a propane tank in San Antonio, we figured out how to put the pit together, and then he made it in his backyard."

Bates's previous experience was limited to a Friedrich rotisserie he used at Noble Sandwich Co., a device he equates to "the Easy Bake version of smoking," so he spent the next 60 days learning how to use his new pit and developing recipes. "Every time you get a barbecue pit you've got to spend about a week or two just learning how the heat travels through, where the hot spots are, where the cold spots are, how quickly it pulls—all the characteristics of the pit," explains Bates.

Now he's acquired three more 1,000-gallon pits: one made by Sunny Moberg, one by Mill Scale Metalworks (see page 286), and another made by a friend who is launching a pit-building business in São Paulo, Brazil. The very first time that last one was fired, Bates's buddy cooked 600 pounds of pork belly on it at Churrascada, the biggest barbecue festival in

Brazil, before figuring out the logistics of shipping it to Texas.

"I think a good cook can cook on anything, and can cook in any environment," Bates states matter-of-factly. "When you truly learn your craft, you're not limited by the tools. It always helps to have better equipment, but I don't think it defines a cook."

Bates's kitchen experience spans from cooking seafood on the Gulf Coast and Cuban cuisine in Portland, Oregon, to Italian food in Austin. He's the kind of chef who will make pasta from scratch on his day off—and his breadth of culinary knowledge shows in InterStellar's menu and one-off specials.

"We've become known as the place to go to if you want something that's not super traditional," says Bates. "We always have something fun and experimental; I'm trying to bring new flavors and items to Texas barbecue."

One of InterStellar's signature sides is a scalloped potato dish that is layered with salt, Parmesan, cream, garlic, and black pepper before it is baked in a smoker. He eschews classic yellow mustard potato salad for red-skinned new potatoes coated in a mayo-based dressing, and serves the same crunchy, vibrant jalapeño slaw he created for Noble Sandwich Co. Depending on the time of year, you'll also find options like bright marinated tomato-and-zucchini salad, roasted beet salad, and creamed corn made from kernels freshly shucked off the cob. And there's classic banana pudding, but it's made from scratch, with flecks of vanilla bean and drizzles of salted dulce de leche layered throughout.

"For me, inspiration comes from my stomach," says Bates. "I'm an old-school cook at heart, and I cook for the enjoyment and pleasure of eating and providing real hospitality to people. I like to actually make people happy. I don't want to challenge them—I want to give them joy. The menu reflects food I would want to cook for myself, and what I would like to serve to my friends and family if I was having a cookout."

As for meats, Bates has achieved brisket perfection, but he only sells through about 40 or 50 briskets a day (which is on the low end for the crowds InterStellar serves). That's because he typically offers 8 to 10 other proteins, too. The peach tea–glazed pork belly, slow-smoked into literal meat candy, is a fan favorite for good reason, as is the Tipsy Turkey, which is brined overnight in hefeweizen to produce an absolutely succulent result. He creates sausages in flavors like jalapeño popper and Frito pie, and serves tender pulled lamb in lieu of pulled pork.

"I think it's really important that we introduce new flavors and techniques so that Texas barbecue can continue growing," says Bates. "You have to honor the style, and it has to feel like Texas. But there's no reason why barbecue can't use lamb and goat and duck and other ingredients."

These less-common proteins often find their way to InterStellar's menu in the form of daily specials that honor Bates's South Texas roots: lamb picadillo tostadas, pulled goat tortas, smoked lengua or cabrito tacos, and pastor lamb chops with pineapple glaze. And you can (and should) always order the brisket

taco on the daily menu: a thick slice of brisket served on a handmade flour tortilla with avocado salsa, onion, lime, cilantro, and cotija. (Though Bates makes his own thick, Corpus Christi–style flour tortillas, you won't find anything here but Mrs. Baird's when it comes to bread. "I'm retired from the bread-making game," he says. "Running a sandwich shop has taught me that making bread is a fool's errand.")

When Bates first opened InterStellar, he decided to immerse himself in Texas barbecue culture by launching a collaborative series called Space Cowboy, whereby he reached out and invited other pitmasters he admired to come cook with him for special one-off events. After connecting with Texas-based chefs in the first year, he started reaching out to guests in different parts of the country, like Hector Carate from Palmira BBQ in South Carolina, Danny Castillo from Heritage Barbecue in California, and Rick Mace from Tropical Smokehouse in Florida. In the spring of 2023, he hosted his first Cross-Cultural Exchange edition with a group of pitmasters from Monterrey, Mexico, barbecue spots RIVS Smoke & Grill, Nomada XXI, Old Jimmy's, and Smokey José.

"I think it's really important that we reach out to different folks and bring them in so people here can try their food, and we can also learn some things from them," explains Bates. "I think of it as the big tribe, although I still believe Texas barbecue is the best version of all."

MILL SCALE METALWORKS

In Texas barbecue, the offset smoker is not just a piece of equipment; it's a revered symbol of culinary craftsmanship. Its submarine-like cooking chamber, adjacent firebox, and offset smokestack have become emblematic of this state's penchant for low-and-slow cooking with indirect heat.

With the increasing popularity of barbecue, offset smokers (or "stick burners") have been in high demand, and a number of pit builders have popped up, but none more esteemed than Mill Scale Metalworks. Backyard smokers covet their creations, and both chefs and pitmasters speak of Mill Scale products as though they've acquired the Holy Grail. Joe Zavala (of Zavala's Barbecue, see page 37) calls his Mill Scale offset (named Selena) "the Ferrari of smokers." Ernest Servantes (of Burnt Bean Co., see page 436) says that—beyond the notable cooking capabilities of his pit—"it's usable art."

Mill Scale Metalworks was started in 2018 by Matt and

culture, and both were obsessed with the high-quality barbecue found all over the city. But they soon found themselves missing the craft of welding.

"And it wasn't just welding—it was woodworking and plumbing and electrical," remembers Matt. "If there was something to be built, we wanted to build it. And if we hadn't done it before, we wanted to learn it. If we needed a tool, we would go buy it. So we're self-taught. We learned the trade from our childhood, but as adults, we really applied it towards fabrication."

They began working at different shops around East Austin, learning architectural steel design, more efficient modes of installation, and better-quality welds executed with stronger materials. From there, they started applying this knowledge to designing smokers and other outdoor cooking instruments, developing their own unique style.

"Before we really jumped into the game, a lot of the offset trailer units were very slick, with candied paint jobs and chrome and TVs and hand sinks and different thermometer readings—lots of gadgets," explains Matt. "We really wanted to strip it down and create something super functional. And we've always believed the philosophy that the best design is the most simple design."

The Johnsons use 500- and 1,000-gallon decommissioned propane tanks for a majority of the pits they build. (They started out by driving all over Texas to

buy tanks piecemeal off farms and ranches, but these days they purchase larger lots.) After the carbon steel tanks are devalved (for anywhere from six months to three years—the longer the better), they go through a rigorous cleaning process that differs based on their history but usually entails pressure washing with cleaning agents and vacuuming.

"There's so much character, and each [tank] tells its own unique story with color, patina, scarification, maker's marks, and manufacturing dates and badges," says Matt. "So for us, it's like dusting off some relic from the past and trying to see where it came from . . . and the cool thing is that we're taking something that would be historically categorized as waste—or hopefully recycled—and we're breathing new life into [it] and giving it a whole other chance to live. And it's gonna be around forever."

The fabrication process, executed by a 10-person team, begins with the buildout of a frame for the unit. Depending on the customization, some smokers are mounted on skids, others on wheeled trailers. Next, they begin cutting and welding all the pieces that will be attached to the cooking chamber created by the tank.

"Our construction process is kind of like mise en place with cooking, where you do all your prep ahead of time and then you begin your dish," explains Matt. "So all the parts, assemblies, and different features of the unit are built in advance. And then we assemble everything at once to speed up the production process."

The team then begins cutting doors, mounting fireboxes (which are made from 250-gallon propane tanks), installing the exhaust system, and attaching the smokestack. On the interior, they install the cooking grates, upper shelves, thermometer fittings, and counterweights on the doors. But one major thing that sets Mill Scale products apart is the fact that, once the Johnson brothers decided to focus their energy on pit building, they began to expand their culinary network and learn as much about food and cooking as they could to effectively inform their design.

"There's a lot of talented fabricators out there that can build really beautiful barbecue pits," says Matt, "but some of them don't function correctly based on the geometry or their understanding of heat and smoke and convection, or what a user is looking for. And so that was really critical in our design process—of understanding who is using it, where it's going, and how it's going to be applied."

The Johnsons established an ambassador program with barbecue experts from around the world representing their products—Tuffy Stone out of Virginia, Leonard Botello IV (of Truth BBQ, see page 121), Charlie McKenna of Lillie's Q in Chicago, and Johan Fritzell and Johan Åkerberg of Holy Smoke BBQ in Sweden. Before they'd even established themselves locally, their very first orders came from the UK, Germany, and Sweden, thanks to the power of social media.

"That was the biggest surprise to us—how far-reaching barbecue culture is, and specifically Central Texas barbecue," says Matt. "It's pretty prolific around the world at this point. Texas is really driving the culture and so the consumer's incredibly educated on what they're looking for, and they have lots of options for who to get it from. There's also a huge respect for the craft and the time it takes not only to build a barbecue pit but also to cook brisket."

Once they'd established a global audience, Mill Scale decided to expand their product line with models inspired by cooking techniques from around the world. Through relationships they forged with Johan and Johan at Holy Smoke BBQ, plus Swedish chefs Niklas Ekstedt (Restaurant Ekstedt) and Carl Phillip Dreyer (Blommeröd), they'd become enamored with Scandinavian cooking techniques and preservation processes. A deep dive into cold-smoking processes led to the design of The Cabinet Smoker, a 7-foot-tall carbon steel cooker with capability for cooking via both direct and indirect heat.

They also became obsessed with the dramatic asado-style cooking practiced in South America, and began experimenting with building domes, iron crosses, and planchas, adding open-fire grills to their barbecue trailers. From this study came their Asado Fire Pit (an elevated, multilevel cylindrical pit with modular grates), the Santa Maria (a parilla-style grill with space for four planchas and hooks for hanging protein), and Fire Tables (designed as a stage for cooking proteins using a multilevel grill, plancha, iron cross, and asado dome).

"So much romance, so much theater!" says Matt. "This culture of cuisine is utilizing every stage of the fire, which was really mind blowing for us. They're using embers, live fire, ash, smoke, direct heat, indirect heat—and they're cooking large cuts of meat, literally with just fire on the ground."

Next, they turned their focus to Japanese styles of cooking with fire to create three different styles of multilevel yakitori grills. With a quickly scaling business and an ever-growing waiting list, they couldn't find the time for a visit to Japan or South America, so these designs took shape through plenty of research, meetings, consultations, and prototypes.

"There's a lot of people that helped us understand how those cooking techniques are applied and how we can do [them] justice and pay respect, but put a Central Texas spin on it," explains Matt. "Understanding that our equipment travels worldwide, we want to offer adaptability for different proteins, wood varieties—or fuel sources—and cook times. Since Texas is very close to our heart and where we grew up and live, we bring this very special state with us wherever our equipment travels. Our offset smokers offer a large, oversized firebox to accommodate different fire management techniques—however, they are designed to specialize in cooking high-level briskets, low and slow, with post oak wood. We bring these intentions into every product and design that we develop."

A custom Mill Scale offset smoker crafted from a decommissioned propane tank can run anywhere from $5,000 to $20,000 or more, depending on the model and any upgrades. Their globally influenced models range from $1,560 for the Yakitori I to $23,400 for The Cabinet Smoker, with many more products detailed on their website. In order to better accommodate backyard cooks, the team also designed a smaller, 94-gallon smoker crafted out of steel pipe, which rings in at just under $5,000. They'll also customize cookers in stainless steel, a favorite of chefs in restaurants, and build 361-gallon, 529-gallon, and 767-gallon smokers using steel pipe.

During the pandemic, the brothers moved their operations out to Lockhart and, after working out of a rural welding studio for several years, they knew it was time for a public-facing shop. In February 2024, they opened a 10,000-square-foot workshop and retail space, where customers can admire their detailed craftsmanship in person and ask questions about the products (a number of the top sellers are on display in the showroom). The shop also features a curated collection of locally foraged tools, grill accessories, YETI products, cookbooks, apparel, rubs, and sauces, and space for classes, events and community activations. Matt's wife, Annie, serves as the operations manager, overseeing everything that happens outside of Mill Scale's welding shop.

"Opening the new facility changed everything for us in a big way," Matt emphasizes. "We were able to expand our team, production, tooling, and capabilities, as well as offer a retail store to welcome folks in to kick the tires in person . . . and we now have a venue for on-site programming and larger scale food festivals to celebrate the culture, community, and barbecue history of Lockhart."

The new showroom is in good company, located right next door to Kreuz Market (see page 295), one of the first smokehouses in Texas and one of the first on record to build a brick pit designed to use indirect heat. While those 1924 brick pits still stand in the same building, which now houses Smitty's Market (see page 391), they need to be restored every 8 to 10 years to replace the metal lining and any broken bricks. When Kreuz moved to its current location in 1999, they built new offset brick pits, but with a resilient steel interior, eliminating the need for restoration.

The Johnsons connected with Kreuz Market's owner, Keith Schmidt, when they moved to town and, to their delight and surprise, he ordered a 1,000-gallon propane smoker from them. Pitmaster Roy Perez, who has been smoking the meats at Kreuz for nearly four decades, is a huge fan of Mill Scale pits, which he says cook more evenly, use less wood, and are much easier on his body than Kreuz's offset brick-and-steel pits. After seeing the results of the first pit, Schmidt ordered two more.

"It was kind of jaw-dropping for us," says Matt, "It was just like this gesture of belief and support. He's in this dynasty and he was able to be like, well, let's see if we can do it better. Let's see what this new-school barbecue thing is all about. It's a huge honor that we're now a part of their history, and we're one of the biggest changes that they have made in the last 100 years. That's something we don't take lightly at all."

Since the new space has allowed the Mill Scale team to expand their operations and increase production, business is booming more than ever before. Their residential equipment lead times range 6 to 12 weeks, while those wanting larger commercial smokers join a waitlist of 6 to 12 months. They've partnered with Sweden's Holy Smoke BBQ to build to their specifications and quality control, then ship to destinations outside the continental US (which have been as far-flung as Kuwait and Singapore).

"It seems like the world is really on fire for barbecue, and it hasn't gone anywhere since we all started breathing on this planet," says Matt. "In the age of convenience and apps and gadgets, people are still going back to the roots of cooking with fire. So we feel like the future is bright."

IT'S THE PITS

The very first barbecue in the United States was cooked over direct fires that were built in pits that had been dug out of the ground. But when meat markets began selling barbecue in the late nineteenth century, they began building their pits from the ground up, while still using a direct heat source. Kreuz Market (see page 295) was one of the first on record to build a brick pit designed to use indirect heat, and those original 1924 brick pits still stand in the same building, which now houses Smitty's Market (see page 391).

Throughout the 1970s, as barbecue became more widespread, more and more pitmasters began to embrace using an indirect heat source for a longer cook. Wayne Whitworth, a metal fabricator who worked in the oil fields surrounded by barbecue enthusiasts, started building pits from surplus oil pipes as a hobby, and when the price of oil fell in the early 1980s, it became a lucrative source of income. In 1983, Whitworth opened a Pitts & Spitts retail store in Houston, where they still craft offset smokers and competition-style rigs using carbon and steel.

It is unclear who was the very first person to use a decommissioned propane tank for the cooking chamber for a pit, but the approach quickly became widespread due to the general availability of the tanks. In the more commonly used offset pit, a steel firebox is welded to one end of the cooking chamber and a tall steel exhaust pipe attached to the other. The flow of air through the exhaust pipe (which is typically controlled by a damper) draws hot air from the firebox over the meat, slowly cooking it and imbuing it with a smoky flavor. In a reverse-flow firepit, the firebox is on the same side as the exhaust pipe. The heat is drawn from the firebox and forced to travel through the cooking chamber before reversing its flow, back to the side where it originated, to exit through the exhaust pipe. Pitmasters who prefer reverse-flow pits say they create a more uniform temperature and cooking environment.

There are a number of fabricators across the state who specialize in building custom pits (a list of them, along with their web addresses, follows). However, lead time has grown so long for some of the commercial-sized rigs, many pitmasters are venturing out-of-state to find theirs.

PITTS & SPITTS
HOUSTON
pittsandspitts.com

MOBERG SMOKERS
DRIPPING SPRINGS
mobergsmokers.com

MILL SCALE METALWORKS
LOCKHART
millscale.co

CEN-TEX SMOKERS
LULING
centexsmokers.com

M&M BBQ COMPANY
TOOL
mmbbqcompany.com

AUSTIN SMOKEWORKS
BARTLETT
austinsmokeworks.com

AJ'S CUSTOM COOKERS
FORT WORTH
ajscustomcookers.co

LONE STAR GRILLZ
CONROE
lonestargrillz.com

LYFE TYME BBQ PITS
UVALDE
lyfetyme.com

MULE SKINNER SMOKE RIGS
BRISTOL
muleskinnersmokerigs.com

BIG PHIL'S SMOKERS
CADDO MILLS
bigphilssmokers.com

MATT'S BBQ PITS
PIPE CREEK
mattsbbqpits.com

CANNON PITS & FABRICATION
GRANBURY
cannonpitsandfabrication.com

EAST TEXAS SMOKER COMPANY
TYLER
easttexassmokercompany.com

EL CUCARACHO SMOKERS
FORT WORTH
elcucarachosmokers.com

BBQ PITS BY KLOSE
HOUSTON
bbqpits.com

MARKET
SINCE 1900

KREUZ MARKET

LOCKHART

Lockhart has long been celebrated as the Barbecue Capital of Texas, attracting pilgrims from across the globe who are eager to pay homage to some of the state's earliest smokehouses.

Lockhart's cowtown legacy began shortly after the Civil War, when ranchers began capturing wild cattle and herding them north to sell to buyers who then shipped them to eastern markets via the newly constructed railway. This cattle drive—which started in South Texas and ended in Abilene, Kansas—was called the Chisholm Trail and, from 1867 to 1884, it was a significant source of income for a number of Texans who were impoverished after the war.

Meat markets began opening in Lockhart, a key stop on the trail, as a direct result of the cattle trade. Jesse Swearingen opened Lockhart's first meat market in 1875, just off the courthouse square. With no way of refrigerating the unsold cuts of meat, he began smoking them over local post oak wood as a practical means of preservation.

"Instead of letting the meat spoil, they would take it out back and cook it," explains Keith Schmidt, owner of Kreuz Market. "Then people could go out back, order whatever they cooked that day, and they served it on butcher paper. Crackers came in barrels back then, and they'd go buy a pickle. There were cabbage knives chained to the tables—and not so people wouldn't steal them. They were chained just close enough to the table to use, but you couldn't stab somebody. Lockhart was a rough town back in the early days. It was the Wild West!"

In 1900, Charles Kreuz Sr., a son of German immigrants, purchased the market for just $200 and changed the name to Kreuz (pronounced "Krites") Market. He developed a German-inspired recipe for ring sausage, using mostly beef and some pork plus salt, black pepper, and cayenne in a natural beef casing. Customers would enjoy these hand-tied, smoked "hot guts" simply, with crackers or bread and a chunk of cheese. Back then, sausage could be ordered "juicy" or "dry," and the other cuts of meat offered were simply "lean" (shoulder clod or chuck) or "fat" (brisket).

The business, which was a grocery store as well as a meat market, went through several changes of hands, all within the Kreuz family, in the early twentieth century. In 1924, Charles's sons—Theodore and Alvin—and his son-in-law Hugo Prove tore down the original metal building and built a two-story polychrome brick structure in its place. They also constructed offset brick pits and built an outdoor seating area, solidifying the market's future as a full-fledged barbecue restaurant.

In 1948, the Kreuz family was ready to retire, and asked their longtime butcher Edgar "Smitty" Schmidt if he would be interested in buying the business. He accepted the offer, and continued to seamlessly run the operation, changing very little until the 1960s. With rising competition from chain grocery stores, Schmidt decided to stop selling dry goods and focus instead on the meat market and quickly growing barbecue operation.

Those wanting to purchase meat from Kreuz Market could enter right in the front of the building, which looked out onto Lockhart's downtown. To purchase barbecue, locals knew to either walk down the smoke-darkened hallway—or just enter through the back—to reach the open-fire brick pits, where meat could be ordered by the pound right off the pit.

In 1978, Edgar acquired the building next door and added even more space for seating—this time indoors and air-conditioned. He filled the brightly lit dining room with long tables and chairs, and decorated the walls with tin soda ads and neon beer signs. Customers now lined up at a separate counter inside to pick up sliced white bread and purchase drinks and extras like pickles, cheese, onion, tomato, and avocado (the only "sides" that existed back then).

As new generations continued to discover and enjoy Kreuz Market, Edgar retired and sold the business to his sons Rick and Don Schmidt in 1984. The brothers continued to remain true to tradition—not a fork in sight at the restaurant, and asking for barbecue sauce was akin to blasphemy—but they did modernize

things by creating systems and methods to maintain product consistency.

"My grandfather made sausage with whatever they cut that day," laughs Keith, who is Rick's son. "Like if they didn't make pork that day, it's all beef today. That's just how they did it—sausage was a way to use scraps. And my dad was like, 'No, we're going to write out a recipe. It's gonna be 85 percent beef, 15 percent pork, here's how much salt, here's how much this and that.' So it would be consistent, because as you started leaving the old days and moving into the modern age, you had competition with other places."

Keith started working at Kreuz Market tying sausage in the summers when he was 12, and continued through high school. Around the same time, a construction worker named Roy Perez (pictured above)

was out of work after the housing market had plummeted. Roy's nephew convinced him to come work at Kreuz, where he started off by making the sausage.

"He told me, 'You don't have to talk to anybody,'" remembers Perez. "He knew I didn't like talking. So I started doing that, and then I saw the way they were slicing meat and it looked like an art form. I thought, 'Man, I would love to do that someday.'"

After mastering sausage making, Perez started learning the ins and outs of fire management, keeping a detailed log of everything he cooked. He learned Kreuz's methods of smoking hotter and faster than a lot of Texas barbecue (briskets are typically finished in about eight hours), and all without using a thermometer. When the pitmaster at the time took off and left Perez alone one day, he was effectively thrown into the deep end and subsequently promoted. Perez admits that for a while after this promotion, he was still calling the post oak "lumber," because it took him so long to swap construction language for barbecue lingo.

In 1990, Edgar's death catalyzed what would become one of the most famous barbecue family feuds in Texas. Rick and Don had purchased the business from their father, but Edgar had left the building and the land to their sister Nina Sells in his will. As they approached the end of the lease, Rick tried to negotiate with her to buy the building, but she was not interested. Sells said she would extend the lease, but would have to increase the price.

"I mean, they didn't like each other that much, but that was nothing new," says Keith. "So he would tell people, 'She's trying to shut me down, she wants to take it away from me.' The real story is somewhere in there, but who knows. It happened real quick; it was no big feud. But the newspapers made it as big as they possibly could, which was great—free advertising!"

Don retired, leaving his brother as the sole owner, and Rick decided that the best move was to build a bigger and better space. Keith, then 28, had been working with his dad full-time for a year and a half when they made the big transition. They designed a pit room and built eight 16-foot-long brick pits inside of it, this time lining them with steel to eliminate the need for constant restoration, as required by the original pits. Their new 25,000-square-foot space also included an area for federally inspected wholesale sausage making and several spacious dining rooms.

However, Rick was set on keeping the feel of the restaurant as close to the original as possible. He insisted on two counters because that's the way it had always been done. One is for ordering meat off the pit, to be carved, weighed, and wrapped in butcher paper. The other climate-controlled counter is for ordering sides, drinks, and desserts. He was also set on continuing butchering in the new location, but once the "Fresh Meat" sign fell off the building three times, he took it as an omen and decided to forgo the meat market, which was becoming less profitable as the years went on.

On September 1, 1999, Perez and the Schmidts hauled a tub of embers from the former site of Kreuz Market to the new location a half-mile away, a ceremonial transfer of coals made with reporters and police escorts in tow. Just one month later, Sells rebranded the original Kreuz Market space and named it Smitty's Market (see page 391) after her dad.

Though Rick was reluctant to make changes, the huge new building provided great opportunity, and Keith pointed out that it would behoove them to evolve to an extent. They now had pit space to greatly expand their meat offerings to include spare ribs, beef ribs, pit hams, chickens, and turkeys, in addition to the sausage, beef clod, brisket, pork chops, and prime rib the family had been smoking for years. And they still use just salt, coarse black pepper, and cayenne—in varying ratios—as their rub on every protein.

"I told him we don't need to change anything, but we can certainly add," says Keith. "You can come in here and get exactly what you got in 1960, if that's what you want, but if you want turkey and mac and cheese and green beans, then you can have that too! So as people started traveling more, and Lockhart became a destination, we had to appeal to a newer audience. We've got people that came here when they were babies who now have kids. So you want to keep that tradition in quality going, but you need to update a bit."

Kreuz Market began offering sides, starting with beans and a hot German potato salad with sauerkraut

Kreuz
MARKET
SINCE 1900
619 N. COLORADO
RBECUE
SAUSA

in it, which they have since switched out for a cheesy baked potato casserole and a separate sauerkraut option. They also offer cold potato salad, coleslaw, green beans, mac and cheese, and poblano cream corn, all gradually added to the menu through the years. And keeping with tradition, they still offer the same "trimmings" that have been available from the beginning: pickles, onions, cheese, avocado, jalapeños, and serranos.

In 2011, Keith purchased Kreuz Market from his father so Rick could enjoy his retirement. With such a strong work ethic passed through the Schmidt family for generations, Rick only knew how to operate at full throttle.

"It was like watching someone get a two-ton rock cut off his back," Keith remembers. "It was a big responsibility to him, and he looked at it more as a stewardship than an ownership. He felt like he needed to keep these people happy . . . and we don't try to make everybody happy here. You can't please everyone when you're dealing with something like barbecue, because it means something different to everyone. My father would have people getting in his face going, 'If there's no sauce, it's not barbecue.' Of course, we'd also have people that weren't from Texas going 'If it's beef, it's not barbecue. It has to be pork.' But the good thing about all of that is that, as everybody learned the different ways, it became more of a community and less of a competition."

The controversial additions of both barbecue sauce and forks were spurred by a location of Kreuz that Keith opened in Bryan in 2015 (which has since closed).

"It was like going to another world," says Keith. "And we had to come up with a sauce because we knew it would never go over [well] there [without one]. So suddenly we had a sauce, which was my maternal grandmother's recipe, and forks, because everybody out there was too prissy to eat with their hands."

In order to maintain consistency—and appease the growing complaints he received with more newcomers visiting—Keith brought the forks and the sauce over to the Lockhart restaurant in 2017. Another big change he spearheaded was opening the restaurant on Sundays. He also started bringing in live music on Saturdays and Sundays, which started as a strategic move to let customers know they were open later in the day than a lot of Texas barbecue joints. (They strive to make enough meat to last until closing time, and stay open until 8 p.m. every night but Sunday, when they close at 6 p.m.)

As they say: the more things change, the more they stay the same. These days, Kreuz is taking on more catering jobs than ever, so Keith brought on a catering manager and has a food trailer he takes out to special events. And nearly four decades later, Perez is still the pitmaster at Kreuz Market, and one of the most recognizable ones in the state, because he is decorated not only with awards, but with Elvis-inspired sideburns and a signature cowboy hat. However, he still can't understand why people ask for his autograph or want to take photos with him.

"I'm sure there's more people that should be more well known but they just had word of mouth to rely on; they didn't have the technology," he says humbly. "I always make sure to pay respects to people like Keith's dad. Rick taught me everything he knew. I'm not gonna ever forget the past."

That history is also preserved on the walls of Kreuz Market, which are hung with yellowed newspaper articles and signed photos from guests like George Strait and Don Walser. There's a six-and-a-half-foot rattlesnake skin mounted on the dining room wall from a snake said to have been killed by a customer many years ago. Near the entrance, there's a black-and-white photo of Rick at the original Kreuz pits taken by Wyatt McSpadden, and a big painting of Edgar at the chopping block, with Rick and Don on either side of him. And those chained cabbage knives—from the very early days of Kreuz—are now suspended on the wall in the hallway, a true relic of Lockhart's barbecue roots.

HARDCORE CARNIVORE

Jess Pryles was visiting Austin from Australia for the first time in 2007 when a bite of smoked beef rib triggered a transformative journey down a whole new career path.

"It was at Artz Rib House, with the red- or white-check tablecloths and the two-sided laminated menu and the paper plates," Pryles recalls. "They were serving back ribs, which is not what's used these days—now you'd use plate or chuck ribs. So they were more bone than meat, but that meant they had that gnawable, nubbly, crispy golden bits along the bone."

Pryles, who owned a cupcake bakery in Melbourne, was in town to put on a pop-up at a popular Austin bakery. At that time, she also had a blog named Burger Mary, where she documented her search for the world's best burgers and Bloody Marys. She returned home and decided to evolve the blog into a website dedicated to her own recipes. However, the natural-born meat lover knew she had much to learn about cooking it.

"I wasn't a competent meat cook at all," Pryles admits. "I always loved eating it, but I relied on boyfriends through the years to do the grilling. And then when I started to learn more about how barbecue was made, I became fascinated with the meat industry and learning more about meat."

When Pryles sought out her first brisket in Australia, she realized how vastly different it looked from the ones she enjoyed in Austin. So she fell further down the rabbit hole, learning everything she could about different cuts of meat, breeds of animals, and feeding practices.

“They would slaughter at about a yearling in Australia and they would wait until at least 18 to 24 months in the States, but (they’re also) bigger cattle with bigger genetics,” she explains. “The cattle industry is older here and y’all have corn and y’all know how to feed ‘em. And they get big—big boys!”

Pryles continued visiting Texas, having fallen in love with the state as well as its barbecue culture. With each visit, she advanced in her barbecue studies a bit further and kept making more connections. A friend introduced her to the legendary late pitmaster John Mueller, who let her cook overnight with him and cut meat in his JMueller BBQ trailer each time she returned to town.

“At this stage, no one was gatekeeping because that whole thing where chefs come to stage for two weeks and then go off to open their own place—that wasn’t happening yet,” says Pryles. “So everyone was very forthcoming with how they did things and what the technique was . . . and there’s no substitute for experience. You go and work two weekends at a smokehouse, and you will learn more than you ever have, just from the repetition and the volume.”

Pryles’s meat journey took her to processing plants, butcher shops, and ranches across Australia and Texas, and she documented it all on her quickly growing Instagram account. She got hands-on experience butchering with an apprenticeship at Gary’s Meats (now called G. McBean Butcher) in Melbourne. She learned how to hunt and process game like whitetail deer, hog, and turkey under the guidance of Marvin Bendele, the director of Foodways Texas. She went on to cofound the Australasian Barbecue Alliance, a key resource for American-style barbecue in Australia, and she became a sought-after speaker at prominent events like Camp Brisket (put on by Texas A&M University), South by Southwest, and various meat industry conferences.

“At the industry stuff, I speak about how to connect to the public,” says Pryles. “And at the public stuff, I teach them what I’ve learned from the industry, like beef grading and dispelling myths and helping people understand basic meat selection, in addition to cookery.”

In 2012, Pryles founded an event called The Carnivore’s Ball, and went on to hold three of them in Melbourne, one in Sydney, and two in Austin.

“[The Carnivore’s Ball] started with the idea of elevating barbecue,” she explains. “So each pitmaster did a different course and we’d have live music in a wedding reception–type venue. It was before this hyperdrive of events happened, so I like to think it was one of the very first events that brought multiple barbecue places into one location—before barbecue festivals were even a thing.”

Pryles permanently relocated to Texas in 2015 and enrolled in classes at Texas A&M University, studying with meat scientists to deepen her understanding of the field. (She would later earn a graduate certificate in meat science at Iowa State University in 2022.) And as her understanding of meat science grew, so did her brand.

In 2016, she launched a line of meat rubs and steak seasonings branded Hardcore Carnivore, and in 2018, she published her first cookbook. *Hardcore Carnivore: Cook Meat Like You Mean It* features recipes for protein-focused dishes from andouille gumbo and char siu skewers to coffee-rubbed kangaroo loin and peach bourbon pork chops. Over the next couple of years, she expanded the Hardcore Carnivore brand to include smoked sausages and tools like butcher paper, high-heat gloves, trimming knives, and brisket-slicing knives. Her line can be found at Bass Pro Shops, Cabela's, Buc-ees, Academy Sports + Outdoors, and H-E-B, and she now distributes to Mexico, Canada, Australia, Scandinavia, and Ireland too.

In more recent years, Pryles has also become quite the TV personality. She has grilled in the middle of Rockefeller Plaza on *The Today Show* and appeared as a judge on Food Network shows like *BBQ Big Race, Beat Bobby Flay*, and *Kids BBQ Championship*. She also hosted *BBQuest*, a show where she visited different barbecue joints and ranches around Texas. The show, which was produced by the Texas Beef Council, lasted for three seasons and got picked up by Hulu. And she just launched her own *Hardcore Carnivore* series on the Outdoor Channel and is currently filming the second season.

"My show is some hunting, some ranches, and it always ends in cooking—all with my sarcastic, acerbic personality and a little bit of swearing, because I'm Australian," she says with a smirk.

Though she can often be found speaking or teaching about meat, emceeing events, and acting as a brand ambassador for companies like Gerber Knives and Kingsford Charcoal, Pryles's passion still lies in cooking. She's taught live-fire cooking classes across four different continents, and is constantly developing new recipes for her website, which she also shares on social media, along with all manner of shopping, butchering, cooking, and smoking tips.

"I especially love cooking any secondary cut," says Pryles, "and experimenting with things like beef shank, with a combination of smoking and braising. I love that you can take something that's an unwanted, tough cut—which is what brisket used to be—and turn it into something incredibly flavorful."

Pryles encourages backyard cooks not to be afraid to branch out beyond the most well-known cuts of meat. "Ask your butcher questions," she advises. "Generally, they're happy to help you learn about new cuts for the smoker."

Next, she stresses the importance of a good pit. She teamed up with Pitts & Spitts to design The Jess Pryles Signature Edition Pit, an offset smoker with a double-size firebox to allow greater control over temperature. Each pit is custom-made in Texas, individually numbered, and marked with her signature.

"All of the top 50 barbecue joints are using at least Prime grade brisket because it's hard to get Select brisket and turn it into something good—and same with the smoker," Pryles relates. "You can't go in and get the cheapest smoker at Academy because it's going to be really thin metal and you're going to lose heat. Barbecue is an expensive hobby for people who are obsessed with perfection."

However, Pryles doesn't discredit the importance of pellet smokers for unmatched convenience and ease. "I believe that the best barbecue does come from offset smokers, but it's so hard to pass up a decent pellet grill, especially for recipe testing," she admits. "Firing up an offset smoker in your backyard is a luxury, like spending your Sunday watching football. It's an all-day activity, and you can't be interrupted to do anything else. So I think pellet smokers have allowed us to use barbecue as a weekly event—and a weeknight event too—instead of just having to wait to find the time to babysit your offset smoker."

Some of Pryles's online content is dedicated to dispelling myths and fear tactics about food safety and the meat industry, and providing factual, research-based information in its place. While the intent is to empower and inspire consumers, even this content creator recognizes that the oversaturation of information on the web can sometimes be overwhelming. In the end, her number-one piece of advice for aspirational backyard cooks is simple: just get out there and do it.

"I feel like there's a lot of information out there, especially for home cooks, like videos and YouTubes and references and materials, and I think it can be really intimidating to read before you try it," she says. "So I would encourage everyone just to go and cook a brisket before you trim it, preen it, mustard it, inject it, dry brine it, look at it over your left shoulder—you know, like these things that people think you need to do. First, you just have to understand your baseline."

Though this meat expert is busier than ever these days, Pryles still makes plenty of time for researching barbecue, so I had to inquire about her go-to bite at Texas smokehouses.

"I like to get the moist for my own enjoyment and the lean to check out the pitmaster," she says deftly. "But my ultimate barbecue bite is a slice of white bread, a torn-off tongue of beef rib, a piece of cheddar cheese, a little bit of barbecue sauce, and some white onions that are gonna make you smell awful in about three hours. And that little bite is quintessential Texas barbecue."

SNOW'S BBQ

LEXINGTON

The top-rated barbecue joints across Texas are known to draw epic lines and sell out before lunchtime. But Snow's BBQ is the only destination where I have arrived under a star-filled sky and watched the sun break the horizon. Since opening in the early aughts, the Lexington restaurant has inspired food lovers from across the globe to embark upon certified pilgrimages to try the acclaimed barbecue and meet nonagenarian pitmaster Tootsie Tomanetz.

On my last visit, I met a group of seven friends from Europe and the UK who travel to Texas annually to eat their weight in barbecue across the state. Their journey lasted 24 hours, and Snow's was their very first stop.

"They travel from all over," says owner Kerry Bexley, who keeps a guest book at the restaurant's door for guests to sign in. "Last I counted, it was 23 different states and 15 countries on a Saturday morning. And if you go count it today, it's probably going to be close to that."

Bexley never imagined his modest barbecue venture would achieve global acclaim. By the time he opened Snow's in 2003, it was just another one of his many entrepreneurial pursuits. In the 1990s, he operated a farm-and-ranch store on the very spot where Snow's now stands, then sold it in 1996. He spent 15 years as a professional rodeo bullfighter and over two decades

as a control room operator at a coal mine. And even today, he still owns and maintains 15 rental properties and manages cattle on his 100-acre ranch in Lexington, demonstrating the hardworking spirit that defines Snow's BBQ.

Before opening Snow's, Bexley had dabbled in barbecue in his younger years, occasionally participating in cook-offs. He'd also grown up visiting City Meat Market in Lexington, where Norma Frances Tomanetz (known to everyone as "Tootsie") worked alongside her husband, White. Tootsie had gotten her start at City Meat Market in Giddings, where White was a butcher. After filling in at the market one day when they were short-staffed in 1967, she ended up working there for a decade, learning how to cook meat on brick pits alongside pitmaster Orange Holloway. Tootsie and White went on to run the Lexington meat market, butcher shop, and barbecue joint for 20 more years before White suffered a debilitating stroke in 1996. They shut down their business, though Tootsie was working under the new owners when Bexley began approaching her with the idea of opening a barbecue joint together.

Tootsie initially declined his offers because she was committed to helping the owners she'd sold her business to. But a few years later, they sat down to talk it over, and Tootsie agreed to cook with Bexley if he could weld direct-heat pits identical to the ones she'd mastered over the years. He set to work building them, with Tootsie consulting on the design.

"Learning how to cook on direct heat and still cooking with direct heat, I prefer that," she says matter-of-factly. "I just haven't cooked that much with indirect heat and, at my age, I'm not going to learn now. I've got my style, and I'm gonna stick to that."

The two spent some time cooking together, Bexley honing his skills on the indirect pit and learning Tootsie's methods as well. In direct-heat cooking, fat from the meat drips onto the coals, resulting in a distinct flavor and crispier bark. It's a labor-intensive process, involving lots of coal shoveling, fire management, focus, and patience.

"She had the reputation and she brought the knowledge on board. I did not have a lot of barbecue knowledge, but I'm very anal about everything so I'm gonna learn to do whatever I want to do," says Bexley. "I love the relationship we have. Has it been challenging? Very much so. She's tough!"

In March 2003, Bexley opened Snow's BBQ, a name inspired by his childhood nickname, Snowman.

"I was born in February and when Mother was pregnant with me, an elderly gentleman asked my older brother, 'Do you want a little brother or sister?' and he said, 'I want a little snowman,'" says Bexley. "So he nicknamed me that and, by the time I got to school, that's what everybody called me!"

From the outset, Snow's BBQ has operated exclusively on Saturdays, carrying on the tradition of selling barbecue after the weekly livestock auction that takes place down the street. But that schedule also worked with the duo's busy schedules. While Bexley juggles his multiple ventures, Tootsie (who has six grandchildren and ten great-grandchildren!) works full-time as a custodian for the Giddings school district, approaching her role at Snow's with the same tireless work ethic that has defined her life.

"I was raised to work," says Tootsie, who grew up harvesting wheat and threshing peanuts on her family's farm. "You got up in the morning knowing there was a job to do, work to be done."

"That's why we get along, is our work ethic," adds Bexley who, in the early years, would sandwich shifts at the mine around cooking at Snow's.

The post-oak fires are stoked each Friday night for the brisket cook to begin on the indirect-heat pits, which are also crafted by Bexley. For the majority of Snow's history, Tootsie would come in at 2 a.m. to get her fire going for the pork steak, chicken, and pork ribs, but as they have more recently switched to cooking the ribs on the indirect-heat pits, Tootsie now comes in closer to 6 a.m.

At Snow's BBQ, simplicity is the secret ingredient. Every cut of meat is seasoned with table salt (not kosher) and 16-mesh black pepper. ("We just sprinkle it on; we don't rub it in," notes Tootsie). During the cook, the pork steak, chicken, and pork ribs are basted with a mop sauce—a tangy, flavorful mixture of Worcestershire sauce, vinegar, butter, mustard, flour, water, and yellow onion. Applied with a hand-sized mop, the sauce helps tenderize the meat while building layers of flavor.

"We're traditional barbecue," says Bexley. "We don't spice it up or dilute it down to make it taste better. You get the meat taste 100 percent. The taste of the meat and the quality of the meat is a crucial part. And another interesting thing is we'll use a Select grade and there's very few in the industry that will use Select grade as opposed to Prime or Choice. It was a cost-effective thing in the beginning but if you cook it right—can we make that Select grade Prime quality? Yes, we can."

The briskets at Snow's are smoked for about six hours before being wrapped in foil—a technique known as the "Texas crutch"—to lock in moisture. Methods like that and their mopping, paired with meticulous fire management and an unwavering attention to detail, ensure their meats are tender and perfectly cooked.

"It's a lot of tender, loving care," says Tootsie. "It's how we tend to it, how we work with it, and how we handle it."

Even after decades at the pit, Tootsie remains humbled and challenged by smoking meat, a craft dependent on so many shifting variables.

"I have young people now—men, usually, in their 40s and 50s—and they have an air about them and they'll say, 'Well, I know everything there is to do with cooking barbecue,'" she says. "Well, thank you, I'm glad you do. But after 58 or 59 years, I'm still learning. I mean there's always something that turns out different or something that's different. No two Saturdays are ever the same."

Though Tootsie has a long history of sausage making, Snow's has the local Hildebrandt Meat Market craft their regular and jalapeño sausage rings. As for the sides, Snow's keeps it classic with just three options. The pinto beans, slow simmered for hours with bacon ends, chili powder, and salt, develop into a smoky stew with just a hint of spice. The vinegar-based coleslaw and German potato salad—featuring bright bursts of pickles and pimientos—are both the creations of Ms. Patsy, a cherished home cook from Lexington.

"Locals could only get Ms. Patsy's potato salad or coleslaw at a wedding or a fundraiser before," says Bexley. "So when we opened up originally, she agreed to make ours. It was a calling card in our earlier times."

Bexley credits those small but meaningful details with helping to attract customers during Snow's early years. "Locals can be a tough crowd in a little bitty town," he says. While they managed that, the demands of the business with his family life and other work were an ongoing challenge. By late 2007, he had settled on the difficult decision to sell Snow's and was in discussions with a prospective buyer. But fate had other plans—a change of heart from the interested couple kept the sale from happening. The very next weekend, writers from *Texas Monthly* stopped by for a visit.

That visit turned out to be a game-changer. Snow's BBQ earned the coveted #1 spot on *Texas Monthly's* Top 50 list in 2008, transforming it from a little-known small-town spot into an overnight culinary destination. Suddenly, customers were lining up as early as Friday night, armed with folding chairs, to claim their place in line (all night long) before the doors opened at 8 a.m. on Saturday. With this sudden onslaught of business, Snow's needed more hands on deck. Bexley asked Tootsie's son Hershey if he would be interested in helping out, and he became a key team member for the next seven years—until brain cancer resulted in his untimely passing, just one year after Tootsie lost her husband, White.

Tootsie dealt with the grief the best way she knew how—by working through it, upon her insistence, and with the support of her barbecue family. The restaurant was just as busy as ever, so Bexley asked a regular customer named Clay Cowgill if he would consider joining the team in 2015. Bexley trained him on the pits and he took over Hershey's roles, and continues to produce all of Snow's brisket and ribs each weekend, as well as for their robust mail-order program. In 2017, Snow's again placed No. 1 on *Texas Monthly*'s list.

"Getting number one in '17, the second time, was really the 'attaboy,'" remembers Bexley. "Now there's so many in the business and so much craft and politics and—we just do what we do and that's it."

And why change anything when the recognitions continue rolling in? In 2018, Tomanetz was inducted into the Barbecue Hall of Fame. She was a semifinalist for the James Beard Award for Best Chef: Southwest the same year. And when Tomanetz was featured in the *Chef's Table: BBQ* series that premiered on Netflix in 2020, Snow's stream of guests just about doubled again.

"After *Chef's Table,* that's when I really noticed we had people from other countries come in," says Tootsie.

Snow's BBQ has continued to rank in the upper echelon of each highly influential *Texas Monthly* list that is released. In addition to Bexley, Tootsie, and Cowgill, Bexley's son Colby has taken on sausage-smoking duties, and his daughters Larissa and Alison work the front of house each weekend. His wife, Kim, has also stepped into a very lucrative role. During the pandemic, Bexley built bathrooms behind the restaurant, and they decided to turn the front of the little building into a merch stand. That has now developed into a whole other business of its own, stocked with shirts, caps, stickers, magnets, YETI tumblers, bandannas, seasonings, and Snow's three different bottled sauces (original, spicy, and sweet spicy).

"It's crazy," says Bexley. "In many weeks, we've sold more in merch than I've sold in barbecue."

Considering they sell an average of 1,200 pounds of meat each Saturday, that is a significant amount of merch. Each Saturday at Snow's is quite an event these days. There's a bar set up in the backyard, serving free beer and cocktails to guests. Barbecue pilgrims form lines to take photos with Kerry and Tootsie and ask to have items signed. (I even watched one fan gleefully procure a greasy rubber glove to take back overseas and raffle off to his followers.)

"Our big deal now with these destination people is the customer service, and hospitality is huge to me," says Bexley. "That's free, and you don't you don't get that everywhere. I can't make them like the barbecue, but I can let them know how important it is that they're here. Do they want to see me? No, they want to see Tootsie most of the time!"

"It's very heartwarming," says Tootsie, who turns 90 in 2025. "But I don't let it go to my head because it's God's leading. It's God's plan that I'm following and I give Him all the credit . . . I'm going to continue, as long as my health is good and God gives me the strength, because I'm happiest when I'm busy."

TEXAS BBQ AROUND THE WORLD

Even a state as big as Texas isn't large enough to contain all the love for its barbecue, and these days, Texas-style barbecue is popping up all over the world. Is it the allure of juicy brisket being lusciously sliced all over social media that proves irresistible to spectators? The cool factor of those massive steel offset smokers, covered in a layer of patina and simultaneously flashy as hell? Or was it Aaron Franklin who single-handedly kickstarted this global movement by showing the world what was possible with a welding torch and a dream? Maybe it's all of these things at once, and the world is more delicious for it. But it does beg the question: If barbecue is made outside of Texas, can it really be called Texas barbecue?

Ponder that question while you're traveling to these spots that follow in the Texas tradition.

HERITAGE BARBECUE

SAN JUAN CAPISTRANO, CALIFORNIA

Heritage started as a pop-up in Danny and Brenda Castillo's Garden Grove backyard in northern Orange County. Danny's job as a corporate chef for Whole Foods Market brought them to the company's Austin headquarters on a work trip, which is when they first experienced Franklin Barbecue (see page 233 for a profile on founder Aaron Franklin), InterStellar BBQ (see page 278), and Terry Black's Barbecue (see page 359), as well as the now-closed Brett's Backyard BBQ in Rockdale. The Castillos fell in love with barbecue on that trip, launched their brick and mortar in the summer of 2020, and the rave reviews have been rolling in ever since—including a Bib Gourmand recommendation from the Michelin Guide in 2021. The Castillos use California white oak to smoke more traditional Texas offerings like Black Angus prime brisket and maple-glazed Duroc spareribs, but they also offer creative specials like pulled pork mac and cheese pie, brisket birria noodle soup, beef cheek barbacoa ravioli, and more. What started as their business's anniversary party has now become the Heritage Barbecue Craft BBQ Invitational, an annual gathering of some of the most celebrated pitmasters in the country—including plenty of friends from Texas. *@heritagebarbecue*

PINCHE GRINGO BBQ

MEXICO CITY, MEXICO

There might not be a better tongue-in-cheek name than Pinche Gringo (which translates to "damn American") for a Texas barbecue joint started by a New Yorker living in Mexico City. Dan DeFossey spent some time in Texas while working for Teach for America before his next job (with Apple) transferred him down to Mexico City. After several years, he was ready for a change—and noticed there was no Texas-style barbecue in the city, despite its proximity to the state. He brought on Roberto Luna as his business partner and the two took a research trip to Texas, visiting greats like la Barbecue (see page 249), Franklin Barbecue, and Micklethwait Craft Meats (see page 271). With no culinary experience whatsoever, they immersed themselves in YouTube videos to learn how to smoke using offset smokers and post oak. Pinche Gringo BBQ opened in 2013, serving traditional sides like beans, coleslaw, potato salad, and mac and cheese (you won't find any limes or tortillas here either—they wanted to keep it as traditional to Texas as possible!) Over a decade later, they now run two successful Pinche Gringo BBQ locations, plus several sandwich shop offshoots and a bar. @ *pinchegringobbq*

HILL COUNTRY BARBECUE MARKET

NEW YORK CITY AND WASHINGTON, DC

Marc Glosserman's grandfather Sam Glosserman was the mayor of Lockhart, the "Barbecue Capital of Texas," from 1955 to 1964, and Marc has many smoked-drenched memories of summers spent there. He decided to bring that style of Central Texas market-stye barbecue to New York in 2007, and then Washington, DC in 2011. Glosserman based the concept on Lockhart's iconic Kreuz Market (see page 295): meats sold by the pound and piled on butcher paper-lined trays. He imports post oak from Central Texas, rubs the proteins with salt and pepper, and smokes everything in Ole Hickory smokers. They also sell Big Red soda by the bottle, have Shiner Bock on draft, and offer Kreuz Market sausages. Some of the sides go beyond the basics of old-school, market-style barbecue joints, however, with additions like white shoepeg corn pudding, sweet potato bourbon mash, and skillet cornbread with ancho honey butter. Exposed brick, worn wooden tables and chairs, plenty of framed Lockhart photos, and a stage for twangy live music set the scene at both restaurants. *@hillcountrybbq*

LEWIS BARBECUE

CHARLESTON & GREENVILLE, SOUTH CAROLINA

El Paso native John Lewis moved to Austin as a teenager and began his barbecue journey in his backyard, playing around with the New Braunfels smoker his parents had gifted him. After a stint in Colorado's barbecue competition circuit, he returned to Austin and made a name for himself by working with Aaron Franklin and then LeAnn Mueller (see page 249), as they launched businesses that went on to gain national attention and countless accolades. In 2016, Lewis decided to strike out on his own, relocating to Charleston to open Lewis Barbecue (he opened another location in Greenville in 2022). Lewis built all his own smokers, which he keeps ripping with local oak. An "All Hail the King" mural showcases a crowned cow (not something you see often in the middle of hog country) and Prime beef brisket is naturally the most popular menu item. There's also Texas hot guts (beef-dominant sausages seasoned with black pepper and stuffed in a pork casing), green chile corn pudding, cowboy pinto beans, and even tallow chips, which can be served with queso or made into barbecue-topped nachos. *@lewisbarbecuechs*

OLD JIMMY'S BBQ

MONTERREY, MEXICO

Eugenio Martinez and Fernando Vela spent many vacations in Texas while growing up just two hours south of the border. When they returned home to Monterrey, they missed the small-town, family barbecue they experienced at places like Louie Mueller Barbecue (see page 240) and Snow's BBQ (see page 308). So in 2015, they opened Old Jimmy's, bringing Texas-style craft barbecue home. Though mesquite grows much more prevalently in the Norestense region, the duo sources oak from local ranches on the outskirts of the city in order to adhere to the Central Texas style. But they also add their own touches to cater to the local palate, toning down the use of black pepper in favor of cumin and Mexican oregano in their rubs, adding tajín to their smoked and grilled chicken, and employing chile de árbol for an extra kick in their sauces. Instead of the standard jalapeño cheddar sausage, they rotate in different chiles and cheeses, such as serrano with Oaxaca cheese, pequín with asadero, and poblano with panela. But you won't find any tortillas here—just white bread purchased at their local H-E-B. Now, in addition to their two locations (one in the neighborhood of Tampiquito and another in La Estanzuela), there are several other Texas-style barbecue joints in Monterrey—and an annual barbecue festival. *@oldjimmybbq*

BLAKE'S AT SOUTHERN MILLING

MARTIN, TENNESSEE

Blake Stoker received a copy of Aaron Franklin's first book from his father for his twentieth birthday and, within months, they'd planned their first pilgrimage to Texas. Upon their return to Tennessee, they had a welder on their ranch build two 500-gallon smokers, and by that summer, in 2016, Stoker was serving his own brisket from a trailer to his hometown of Dresden. He continued to visit Texas year after year, befriending some of the best pitmasters in the state (he's visited over 20 times now). Attracted to the simplicity of Texas barbecue and its minimal use of seasonings, Stoker uses kosher salt and coarsely ground pepper for his rub, then adds some coffee grounds in for color, nuttiness, and chocolate notes. He sources white oak native to Western Tennessee, with some pieces of red oak and cherry making their way in from time to time. Stoker eventually found a permanent location in a defunct mill in Martin, and he and his family spent several years renovating it before opening in the spring of 2023. Though his smoking methods remain true to Texas, Stoker has started to incorporate some hints of Tennessee barbecue into the menu over the years—for example, offering baby back ribs by the half or full rack in lieu of spare ribs by the pound, because the former are more popular with the locals. Pimento cheese with seasoned crackers also makes an appearance on the menu, as do sweet baked beans and vinegar coleslaw. *@blakesatsouthernmilling*

DAMPF GOOD BBQ

CARY, NORTH CAROLINA

Nick Dampf grew up in St. Louis, Missouri, and moved to Dallas as a kid before bouncing around the Midwest and landing in North Carolina. Throughout these itinerant years, he tried his fair share of barbecue, and Texas was always his favorite style due to its blend of simplicity and attention to detail. He and his brother Bryce launched their first pop-up in 2021 in Smithville, a small town 30 miles southeast of Raleigh. The locals were more accepting of the beef-centric menu than they were of the brisket prices, so they moved their operations to Cary, a wealthy suburb of Raleigh, in 2022. They source Red Angus from regional farms, seasoned simply with salt and pepper, and use an aged white oak similar to Texas post oak for smoking. Beef is the most popular item on the menu, but locals still love their pulled pork sandwiches topped with slaw, so Dampf also makes a delicious compromise in the form of bacon brisket, a melt-in-your-mouth, slow-smoked pork belly. *@dampfgoodbbq*

HOUSTON'S BARBECUE

MELBOURNE, AUSTRALIA

After working in IT for 20 years, Kit Houston got a job grilling sausages on busy weekends at a brewery. This awakened an interest to go beyond what Australians know as "barbecue" (grilling) and learn "American barbecue" (smoking). Houston bought an offset smoker and began practicing in his backyard, then sold his meats at another local brewery and out of his driveway. He and his wife, Prue, took an epic barbecue road trip across Texas to experience spots like Stiles Switch BBQ and Brew (see page 385), Franklin Barbecue, Snow's BBQ, Micklethwait Craft Meats, and Louie Mueller Barbecue. The Muellers have had a huge influence on the Houstons, particularly in their well-peppered beef rib. After opening their restaurant in 2019, they even flew Wayne Mueller out to Australia to teach classes. They use redgum, a local hardwood, for smoking Australian beef, which has a more robust, beefy flavor than American beef, due to the cattle being much older at the time they are slaughtered. The proteins and sides all run Texas traditional, save for a couple of differences—"barbecue boxes" take the place of butcher paper–lined trays, and Alabama white sauce makes appearances throughout the menu. And, much like a number of Texas joints, Houston's has developed a following for their smashburgers made from brisket trim. *@houstonsbbq*

FOX BROS BAR-B-Q

ATLANTA, GEORGIA

Twins Justin and Jonathan Fox were born on Texas Independence Day and grew up in Fort Worth, but relocated to Atlanta in 1999 when Jonathan got a graphic design job in the Georgia capital. At that time, there was nowhere to find the brisket they loved from their youth. So they bought an offset smoker and began feeding their friends during backyard barbecues, slowly perfecting their dishes before opening Fox Bros Bar-B-Q in 2007. They use a hickory- and oak-fired Oyler rotisserie to smoke their spare ribs, pulled pork, brisket, and housemade jalapeño-and-cheese sausage, and Brunswick stew makes an appearance on the menu as an homage to the region. Frito pie, served straight out of the bag, is one of their most popular sides and chicken-fried steak specials appear on Thursday. Over the years, they have grown to four different locations around Atlanta. *@foxbrosbarbq*

HOLY SMOKE BBQ

NYHAMNSLÄGE, SWEDEN

Sweden has a tradition of smoking meat for preservation purposes, but Texas-style barbecue was a completely foreign concept until Johan Fritzell opened Holy Smoke in 2014. Fritzell's background is in the graphic design industry, and the establishment started as a passion project—it is still only open from Easter until mid-October due to the region's brutal winters, which leaves plenty of time for barbecue research the rest of the year. He's learned much from trips to Texas, with visits to top spots like Franklin Barbecue, Louie Mueller Barbecue, and Snow's BBQ. The latter was particularly inspirational to him since Holy Smoke is in a very remote part of southwestern Sweden. Fritzell uses American red oak that's harvested locally, the closest they have to post oak, and imports beef from Creekstone Farms, while chicken, pork ribs, and sausages are sourced locally. He has now acquired four offset smokers from Mill Scale Metalworks (two 1,000-gallon and two 500-gallon, for brisket, beef ribs, and pork ribs), an Oyler 1300 rotisserie (for pork shoulder, chuck, chicken, pork belly, and beans) and a Mill Scale cold-smoking cabinet for fun experiments. *@holysmokebbqsweden*

LONGHORN TEXAS BBQ

CAIRO, EGYPT

Egyptian-born Tamer Amer started working in the hospitality industry while in college in Dallas, and went on to manage restaurants there and in Los Angeles. In 2008, he moved back to Egypt to open his first restaurant (Fuego Grill and Sushi Bar in Cairo), which eventually expanded to four locations. In 2018, Amer decided to start a concept that hadn't yet been done in the Middle East, and settled on a Texas barbecue place, inspired by visits to Franklin Barbecue during his time in Texas. He had 1,000-gallon pits from Arizona's Camelback Smokers and Lone Star State artifacts shipped out to Egypt, and hired Texicana BBQ Consulting, who brought on Jonny White (of Goldee's Barbecue, see page 16) and Chuck Charnichart (of Barbs-B-Q), to come out to Cairo and spend six months developing the menu and train all of the staff. They created a peak product from certified Angus brisket imported from Greater Omaha Beef and Creekstone Farms, and acacia and oak sourced from the Egyptian countryside—a combination which is both sustainable and the closest to central Texas post oak. Amer saw such success that he opened a second location in Cairo in 2021 and is currently working on a beachside location on the north coast of Egypt. *@longtexasbbq*

HOODOO BROWN BBQ

RIDGEFIELD, CONNECTICUT

After taking a "guys' trip" to Austin, Texas that included visiting a dozen different barbecue places, Cody Sperry returned home to Connecticut and began his backyard education on a Big Green Egg. After seeing success with barbecue catering, he decided to open a Texas-style joint called Hoodoo Brown BBQ in 2015. In addition to all the Texas barbecue staples, they offer standout items like a cracklin'-inspired pork belly with fresh tomato relish, feature sausages in flavors like chopped cheese and turkey shawarma, and specials like birria grilled cheese and brisket pizza with caramelized onions, candied jalapeño, ricotta, and barbecue sauce. Good luck leaving room for desserts—but you must, with offerings like banana bourbon cream pie and s'mores ice cream cake. *@hoodoobrownbbq*

MELT

PARIS, FRANCE

After experiencing Mighty Quinn's Barbeque in New York, Antoine Martinez and Jean Ganizate traveled to Texas to study barbecue. Their research led them from Austin to Dallas, where they connected with Jeffrey Howard, who was the pitmaster at Pecan Lodge at the time. They convinced him to move out to Paris, where they lived, to open MELT in 2016. They use oak to smoke all the meat, which includes beef ribs, beef cheeks, pulled pork, maple bacon, and half chickens. And it's hard to say whether it was the melt-in-your mouth brisket or spare ribs that inspired the name. Sides include buttery cornbread, Asian-inspired button mushrooms, fried Brussels sprouts, broccoli bacon, fennel salad, and more traditional potato salad and coleslaw. Due to the restaurant's popularity, it has now grown to three locations plus two MELT Delis specializing in sandwiches. *@melt_slow_smoked_barbecue*

BRISKET COUNTRY

In the highly competitive, and, honestly, quite oversaturated, world of Texas barbecue, great food alone isn't enough to ensure success.

"Nowadays, with the number of barbecue places that are open, differentiating yourself from everyone else—besides just with the food—is essential," explains designer M. Brady Clark, whose love of food, plus a need in the industry for design and branding, led to the formation of Brisket Country, the world's first creative studio dedicated to Texas barbecue.

Clark was born in Southern California to a self-proclaimed culinary anthropologist. His father ran restaurants for Burt Reynolds in the 1980s and served as an executive chef all over the US, specializing in Mexican and Latin American cuisine.

"So he cooked a lot, but we went out to eat all the time and, to a fault, that's all he talks about," says Clark. "It was all about food, so you can't help but be wired to that."

When Clark moved to Texas in 2006, inspired by a friend who'd recently relocated to the area, he was working for Billabong, doing menswear design. Two years later, he started working with Thunderwear Apparel, Inc., crafting high-end custom apparel for the entertainment industry—like a highly coveted satin jacket with custom labeling he made for Elton John's fortieth anniversary show at Dodger Stadium.

Clark's first introduction to the world of Texas barbecue came through a serendipitous encounter with Daniel Vaughn (see page 26). Clark's friend Chet Garner, the host of a Texas travel series on PBS, couldn't make a bacon competition he was supposed to judge, so he asked Clark if he wanted to go in his place. Vaughn, also a judge, was working on his book, *The Prophets of Smoked Meat*, at the time and needed art for his book. He had been recording what type of wood was used to smoke at over 200 different barbecue joints, and he wanted them categorized and mapped on the state of Texas. After the two connected and joined forces, Clark designed a wood map called Texas by the Cord. The poster was screen printed in 12 colors on French paper and has gone on to become an important piece of Texas barbecue history.

"Daniel and I were doing that project, and then Texas barbecue sort of proliferated—West Coast, East Coast, worldwide," says Clark. "Texas barbecue is everywhere."

After working on that book project with Vaughn, Clark started getting more requests than ever for barbecue-focused design. And with each job he accepted, he'd get another through word of mouth. In 2010, he started his Brisket Country Instagram account to showcase that work. Since then, he says the moniker has taken on a life of its own, so he started designing a line of Brisket Country merch like shirts, hats, posters, patches, and stickers.

"Barbecue people talk like schoolgirls—for good, mostly, and sometimes bad," laughs Clark. "But when you do good work, then it spreads. So I've gotten to work with a ton of awesome people—the barbecue family, as they say. I'm sort of this guy behind the guy, in the shadows, helping a lot of people in barbecue."

Clark has worked with a number of businesses in Texas, plus Texas barbecue concepts outside the state, from Heritage Barbecue in California to The Smiddy BBQ in Edinburgh, Scotland. His scope of work spans graphic design, signage, packaging design, custom merchandise, and interior design. But oftentimes he begins with branding on a conceptual level in order to help his client create a visual identity.

"I partner with clients to help bring their story to life in a visual way at inception or help them rework how their existing identities, store interiors, merchandise look and feel to make their businesses grow to be successful," explains Clark.

In his work for butcher and culinary consultant Jess Pryles (see page 304), he's helped to visually conceptualize her Hardcore Carnivore brand, which includes a cookbook and products like rubs, knives, and other gear. Clark has designed curry sauce labels for Khói Barbecue (see page 161) and is helping pitmaster Don Nguyen maintain his brand identity as he evolves his Vietnamese-inspired Texas barbecue pop-up into a Houston brick and mortar. He's also established aesthetics and created logos for a laundry list of businesses, including Convenience West, Brotherton's Black Iron Barbecue, Brett's Backyard BBQ, Camp Brisket (see page 175), and many more.

"We work together on identifying colors, iconography, creative concepts, and chart the best course for those unique aspects to shine," says Clark of his process. "Putting it simply, I create a unique toolbox, based on identified goals and story points, [for] them to use in all aspects of their business."

Visit a few barbecue joints across the state, and you'll quickly notice recurring elements like rustic wood, Western font, Texas flags, and license plates prominently displayed throughout the interiors. When designing, Clark aims to give each business its own distinct identity without leaning on overused Texas barbecue aesthetics.

"I mean, there's smoke, there's cattle, there's wood, there's the shape of Texas," he says. "There's a suitcase full of icons and ideas that *are* Texas, and the challenge is always trying to differentiate clients but also figure out new takes on old ideas."

But in each of his distinct projects, Clark's signature style shines through. He uses a carefully curated, punchy palate of contrasting colors, and finds inspiration in vintage typography and retro design motifs, which pair well with the craftsmanship of barbecue.

"A number of people told me that I can capture someone's story and make their business or their product unique, but it still fits within the quality of my design," he says. "I love old typography and letterpress type. And 'perfectly imperfect' is one of my mottos. I used to intentionally make things wonky just to make it not seem so clean-cut or streamlined and computerized. It even harkens back to typesetters having to pull blocks for each letter and putting them in the machine and hand-pulling it. None of us are perfect, so it speaks to humanity and hard work, and gives it personality."

Clark also supports businesses through transitions, whether it's a complete rebrand, a redesign, or refining an existing visual identity. He helped chef John Bates rebrand Noble Sandwich Company into InterStellar BBQ (see page 278), a modern Austin barbecue concept with a playful, intergalactic theme. When Bates started hosting Space Cowboy events—inviting pitmasters from all over to come collaborate with him at the restaurant—Clark designed and printed intricate posters for each one.

When pitmaster Andrew Castalan took the reins at Cattleack Barbeque (see page 30), Clark helped him with a brand refresh while maintaining important foundational elements. For example, the longhorn with pronged horns had become synonymous with the lauded restaurant, so Clark kept it, but streamlined its design and changed both the font and colors.

"I wanted to do justice to the previous chapter while refreshing the design and aesthetics," explains Clark. "I like to create stuff that can then become merch they can sell and be that billboard that people wear all over the world. Merch can tell your story when someone's not at your location. I've been able to help

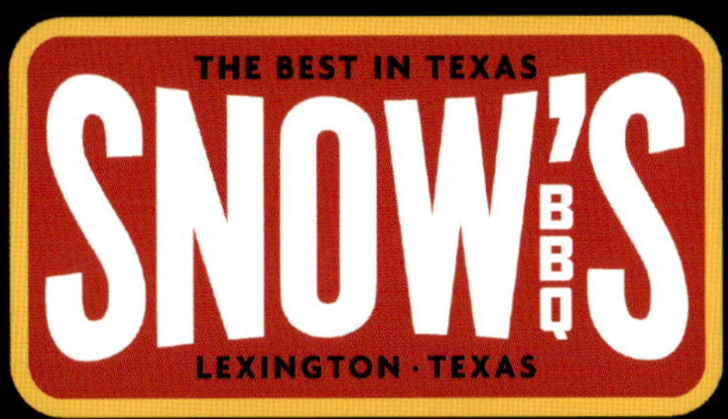

foster that idea with clients, let them know they need it and it needs to be unique and fit them."

In a commodity-based industry like barbecue, where business owners are at the mercy of rising meat costs, merchandise is a juicy opportunity to diversify revenue streams, boost online sales, and amplify brand loyalty. One business that has really seized this opportunity and thrived is Snow's BBQ (see page 308) in Lexington. The beloved barbecue joint is only open on Saturdays, and adding a robust inventory of merchandise has significantly increased their online sales for meat, sauce, and seasonings too.

Snow's owners Kerry and Kim Bexley even built a dedicated souvenir shop in the restaurant's backyard. After braving the epic line that forms outside Snow's before the sun rises, customers can commemorate their experience with branded T-shirts, sweatshirts, hats, koozies, and YETI tumblers designed by Clark. And not only do they all want photos with Kerry and nonagenarian pitmaster Tootsie Tomanetz, but they usually ask for signatures too.

"What I do now for barbecue is what I did 10 years ago for the music industry—making merch and show posters and gig posters, but for culinary, for barbecue," says Clark. "These guys are now the rock stars."

South Texas Style
EST. 2016
PIT SMOKED
BARBECUE
Low & Slow

EAKER BARBEQUE

FREDERICKSBURG

Fredericksburg is well-known for its Teutonic influence, and its Main Street has plenty of restaurants and breweries serving traditional German cuisine. Just past the town's main stretch of shops, you'll see a line winding its way down the sidewalk. Those folks aren't waiting for schnitzel or wurst, but rather Eaker Barbecue's spicy-sweet gochujang ribs and addictive kimchi fried rice.

Neither Lance nor Boo Eaker (pronounced "acre") ever imagined they would own a restaurant, much less a celebrated Hill Country barbecue joint. They were both settled into established careers and didn't even get into cooking until a little later in life. But once they discovered their shared passion for it, they saw the potential to turn it into a thriving business.

"I tend to get obsessed," admits Lance. "I've gone through this in a proper Texas route: homebrewing, guns, and golf were all previous passions. And then barbecue was the one that got me to quit my job."

While growing up in Uvalde, Lance says his dad would grill steaks every now and then, but barbecue was never a big focus in his family. However, his dad and brother owned a tree trimming company, so cords of wood were always stacked in their driveway.

"I guess I had more connection to the actual wood than the barbecue," says Lance. "My dad worked with mesquite, so that's what I know and appreciate."

Boo (short for Bookyung) grew up in Seoul, South Korea, where she was spoiled by her mom's delicious homemade food.

"My mom was an excellent cook," says Boo. "She wanted to go to cooking school but never had a chance because she was a stay-at-home mom. She had the best kimchi in the whole neighborhood, and she made housemade mayonnaise, peanut butter, dumplings—everything!"

However, despite Boo's interest in picking up those kitchen skills, her mom would insist she didn't need to learn yet. Boo remembers, "She would say, 'Oh, you have plenty of time to learn when you get married, and then you've got to cook for half of your life. Just enjoy what you have!'"

After going to school for graphic design and working as a visual merchandiser in Korea, Boo immigrated to San Antonio to study at the Juren Sullivan Center for Fashion Management at the University of the Incarnate Word. She intended to return home after graduation, but life had other plans for her. That's where she met Lance, who was an IT manager at the time.

"She'd just started cooking when we first started dating," remembers Lance. "She could cook three things: she could fry an egg, she could cook kimchi fried rice, and she could make ramen!"

After graduation, Boo received a job offer for a designer position with an upscale baby clothing company, so the couple relocated to Houston in 2003. It was there that Lance started grilling, almost as a default to his newfound roles of husband and father.

"I rented my first house, so I buy a grill," he narrates. "And then we buy a house, so I bought a smoker. I was like, 'Okay, I'm a Texan, I'm married, I've got kids, I've got to do this.'"

And that's where his obsession took hold. Lance used his $200 Char-Griller from Lowe's so often, he burned out the firebox, replaced it, and burned it out again with repeated attempts to perfect brisket and ribs using a blend of post oak and the mesquite he grew up around. His brother and father-in-law (who had moved with Boo's mother to Texas to help with child-care while the Eakers both worked full-time) were frequent taste testers and motivators, constantly encouraging Lance to make barbecue for a living.

"If I cooked a brisket today and it was like what I used to make, I would literally throw it in the trash," laughs Lance. "But the cheerleaders matter, right? You always need the friend that's brutally honest to guide you in the right direction, and you need the cheerleaders to keep you moving. So we had both of those to an extent."

After years of honing his pit skills, Lance established an LLC in 2016 and started to buy better equipment to work toward selling his barbecue publicly. In 2017, he began cooking three or four briskets at a time to sell at the local farmers market, and when Hurricane Harvey hit Houston, Lance was given a real opportunity to test his cooking skills on a large scale. When their neighborhood flooded, several of their neighbors lost their homes, and volunteer crews arrived to help clean up. Friends and colleagues started donating food, and Lance ended up smoking meat to feed over 300 people.

After that experience, the couple ordered a food truck and Lance put in notice at his job, as they planned to live off Boo's salary while getting the business up and running—but when she was unexpectedly laid off, they had no choice but to go all-in. Luckily, they'd already built up a following through the farmers market plus friends, family, neighbors, and their kids' school communities. When they launched the Eaker Barbecue food truck in 2018, they first dropped their anchor in a park near their house before relocating to the lot of a Jewish grocery store, and then rotated to busy bars like Truck Yard and Kirby Ice House.

At that point, word was really getting around about Eaker's supple Prime brisket, peppery dry rub ribs, tender pulled pork, and delicious sides. Boo, who started her real cooking journey as soon as they had kids, had developed dishes like an elevated version of Lance's mother's chunky mayo-mustard potato salad with dill and hard-boiled egg, and a rich, fluffy creamed corn based on one they loved from Rudy's Bar-B-Q. She also started gaining a following for the desserts she added to the menu, like sea salt chocolate chip cookies and melt-in-your-mouth lemon cookies dusted with confectioners' sugar.

When they were invited to participate in The Throwdown, a Houston barbecue festival known for its culinary ingenuity, Lance and Boo brainstormed upon a new, creative dish they could offer. Eventually, they saw that they only needed to turn to the way they eat at home, where leftover barbecue often finds its way into rice and ramen, and kimchi is a daily staple. So they featured a kimchi fried rice with brisket and sunny-side-up quail eggs, and found huge success. The next February, in 2019, they were invited to participate in Super Beef Sunday, an annual Super Bowl Sunday barbecue event held at St. Arnold Brewing Company. This time, Lance was inspired by his brother-in-law to develop gochujang pork ribs. The Korean chili paste is traditionally used on ribs as a mop while grilling, but Lance instead marinates the ribs in gochujang, smokes them, cuts them, then brushes them with more sauce, and torches them to caramelization for added texture and flavor. A sprinkle of green onion and sesame seeds completes the dish, which was an immediate hit.

By popular demand, gochujang ribs replaced the regular ribs on Eaker Barbecue's food truck menu, and kimchi fried rice became a regular offering as well. With these additions, Eaker Barbecue was getting

plenty of attention from local publications, and landing on "Best of" lists for Houston food trucks.

But running a food truck is no easy feat, and especially not during the excruciatingly hot summer months.

"Outwardly, we were very successful," says Lance. "But we were running a protein-heavy food truck. To make the same money as a traditional food truck, we'd have to do three to four times the revenue because the profitability is not the same."

They started to weigh other options, including the many opportunities that were starting to come their way. They were approached by three or four food halls, and almost signed on with one of them.

"We were to the point of sitting with an attorney and redlining the contract, and something didn't feel right, so we backed out," remembers Lance. "And then a month later, COVID happened and they were shut down."

During that time, Boo, Lance, and their children decided to get out of the city for a respite in the Hill Country. While staying in Hunt, located about 45 minutes from Fredericksburg, they watched the sunset darken into a sky full of twinkling stars. Boo, who never thought she'd live outside of a big city, looked up and said "I feel 10 pounds lighter. I could totally live here." That was all Lance, who'd always dreamed of ranch life, needed to hear. *Houston Chronicle* barbecue editor J. C. Reid suggested they look into finding a place in Fredericksburg, which attracts a steady stream of visitors but lacked high-quality barbecue. An overdue visit to the town sealed the deal and they started seeking out a space.

The spot the Eakers landed on previously housed a sandwich shop, which had closed during the pandemic. They signed a two-year lease and were even able to secure $50,000 in grants, which greatly helped with the build-out of the restaurant. Now, Lance is using two Cen-Tex offset smokers (one named Ms. Lucky and another named Faith), plus another smoker and live-fire table on a trailer named after their fathers, Harold and Sensei Woo, both hard workers who inspired them.

"And so the idea was that, with a whole lot of faith, a little bit of luck, and a whole lot of hard work, maybe we'll be successful!" says Lance.

Cooking on a 1,000-gallon offset for the first time, Lance found he had to make some adjustments to his methods. He used to fuel his old smoker with two-thirds mesquite and one-third post oak, but found it wasn't necessary to take the edge off the mesquite when using a bigger pit. In fact, he started rubbing his meat with Diamond Crystal kosher salt and a chunkier 14-mesh black pepper, which helps to capture the mesquite smoke even more.

"When you're cooking on a very small pit, you have a heavy smoke concentration in the chamber," he

explains. "So it's very easy to not have a clean fire with mesquite and then it gets super bitter. . . . In one of these (big pits), your meat-to-space ratio is vastly different, so you have more expanse for that smoke to distribute, and you're not going to get as much smoke on the meat. So running a bigger smoker and running good seasoned mesquite, you don't have that bitter problem. It has a better flavor—it reminds me of growing up and it's a differentiator. Everybody's got brisket dialed in and it starts to taste the same. But I like a little more flavor to it."

His pork ribs and pork butt (which becomes pulled pork) are rubbed with almost the same blend of salt, pepper, garlic, onion, paprika, and chili powder, and his turkey gets a simple rub of pepper and olive oil, which Lance says helps keep it moist while giving it good color when it smokes. As for sausage, the Eakers had taken a class with Bill Dumas, the Sausage Sensei (see page 431) years prior, but couldn't find the time or space to develop the program while running the food trailer. In their restaurant, they make several kinds of sausage using brisket and pork shoulder trimmings: Hill Country sausage inspired by the meat markets of Central Texas, jalapeño and cheddar, brisket boudin, and Hatch chile queso.

Boo was also able to really expand the sides offered in the new space, developing a super-rich baked macaroni and cheese (made with Gruyère, mozzarella, and cheddar), borracho beans simmered with Shiner Bock, and a banchan-inspired Korean cucumber salad made fragrant with fish sauce and showered with sesame seeds. Kimchi is also a daily offering, and Boo makes around 100 pounds of it a month using her mom's recipe—napa cabbage fermented for several weeks with gochugaru, fish sauce, and pre-fermented shrimp. Originally, they were making kimchi just for the kimchi fried rice, but customers started requesting it by the quart, so now they offer it as a side too.

"In Korea, you always have kimchi on your table," says Boo. "And it has probiotics, which is good for your gut, so it is naturally great with barbecue. That's what it's intended for—to help you digest fatty foods."

Lance says about 70 percent of Eaker Barbecue's business is local, but on the weekend that percentage flips due to the influx of visitors. So they run both weekday and weekend specials to keep their regulars coming back for more. They've featured japchae, Korean fried chicken sandwiches, Korean fried rib bowls, and a Korean Philly cheesesteak topped with provolone, sauteed onions, and kimchi. They also serve sticky, sweet pork belly burnt ends enhanced with different sauces each week: gochujang, hot honey, peach bourbon, raspberry chipotle, and jalapeño, to name a few.

Boo continues to make her best-selling cookies, but she's sweetened the menu with a few other desserts too. She developed a pecan pie bar—with a cookie-like crust plus more nuts and less sugary goo than one would expect in a traditional pecan pie. Inspired by Misty Roegels's banana pudding at Roegels BBQ Co. (see page 220), Boo developed a Boo-zy Banana Pudding (with Misty's blessings), laced with bourbon and topped with bourbon-caramelized banana slices.

Just four months after opening in Fredericksburg, Eaker Barbecue was named a Top 50 barbecue joint by *Texas Monthly*, a distinction which doubled their revenue and acted as great advertisement for the new restaurant. And when you visit Eaker, it's always a family affair at the buzzing joint: Boo and Lance's 15-year-old son Brandon helps out behind the counter, and 11-year-old Bradley puts on gloves and assumes the role of "Bun Boy," toasting buns to order.

Next, the Eakers have set their sights on the space next door, which they are going to develop into an outpost with a takeout line for locals who call in pre-orders, a cold case for vacuum-sealed meats, and a shop with spices and rubs and housemade breakfast items (kolaches, koblasnik, breakfast tacos, and sweet pastries). Lance has also been perfecting his coffee game, and is developing an espresso program he'll offer next door too.

"I went from a $400 cheapo espresso machine to a $1,600 one," he says. "And then went from a $30 grinder to a $400 grinder. It's my latest obsession."

COOPER'S OLD TIME PIT BAR-B-QUE

LLANO

If the aroma of smoke isn't enough of a siren's call to Cooper's Old Time Pit Bar-B-Que, you can't miss the restaurant as you're driving through Llano. The long, brick-red building contrasts the blue sky, and a white aluminum sign announces its name in large, Western-style font. Another sign teases "Home of the Big Chop," and a smaller one, next to the door leading inside, reads, "Place All Meat Orders at Pit."

At Cooper's, they do things differently than most other Texas barbecue joints. Guests line up against the wall, then come right up to a holding pit and point to their proteins of choice, which are sliced to order and added to a tray. And that's the way they've been doing it since 1953, when a rancher named George Cooper opened the first location in Mason, Texas.

After nearly a decade of success there, George's son Tommy brought a location of Cooper's to Llano in 1962. Current owner Terry Wooten worked there in high school, running the pits alongside Tommy's son Barry as Cooper's became a cornerstone of the Llano community, with a good number of regulars who ate there multiple times a week, if not daily.

Then, Tommy was tragically killed in a truck accident in 1979. Kenneth Laird, another former Cooper's pit hand, took over the lease until he moved to the other side of town to open his own spot in 1986 (Laird's BBQ, which closed in 2018).

In the early '80s, Terry Wooten was running a successful real estate brokerage in a booming economy. But by the mid-1980s, the market for Hill Country ranches had slowed and he was in need of supplemental income to support his wife and two children. When the restaurant came up for lease in 1986, he took a leap of faith and decided to take over operations. He got the keys to the empty building the night before Labor Day and managed to stock inventory and prep enough food to get up and running the very next day.

Terry brushed up on his barbecue skills and brought on three friends and his family to help run the restaurant. His wife, Karen, worked the cash register, while their sons Jason and Chad (who were 11 and 16 at the time) started working both front and back of house. Barry, who had worked alongside Terry at the original Cooper's, returned from college to help out as well.

"I can remember washing dishes at 11 and 12 years old," says Jason. "I saved up my money and bought my first car from all that when I was 14 because I wanted to work on a car and fix it up!"

About a year in, Terry hired his first full-time employee, Gaudencio Vences, who went on to become his pitmaster for the next 12 years. Karen and Terry worked at the restaurant from open to close for seven years, every single day but Christmas, and, all the while, Terry continued to run his real estate business. (He even put a trailer in the parking lot so he could throw off his apron and meet clients in his makeshift office!) Jason left Llano to get a degree in Restaurant Hotel Institutional Management from Texas Tech, then returned to help his dad run the business. As the barbecue business continued to thrive, Terry continued to expand the space and fine-tune operations—but he never changed the unique cooking processes for which Cooper's is known.

Central Texas barbecue joints are known for using the Czech-German method of cooking meats low and slow in an offset smoker using post oak, which penetrates the protein with its gently smoky flavor. But Cooper's resides in the Hill Country, just to the west of Central Texas, and they have always cooked over direct heat, using mesquite, which grows best in the region's soil. This style of cooking, also known as "cowboy cooking," was born out of necessity and formulated by cowboys, who used wood from wild mesquite trees to cook at their camps while on cattle drives.

"We cook a little bit hotter and a little bit faster than your offset does," explains Jason. "We get our flavor from the meat dripping down, hitting the coal, and making that smoke when we're cooking. There's still a lot of smoke involved, but it's not wood smoke wafting through the pit."

For years, the Wootens employed a crew to cut down and process mesquite wood, burning it down in large steel chambers. Someone with a long-handled shovel would then transport the coals to the bottom of their smokers and spread them out evenly below the cooking rack. They also started incorporating custom-made rotisserie smokers that featured a special drawer for loading lit charcoal. But as the business continued to grow, they found it was becoming impossible to keep up with harvesting their own wood, so they began to source organic mesquite lump charcoal from Mexico instead. It weighs just 25 percent of what it would weigh in wood form, so 10 bags equals a whole pallet of wood, making it a much more efficient process.

"People in Llano don't cut oak trees down," says Jason. "You just don't do that! It's so pretty out here in the Hill Country, so everybody likes to protect our scenery. But [mesquite] is what we would use, even if we did have a different choice. Because we like how hot it burns and the coal that it makes."

Brisket cooked over direct heat, for example, can be done in as little as five hours (as opposed to the 10 to 12 it averages when smoked with indirect heat). When used this way, mesquite smoke adds a slight sweetness to the meat, but it doesn't give it the more prominent smoke flavor that some barbecue purists may seek. At Cooper's they sear their briskets first to seal in moisture, and then cook the meat slow enough to yield a tender, moist interior. However, you won't find the smoke rings and butter-soft rendered fat created by extended smoking with cooler, indirect heat.

Cooper's has a wide array of meat offerings, and everything is seasoned with the same spice blend ("Salt, pepper, and various spices is all I can say," Jason offers). In addition to the brisket, snappy pork-and-beef ring sausage, moist, flavorful turkey, and pork loin, there's also generously seasoned whole and half chickens, juicy slabs of prime rib, and sliced sirloin that is flame-kissed on the outside while medium-rare on the inside. Both the pork and the beef ribs (which are chuck short ribs, smaller than the massive beef ribs found at most barbecue spots) are also crisped on the exterior, with a good amount of chew: perfectly tender but not falling off the bone.

Cooper's is also known for a few unique items. One is cabrito, or goat, which is very rare to see in any Texas barbecue joint—especially one in the Hill Country. Cooper's cooks the whole goat, cut into pieces, on the pit and it results in a tender and sweet, not gamy, meat. Tommy had introduced a 2-inch-thick, bone-in pork chop, but it became well-known when Terry started advertising it in 1992 (inspired by Burger King's "Home of the Whopper" campaign), by adding the big "Home of the Big Chop" sign outside. Now, visitors travel from near and far for the thick, juicy chop, easily the most famous cut they offer. And around a decade ago, Cooper's started featuring whole sirloin steaks each Thursday through Saturday. The steak night special comes with a potato (which is also seasoned and smoked on the pit) and another side.

One benefit of ordering right at the pit (beyond getting a visual to help narrow down your selection) is getting to let the cutter know how thick you want your slices. If you want sauce, they'll dip your meat directly in a pot of thin, vinegar and tomato–based sauce kept in a pot on the pit. Unlike thicker, bolder barbecue sauces, this one is meant to complement without overpowering.

Though tradition plays a big role at Cooper's, the family also isn't afraid to innovate. In 2008, the company began franchising, starting with a location in New Braunfels, which Terry and Jason oversee. Fort Worth was next, in 2010, and Barry runs that one. An Austin location opened in 2016, also run by Terry and Jason, and Jason's brother Chad operates the College Station location, opened in 2019.

And, for anyone wondering—the original Cooper's opened by George Cooper still stands in Mason, but it's been under different ownership for years.

There are different pitmasters at each location running the same style of open, flat pits. Once you're handed a tray with all your meat selections wrapped in brown butcher paper, you'll head inside to pick out sides and desserts. Karen created the recipes for the original sides—just coleslaw, potato salad, and beans—back in 1986 when the Wootens first took over the lease. Before that, only chips and pickles were offered alongside the barbecue. The coleslaw is creamy and classic, while the potatoes are whipped into a tangy cloud, and Cooper's peppery and mildly chili-spiced pinto beans are a fan favorite, available for the taking in a pot in the corner (alongside the pickles, onions, sliced white bread, and another pot of barbecue sauce).

The indulgent mac and cheese (as well as a jazzed-up, bacon-and-jalapeño version) was developed about a decade ago by Jason and team, followed by smoky bacon-boosted green beans. All of these sides are ordered in a cafeteria-style line, and there are also extras like rounds of cheese and creamy horseradish sauce (essential for the prime rib, and also delicious on the sirloin). Dessert offerings include cobbler (choose from peach, blackberry, apple, or pecan and make it à la mode with a scoop of Blue Bell vanilla ice cream) and banana pudding, which was developed just a few years ago by Chad's wife, Darla, and is made with Mexican vanilla and fresh bananas.

Once your proteins have been weighed and you settle up for your meal, find a seat in the dining area, where picnic tables with brown peeling paint are lined up, mess hall–style, while a row of mounted deer look on. Each table is set up with a roll of paper towels, a bucket of whole pickled jalapeños, salt, pepper, and condiments. You'll open up each packet of meat and dump them on a piece of white butcher paper, which turns your tray into a plate.

"Well, you definitely don't come for the atmosphere, do ya?" says a woman across from me visiting from

South Dakota with her husband. With Cooper's widespread notoriety, this community-style seating format means you end up sitting with people from all over the globe. The Midwesterners marveled at the meats and asked me questions about Texas barbecue, since they'd be in the area working remotely for a period of time. I explained why Cooper's is special, with its unique style of direct heat pits, and gave them some recommendations for Central Texas–style barbecue too.

Before leaving, I stop once more to observe the outdoor pit area, a true sight to behold: six flat brick pits with counterweight pulley systems stand like monuments, with silky smoke seeping out from under closed steel lids and up out of smokestacks. These workhorses have been going for over seven decades, and have even fed a couple of presidents (Lyndon B. Johnson and George W. Bush).

I also couldn't help but notice the office next door: Terry Wooten Real Estate. When I followed up with Jason, I asked if Terry (now in his 70s) is still doing real estate.

"Oh, yes," says Jason. "He's kind of like that Toby Keith song, 'Don't Let the Old Man In.' That reminds me of my dad because he just keeps going and he's a busybody! He might be out at the pit one day or you might be working with his horses the next day and doing real estate the next. That man will do anything to stay busy!"

MILLER'S SMOKEHOUSE

BELTON

Dirk Miller had been running Bang & Bow Taxidermy and Deer Processing in Belton for four years when his son Dusty, recalling the sticky chicken and country-style ribs his father used to cook on hunting and camping trips, suggested they start a little restaurant in the front of the shop to utilize their sausage-making equipment during the offseason. That's how this Texas fairy tale begins.

Never once did the Millers let their lack of restaurant experience get in the way of this vision. They settled on the name Miller's Smokehouse and Dusty, who was a freshman in college in 2008, took $1,000 saved from a valet parking job and headed to Sam's Club to get some start-up supplies. Father and son began selling sausage wraps and pulled pork sandwiches out of the taxidermy shop, mainly relying on friends and family, who became supportive customers. Then they decided to step things up by borrowing a smoker from a friend, which they used to smoke one brisket a day.

"There have been so many amazing people who have come into our lives and left the business better than they found it," says Dusty, "There has also been a whole lot of, 'Let's try it!' Never being scared to try something new and always being open-minded to better ways of doing something is important."

Next, the father-son team bartered taxidermy work to buy their first offset pit—and their second—then they built upright pits out of 55-gallon steel drums, which they used to smoke sausage and chicken in the alleyway. Pretty soon, they were selling more smoked meat than taxidermy or deer processing services.

In 2011, Dusty had just graduated from Baylor with a degree in accounting and began digging deeper into the finances of the smokehouse. They decided it was time to turn their barbecue hobby into a real business by modifying their portions and pricing, expanding their hours, and turning the former deer processing shop into additional dining and kitchen space (which required relocating the taxidermy business to a nearby building).

By 2012, Miller's Smokehouse had really gained momentum. Dirk had become known not only for his Certified Angus Prime brisket, with its buttery rendered fat and thick, sturdy bark, but also for his peppery pork ribs and different variations of housemade beef and pork sausage (known as Miller's Grillers). The Millers primarily smoke with live oak, due to its local availability, and they mix in post oak too.

"We love post oak—it burns well and puts off a great sweet flavor—while live oak has a generally stronger flavor," explains Dusty. "They both cook the meat the same way, and keeping a clean fire and sourcing well-seasoned wood are the more important variables in our process."

Meanwhile, Dirk's wife, Lisa (known to everyone as "Momma") Miller, began baking for the restaurant while still working full-time in a real estate developer's office. Lisa had learned to bake from her grandmother, and Dusty remembers a childhood filled with the baked goods she crafted for him and his siblings, Dylan and Samantha.

"Grandma Grier was a very talented Southern baker," recalls Lisa. "She could cook anything—biscuits, ham, sweet potato pie. And she was a pound cake queen! She had already passed away by the time we got going on Miller's. She never saw any of this and she would've loved this. She would've been in the kitchen cooking with us. But this way I get to share a piece of her with the people who come in and eat."

Lisa makes her grandmother's pound cake for the restaurant, which she serves with whipped cream and strawberries. She also makes a chocolate version, which she frosts with a fudge icing to create her Chocolate Pudding Cake. Once Lisa established a bake shop, Miller's developed an even larger fan base for her cloud-like cinnamon rolls, decadent sopaipilla cheesecake pie, and oatmeal cream pies, along with a roster of rotating seasonal pies from coconut cream to key lime. As they began to accumulate more ovens and mixers, Lisa began making all their potato rolls, and then flour tortillas. Even the vanilla wafers in the banana pudding are homemade.

"And all of these things are things I had no idea how to make until Dusty had the idea we should start making them from scratch," says Lisa. "We just learned through trial and error and dumping out lots of batches to get it right. We also do a test kitchen altogether in the bakery as a team. The piecrust we use now is the third version. We're always trying to make things better, so if someone comes in and has better ideas, we try them."

They use the same method on the savory side of the kitchen. Whenever a new menu item is up for consideration, the culinary team comes together to taste, fill out feedback forms, and evaluate. They won't move forward with an item until everyone is on the same page. When they first launched, they started with the two most essential sides: beans and potato salad. They then went on to add homestyle offerings like green beans, buttered potatoes, and macaroni and cheese, plus lighter, more refreshing items like a crunchy coleslaw and broccoli salad made with raisins, almonds, and crisp bacon. They also developed a chicken salad using their smoked half-chickens, which are rubbed with their house all-purpose blend of salt, pepper, garlic, onion, paprika, celery, and turmeric.

"We strongly feel that a special part of what we do is working as a collaborative group to put out the best product that we can," says Dusty.

When Miller's landed on *Texas Monthly*'s Top 50 list in 2013, they expanded into the building next door, turning it into a prep kitchen and a bakery for Momma Miller, who was able to quit her day job to manage the Miller's Smokehouse bakery full-time. In the last decade, the business has just continued to evolve, and Dirk's barbecue program grew to require five 1,000-gallon offset smokers. In 2016, they moved from their 1,600-square-foot space to a 7,000-square-foot space down the street. In 2018, another passion became a successful business, as they added a coffee bar to Miller's Smokehouse.

"It started as a hobby and caffeine addiction, then we realized how well it paired with the smokehouse offerings, and now it's a full-blown business of its own," explains Dusty.

Soon after the coffee bar opened, Dusty began importing beans from all over the world (Guatemala, Costa Rica, Brazil, Ethiopia, and beyond) and the coffee team started to roast them in the warehouse that housed the deer processing business (which they shut down completely in 2017). Dusty opened a coffee shop in Salado (there are more to come), and named it Muscovy Coffee Roasters after the ducks that live in downtown Belton on the banks of the Nolan River.

"They are rough-looking birds who embody underdog mentality," explains Dusty. "With the spirit of the tough little duck from under the bridge, we want to grow the coffee company. The duck also serves as a reminder of where we come from, our little community, which we are quite fond of. Humble, but strong."

Miller's bake shop makes a whole line of goods just for Muscovy Coffee Roasters, like kolaches and taquitos stuffed with their barbecued meats, biscuit pinwheels, pop tarts, cake pops, and quick breads. Miller's also incorporates elements of coffee throughout the restaurant, from the barbecue sauce and bacon to the rib brine and Momma Miller's desserts. They even grind beans fresh daily and mix the grounds with salt, pepper, and garlic to make their brisket rub.

"Coffee plays a huge role in fueling us throughout the day, but it also allows us to add a unique touch to what we do culinarily," says Dusty.

Now a coffee shop and barbecue joint, the next logical step was to develop a breakfast menu. Miller's features breakfast tacos, bowls, and sandwiches—with cornbread and biscuits made in-house—plus signature items like Ribs & Cakes (bacon ribs served over hotcakes and drizzled with maple syrup), cinnamon roll pancakes, hotlink hash, and more.

But right when they launched this new menu, the pandemic arrived. No strangers to adaptation, Miller's pivoted to become a take-out restaurant and grocery store with curbside pickup during the pandemic. You can still order many of the same items on their website for easy pickup: their juicy brined smoked turkey and chickens, whole racks of St. Louis–style ribs, whole briskets, housemade Wakin' Bacon, quarts of beef tallow, Momma's cornbread and buttermilk biscuits, bags of Muscovy coffee, and bottles of both their original (sweet and thickened with molasses) and tangy (brightened with mustard and apple cider vinegar) sauces.

The smokehouse, now busier than ever, replaced their offset smokers with rotisserie smokers from M&M BBQ Company (see page 76), which have allowed them to increase their production while maintaining quality.

"Our wood consumption has gone down drastically, we are putting out our most consistent product, and we are getting to cook new items due to the efficiency of these pits," says Dusty. "Sometimes, it feels like you do the same thing every day, but it's always different, and it's so important to strive for consistency in product and service."

These days, Miller's employs over 100 employees, with 10 on Lisa's bakery team. ("We're open seven days a week, so it takes a lot of little bodies to keep things a-goin'!" she says). Dirk has moved out of the pit room into the kitchen, while Bradley Knight and Arturo Miranda lead the pit team, and Dusty oversees finances and management for both Miller's Smokehouse and Muscovy Coffee Roasters. Dusty emphasizes that it's the partnership and collaboration of the whole team that has made their growth possible.

"A service-oriented business really relies on people truly caring about their team in order to work well together," he says. "This business has brought so many sacred relationships into our lives, and we have really learned the importance of people being on individual journeys of self-improvement in order to come together as a successful team."

"It's about just locking arms and having each other's backs—both your family and your employees," adds Lisa. "And it's important to always keep that underdog mentally. It doesn't matter if you're in the Top 50 or not—it can always go away. You have to always keep striving to be better."

Beyond her baking expertise, Lisa says her grandmother, a widow who would open her home to feed the other widowers from her church, was also a huge influence in the way she perceives hospitality.

"She showed me what hospitality really means," Lisa says. "We always want people to feel welcome—not just come in and eat but come to a place where people know who they are and love them and want them here. That's the difference between playing restaurant and hospitality."

SOUTHSIDE MARKET & BARBEQUE

ELGIN, BASTROP, AUSTIN & HUTTO

Texas barbecue history can get a bit convoluted. Some of the state's pioneering barbecue joints have experienced several changes in ownership, location, and business name, making exact origin stories difficult to trace. Lack of early documentation and a few famous family feuds have added to the complexity. But based on anecdotal evidence and extensive research, Southside Market & Barbeque is widely regarded as the oldest barbecue operation in the state.

In 1882, William Moon started raising and slaughtering cattle on his 88-acre homestead in Elgin. He carried the fresh beef to town by horse-drawn wagon and sold it door-to-door, trying to off-load it before it spoiled. Then in 1886, the itinerant butcher opened his first brick-and-mortar meat market on Central Avenue in Elgin, where he sold barbecue out of the back as a means of preserving the cuts that didn't sell.

The earliest documentation of the name Southside Market is found in a local paper printed in 1918. And over the next number of decades, Southside went through many changes of ownership, with little to no records on file. (It is said that the business would often change hands after a late-night poker game.) Much of that lore was passed down through word of mouth by butcher Bud Frazier, a colorful character who worked at Southside from 1895 to 1971.

Bryan and Rachel Bracewell are the seventh (documented) owners of the business, taking over from Bryan's grandparents Ernest and Adrene Bracewell. Ernest was a San Antonio–based meat salesman who transferred to Austin in 1966, and Southside Market (located just under 25 miles east of Austin) was one of his accounts. Ernest got to know the owners (Jerry and Edwin Stach) and bought it—as well as Moon's original slaughterhouse—from them in 1968.

"Back in the old days, I grew up riding in the truck with my grandfather to go get the cattle," remembers Bryan. "On Mondays, we would go to the feedlot, get a trailer load of cattle—calves, steers, and heifers—bring them back. Tuesday morning was slaughter day, and then that was the meat for the week in the butcher shop."

When Ernest took the reins, Frazier was crafting sausages they called "hot guts" using ground beef trimmings, beef tallow, salt, pepper, and cayenne pepper stuffed into pig intestines (the "guts"). No actual recipe existed—Frazier just eyeballed the ratios as he had done for so many years before—so Ernest observed him for a couple of months to standardize the recipe, which is still used to this day.

"What we believe is that we're making the same sausage now that was made back then," says Bryan. "Back in those days, [they were] called hot guts, even though 'hot off the pit' is what they were talking about. It wasn't real spicy, but it was a little bit spicier than it is now. My grandfather took some of that cayenne pepper out of the sausage, and put it into the hot sauce on the tables. And he did that because, when he bought Southside, it was not a real family environment. He felt like he needed to clean it up and knock off the rough edges, and one of the things he did was bring down the spice level in the sausage so it was welcoming to the whole family and not just Papa."

That was just one of many changes made by Ernest during a period of great transition. Back in those days, "barbecue" was the generic term for all of the scraps that hadn't sold in the market—that is, until the 1970s, when Ernest switched to using boxed meat by the cuts. During that same period, Adrene developed a tomato-based barbecue sauce.

Southside remained in its original downtown location for 24 years, but by 1992, it had outgrown its space and the lack of parking had become problematic, so Ernest purchased the old Security National Bank on Highway 290 and relocated the business with the help of his son, Ernest Bracewell Jr. With the new building came new flat offset pits, made by a local builder using white bricks, as well as a wood-fired Oyler rotisserie smoker.

"The rotisserie gives us the opportunity to cook overnight," says Bryan. "There's anywhere from six to eight hours where those pits are by themselves. We load up the firebox with wood and it's got an internal damper system where it'll maintain the internal temperature in the pit. And so there's a little bit of cheating there, I guess, but it allows us to go home and sleep."

Meat at Southside is smoked in the Central Texas tradition: using only salt and pepper as a seasoning and post oak for the smoke. Brisket, ribs, and chicken are cooked on the rotisserie pit, while sausage, lamb ribs, and pork steaks are cooked on the brick pits.

"Our more experienced pitmasters use the brick pits, because there's no thermometers or gauges," says Bryan. "You don't have an internal damper system there—the amount of wood you throw on it is how hot your pit is going to be. And there are spots on the pit that are hotter than others. And so, it's more labor intensive, knowing how to manipulate the pit and the wood and fire to make all that work for you."

Pickles, onions, pickled jalapeños, cheddar cheese, and crackers were the only semblance of sides at the original location, so that is another big change Ernest and Adrene made once they had a kitchen in the new location. Adrene developed a recipe for creamy, mayo-based potato salad and, thanks in part to her upbringing in South Texas, had already perfected a peppery, slow-cooked pinto bean recipe, and they served these at caterings before bringing them onto the restaurant menu.

"Grandpa cared about those more than anybody else," remembers Bryan. "He was the patrolman on overseeing the pinto beans."

Bryan began working at Southside when he was 12, just as his own father had. He remembers earning a wage of $3.75 an hour for bussing tables, sweeping the sawdust-sprinkled floors, and gathering up crates of returnable glass soda bottles before moving up to working the line, and graduated to the pits by the time he was 14. Bryan says he never questioned pursuing barbecue; it was simply the path he was destined to follow.

"I never remember making the decision that that's what I was going to do," says Bryan. "It was just part of who I was and part of growing up in a small town. If Grandpa would have been a fireman and I grew up in the fire station, maybe I'd be a fireman today."

As he neared the end of high school, Bryan chose his college based on where he could advance his knowledge of meat, enrolling at Texas A&M University in College Station.

"Back then, they didn't have a Meat Science degree like they do now, so I took my degree in Food, Science, and Technology, and I just took every meat class that I could," says Bryan. "I worked at the Meat Science Center as a student worker, I was on the meat judging team, and I basically just hung around all that stuff as much as I could. Growing up in a small-town family business, a lot of times you just do what you're told and you don't ask questions. It wasn't invited to ask questions. I went to Texas A&M to learn why we were doing what we were doing, the science behind all that, and whether what we were doing was right or wrong. So most of the training that helped me really understand the meat industry came from that time at Texas A&M, and I was able to craft my classes based on what I knew was waiting on me back home."

Bryan returned from college, filled with ideas and ready to implement change based on his newfound knowledge—but soon learned that the elder Bracewell might not be too keen on immediate changes.

"I quickly realized that change for the sake of change wasn't going to happen just because I had the idea, just because I learned something," recalls Bryan. "And I think there's some wisdom in that. So what I learned was I had to prove it up. If I ever wanted to implement a change, I had to do my own research and development and then bring the results to my grandfather. To his credit, he was always very hands-on—'Show me, let me see, let me taste it.' And he wanted to know the numbers. So as long as I had the numbers in my hip pocket—on the spreadsheet or written down—and I could prove to him why this was a better decision from a quality standpoint or from a cost standpoint—he may not [have] always liked it, but he never told me, 'No, you can't.' He did give me guardrails that I had to work within."

Ernest and Adrene worked until they were 80 before passing the torch to Bryan and Rachel in 2010. While plenty of historic barbecue joints in Texas pride themselves on not changing a thing, Bryan says just about everything has changed at Southside—besides the recipes.

"We've been around for 143 years, and this business is ever evolving," says Bryan. "We've got more technology, better equipment. The way we cook the brisket, how long we cook them, the doneness to which we cook them to, how we cut them. And it wasn't one change, it was small tweaks over time. And we've always tried to just change one variable at a time, instead of changing too much. So, when it hasn't worked out, we can go back."

Bryan decided to start expanding the business, starting with a second location in Bastrop. He says it took five years to get their stride before he felt comfortable opening an Austin location. And then he broke ground on a fourth location in Hutto right before the pandemic and opened that one in October 2020. But before all of this expansion, Bryan developed a plan to do so without sacrificing the integrity of the original.

"My biggest fear at the time was to have somebody say, 'Well, it was a pretty good barbecue joint when the old man had it, but when the young kid took over, it just went downhill,'" he says. "And so my goal in life was to make sure that opening a second restaurant helped us have better quality at both spots. It took us some time to figure that out, and I believe that that ultimately did happen. We're better in Elgin, because we didn't want to be bad in Bastrop."

In order to maintain consistency, a lot of the prep work still takes place at the original Southside. Briskets are trimmed in Elgin, and then that trim goes into the sausages, which are made in the on-site USDA-inspected plant (Bryan secured that federal certification in 2002 in order to be able ship smoked meats beyond state lines). Using a massive kettle, all the beans are stewed, sauce is simmered, and potatoes are cooked in Elgin too. All the pits are the same at each restaurant so cooks can go to any location and find familiar cooking processes.

While most barbecue operations that started out as meat markets eventually eliminated the market to focus on restaurant operations, Southside has maintained its meat market tradition and carried it on in each of its four locations, using the same zero-waste mentality that brought about smoked meats to begin with.

"We don't compete with big-box grocery stores," says Bryan. "We don't have chucks and rump roasts or hamburger meat, but we carry everything that we have on the barbecue menu. Whatever it is, it sits in the butcher case for one day. Then it gets seasoned and we try to sell it the next day. If it doesn't sell, it goes on the barbecue pit."

One of Southside's top-selling items, the Sausage Slammer, was born of the meat market. When pan sausage took a dive in sales, the butcher at the time (named Hank) came up with a new way to present it. He stuffed a fresh, deseeded jalapeño with cheddar cheese, wrapped it with pan sausage and then wrapped the whole package in bacon. Now they make pan sausage just for the Slammers, which are sold hot in the restaurant, ready-to-cook in the market, and are also distributed by H-E-B.

One unique Southside offering held over from the old days is lamb ribs. Bryan says goat and lamb were much more common back in the restaurant's early days. They dipped down in popularity but never got taken off the menu, and now they're seeing a resurgence.

"We're selling more lamb ribs now than we did at any point in my career here," says Bryan. "So I think that's kind of a cool story—that we were just too stubborn to get rid of it and now it's coming back."

While all of these successes speak to the business acumen of the Bracewell family, there are, of course, factors that cannot be controlled. These days, Bryan is up against the continuously rising prices of meat.

"What's worried me the most is that barbecue [used to be an] everyday meal for the everyman—cheaper cuts of meat that you could get a good value on and didn't break the bank," he says. "We had folks that would come in and eat three or four or five days a week. But over the past 15 years, the price of meat has just really gone crazy. That's really changed the dynamics, and I worry about our customer base. We've already had to adjust our cooking styles or customer service or hospitality to stay relevant to a

new generation, and I see that working. But we've had to be very intentional to stay relevant as an old-time barbecue joint."

There might not be sawdust on the floors anymore, but the limestone columns and wood-paneled walls hung with mounted bucks harken back to a much more rustic version of Elgin. Large framed black-and-white photos of the Bracewell family document the Southside's early days along the walls while customers of all different ages share trays of smoked meat at long wooden tables.

"One advantage that I believe we have is we've got guests that have been coming to us for generations," says Bryan, who goes on to describe a card he keeps on his desk from a customer who came into Southside with his grandparents and now brings his own grandchildren in. "There's five generations of people. And that's pretty darn cool, I think. But it's also a tremendous responsibility—to do things right and to keep it close enough to the same where it doesn't alarm anybody. Because, in their mind, that's their family's barbecue joint—it's not mine."

OPEN EVERYDAY
BLACK'S BARBECUE
GIANT BEEF RIBS!

THE ORIGINAL
BLACK'S
BARBECUE
OPEN 10 AM
EXIT
OPEN 8 DAYS A WE
OPEN 10 AM
BLACK'S BBQ
88 years!

THE ORIGINAL BLACK'S BARBECUE

LOCKHART, NEW BRAUNFELS, AUSTIN & SAN MARCOS

When you visit the original Black's Barbecue in Lockhart, be sure to take special note of the cutting blocks used to slice meat behind the counter. The oak slabs have cut so many thousands of pounds of meat over the years, they need to be rotated and sanded down annually. And about every 30 years, these barbecue heirlooms need replacing.

Black's Barbecue, like many of the first barbecue operations in Texas, began as a meat market and grocery store. Edgar Black Sr. was a rancher living between Lockhart and Bastrop, in a community called Delhi, when the Great Depression hit in 1932. His only real assets were 50 head of cattle, so he and his friend Joe Roble, who owned a building in Lockhart, shook hands to open a meat market. Black transported the cattle to Lockhart in a cattle drive, and pastured them across the street from the building. Each week, he would slaughter and butcher one of the cows to sell fresh meat in the market. He began smoking the unsold meats as a means of preservation, since refrigeration was sparse and unreliable, and began crafting sausage as another means of eliminating waste.

Within Black's Market's first year, Edgar Sr. added some groceries to his business model. Both the grocery store and meat market took off, so when a larger space became available across the street in 1936, he relocated the operation. He named the grocery and meat market Northside Grocery & Market, and opened a separate Black's Barbecue in an adjacent building. Edgar Sr.'s son, Edgar Black Jr., returned from fighting in World War II and graduated from Texas A&M with a degree in accounting in 1949. He married Norma Jean, a daughter of German immigrants, and together they worked with his dad until Edgar Sr. passed away in 1962.

"The second generation, my grandfather and grandmother, were the ones who really dedicated themselves to the craft of barbecue, figuring out how to make this tough cut of beef that nobody really wanted taste amazing," says Barrett Black, the family's fourth-generation pitmaster. "Barbecue then was just the meats that didn't sell in the meat market, so the menu would say 'smoked beef.' My grandfather was one of the first people to say, 'Brisket! That's going to be our beef!' And when he got tired of little bits and pieces of the brisket burning and getting crusty, he came up with a method for trimming it, and then started using those trimmings to make the sausage. They standardized our sausage recipe, and really helped define what we consider Central Texas barbecue today."

Black's still crafts sausages using the very same recipe, then shapes them like horseshoes with a cotton string connecting the ends. Seven thousand of those

ring sausages a week are then hung to smoke in offset brick pits designed by Edgar Jr., with two fireboxes and one chimney, a unique design Barrett says he still hasn't seen elsewhere. Edgar Jr. also discovered that drier wood made much better tasting barbecue, so he began purchasing cords of post oak and seasoning the wood behind the restaurant. To this day, Black's is one of few Texas barbecue restaurants that does its own curing, stacking 80 or more cords at a time behind the building and letting them sit for at least a year.

Black's did a lot of innovating in the way that they cooked, but they were forward-thinking in other ways too. In fact, they were the first restaurant in Lockhart to integrate their restaurant and their workforce. Kent remembers his mom and dad taking down the "Colored Only" signs, and then successfully pushing for integration at other places in Lockhart, like the local swimming pool and the Little League teams.

"Some of my dad's friends would ask him, 'Where are those African people going to sit? And my dad would say, 'If they got 50 cents to buy sausage, they're gonna sit anywhere they want to,'" remembers Kent. "Some people said 'Well, we're never gonna shop with you again!' and we'd say 'Well, we're gonna miss you, but it's the right thing to do. And we're going to do it.' And then slowly the rest of the community followed—very slowly. . . . So we're real proud of our business, but we're equally proud of what our family has done culturally."

Edgar Jr. also taught classes in distributive education in the mornings before work, where he would educate students how to apply for jobs and interview, then he'd help them secure work. He would leave from there to go work at the restaurant and grocery store, despite his own constant health problems and many major surgeries. Norma Jean steered the ship each time he was out recovering, and she also ran into a lot of discrimination, such as vendors who refused to take orders from her because she was a woman.

"[Edgar] had enough of it so he called the main offices and said, 'I can't make it down there all the time because I'm sick a lot,'" remembers Norma Jean. "'So she's taken over and if y'all don't take her orders, you're not getting them from me, so make up your mind what you want to do!'"

Norma Jean also developed some of the recipes Black's still serves today. After getting so many requests for sauce, they decided to offer one in the 1970s, and she developed a tangy, tomato-based recipe with the help of familial taste testing. She also created the creamy potato salad, the peach cobbler, and the pinto beans, which still bear her name: Norma Jean's Beans.

"They have enough spice to be tasty, but they're not spicy," Norma Jean describes her namesake offering. "They're not too thick and not too watery. And the beans are not too hard, and not too soft."

Kent started working at the restaurant with his parents when he was just six years old, serving snow cones from a machine out in the front, before he went on to clean tables, cut meat, run the cash register, work at the grocery store, and work in the sausage kitchen through the years.

"I was working 12-hour days on Saturdays and in the summer and I was bringing home $20 a day which, in 1958, was a lot of money," says Kent, "So I grew up in the family business and spent as much time here with the family as I did at home, maybe even more here. We had three businesses right here, so when you worked, it was just kind of a carousel. I'd be up here working the grocery store and then I'd put on a different apron and go over to barbecue to cut meat and then they might need me in the sausage company next."

After 50 years—and with Edgar facing increased health setbacks—the Blacks decided to shutter the grocery store in the 1980s to focus on the barbecue operation and sausage production. Edgar and Norma Jean had insisted their sons Kent and Terry get college degrees so they had a backup plan in case the barbecue business failed. So Kent graduated with a law degree from South Texas College of Law in Houston, married his wife, Candy, in 1983, and opened up a private law practice next to the family business. He then went on to serve as a municipal judge and work as a state prosecutor on daycare and nursing home abuse cases.

Meanwhile, after Terry graduated from the University of Texas with a degree in accounting, he handled Black's Barbecue's bookkeeping from an office across the street from the business. When Edgar had a heart attack in 1991, Terry stepped in as president of the company, while Kent was helping to run restaurant operations.

"My parents continue to work here into their 80s—not because they had to, but because they liked doing it, and their customers were their friends," says Kent, who took the reins in 2015 when Edgar and Norma Jean decided to retire. "When I bought the company from our parents, my business plan was very simple. It was three words: don't change anything."

Terry's son Mike had begun working at the restaurant when he graduated from college in 2010, and he immediately fell in love with barbecue, but didn't get along so well with his Uncle Kent. He decided to team up with his brother Mark, and the brothers opened up their own Black's Barbecue in Austin, but they very quickly received a cease-and-desist from Kent for using the family name without permission. They came to an agreement with his attorney and renamed the business Terry Black's Barbecue (see page 359), but the whole debacle has become one of the biggest barbecue family feuds in Texas, punctuated with lots of not-so-passive-aggressive billboards, a practice that got especially contentious when Black's opened a location in Austin and Terry Black's opened one in Lockhart.

These days, that's all water under the bridge, as both branches of the family operate four successful locations of their own businesses. Black's opened a location in San Marcos in 2014, where Kent built an exact replica of the Lockhart pits. That same year, they opened an Austin location, which serves meat smoked in the Lockhart pits. Kent's stepson Eric Lenderman lives in New Braunfels, where he is the pitmaster at the fourth location of Black's, which opened in 2016. Candy acts as chief financial officer ("If I need 10 bucks for a pizza, I have to ask her for a username and a password!" says Kent). And though Edgar Jr. passed away in 2017 at the age of 91, Norma Jean still appears at the restaurants, always examining everything with an eagle eye developed by running the business for over 60 years.

"Her code name is Elvis," says Kent with a smile. "And when she walks in, we all sit up straighter, make sure our hats are on, go 'Did I shave today?' And then it quickly goes around the company—'Elvis is in the building.' When she leaves, we all kind of exhale like—'Elvis has left the building!'"

Now approaching their 100th year in business, Black's remains true to the cooking methods first used by Edgar. Briskets are cooked low and slow, typically for 12 to 13 hours, but they don't rotate them or wrap them in butcher paper. They simply use salt and pepper on high-quality meat: specifically Certified Angus Beef raised by small ranchers all over Texas and United States.

"My dad used to say, 'It's not what we put on it that makes it so good—it's what we *don't* put on it,'" emphasizes Kent. "Brisket's a great cut of meat just the way God made it. And we want to enhance it just a little bit, but we're just trying to bring out that greatness and not mess it up with apple juice or oranges or stuffing it with cloves—nothing wrong with that, but that's not what got us here 92 years ago."

That's not to say they haven't expanded their offerings through the years. Kent was one of the first Texas pitmasters to add beef ribs to the daily offerings, joining pork ribs, pulled pork, and quarters of smoked chicken. The family gradually added green beans, creamed corn, sweet potato casserole, and mac and cheese to the menu.

"We've been successful with the way we cook our meats, but sides are fair game," says Kent. "You know, people's tastes change."

The most recent additions have been Barrett's creations, like Mexican street corn and candied brisket ice cream, which joined their traditional banana pudding and cobbler dessert offerings. When Barrett appears on television or at festivals and special events, he also develops a number of unique and playful offerings, from smoked lamb neck masa cakes with Mexican Coke mole sauce to a flaming bourbon maple jalapeño doughnut sausage sandwich, which is lit with a blowtorch.

But the name of the game is tradition at the original Lockhart location. Guests slip into wooden booths to feast from their heaping butcher papered–trays on red and white–checkered tablecloths. The wood-paneled walls are hung with massive longhorn cattle horns and photos of the family through the years, posing with greats like Lyndon B. Johnson and George Foreman. Now that they're operating in four locations, Kent and Barrett want to be sure that their staff of 150 understands and appreciates they're not just serving barbecue, but upholding a legacy.

"We try to have every new manager spend two or three weeks in Lockhart to really learn, feel, and experience the history and the aura of 90 years of Texas barbecue, so they gain a reverence and a respect for it," says Barrett. "I think about the struggles [my ancestors] went through and it just makes me so grateful for what they built . . . so I always make sure people know that we are standing on their shoulders."

And now that Kent and Candy have seven grandchildren, things are looking bright for the fifth generation of Black's pitmasters. Barrett's five-year-old son Luke has even appeared on a cooking show alongside his dad already.

"We're trying to be the keepers of the flame, cooking just like my grandfather did. We feel an honor and responsibility to not let that style of cooking disappear," says Kent.

TERRY BLACK'S BARBECUE

AUSTIN, LOCKHART, WACO & DALLAS

Generally speaking, if you wait until lunchtime to line up for Texas barbecue, you've likely missed the boat. The most beloved places will attract a line of devotees starting early in the morning (sometimes even before the sun has risen), open their doors around 11 a.m., and begin selling out of items a couple of hours later. It's an interesting phenomenon, and one of the things visitors to Texas are often surprised by. But Mike and Mark Black set out to change that with Terry Black's Barbecue—and they have. It's one of the few top-rated barbecue joints in the state where you can walk in and choose from a full menu of offerings from open until they close (which is 9:30 p.m. Sunday through Thursday and 10:00 p.m. on Fridays and Saturdays).

"There's a lot of good barbecue restaurants in Austin, Texas—probably 10 or 15 that, on any given day, could be considered the best," says Mike. "And Mark and I knew that when we came to Austin, we were gonna have to do things differently and separate ourselves . . . so we said we're gonna outwork people. We're gonna have a restaurant that serves a.m. and p.m. And by doing so, we're gonna get more people in the doors to spread the Terry Black's gospel."

The Black brothers were just a few years out of college when they began this endeavor. But having been born into Lockhart barbecue royalty, they were no strangers to this world. In 1932, their great-great-grandfather Edgar Black Sr. opened a meat market in downtown Lockhart, which grew into the town's biggest grocery store. Smoking was introduced as a way to preserve meats, starting with the ring sausages for which they were known. When Edgar Black Jr. took over the market with his wife, Norma Jean, they transitioned the business into a full-fledged restaurant, Black's Barbecue (see page 353). After graduating from Texas State University with a finance degree in 2010, Mike began working for his grandfather and soon fell in love with the barbecue business.

"Not only did I like the process of cooking, but I really enjoyed the relationships with the employees," he remembers. "The restaurant wasn't crazy profitable—most restaurants aren't—but I saw that there was money to be made, and I saw that there were a lot of improvements to be made, too."

When Edgar Black Jr. had a heart attack in 1991, Mike and Mark's dad, Terry, ran the company until 2011. It was then that his brother Kent left his career as an attorney for the state and purchased the business from his parents when they retired. That was when Mike remembers he and his dad being ousted from the business.

"He and I never really got along and he didn't like me being there," recalls Mike. "We just did not see eye to eye and I saw the writing on the wall, so I said, 'Well, we're young. Let's go compete. Let's open a barbecue restaurant in Austin.' And it's been a blessing in disguise. We've learned so much from it and, as a family, we've grown closer."

Mike teamed up with his twin brother, Mark, and, with the support of their father, mom, Patti, and sister Christina, they opened Terry Black's Barbecue in 2014. Patti helped them with recipe development and Christina leads the accounting side of the business. And though their dad Terry, the restaurant's namesake, "never cooked a brisket in his entire life," according to Mike, he helps out in a myriad of other ways, from maintenance to operations.

In the 1950s, the Barton Springs Road building was home to Holiday House, a popular burger joint that also featured such oddities as a live alligator named Charlie in the front and an aviary in the back. But after it closed, a string of unsuccessful businesses tried and failed in that spot. In fact, friends worried the Black family was taking on a cursed location.

"We looked at it and said, 'No, this building screams barbecue—barbecue will be successful here,'" remembers Mike. "And we went in, just blessed to kill it from day one . . . we created one of the top restaurants in the United States. Depending on the week, we serve 15 to 20,000 people a week out of that location."

They do so by cooking 24 hours a day (in three 8-hour shifts), 364 days a year (every day except Christmas). It's a hardworking team, many of whom have been with them from the beginning.

"I think the most important thing is we've got an amazing staff," says Mark. "Barbecue's such a tough business. It's not like a steak house or a regular restaurant where you cook and leave for the night and shut the place down."

A welder friend crafted their first four offset smokers, and they've now added a fifth, made by Sunny Moberg. Terry Black's Barbecue maintains a very robust online shipping program that eliminates waste: any extra proteins get vacuum sealed, frozen, and shipped around the country via Goldbelly. They also designed the restaurant to include four cutting blocks, which helps move people quickly through the line. And when the line does stretch outside, there's plenty of shade, fans, and a bar to mitigate the pain that often comes along with waiting for barbecue.

While the Blacks are very proud of their unparalleled efficiency, they've also vowed to never sacrifice quality for quantity, which is one of the things Mike says he and his uncle butted heads over. The Black brothers spend six days a week sourcing the highest-quality meat they can find, and their team makes all the sides and desserts from scratch, right down to the piecrust.

"We knew what was good barbecue, but I think, more importantly for us, we knew what was bad barbecue," says Mark. "We knew coming in, with our experience,

what we wanted to deliver. And we're not really big cheffy types—we just wanted to do good, homemade recipes but stick to the basics."

Before opening, they went through rounds of recipe-testing with family and friends to create unimpeachable versions of sides like potato salad (made with baked potatoes for a nice chunky texture), pinto beans (with just the right amounts of chile and salt), creamed corn (delicately spiced with tarragon), and green beans (lightly seasoned with a distinctly fresh snap). Just like the setup at Black's Barbecue, the line leads guests to a counter where servers scoop sides into cups, cafeteria-style, before they continue to the meat-cutting blocks.

A mural inside their expansive dining room reads "Brisket is King." The letterboard facing Barton Springs typically preaches the same. And, considering they go through 50,000 pounds of brisket each week, there is no doubt about the truth of that statement within the world of Terry Black's. Even their lean cuts are impossibly succulent, with a dark, thick bark developed through hours of low and slow smoking over post oak. Black's is equally as well-known for its massive beef ribs and tender pork ribs. And, incredibly, all their proteins are rubbed with the same simple 1:1:1 ratio of salt, pepper, and seasoned salt.

When designing their next two locations, the Black brothers made sure the pits were the first thing guests see upon arrival. The Dallas restaurant opened in 2019 with five Moberg smokers, followed by the Lockhart locations in 2022 with eight more pits, and a Waco location in 2024 with six more pits (and an attached oyster bar). They encourage anyone who's interested to request a pit tour while visiting.

"If you can teach someone something, then you can make them a customer for life," says Mark. "So we want to bring you into the pits, show you how we do things, and talk barbecue with you."

While some barbecue places are very secretive about their techniques, the Black brothers say Terry Black's is an open book. They're not worried about competitors knowing the methods behind their meat. But they also know firsthand that there's nothing wrong with a little competition.

"The more and more places that pop up in Austin, everyone's just getting busier and doing well," says Mike. "It's become a destination where people from all over the world are coming to experience barbecue. So we think competition is good in the sense that it drives business."

That spirit of friendly rivalry has served them well. In 2024, Terry Black's earned a prestigious Michelin Guide Recommendation, a testament to their meticulous craft and unwavering commitment to quality.

DISTANT RELATIVES

AUSTIN

These days, you'll find a lot of pitmasters pushing the industry forward by embracing new trends. But in opening Distant Relatives, Damien Brockway did just the opposite—he looked to his ancestors for guidance and inspiration.

Brockway grew up in Connecticut, where cooking and coming together over food was always a part of his family and community life. After attending the Culinary Institute of America in Hyde Park, New York, he went on to cut his teeth in the kitchen of establishments like Clio in Boston and One Market in San Francisco before moving to Austin, where he took on the role of chef de cuisine at Uchi and then executive chef at Counter 3.Five.VII. But despite his fine-dining pedigree, barbecue is what he found himself enjoying the most when he cooked for friends and family.

After reading *The Cooking Gene: A Journey Through African American Culinary History in the Old South* by Michael Twitty, Brockway was inspired to track his own ancestry and heritage. His mom helped him gather photos, recipe cards, and documents, and a neighbor started seeking out vintage culinary books and publications for his project. In these resources, Brockway discovered connections to ancestors from Nigeria, Mali, and Cameroon, and began delving deeper into his own memories and experiences. All of these elements came together to inform Distant Relatives, which reflects his own origin story while tracking the influence of the African Diaspora in the United States.

Brockway opened his trailer in February 2021, first in the parking lot of an East Austin tire shop, before relocating to bustling Meanwhile Brewing later that year, in July. He loads the firebox of his Mill Scale Metalworks offset pit with 100 percent Texas pecan, which is exceedingly rare in this part of Central Texas.

"Post oak smoke and barbecue are fantastic, but our flavor profile demands otherwise," explains Brockway. "We use pecan, which is the largest species of hickory and the Texas state tree, not only because of hickory's historical significance in the history of American barbecue—and by default also African American barbecue—but also for its delicate, round, subtly sweet smoke which balances well and allows room for our spice profile, alongside the fact that we also barbecue vegetables."

Brockway sources from local farmers and ranchers through relationships with Farm to Table ATX and Urban Roots Farmshare, and his beef comes from Goodstock by Nolan Ryan. Each protein is spritzed on the pit with its own vinegar-Worcestershire blend, each one enhanced with a proprietary spice blend made from aromatics of African origin, like grains of paradise, African bird chiles, and benne seeds.

"Vinegar has always played a crucial role in the seasoning of barbecue, all the way back to the times when it was predominantly enslaved Africans tending the fires," says Brockway. "Worcestershire's origins itself don't go back to Africa, but were inspired by India and the ingredients of molasses, tamarind, and preserved fish do speak to elements of the African Diaspora and its core flavor profiles, as well as the narrative of plantation labor."

Rather than hawking smoked meats by the pound, each one of Brockway's proteins is paired with its own unique accoutrement inspired by the mop sauces that were traditionally slathered on meats while on the pit: the beef brisket comes with a smoked mustard-and-butter sauce and the pulled pork gets a tamarind-and-molasses barbecue sauce. The chicken leg is brightened with a chili-and-vinegar dip, while the pork spare ribs are coated with a spicy dry rub, then served with onion.

There are always sandwiches available, made from the current meat offerings, as well as a selection of seasonally rotating vegetables and pickles. Brockway's mother inspired the black-eyed peas with burnt ends, as well as the spicy smoked peanuts, ham preparations, and different variations of greens (like collards with barbecue broth, spring vegetables, and benne seeds). Brockway created a slaw using green mango, a staple fruit of Cameroon, but this dish was also inspired by his wife's Thai heritage. Red peas, okra, and Carolina Gold rice all make appearances on the rotating menu, and his chicken is inspired by the barbecue chicken he encountered at large gatherings growing up. In lieu of traditional barbecue peach paper, proteins and sides are all artfully presented on trays lined with Distant Relatives' signature black and white–checked lining.

Since Brockway's passion project earned a spot on *Texas Monthly*'s Top 50 list in 2021, customers have started lining up before opening on weekends, and they typically buy up all the barbecue by mid-afternoon. Brockway was also recognized as James Beard Foundation semifinalist for Best Chef: Texas in both 2022 and 2023, and the trailer was presented with a Michelin Bib Gourmand award in 2024. With all of his continued success, Brockway has doubled his pit capacity and looks forward to eventually opening as a brick and mortar with indoor seating. Until then, you can enjoy this thoughtful take on Texas barbecue alongside Meanwhile Brewing's well-crafted lagers and ales.

ROLLIN SMOKE BBQ

AUSTIN

If you're not hungry before you come across Rollin Smoke BBQ's Instagram page, you will be soon after. Sure, there's the expected glistening trays of meat nestled with boats of cheesy sides and vivid pickles. But there's also pastrami burnt ends tucked into a gooey, melty Reuben and smoked carnitas oozing out of quesotacos on a freshet of cheese. Weekends bring brunch specials like a barbacoa frittata drizzled with green sauce and finished with jalapeño slices and pork pozole verde smothered with smoked biscuits, pickled red onions, and an egg.

"We ate some gummy vitamins and decided to throw some of our fire-smoked cheesy hash in a waffle maker," one post read. "Then kept throwing things on 'til it toppled over."

That particular creation, called the Harvey Cruz, featured pit-smoked carne guisada, chipotle cream, crushed house bbq chips, and an egg stacked on a cheesy hash waffle.

The barbecue masterminds in the graffitied Rollin Smoke trailer, with its recognizable pink pig, are always thinking up something deliciously wacky, and owner Kyle Stallings says a lot of that inspiration comes from his mom, who he fondly remembers cooking dinner every night after working all day as a teacher to support the family as a single mom.

"Most of my inspiration comes from my mom and nostalgic plays on the food she made when I was growing up in Tyler," remembers Stallings. "We just always try to come up with something a little different."

Stallings moved to Austin over 20 years ago and worked in a number of restaurants, from Chili's to Alamo Drafthouse to Carrabba's, in both front and back of house roles. After a stint in Northern California, he returned in 2012 and began working in a barbecue truck—called Rollin Smoke—that a couple of his friends (Tony Hamilton and Eliot Akers) had opened on West 5th Street the year before.

"I just fell in love with everything involving barbecue," he says. "I became obsessed with trying to learn how to do it, and do it my own way."

He immersed himself in the few videos that were available online at the time, and otherwise learned through a lot of trial and error. When one of the partners decided to pursue a different career path, Stallings took over operations (the other partner still remains, though silently). After two years downtown, they relocated the trailer to East 6th Street, where it operated across the street from Hotel Vegas (a popular East Austin bar with nightly live music). This location and their late-night hours (which are very rare in Texas barbecue) certainly helped build a strong fan following for their sandwich- and taco-heavy menu. When the pandemic hit, however, they pivoted to daytime hours.

In 2023, Rollin Smoke had the opportunity to join the Arbor Food Park on East 12th Street, alongside some other popular food trailers. Stallings changed the menu this time to focus more on barbecue by the pound rather than handhelds, though he still features favorites like The Silky (pulled pork topped with spicy slaw on a sweet bun), The Playboy (brisket, pulled pork, and sausage piled high on a sweet bun), and Players Pie (a brisket-based Frito pie topped with BBQ sauce, onions, cilantro, and chipotle cream). Then, in late 2024, a new West Texas–themed east side bar named Chalmers invited Rollin Smoke to lay its roots in their spacious patio. Now, with more visibility and a steady stream of bar patrons, Stallings is busier than ever—and back to some later hours (9 p.m. on Thursday and Sunday, 10 p.m. on Friday and Saturday).

The meats by the pound are listed along with their sources: prime brisket from Goodstock, Chairman's Reserve pulled pork, Prairie Fresh spare ribs, Comfrey Farms pork belly burnt ends, and Texas Sausage Company sausage. A sandwich board on the ground details specials in bubbly chalk letters: pit-smoked carne guisada, 28-hour brined chicken, and smoked pimento cheese dip with chipotle saltines.

Stallings uses a 500-gallon Moberg offset smoker to smoke all the meats at the trailer with 80 percent post oak and 20 percent pecan. (Hickory is the wood of choice in East Texas, where he's from, and pecan is a close relative that's easier to come by in Central Texas. He likes the added smoke and flavor it brings.) Stallings uses just salt, pepper, and a little garlic as a rub for the chicken, which he says makes it the most Central Texas–style dish they do. The all-purpose rub he developed for everything else is a combination of salt, pepper, garlic, cayenne, paprika, chili powder, brown sugar, and white sugar.

As an homage to his roots in East Texas (where sauce is boss), he's developed four different ones: a Big Red sauce (sweet with a little spice), a sweet bourbon sauce (made with local Fierce Whiskers whiskey), a Carolina Gold mustard sauce, and Ladybird Sauce, a play on an old-school recipe developed by Lady Bird Johnson.

Confined to the space of the food truck, Stallings and his team have to think outside the box when it comes to space. They pickle their own onions and jalapeños, but don't have room to make their own pickled cucumbers. They get their tortillas from H-E-B fresh daily (because there's no space to make their own, but also because "they do a pretty darn good job," says Stallings). He even uses the pit to smoke chocolate chip cookies and fruit cobblers on the top rack each weekend.

"We never had much kitchen equipment, so we've always been forced to try to do things on the smoker and see how it turns out," he says. "Turns out, it works."

MUM FOODS SMOKEHOUSE & DELICATESSEN

AUSTIN

"Barbecue sort of found *me*—like it does so many of us," says Geoffrey Ellis, the owner of Mum Foods Smokehouse & Delicatessen in Austin. Ellis created the concept as a tribute to the two culinary traditions that shaped his upbringing: the bold flavors of Texas barbecue and the comforting classics found in New York's Jewish delis.

Born in Lubbock, Ellis moved to Austin in 1996 and says some of his first Central Texas memories involve trips to Kreuz Market and Smitty's in Lockhart, and Louie Mueller Barbecue in Taylor.

"Those [places] made a huge impact on me, in terms of understanding what the native cuisine of this area was," remembers Ellis. "I never, ever forgot the way they smelled, and the way the walls looked, and the characters there. I was always sort of enamored with the history and the simple beauty that those places represented."

As a child, Ellis spent summers in New York with his grandparents, staying in the same Queens apartment where his mother grew up. His grandfather, a Lower East Side jeweler who worked just down the street from Katz's Deli, would take Ellis to delis around the city to compare and contrast pastrami.

"When I moved to Austin and experienced the barbecue places here, it clicked with me that the delis back East were like the barbecue places here, in that they attracted similar characters, similar kinds of people worked at them, and people argued over who had the best pastrami, just like they argue over who has the best brisket here," says Ellis. "Everything clicked for me when I realized that Central Texas barbecue places and delis were sort of kindred spirits."

Back in Texas, Ellis's parents were very supportive of his interest in food. Ellis helped them cook at home, and they took him and his sister to farmers markets and exposed them to fine dining. When Ellis's older sister moved to San Francisco, she sent him one of Alice Waters's Chez Panisse cookbooks. Discovering the iconic restaurant—and its farm-to-table philosophy—at a young age deeply influenced Ellis.

"That was the first time that I realized that food came from somewhere, that there could be seasons," he emphasizes. "That cookbook opened my eyes to wanting to do this as my career—that really turned things on for me."

While studying food science and nutrition at Texas State University, Ellis worked at well-respected Austin restaurants like Jeffrey's and Café No Sé. It was during this time that he also visited his sister in San Francisco for the first time. She introduced him to a then little-known bakery called Tartine, where locals in the Mission District lined up for its now-legendary bread. During the visit, Ellis had a chance to chat with baker Chad Robertson, sparking his fascination with sourdough. When Tartine released its first cookbook six months later, Ellis eagerly dove in, following each recipe step-by-step in an attempt to replicate their bread—despite lacking all of the equipment and specialty grains.

After plenty of practice (and a postgraduate stint slinging wood-fired pizza in Oahu), Ellis decided to take his bread to market—literally. In 2012, he and his partner at the time, Mattison Bills, started selling sourdough from a booth at the Lakeline and Barton Creek farmers markets under the name Mum Foods. (Mum was the name of their sourdough starter, a nod to mother cultures.) The loaves sold well, but they needed something else to capture customers more frequently and bolster sales. So they began buying meat from local ranchers and smoking it with post oak to sell on market days.

"There was nobody else doing barbecue at the farmers markets, which were becoming really popular, so it seemed like a no-brainer," recalls Ellis. "And it was great to be able to support the local ranchers as we grew. . . . I always felt like Texas barbecue should be made with Texas beef. So I didn't understand why people were buying beef from Kansas City or Nebraska to make barbecue here in Texas. It's unfortunate because so much emphasis is given to pitmasters and wood and what kind of smoker they use. So we put an emphasis on Texas beef and I'd like to think we're a part of the growing number of people who will make that demand so the farmers and ranchers grow the supply chain to meet our needs."

For the first year, Ellis and Bills smoked and sold beef ribs, brisket, turkey, and housemade sausage by the pound. Then one day, they found themself with a surplus of brisket from one of the ranches. Since it was more than they could sell that week, they decided to try making pastrami. Ellis started with a recipe from Michael Ruhlman's book on charcuterie and made a few tweaks to it, submerging the briskets in a simple brine of water, kosher salt, curing salt, and sugar for 10 days. After brining, the briskets are rubbed with a 50-50 blend of freshly ground black pepper and coriander, and then smoked for 9 to 10 hours.

"And that product then is the same as what we create now," says Ellis. "I mean, it was pretty much perfection from the first time we tried it."

There was a huge demand for the pastrami as soon as they started selling it, so in 2014, they expanded Mum Foods to Mueller Farmers Market too. When Daniel Vaughn visited and declared it the best pastrami in the state in *Texas Monthly*, Mum's popularity continued to soar. In 2019, Mum Foods opened its first brick and mortar in a little converted bungalow on Austin's east side. Restaurateur Sam Hellman-Mass had plans for the space, but offered it up for Mum to take temporary residence for an extended pop-up.

Though the market operation had focused on meats by the pound, Ellis and Bills expanded Mum to focus on sandwiches. They began offering pastrami stacked on their signature rye sourdough, slathered with housemade yellow mustard and accompanied by lacto-fermented kosher dill pickles. They developed the Rachel, a pastrami sandwich topped with melted Swiss, red cabbage coleslaw, and housemade Russian dressing. Each day they also offered a blackboard of creative offerings like Chinese cabbage and smoked chicken salad, pastrami chili, and a porchetta sandwich with roasted broccoli, fresh basil, and garlic mayo.

Later that year, Ellis and Bills decided to part ways. Bills sold her share of the business and went on to open Three Six General (see page 441), and Ellis continued to operate at three farmers market locations while searching for a permanent brick and mortar. He'd recently bought a house in Austin's Windsor Park neighborhood and saw a need for more food in the up-and-coming area. He set his sights on a huge space that had previously been a barbecue restaurant—and even had a smokehouse attached. After securing the lease, Ellis opened the current iteration of Mum Foods Smokehouse & Delicatessen in late 2022.

Ellis brought on pitmaster Travis Crawford, who'd spent time cooking at LeRoy and Lewis Barbecue and the now-shuttered Valentina's Tex-Mex BBQ. Mum uses strictly salt and pepper to season the meats they smoke over post oak on two 1,000-gallon offsets made by Bison Smokers (a North Texas company started by a shop teacher): Wagyu brisket and pastrami, Berkshire pork spareribs, natural turkey from Greener Pastures, and all-beef ring sausage in homage to the barbecue joints of Lockhart.

"Central Texas barbecue has very few tenets, and I feel like we are obligated to follow those," says Ellis. "That's the tradition that's been handed down to us."

Now with much more space for smoking meat, baking bread, and preparing sides, Ellis was able to fully marry the concepts of Texas barbecue and the delis he grew up visiting.

"Spiritually, religiously, I'm not a practicing Jew, but I've connected with my ancestry and my heritage through food," says Ellis. "For me, the deli is my synagogue. That's my way to connect with my grandfather, and to give back and keep telling [our] cultural story."

Ellis uses locally grown and milled Barton Springs Mill flour to make smoked beef tallow brioche, which is used as a vehicle for hot barbecue sandwiches, plus cold deli sandwiches made with smoked chicken salad, pimento cheese, or egg salad. He uses his signature rye sourdough for hot sandwiches made with hand-carved pastrami and corned beef, which is made from brisket that has been brined but not smoked. ("They're so similar, I consider them links in the same chain," says Ellis.)

Mum ferments a half-sour and full-sour kosher dill pickle all year long. Since cucumbers have a short growing season in Texas, Ellis says he does have to source them from Florida for part of the year. But he also preserves produce the rest of the year based on what's thriving locally and seasonally—from mushrooms and green beans to golden cauliflower and purple scallions. Mum also ferments their own sauerkraut in-house, and pickles mustard seeds for the housemade yellow mustard. After burning through several Vitamix blenders with the thick condiment, Ellis discovered a game-changing tip in Hawaii: using a drill and a paint mixer to efficiently produce 10-gallon batches!

In addition to more traditional barbecue sides like potato salad and coleslaw, Mum simmers savory collards in smoky pot liquor, and crafts exceptional shells and cheese by making an American-style cheese from aged Vermont cheddar emulsified with sodium citrate. There are always a couple of salad options on the menu (featuring house pickles, seasonal veggies, and playful inclusions like rye bread crumbs), plus seasonal veggie specials. Another big draw is the lauded matzoh ball soup, developed from Ellis's Grandma Rachel's recipe.

"I'm sorry to say this, but I think we've taken it to another level," says Ellis. "Because we smoke all the chicken bones, we make the stock from scratch, and we use a lot of chicken fat in our matzoh ball because we have those drippings ready to go."

Ellis also draws inspiration from his grandfather's Depression-era recipe for custardy chess pie, making one key enhancement to the original: browning the butter before blending it with eggs, milk, sugar, vanilla, and vinegar. The browned butter imparts a deep, nutty richness, while finely ground cornmeal floats to the surface during baking, forming a beautifully golden top layer. Ellis also uses brown butter in the graham cracker crust of the cheesecake, which is a cheffed-up take on New York cheesecake: goat cheese joins the cream cheese base for a bit of tang, rose water and orange blossom water are added for floral complexity, and the cakes start off in a ripping hot oven to achieve the caramelization of a burnt Basque cheesecake.

Mum Foods has been basking in well-earned acclaim recently. In 2024, Ellis was named a James Beard Foundation Award semifinalist for Best Chef: Texas, and by year's end, Mum Foods earned a coveted spot as a Michelin Guide Recommended restaurant. The growing recognition has brought a surge in business, prompting Ellis to find ways to expand without compromising his core values.

"Now we do work with wholesalers—because at the scale we're at now, we have to," he says. "But when we get on board with them, we lay out our criteria very early on—that we're only buying Texas beef, and it must be free from hormones and antibiotics."

Ellis remains committed to sourcing local produce whenever possible and continues to anchor Mum Foods in Austin's farmers markets (Mueller, Lakeline, and Barton Creek).

"[The markets] are our lifeblood, and I think they keep us connected to our roots," he says. "They keep me interacting with farmers, and they keep me learning about what's coming out seasonally. So they're profitable, and they are successful, but at the end of the day, they also keep us grounded in our history."

KG BBQ

AUSTIN

Kareem El-Ghayesh's first bite of brisket lit a fire inside of him, inspiring a move across the globe and an entirely new career path.

El-Ghayesh grew up in Cairo and came to the United States for the first time in 2012 to visit his uncle in Cincinnati. During that excursion, he planned a side trip to Austin to visit a friend. That trip proved to be fateful—he was so moved by his first tray of barbecue that he returned to Egypt and began practicing at home using a Weber grill, Franklin Barbecue's first cookbook, and instructional YouTube videos. He also befriended Cairo butchers and eventually found one to regularly supply his brisket (a cut that proved to be just as difficult to source as oak, which is an expensive wood in Egypt, and typically imported only for furniture making).

El-Ghayesh had grown up watching both his grandmother and mother cook, then helping them make traditional Egyptian dishes like lamb shank in tomato sauce, stewed okra, roasted duck, and desserts like baklava and kanafeh. As you might imagine, Texas barbecue was completely new territory.

"We love beef in Egypt, especially tenderloin, but all the barbecue is so different from here. It's just skewering things and grilling over live charcoal, and there is a high culture of slow-roasting in the

2019 WFC
BBQ TEAM
WESTERN
PREMIUM
BBQ PRODUCTS

oven" says El-Ghayesh. "But I think the flavors of the Middle East go really well [with Texas barbecue] because of how opposite they are. They're brighter and fresher, crisper—lots of vegetables, lots of herbs. So they really complement barbecue and the richness and heaviness that we are used to eating: mac and cheese and beans and sides that are actually heavier than meats themselves."

El-Ghayesh graduated Cairo University with a business degree, but was growing increasingly discontent in his corporate finance career. He'd been toying with the idea of starting a food business and, in 2015, he saved up vacation time for a hands-on deep dive into the world of Texas barbecue.

"Learning from people here, the real masters, seemed like the legit way," says El-Ghayesh. "It's like learning basketball from LeBron James. You're learning from the people who are immersed in it and doing it successfully."

El-Ghayesh ate barbecue all over Austin, connecting with as many owners as possible and asking a few to teach him their craft so he could bring Texas barbecue to Egypt. He was put off by a number of pitmasters before Bill Kerlin (of Kerlaches) agreed to teach him in exchange for labor at the (now-shuttered) Kerlin BBQ. El-Ghayesh returned to Cairo to quit his banking job, pack his bags, and become fully immersed in Texas barbecue culture.

"Every single pitmaster, or mentor as I like to call them, taught me something different," he says. "Kerlin taught me the basics. He's a really good pitmaster; he does everything traditionally. He knows what he's doing with fire and wood, meat and smokers. So he really gave me the fundamentals and a great introduction and a push into the world."

Next, El-Ghayesh went on to work at Valentina's Tex-Mex BBQ under pitmaster Miguel Vidal while pursuing a culinary degree at Austin Community College. These two experiences together helped him begin the Tex-Egyptian concept that would become known as KG BBQ, producing outstanding dishes like pomegranate and za'atar–glazed pork ribs; Mediterranean-style pork sausage with sun-dried tomatoes, green olives, and feta; lamb-bacon ribs with mint-serrano chimichurri and brisket shawarma bowls served over Egyptian rice and sprinkled with pine nuts, pistachios, golden raisins, and a drizzle of tahini.

"I would say that the inspiration came from Miguel, seeing this fusion happening firsthand, and seeing that it really works," says El-Ghayesh. "He's so dedicated and so proud of his culture and food. He loves barbecue and puts a spin on it that way. My cooking style is also very influenced by him."

After Valentina's, El-Ghayesh continued to gain experience at a number of other top Austin barbecue spots, including brief stints at [the now-shuttered]

Freedmen's Bar, Rollin Smoke BBQ (see page 367), and InterStellar BBQ (see page 278). He also spent a year and a half cooking on the line at Lamberts, took a glimpse into the meat processing industry at Lone Star Meats, and took on a role at Salt & Time to learn butchery and sausage-making. He started his first barbecue pop-up at South Austin honky-tonk Giddy Ups in 2017, initially serving traditional Texas barbecue. His catering business and private cooking classes were ramping up when Dia's Market in North Austin asked him to cook for their anniversary party. That's where he served his first Tex-Egyptian menu, and it was so popular they asked him to turn it into a monthly pop-up. When COVID-19 put a pause on those, El-Ghayesh developed a small supper club to share his Egyptian food and culture, complete with a curated soundtrack and belly dancers.

The unique experience gained a lot of traction on social media, and when El-Ghayesh re-launched his pop-ups in 2021, he immediately had a line stretching down the block outside Dia's Market. That made it clear it was time to take the next step, and he paused operations to start gathering investors, buying supplies, and designing a food truck. After a few pop-ups at Oddwood Ales in East Austin, he opened for business in October 2022. A black trailer parked along Manor Road now houses his 1,000-gallon offset smoker built by Primitive Pits in Atlanta.

"Its name is King Tut," says El-Ghayesh, who can typically be spotted in a cowboy hat, leather-accented apron, and pearl snap shirt, grinning beneath his big mustache. "Our plan is to name every smoker after an Egyptian king."

While El-Ghayesh's culinary education and barbecue training informed his masterful fusion, his Egyptian family inspired many of the dishes on the menu. His mom's mac and cheese (known in Egypt as macarona bechemel) was the first dish he learned to cook as a teenager. Now he tops it with pulled lamb, sumac-pickled onions, pomegranate barbecue sauce, and za'atar for a dish he calls the Egyptian Cowboy. His recipe for baladi salad (a tangy, vinegar-heavy mix of tomato, cucumber, red onion, and pomegranate) is as close as he could come to his uncle's. Oum ali is a cinnamon-spiced Egyptian bread pudding typically found at celebrations and parties, and El-Ghayesh makes his with mixed nuts and puff pastry—and bakes it right inside King Tut.

"Every single thing is cooked on the smoker," says El-Ghayesh. "It's not a very even smoker, but we use that to our advantage. Like when we're cooking at 250°F, some of the spots can go up to 375°F or 400°F. So we use that as our oven. And then kofta and chicken kebabs we'll just cook on the hotter side for more of a charred, grilled flavor."

Compared to a lot of Central Texas barbecue (which typically centers around simple salt and pepper seasonings), El-Ghayesh dives deep into the spice cabinet to create his signature proteins. He starts everything with his brisket rub of salt, pepper, garlic, and oregano. His pork ribs also get coriander and fenugreek, the lamb shoulder gets sumac and cinnamon, and lamb chops get paprika, cayenne, and some other proprietary spices. Chicken is the one protein that gets a marinade—yogurt, honey, garlic, lime, sumac, tomato paste, salt, and pepper.

KG BBQ's unique sides add fat-splicing acidity to each tray, as well as splashes of color. In addition to the baladi salad, there's a beet-dyed "pink potato salad" made with fresh dill and jalapeños, and a Mediterranean rice bowl that gets its bright yellow hue from turmeric, contrasted with pops of pomegranate arils and candied nuts.

"In the Middle East, we always have a centerpiece, and we always surround it with all these beautiful, colorful, vibrant pickles, sauces, and condiments," says El-Ghayesh. "I put a lot of love in what I do, but I also put a lot of effort into making the plate that you get look really beautiful, as opposed to the regular brown-and-yellow barbecue trays that we're used to."

As a result, KG BBQ's technicolor spreads have become popular for weddings and celebrations, and El-Ghayesh maintains a steady flow of catering business. He has also been getting so many requests for halal barbecue that his latest expansion plan includes opening a brick and mortar and keeping the food truck where it is, but turning it into a halal operation. He looks forward to continued expansion, which would allow him to offer things like Egyptian pita, a sourdough bran flatbread that he says will be "a game-changer" for KG BBQ.

But one could say El-Ghayesh has already changed the game. Just a month after opening his trailer, *Austin Monthly* named KG BBQ one of the city's best restaurants and, another month after that, El-Ghayesh was named a semifinalist for the prestigious James Beard Foundation's award for Best Chef: Texas. And in 2024, KG BBQ was awarded a Michelin Bib Gourmand rating.

"*Texas Monthly* was my biggest goal, really," says El-Ghayesh, somewhat incredulously. "I was like, 'If I make it to *Texas Monthly*'s Top 50, I can die happy, I can go to my grave peacefully.' And then James Beard came out! I feel humbled and grateful that my food fits so well in Texas and people like it. Texas barbecue is a beautiful blank slate to work with. You have high-quality meats and you have salt, pepper, and live fire. You can take these flavors and just go in endless directions. And people are coming here, getting inspired and bringing their own flavors, cuisines and cultures into barbecue. I think this is where it's headed. It's about different fusions now."

AUSTIN'S ORIGINAL
STILES SWITCH
BBQ and BREW

STILES SWITCH BBQ AND BREW

AUSTIN

Growing up in Taylor, Texas, a town made famous for its barbecue thanks to Louie Mueller Barbecue (see page 240), Shane Stiles has always felt a deep connection to the craft.

"It's simple," Stiles states matter-of-factly. "It's delicious. It's a fascinating process from start to finish. There is really no other cuisine like it, in my opinion."

He and his father frequented Louie Mueller to worship at the legendary "Cathedral of Smoke." If Bobby Mueller (the first Texas pitmaster to earn a James Beard Award for his restaurant) wasn't behind the counter serving them himself, his right-hand man, Lance Kirkpatrick, was.

"Bobby was my mentor for over eight years," says Kirkpatrick. "He taught me all of the basics of barbecue as he understood them. He taught me how to manage the fire to get the results you want. Bobby taught me how to trim each cut of meat, as well as temperatures to use for each cut. Bobby taught me sausage making, a skill I developed over five years of making the sausage for Louie Mueller. But beyond that, he taught me the importance and reverence of barbecue, and what it means to people."

In 2008, Bobby Mueller passed away suddenly and Kirkpatrick took the reins as pit boss until he decided to change tracks and open a high-end restaurant two years later. But the venture was ahead of its time for the small town, and he closed it shortly afterward. When Stiles moved to Austin in the early 2000s after graduating from Texas A&M, he was surprised to find a lack of high-quality barbecue in the state's capital. He was working in commercial printing, but started to think more seriously about opening his own barbecue joint. His dad, who still lived in Taylor, let him know that Kirkpatrick was now a free agent.

"My dad said, 'You might have an opportunity here to get Lance on board with your idea for a barbecue joint in Austin,'" remembers Stiles. "So, I called him up the day after he closed (his restaurant) and pitched him my idea—and the rest is history. The stars aligned, and here we are, 12 years later with three restaurants."

Stiles named the restaurant after a historic railroad stop that stood on land once owned by his family just outside Austin. Stiles Switch opened in December 2011, in Brentwood's Violet Crown Shopping Center (which was the city's first when it opened in 1951). The iconic complex is also where The Emporium scene in *Dazed & Confused* was filmed.

At Stiles Switch, Kirkpatrick has adapted his techniques, moving from the fast and hot methods of Louie Mueller's huge brick pit (where all the meats were loaded up simultaneously each morning) to using four 1,000-gallon Moberg smokers (named Pancho, Lefty, Dolly, and Kenny) that allow for more precise temperature control, each one designated to cook a different protein over post oak.

While Bobby only used salt and pepper as a seasoning, Kirkpatrick has developed a housemade seasoned salt and uses it to enhance the flavors of most proteins, and proprietary sauces for others. Briskets are wrapped in butcher paper for the final hours of cooking, pork ribs are seasoned with salt and pepper before receiving a sauce glaze and foil wrap, and chicken is basted with a mix of butter, beer, garlic, and apple cider vinegar.

Stiles Switch was one of the first modern Texas barbecue joints to craft their own sausages in-house. They drew inspiration from the original recipes Kirkpatrick learned from Mueller, but he and the rest of the sausage team have developed and perfected a number of flavors over the years. Each day they offer an original link, a jalapeño-and-cheddar link, and a creative Sausage of the Month, all hung and smoked in a Moberg vertical smoke cabinet.

Long before Texas barbecue joints were known for the type of culinary innovation now pushing the industry forward, Stiles Switch was testing the boundaries of barbecue. Oak-smoked wings appear on the daily menu, tossed in your choice of housemade sauce (garlic parmesan, Alabama white, buffalo, or honey BBQ). They were one of the first spots to offer a Frito pie made with chile con carne, and their creative sandwiches stack contrasting elements like pulled pork, pork rinds, and coleslaw (as seen in the Boss Hog).

The restaurant features weekly specials like smoked prime rib on Wednesdays and smoked brisket burgers on Thursday, and has become known for its 12 Days of Smoked Meat, an annual December event featuring unique smoked meat dishes like chicken-fried beef ribs and smoked tomahawk steaks.

They also offer classic sides like pinto beans and coleslaw alongside more modern offerings like cheesy tater tot casserole, cucumber tomato salad, and sweet serrano fried Brussels sprouts. And the corn casserole, a cherished Stiles family recipe, immediately became a customer favorite. In addition to classic desserts like banana pudding and peach cobbler, the team developed a rich chocolate cake (Stiles's favorite), creamy tres leches, and a layered Oreo pudding.

Stiles's wife, Catherine, handles all PR, events, and marketing for the restaurants, and in 2014 she established a beverage company called Barbecue Wife. She launched with Barbecue Wife Bloody Mary Mix, made with smoked sea salt, smoked black pepper, and a bit of Stiles Switch mop sauce, and followed up with the Texas Smoked Honey Margarita Mix, made with fresh lime juice and smoked Texas wildflower honey. She also highlights other women in barbecue on her website with interviews accompanied by portraits taken by photographer Wyatt McSpadden.

"When I first entered the space of barbecue, I quickly noticed how many amazing women were involved in the business, but their stories were not usually being told by mainstream media," she says. "So with Barbecue Wife, I really wanted to highlight these women."

In 2018, Stiles partnered with Chef Todd Duplechan to open The Switch in Dripping Springs, which offers both barbecue and Southern cuisine with a Cajun twist. In 2020, they expanded to another location of Stiles Switch in Cedar Park. Stiles is very hands-on at each location and assists with every aspect of the business, including cooking with the rest of his team.

"I hope [Texas] barbecue can continue to evolve and continue to push for better quality and techniques practiced and handed down," says Stiles. "Our motto with our crew is to always be better than the day before, to keep pushing to improve. I hope that rings true for Texas barbecue as a whole."

LONE STAR
LONE STAR

SMITTY'S MARKET

LOCKHART

Smitty's Market provides one of the most uniquely exciting barbecue experiences in the state. Upon entering through the back door (that's the main entrance these days), you are immediately hit with the unmistakable heat of fire. As you move up in line (which is typically present, but fast-moving), you'll see open fires raging on the cement floor at the base of the brick offset pits. The brick walls are darkened with soot and streams of daylight pierce through the smoke to illuminate the otherwise dungeon-like space. When it's your turn to order, pit hands (wearing impressively clean white aprons) will lift the ash-coated steel lids of the pits to retrieve the cuts of your choosing. They'll carve and weigh each meat to order and wrap it all up in pinkish brown butcher paper.

"I want people to walk in there and feel like they're in someplace from the '20s and '30s," says owner Nina Sells.

The original building's ties to barbecue actually date back to 1875, when it opened as Lockhart's first meat market, and leftover meats were smoked out of necessity due to lack of refrigeration. In 1900, a German immigrant named Charles Kreuz Sr. purchased it and renamed it Kreuz Market (see page 295). The business, which functioned as a butcher shop, grocery store, and barbecue operation, went through several more changes of ownership within the Kreuz family through the years. Edgar "Smitty" Schmidt started working there in 1933 when he was just 13 years old. When the Kreuz family was ready to retire in 1948, they asked if he would be interested in purchasing the business, and he did just that.

Schmidt continued to honor the traditions of Kreuz Market, serving the same German-inspired ring sausage Charles Kreuz had developed at the turn of the century, made with mostly beef and a little pork, and seasoned with salt, black pepper, and cayenne. He continued to smoke the meat market's leftovers out back on the offset brick pits the Kreuz family had constructed in 1924. The meat was served with white bread or crackers, and customers could choose pickles or cheese as accompaniments. Schmidt used the meat market's butcher paper in lieu of plates, and there was not a fork in sight. Instead, customers used their hands to enjoy the hot-off-the-pit meats while sitting on benches in a hallway that connected meat market to pits. Communal knives, attached to chains, were used to cut their meat if needed.

In 1978, Edgar had the opportunity to purchase the dry goods store next door, so he turned it into a sunlit, air-conditioned dining room, with long tables and chairs, the walls decorated with ads for Big Red and Coca-Cola. He also added indoor restrooms and a counter for customers to pick up their bread, crackers, drinks, and trimmings like the traditional pickles, onions, and cheese, plus tomato, avocado, and jalapeño and serrano peppers. (Sells says some

customers still like to make their own pico de gallo or guacamole using these á la carte items.) They did, however, remain a proudly sauce-less establishment.

In 1984, Edgar retired and sold Kreuz Market to his sons Rick and Don Schmidt, who ran it as the Kreuz family and their dad had. But in 1990, Edgar's passing prompted a rift that would shape Texas barbecue history.

"It was a family disagreement," explains Sells. "Dad wanted to retire and it was hard for the brothers to accept their little sister being a part of it. They wanted the business, so dad conveyed the business to them. Things happened, Dad got upset with one of my brothers and, next thing I know, he said he changed his will and he left both buildings to me."

Sells's brothers leased the building from her for the better part of a decade before trying to negotiate with her to buy it. But she wasn't ready to sell. She did offer to extend the lease, but with a slight rent increase. Don chose to retire, while Rick decided to move the entire operation. With the help of his son Keith (who now owns Kreuz Market), he designed and built a new building just a half-mile away.

"I didn't mind Kreuz Market," insists Sells. "I didn't *want* them to leave! But you know, we had to face what was coming. And I said 'Well, whatever we do, the building was built for a barbecue place and Smitty's was the perfect name. I had a lot of support. I couldn't have done it just by myself. But it was good for both of us and it was good for business because of the publicity—worldwide publicity!"

Within a month of Kreuz Market moving out, Sells was able to rebrand the space, naming it after her dad, and continue operations. She had worked in the meat market for a period of time in her 20s, but she'd never operated the pits. She was also working full-time at the courthouse, while her husband Jim was an agricultural teacher in town. So her youngest son, John Fullilove, who was working as a wastewater operator for the Guadalupe-Blanco River Authority, made a quick career change to come manage the pits at Smitty's. Her older son, James Fullilove, also left his job at FedEx to join the team, along with Jerry Mendoza, who took the lead on sausage production. (John sadly passed away in 2023, but James and Jerry still lead the pit team today.)

The meat menu people knew at Kreuz Market stayed primarily the same at Smitty's. Everything is smoked at a higher temperature than it is at the more modern Central Texas barbecue joints, with brisket finishing in 5 to 7 hours, armed with a crispy bark. An old sign by the pits still advertises "lean" meat (shoulder clod), "fat" meat (brisket), sausage (they make 6,000 to 7,000 a week, sold hot, cold and by the box), plus pork chops and prime rib (which both tend to sell out quickly). Smitty's also added pork ribs, turkey, and chicken (just on the weekends). All the meats still get rubbed with the same blend of salt, black pepper, and cayenne and smoked with post oak. The pork ribs are also sauced after they're cooked, then returned to the pit to caramelize.

Though Kreuz Market never had sides, Sells says her dad did have a bean recipe he would make for caterings (which they would call "feeds" back in the day). He'd written that recipe on a torn-off piece of butcher paper, and Sells gave that to her sons when the family first launched Smitty's.

"I said, 'This is your Papa Schmidt's recipe on this butcher paper,'" she remembers. "If you want to go get the ingredients, we'll see if we want to change tradition and sell beans."

They did indeed decide to change that tradition, and they also recreated Sells's mom's recipe for scoopable potato salad, as well as a creamy, traditional coleslaw. Over the next few years, they added mac and cheese, green beans, and creamed corn to the menu, and they eventually broke down and created a barbecue sauce too: sweet and tomato-based, with a touch of spice.

"It's hard to know what people are wanting and accommodate them, but then also stay true to tradition," says Sells, admitting that they initially hid the sauce and only took it out by request, until its popularity forced it into the light. "But still not forks! We're still hanging onto that!"

EXIT

BAR-E
BARBEQUE & SAUSAGE
CITY MARKET
LULING, TEXAS

NO OUTSIDE DRINKS
OPEN
CITY MARKET
T SHIRTS
NOW ON SALE
~ INQUIRE AT ~
FRONT COUNTER
LARRY GATLIN
iques
next
block

CITY MARKET

LULING

The small town of Luling, Texas, is known primarily for three things: oil, watermelons, and barbecue. But, while many of the oil wells have dried up and the annual Luling Watermelon Thump takes up just four days a year, the barbecue at City Market draws lines of visitors every day but Sunday, when it's closed.

City Market, like Kreuz Market (see page 295) and Black's Barbecue (see page 353) in nearby Lockhart, began as a meat market and grocery store, where pit-smoking with post oak naturally evolved as a way of utilizing unsold meat. Willie "Buddy" Ellis opened the market for his parents, Lanos and Delma Ellis, when he returned from the Korean War. Lanos and his brother Howard were ranchers who had learned the barbecue business while working at Kreuz Market. Lanos ran City Market's operations, while Howard manned the pits, using meat from their nearby ranch, Bar-Ē, which was slaughtered locally too.

Joe Capello tagged along with his brother when he started working at City Market in 1959. Just a young teenager at the time, Capello worked there as a busboy in the summer. When he no longer had a way to get to Luling, he started working at Kreuz Market in Lockhart, where his family lived, and he was working as a meat cutter at Northside Market (which later became Black's Barbecue) after high school when he was drafted into the Army.

After spending two years in Vietnam, Capello returned to Luling in 1969. Now he had a car and a wife, but he needed a job. So he returned to City Market and began working there full-time. Now 77, Capello still works five 12-hour days a week, managing the restaurant and manning the pits at this barbecue institution where not much has changed—and with the success they've found in more than six decades, not much needs to.

When you enter the wood-paneled interior of City Market, it does feel like you've taken a step back in time, with its mismatched wooden tables, beige floor tiles, metal folding chairs, and framed black-and-white photos documenting Luling's 1920s oil boom. A line dissecting that dining room leads to a smoke-darkened area behind a door in the back, where you'll order meat right off the open brick pits. The pit hands, all wearing crisp white button-downs, carve to order on a cutting block, and ask if you want pickles (dill or sweet slices you scoop into a cardboard boat), onion (sliced and wrapped in plastic wrap), and white bread or crackers.

"When we first got started we used to cut up the whole steer," remembers Capello. "You could get a ribeye for $1. . . . We would use the briskets and the shoulders for barbecue and the rest of the trimmings would go into the sausage."

The Piggly Wiggly grocery chain came to town sometime in the late 1970s, putting lots of mom-and-pop

operations out of business. Seeing the writing on the wall, the Ellis family decided to close down the meat market and focus on the barbecue operation, which had seen such success they needed to move to a bigger location down the street in the mid-1960s. Once Howard retired in the 1980s, Buddy promoted Capello to full-time pitmaster.

The pits where you place your order at City Market are holding pits. Most of the cooking happens on two identical offset pits out back in the garage, where Capello smokes the same three items he's been perfecting over the last 50 years: brisket, pork ribs, and sausage. The sausage is made fresh every day by grinding 95 percent brisket trim and 5 percent pork trim and stuffing it into pork casing. Both the pork ribs and brisket are seasoned with salt, black pepper, and red pepper ("No secret ingredients!" promises Capello. "Just a regular rub!"). He then glazes and smokes the ribs for one to two hours and the brisket sees smoke for anywhere from eight to 12.

"You start it off in the hot part of the pit and then you move it to the back of the pit, where it'll just sit there and start getting tender," Capello describes. "No thermometers! I can tell by just looking at it when it's done."

Capello is known for wearing a hard hat while he works, but it's more for tradition than safety purposes. It was given to him decades ago by Buddy's mother, Delma.

"She said she thought I would look good with that hard hat on, and I've been wearing it ever since," says Capello. "It used to be white but now it's got a tan color to it. It goes with the building! People wonder why I'm wearing a hard hat when other people are wearing baseball caps. Well, this one doesn't wear out."

Delma also gifted the barbecue world with something very significant: a style of barbecue sauce so influential, it's replicated at joints all over the state and referred to as "Luling-style." Her recipe for the amber-hued, pepper-flecked sauce is a secret, but Capello confirms it has mustard, ketchup, and vinegar in it. (And, judging by the balance of sweetness and tang, I'd also guess brown sugar.)

They blend 16 gallons of the renowned sauce fresh each day and, though they don't commercially package it, you can purchase it by the Styrofoam cup or small glass bottle at the cash register. That is also where you get slices of cheddar cheese (which they've always offered, to pair with sausage) and the two available sides added in the '90s: a sweet mayo potato salad (not made in-house) and toothsome pinto beans they simmer in a pot with brisket rub and bacon. And a few years ago, they added banana pudding to the menu, also made fresh daily.

Lanny and Randy Ellis took over operations when their dad Buddy passed away in 2015, and they continue to run City Market today. Most of the staff has worked there between 25 and 45 years, including two other Ellises (Lanny's son Arin and Howard's son Roger). These days, the restaurant goes through about 30 to 40 briskets during the week and 60 to 70 each Saturday, and 2,100 rings of sausage each day. In fact, they added a gas-fired rotisserie in the aughts, which they use to cook overnight in order to have enough meat to make it until closing time each day. And, after all these years, Capello is pretty good at predicting those counts.

I had to ask him what it is about barbecue that has kept him doing it for all these years—and at City Market, which was designated a Texas Treasure business by the Texas Historical Commission in 2022. "I'm still trying to figure that out!" Capello says with a laugh. "I guess I enjoy that people enjoy eating what I cook. People see me and say, 'I thought you were going to retire!' I keep telling them, 'Maybe next year!' But I've been saying that for many years. We'll see, maybe next year!"

BLACK BOARD BAR B Q

SISTERDALE

Black Board Bar B Q is set in a beautifully refurbished red barn, made from local limestone and cedar, and nestled on a pastoral, three-acre plot in Sisterdale. It's the ideal setting for enjoying Texas barbecue—which is probably why the building has a history as a barbecue destination.

Partners in life and business, Joe Rodriguez and Melissa Garza met just a stone's throw from here in Boerne, where Rodriguez was working as a chef for the fine-dining restaurant Cypress Grille, and Garza was a server. After Rodriguez worked there for nearly a decade, the two decided to move to Far West Texas in 2017. Rodriguez had accepted the role of sous chef at the Gage Hotel in Marathon, where he was looking forward to a break from executive chef hours and responsibilities. (Before he was at Cypress Grille, Rodriguez attended Texas Culinary Academy, then worked for Cafe Central in El Paso, then Bin 555 and Il Sogno in San Antonio.)

However, life had other plans for him. The chef that hired him quit just a few months later and Rodriguez found himself back in an executive chef role once again. While in that role, he spent a lot of time at Brick Vault Brewery & Barbecue (see page 508), which was under the same ownership as the Gage Hotel. At the time, the Reese brothers (see page 454) were working out there with pitmaster Phillip Moellering and,

Authentic
Family Style
A La Carte
Texan
MEATS
SMALL BITES & SIDES
Shiner
830-524-6858
PLEASE WAIT
Jake
Kristie
Lainey was here

though Rodriguez never ran the pits himself, he did a lot of observing as they fine-tuned their meat-smoking methods.

"I've always been intrigued by Texas barbecue and I've always liked messing around with wood, fire, smoke, and all that junk," says Rodriguez. "When I was in culinary school, I bought one of those crappy offset pits at Home Depot. A friend of mine's sister was graduating high school, so they contracted me to cook two briskets for her party. From what I remember, it didn't come out too bad but, looking back now, I'm pretty sure it wasn't great. But everybody loved it!"

After five years at the Gage, Rodriguez was feeling burnt out again. In that remote part of Texas, it's very hard to find employees, so he found himself handling all the hotel's weddings and banquets on top of its restaurant, and helping out with an on-site coffee shop as well. Rodriguez and Garza started plotting to buy an old café in town, and began to look into the financials behind it. But at the same time, Garza's dad found a place for sale in the Hill Country while he was riding his motorcycle one day. He called them, excited to share the news—and to get his granddaughter back in his orbit.

The couple moved back to the area and partnered with Garza's parents to take over operations of Black Board Bar B Q in September 2022. Jack Gandolfo had taken over Maywald's Sisterdale Smokehouse in 2016, turning it into Black Board Bar B Q. Though Gandolfo was moving to Idaho, he wanted to ensure that the restaurant would live on as a barbecue joint, so he turned down several other offers before agreeing to terms with Rodriguez and Garza. They worked with him for a couple of days before taking the reins of the existing restaurant. Although there were certainly things they wanted to change, they decided to do so gradually.

"We took a really long time to put our own spin on things because there was already a built-in customer base," says Garza.

"We just wanted to respect people's threshold for change," adds Rodriguez. "We kept some of the menu items, but we just tweaked them to make them better—especially the smoking method, [because] what he was doing was overly smoky and acrid tasting.

That was number one [priority], to get that under control. And then little by little we [started] changing other things to make it our own style."

Rodriguez started sourcing high-quality proteins from Nolan Ryan Beef, 44 Farms, and Creekstone Farms for consistent, well-marbled cuts. Gandolfo had been using a Fiesta brand brisket rub, so Rodriguez came up with a proprietary, more pepper-forward blend of paprika, garlic powder, black pepper, salt, and cayenne. The ribs were previously spiced heavily with piri piri—a popular Portugeuse spice blend—and cayenne, so Rodriguez lessened the heat and developed a rub using piloncillo, brown sugar, granulated honey, salt, pepper, and paprika for a savory and sweet finish. He uses the same rub on the pork shoulder that becomes pulled pork. Half chickens are brined overnight with brown sugar, garlic, salt, and fresh thyme, then rubbed with brisket seasoning before smoking. Rodriguez also introduced a sausage-making program, utilizing brisket and pork belly trim to make one confit garlic link and another with cheddar and jalapeño added.

When Rodriguez took over the existing pits, all he had to work with was an Oyler in bad need of a deep clean. He revived that rotisserie and still fuels it with post oak wood to smoke ribs, chicken, and sausage. However, he also built a brand-new pit room to house his new custom-made, 1,000-gallon offset smoker crafted by Mill Scale Metalworks (see page 286). He uses it to smoke brisket, pork shoulder, and sometimes ribs, and the improvement in quality, texture, and flavor is notable.

After Rodriguez got all the proteins dialed in, he began making changes to the other menu items. Luckenbach Lollipops—semiboneless quail halves, with the leg bone Frenched to serve as a handle, coated in panko, and fried—were a popular menu item, and not one typically found in barbecue restaurants. Rodriguez began marinating the quail in buttermilk before battering it to make comforting chicken-fried quail (now listed on the menu as Quail Lollipops). The previous owner had been using waxy, pre-shredded Parmesan for truffle fries, so Rodriguez switched to freshly grated Parmesan, which results in delicate, meltable threads. Gandolfo's mac and cheese was made using cream cheese, but Rodriguez switched to the signature dish he created while at the Gage, using cheddar, fontina, Parmesan, and black pepper for a decadent take on cacio e pepe. Gandolfo's slaw was Asian-inspired, but Rodriguez phased that out for a creamy jalapeño slaw with jicama, carrots, and red bell peppers.

Gandolfo had always refused to offer beans, but Rodriguez developed a recipe for charro beans cooked with onion, garlic, dried New Mexico red chiles, avocado leaves, bay leaves, oregano, and chunks of smoked pork belly. He also got rid of a creamed corn dish (made with canned corn, onions, and peppers) and instead began making elotes. After smoking the corn in the rotisserie, he peels the husk down to brush the ears with mayo, and sprinkles cotija and tajín over them before serving. Rodriguez also got rid of the sriracha they had been using as hot sauce, and is fermenting his own hot sauce in-house, which he also uses in a spicy aioli.

"We just want to showcase a little bit more of our Hispanic roots as much as we can without freaking people out," says Rodriguez with a chuckle. "It's a little different out here."

Rodriguez taps into his prolific background as a fine-dining chef for specials like smoked pork chops with tomatillo and jalapeño chutney, smoked beef birria poutine, pulled lamb shoulder pita tacos, and smoked pork shank adobada with morita chile and grilled peach salsa. Weekends bring craveable brunch offerings like buttermilk-brined tallow fried chicken with cornmeal waffles and maple syrup. And Rodriguez's pastry skills shine with sweet specials like Mexican Tiramisu (made with Galletas María, cinnamon, allspice, clove, grated Mexican chocolate, and a housemade cajeta) and key lime cheesecake with toasted coconut masa shortbread and citrus Chantilly cream. And his brown butter chocolate chip and sea salt cookies and Shiner Bock caramel and smoked pecan brownies are always on the menu.

"We want to step up the dessert game and not just do banana pudding," says Rodriguez. "We want to create something different, where you're like 'Oh man, I didn't know you could get that at a barbecue place.'"

Black Board Bar B Q also features a selection of natural wine at the front, displayed right underneath the beer and soda cans. Among the bottles on offer are two pet-nats from Saint Tryphon, a neighboring Boerne vineyard specializing in minimal-intervention wine.

Another thing Garza—who manages the front of house and handles payroll—has been slowly tweaking is the restaurant's interior. It was plastered with flags when they first took over, and there are still a good amount of them hanging from the ceiling and walls after she thinned them out. She also kept the restaurant's eponymous blackboard, but it no longer displays the menu. The day's offerings are now on smaller boards behind the counter, while the big board is open for chalk doodles and messages from customers. The restaurant's dining room—with its weathered exposed beams and corrugated tin paneling—really speaks for itself, much like the food, so Garza and Rodriguez have opted to keep things simple with spindle bow back chairs and wooden tables topped with Mason jars containing fresh-cut flowers.

"I feel like we're so aligned with our vision and our values," says Garza. "Joe and I have such a shared vision and expectations for what we want to provide people, both food-wise and quality-wise. . . . Even as a consumer, this is the experience I want to have when I walk through the door. The food, the atmosphere, the service—it's all amazing."

VICTORIAN'S BARBECUE

MART

Many Texas pitmasters have taken unconventional paths to barbecue, but Joey Victorian's journey is uniquely tied to the strings of a fiddle.

Growing up in a Creole household with roots in Lake Charles and Lafayette, Louisiana, Joey was surrounded by the vibrant flavors of his mother's cooking. Then, when he was eight years old, Victorian began attending fiddle contests at the Houston Astrodome. Between competitions, he and his best friend would wander outside to the Houston Livestock Show and Rodeo BBQ Cookoff in the parking lot, where the smoky aromas and vibrant atmosphere ignited his earliest barbecue memories.

After spending a decade attending the cookoff, Victorian told his then-girlfriend he wanted to make barbecue for her family. But his enthusiasm quickly outpaced his skill. "I had only been around barbecue—I didn't really cook barbecue," Victorian recalls, laughing about his early attempt at grilling chicken, which he burned after saucing it before placing it over fire. "I thought I could just pick it up and it wouldn't be any problem, but I was terribly wrong."

That night, his girlfriend's dad took them out for dinner. But he later built Victorian a barbecue pit, encouraging him to hone his skills. Through trial and error—and plenty of failed attempts—Victorian began to improve, eventually entering barbecue competitions.

"I would watch what other guys were doing, try to mimic it, or ask questions," he says. "Until YouTube and TV shows like *BBQ Pitmasters* came along, there weren't many resources. You really had to fail—or read books."

Though Victorian was always pushing himself to improve upon his barbecue, his main priority at competitions was having a good time, and making sure everyone who visited his tent did too.

"[Competition barbecue] is highly focused on partying and barbecue—and I split my time doing exactly that," he laughs. "Then I got older and I didn't feel like partying that much anymore. So I decided, once I hit 40, that I wanted to dive straight into barbecue for a living. I was like, "If I don't do what I love now, I'm gonna get older and regret everything.'"

In 2016, after decades working as a welding inspector in Houston's oil industry, Victorian made a bold career change. He used his savings to create a line of Creole seasonings called Dirrty Swamp, which found success on the shelves of H-E-B and Kroger. With the profits, he purchased a food trailer and enlisted the help of pitmaster Ara Malekian of Harlem Road Texas BBQ (see page 166) to customize it and navigate the permitting process.

Victorian gave up competition barbecue to focus on the trailer, which was parked in Houston's Heights neighborhood. He planned to open a brick-and-mortar in downtown Houston, but decided instead to

seek out a space in a small town somewhere outside the city. It was during this search that Victorian discovered the small town of Mart, which travelers pass through on their way from Houston to Waco.

"Mart is between Houston and Waco. It's easy to get to from Austin, Dallas. It's kind of centralized, and I've always said that barbecue is community and barbecue is also a destination," says Victorian. "People love to travel for barbecue."

He found a 1500-square-foot building that was originally built as a drugstore in 1901, and had housed several different restaurants and offices through the years. He put a bid in on it and, at the same time, a casting director had reached out to him about being on a barbecue reality TV show.

"The day they called to tell me that I was on the show was the same day that I picked up the keys from my brick and mortar," recalls Victorian. "So it was a pretty exciting day!"

Victorian traveled to Georgia to film *The American Barbecue Showdown* for Netflix, where the Tri-Tip King of Texas (a name given to him by the late John Brotherton) became known for his calm demeanor and signature Stetson. His Texas barbecue with Creole flair got him halfway through Season 2 before he returned to build out his new restaurant in Mart. After a year-and-a-half buildout, done with the help of friends and family, Victorian's Barbecue opened in

early May. So when *Barbecue Showdown* aired at the end of that same month, it was the best publicity he could've asked for.

At his restaurant, Victorian uses a 500-gallon offset smoker crafted by M Grills, a hog cooker from Galindo Smokers, and an 11-foot, three-door Bewley pit that pitmaster Kevin Bludso gifted him after they were on *Barbecue Showdown* together. While post oak, white oak, pecan, and mesquite are all prevalent in the area, Victorian prefers to stoke his fires with red oak.

"I like the taste of my food from the red oak," he says. "It gives it a little more smoky barbecue taste then just the post oak. But if I'm in a pinch and I can't find red oak, I will use post oak if I have to. But lately I've been buying so much of it, they keep it on hand for me now."

Though Victorian doesn't sell his seasonings in grocery stores anymore, he does continue using those same blends. His brisket-and-steak seasoning is heavy on the pepper, plus salt, garlic powder, onion power, and mustard powder. Since his seasonings are pretty low in sodium, he also adds Lawry's to introduce more salt to larger pieces of meat.

Victorian sources his beef from 44 Farms, just 60 miles south of Mart, showcasing brisket daily, tri-tip on Saturdays, and, occasionally, picanha (a cut from beef sirloin). His spareribs are seasoned with bold Creole spices, and he sometimes highlights a Creole-stuffed pork loin. Those vibrant flavors extend to his Creole-inspired specials, including crawfish étouffée, shrimp Creole, and jambalaya.

Victorian's wife, Kelli, lends her touch to a variety of sides, including his mom's signature mustard-based potato salad, hearty red beans and rice, and savory boudin balls. Together, they created a standout Creole corn dish, or maque choux, blending creamed corn, tomato paste, onions, bell peppers, and Creole seasoning. The menu also features Tex-Mex-inspired charro beans, bursting with flavors from tomatoes, onions, jalapeños, and cilantro. Victorian's ultra-creamy mac and cheese, made with cheddar and gouda, gets a playful finish with a sprinkle of spicy Takis. Fresh, crunchy cucumber salad and a tangy vinegar-based slaw—mayo-free by Victorian's design—add brightness to the lineup. For dessert, they keep it classic with housemade banana pudding, a local favorite so popular it's often ordered by the pan.

Victorian is expanding his vision, repurposing a historic building nearby into a versatile event venue where he can host and cater parties and receptions. For him, barbecue isn't just a profession—it's a passion and a way of life.

"They say if you love what you do, you don't work a day in your life," he muses. "I say no, you work even harder to keep doing what you're doing because you love it so much."

GUESS FAMILY BARBECUE

WACO

Growing up in the tiny town of Jayton, located between Lubbock and Abilene, Reid Guess learned early on that hard work and resourcefulness were essential, as businesses were scarce and the closest city was a 90-mile drive away. His father, a welder, built barbecue pits as a side project, and soon the family found themselves taking on barbecue catering jobs. By seventh grade, Guess had already built his first pit and was helping cater local golf tournaments and weddings.

After high school, Guess moved to Austin to enroll in culinary school, then honed his craft at notable establishments like Bess Bistro, 219 West, and Perla's, before landing a grill cook position at Lambert's, where he got to craft elevated barbecue for Austin restaurant group MML Hospitality. As the restaurant grew, Guess stepped into the role of its first sous chef, and then moved up to lead chef.

"Through all the different styles of cooking I did, I was best at barbecue because it was ingrained in me," says Guess.

Meanwhile, he met his wife, they had two kids, and Guess found himself regularly in Waco, where she grew up and her family still lived.

"It was a food desert, in my opinion—not now, but it was then—and it seemed like they needed a good barbecue spot," Guess recalls. "When our kids became school age and Austin started doing that explosion thing that it's still doing, it was hard for us to do the things that we loved. It was time to move, and it just made sense to move here."

After six years at Lambert's, Guess was ready to branch out on his own, and he felt like Waco was the perfect place for his vision of high-quality, small-batch barbecue. In 2017, he opened a food truck called Guess Family Barbecue, where he plated and served meat smoked with oak on a pit he built himself—but this time, it was customized for his own concept.

"I was able to build it exactly like I wanted it and, having so many briskets under my belt already, I feel like I had a pretty good advantage," says Guess. "There's zero bells and whistles on my pits. There's no counterweights because that doesn't help the briskets cook. Everything is designed for the meat, not for the pitmaster. They're not as flashy as the Mobergs and Mill Scales, but I think they work better."

Guess focused on sourcing high-quality meat—like antibiotic-free, all-natural Angus beef from places like 44 Farms and Double R Ranch—and seasoning it simply. His brisket is rubbed with salt and pepper and smoked for an average of 12 to 14 hours. But he does have a secret weapon: a tallow he makes from brisket trim and infuses with garlic, thyme, and shallots. When the briskets are wrapped in butcher paper at the end of the cook, he slathers it with this aromatic rendered fat.

The pork ribs get salt, pepper, and a little brown sugar, too, which yields a crisp, caramelized exterior. The chicken-and-turkey rub is a little more involved, with prominent paprika and celery seed, and he lets this seasoning work itself in for two days before cooking them at a very high heat, locking in flavor and moisture. While many places wait until they have the space of a brick and mortar to make their own sausage, Guess established a sausage program right out the gate, and taught his 16-year-old nephew how to grind and stuff the roasted garlic and cheddar chipotle links.

Guess used the pit to make sides like his beans with brisket ends, cheesy, locally milled grits, and green chile mac and cheese. He developed a broccoli salad, which has since been replaced with collard greens, made in a broth enriched by savory pork scraps. And his coconut cream pie, though beloved by the people who ordered it, has been replaced with classic banana pudding.

“People aren’t as adventurous here,” says Guess. “When they go to eat, they want a certain thing.”

Though he focuses on perfecting the classics and giving the locals what they want at Guess Family Barbecue, he gets to branch out and scratch his fine-dining itch when hired by Waco residents for private backyard events.

In September 2019, Guess opened a brick-and-mortar location in a 1950s building that had housed several other restaurants through the years (including a barbecue joint at one point). He built a smokehouse in the back for three 1,000-gallon pits and one 500-gallon mounted on a trailer. But he was only open for three months before he had to close due to the pandemic. Local restaurateur Cory McEntyre and one other investor decided to invest in Guess Family Barbecue, helping Guess pay rent during the unexpected six months of closure.

After reopening in 2020, Guess Family Barbecue has maintained its place as a cornerstone of Waco’s food scene. In addition to classic barbecue served market style or by the sandwich, Guess offers specials like the super popular chicken-fried steak with bacon grease gravy on Thursday, and a Sunday brunch with dishes like barbecue hash, pulled pork pancakes, and a breakfast sandwich with fluffy eggs, melted cheese, and brisket jam.

Though weekends can get quite busy—particularly the Sunday brunch service after church lets out—Guess’s small team (which sometimes includes his kids, Elliot and Emmi) runs the kitchen like a well-oiled machine.

“I don’t want to have a line out the door,” says Guess. “I just want a simple, easy life where I make barbecue and it pays the bills.”

VITEK'S BBQ

WACO

Vitek's BBQ has built a long-standing legacy thanks to the Vitek family's ability to adapt with the changing times. The story begins in 1915, when butcher William Martin Vitek (pronounced "Vee-tech"), the son of Czech immigrants, opened a grocery store and meat market in Granger called Vitek's Grocery and Meat Market. Shortly after opening, William and his wife, Hattie, moved 60 miles north to Waco. The business changed locations several times during its first decade as it weathered the Great Depression and, when William passed away, his son William "Willie" Frank Vitek took over.

As the small town of Waco developed over the next several years, so did Vitek's. Willie built Vitek's current location in 1958 and developed the homemade sausage recipe they still serve today. That same year, construction of I-35 began in Waco. Many businesses were unable to stay open due to the highway construction, but Willie and his son Billy Joe kept the business afloat by cooking barbecue on a portable pit, serving chopped brisket and hot link sandwiches to customers.

As larger chains moved into town in the second half of the twentieth century, lots of family businesses were forced to shutter their doors. However, quick-service restaurants were simultaneously rising in popularity, and Vitek's was well positioned for that shift. When Willie suffered a heart attack in 1972, Billy Joe and his wife, Susan, took over the business as the third-generation owners, changing the name from Vitek's Grocery to Vitek's BBQ. They originally operated a takeout-only business model, with just a single picnic table on site, but soon transitioned into a quick-service restaurant.

As the restaurant evolved, so did the menu. Pulled pork, turkey, and whole and half chickens joined the lineup alongside brisket and sausage, all smoked with oak. Sides grew to include beans, coleslaw, potato salad, and three-cheese macaroni. In the early 1980s, construction workers from a nearby project were seeking out a cheap and filling meal, so Billy Joe and an employee who was a student at nearby Baylor University created the Gut Pack, which is now a huge part of Waco's barbecue identity. The hearty dish features layers of smoked sausage, chopped brisket, pinto beans, and shredded cheddar heaped over Fritos, drizzled with barbecue sauce and served with onions, pickles, and jalapeños on the side.

The Gut Pack was recognized in a variety of publications and outlets, from *Texas Monthly* to *The New York Times*, and was named the "#1 College Eat in America" by the Cooking Channel. Today, it is still the restaurant's top seller. Customers can order the truly gut-packing meal by the full or half serving, add a scoop of mac and cheese to the top to make it a Mac Pack, or get a baked potato as the base to make it a Spud Pack.

In 2006, Billy Joe and Susan retired, leaving the restaurant to their daughter, Julie Vitek Keith. When Julie and her husband, Jason, came in as fourth-generation owners, the business was still entirely analog. So they computerized operations, increasing efficiency with a point-of-sale system. They diversified the menu further with the addition of tacos, nachos, and chips and queso. They also expanded the dining area and added a spacious and dog-friendly beer garden. The business is now more popular than ever with both locals and students from Baylor, carrying on Vitek's tradition of serving the community in a Waco that is constantly growing and changing.

HELBERG BARBECUE

WOODWAY

On my first visit to Helberg Barbecue, I snapped a photo of a big banner in the dining room that summed up Phillip and Yvette Helberg's origin story and values. It ended with these lines: "It's never been easy, but that's why we love it. There's no secret ingredient. It's all salt, pepper, and a whole lotta prayer." This sentiment would prove to contain more truth than even they could know.

Phillip, who grew up in The Woodlands, met Yvette on a cruise to Hawaii. She and her family were there celebrating her 21st birthday, and he was working on the ship to save up money for an outdoor leadership course in Patagonia. He never did take that course, but he did end up relocating to California and marrying Yvette. And when they moved into a new home in 2016, Yvette's mom got them a smoker as a housewarming gift.

"Once I started cooking with fire, I was hooked," says Phillip, who read Aaron Franklin's first book and began taking road trips to Top 50 joints whenever they were back in Texas visiting his family. "What first got me was the challenge of barbecue and the obsession with perfecting it, specifically brisket. Once I met several pitmasters and discovered the professional community and the surrounding culture of barbecue in Texas, I knew it was where I wanted to make a career."

The couple founded an event company called Helberg Ranch in Rancho Santa Margarita, California. Yvette handled marketing while Phillip crafted barbecue using a steel offset smoker. Though the location was great for racing mountain bikes competitively (which Phillip was doing at the time), it wasn't proving to be a good place to run a lucrative business. Yvette had especially loved Waco on their trips through Texas, so they decided to bring their barbecue back to the motherland, picking up a food truck via Craigslist along the way.

Helberg Barbecue began in 2018 outside of Pinewood Roasters, where Phillip and Yvette served brisket-stuffed zwiebacks (an Eastern European pastry similar to a klobasnek) in the morning before switching to their barbecue menu at 11 a.m. Then they started serving at Valley Mills Vineyard's tasting room just outside of the city on weekends. But their trailer days only lasted just over a year; by May 2019, the Helbergs opened their brick and mortar in Woodway, just west of Waco.

Phillip uses two Moberg offset smokers (one 1,000-gallon and one 500-gallon) and an M&M BBQ Company wood-fired rotisserie, and he also has a hybrid offset-direct heat cooker built by Moberg, as well as Mill Scale Metalworks open-fire cooking tables he uses for events. His "Texas trinity" (brisket, pork ribs, and sausage) remains pretty traditional for Central Texas. His Prime briskets get a rub of kosher salt and 16-mesh black pepper. Ribs get rubbed with Helberg's all-purpose house blend (salt, pepper, and some savory spices). And they make two types of snappy housemade sausage: one traditional Central Texas–style beef link, and another with jalapeño and pepperjack.

While all these more typical offerings are perfectly executed, my favorites at Helberg are the creations you won't find anywhere else. Their citrus-marinated pork steak has earned quite the fan following, and for good reason. In lieu of making pulled pork, Philip cuts pork shoulder into thick steaks. Then he marinates them overnight in an orange-lime-garlic-jalapeño marinade, seasons them with orange pepper and 16-mesh black pepper, and smokes them in the offset for a few hours, flipping them every so often. The standout finished product, which gets bathed in the reduced marinade, is bright with a touch of spice, succulent and unforgettable. Phillip stuffs his turkey breasts with pesto, ties them with twine, then rubs them with a garlic-herb seasoning before smoking. They are then slathered with beef tallow before they're wrapped in butcher paper to rest, and the whole process makes for an incredibly supple and herb-laced turkey. The chicken is also not to be missed: half chickens are brined in pickle juice, rubbed with Helberg's house all-purpose seasoning, then smoked just enough to cook through. Then each bird is fried to order in beef tallow, locking in moisture and flavor.

The sides follow a similar path, with traditional offerings like mustard potato salad and ranch beans offered alongside more inventive creations like roasted street corn salad, bright chimichurri slaw, and smoked cheddar mac and cheese, which is enrobed in a classic mornay sauce. They craft their own crunchy refrigerator pickles and two unique barbecue sauces: one beer-mustard sauce in honor of Phillip's German heritage and a red sauce with Mae Ploy, a Filipino sweet chili sauce, inspired by Yvette's family. Helberg Barbecue has also become known for its fluffy banana pudding, which Phillip adapted from his grandmother's recipe, and spiced up with ginger snaps from local Slaton Bakery in lieu of vanilla wafers.

The Helbergs also became known for their creative specials, like Filipino burnt ends over garlic fried rice, smoked tarragon chicken salad on toasted focaccia, brisket banh mi, smoked tri-tip French dip sandwiches, bodega-style chopped cheese with ground prime brisket, and sweet tea-brined pork chops with Texas peach chutney and goat cheese grits.

"Texas is saturated with great barbecue, even more so now than when we started, so it's more important than ever to offer something that makes your place stand out," says Phillip. "We made that a high priority from the very beginning because we saw how quickly the industry was growing and we knew that just serving great proteins and basic sides wasn't going to have much longevity."

While Phillip focused on the proteins, Yvette handled most of the sides and worked service until becoming pregnant with their son. They were also becoming a great deal busier, so they hired help so she could focus on taxes, legal compliance, and other administrative responsibilities. Before long, they had grown to 30 staff members, including six managers, enabling Phillip to focus on leadership, training, quality control, and menu development. After being listed as one of the Top 25 Best New BBQ Joints in Texas by *Texas Monthly* immediately after they opened, it was no surprise that the magazine named them a Top 50 joint in 2021.

Then, in late November of 2023, their momentum came screeching to a halt when an electrical shortage caused a fire in the propane tanks that spread to the building. The restaurant's Ansul system slowed the fire, but could not put it out entirely. Luckily, no one was injured, but the heat damage to the building was irreparable. Thanks to a GoFundMe relief fund, the Helbergs were operating a drive-through out of a new trailer on the same property just one month later (and three days before Christmas). They continued to take on catering jobs and work out of the trailer into 2024, relocating to a property just down the road. In the summer of 2024, they broke ground on a new 7,800-square-foot space, which they are hoping will open in 2025.

"Our faith has grown during this time of uncertainty," says Yvette. "We have learned the importance of community and just how crucial they are to our success. Whether that be our church community, barbecue community, or surrounding communities, all have played vital roles in us still being here today. And our staff—we've learned they care about what we do and our purpose. Those that we still employ had the opportunity and means to look elsewhere, but stayed—and for that we are thankful."

Their new space will allow them to have a bigger dining room, a larger pit room for Phillip's arsenal of smokers, more parking than ever before, and a covered outdoor dining space with a small area for kids to play. It will also enable them to sell vacuum-sealed sausage packs and raw cuts of meat out of a small market area.

"This has been far from easy, but remembering why we do this—and that, ultimately, this is all in God's hands—brings us comfort," says Yvette. "When deciding whether to build back up or call it quits, we truly felt God steering us towards building back up. We are excited to see how God uses this space and us as we look ahead! The challenges are far from over, and we are still in the thick of them, don't get us wrong. But we trust there's a bigger purpose beyond the trial that we just don't see yet."

SOUTH TEXAS

2M SMOKEHOUSE

SAN ANTONIO

While waiting in line to get into San Antonio's 2M Smokehouse, you will most likely be greeted by a gray tabby who circles the restaurant's grounds. This is Truman, a cat who showed up looking malnourished one night while Esaul Ramos was manning the pits, and is now a full-time resident and unofficial host.

"I'm actually allergic to cats, but I love animals," says Ramos. "So I gave him some raw meat and I just kept feeding him, and now he's my best friend! He eats better than most people, I'll tell you that!"

There was a period of time when Ramos called this place home too—at least Thursday through Sunday. When he and his business partner Joe Melig first opened 2M in 2016, they were sleeping at the establishment in camp chairs while they tried to work out a cook schedule. One day their landlord, who owned a mattress store, showed up with a mattress so they could take turns sleeping more comfortably in between pit shifts.

Thankfully, those days are long gone, and now Ramos and Melig have since expanded to include a 2M food truck and a second restaurant. And they did it all through hard work, faith, and the fervent desire to succeed. Like the motto on the front of the bright turquoise restaurant announces, this is "barbecue con ganas."

"Because you've got to have balls to do this—to tackle the impossible," says Ramos. "Growing up my whole life, my dad was always like, 'Do it con ganas!'"

Ramos grew up in a big Mexican family where smoking meat and entertaining was the norm. His dad normally manned the pit—until Ramos decided to relieve him of those duties when he was in middle school.

"A lot of chefs and cooks will tell you they spent a lot of time with their mom in the kitchen, but I never did," says Ramos. "I loved eating, but I just didn't care to cook it. What happened was we would have barbecue get-togethers with family on the weekends, and my dad would have too much to drink sometimes. At first things are coming out good, and then after a while things start coming out dark. So one day I just asked him, 'Hey, Dad, can I cook?' After that, I just kind of took it and ran. It became a hobby, then an infatuation, and now it's a career."

Melig also got into barbecue around the same age, helping his dad with caterings for their small-town church. When Ramos's family moved and he enrolled at Southwest High School, the two became fast friends, and started smoking together on Melig's dad's smoker, which was crafted from an old oil drum.

"Every weekend, we would put our money together and buy briskets and cook them for our families," remembers Ramos. "I feel bad for them now, but it is what it is. Somebody's got to be the guinea pig so we could get here!"

They continued smoking together throughout college, holding the occasional pop-up and eventually charging money for them too. After graduation, Melig secured a job testing and analyzing ballistics for Southwest Research Institute, and Ramos was working as a bus driver for VIA, San Antonio's transit system. But when he lost his job, he started to think about what he *really* wanted to do.

Ramos had already been visiting Austin and working his way through the city's top barbecue restaurants, starting with Stiles Switch BBQ and Brew (see page 385), which blew him away. He also started frequenting la Barbecue (see page 249), where John Lewis was the pitmaster at the time. He befriended Lewis and started working for him in 2014. Ramos credits la Barbecue for teaching him how to trim his brisket, make sausage, craft barbecue on a large scale, and run a business. The wheels started turning, as he imagined what his own business could look like. Though craft barbecue was thriving just 80 miles away in Austin, all San Antonio had at the time was very basic, old-school barbecue offerings.

"Growing up in San Antonio, it was all meats—no one really cared about the sides," says Ramos. "So I wanted to bring what I learned (at la Barbecue) over here, and I wanted to mesh that with the flavors I grew up with—the flavors my grandma or my mom would put in their dishes. . . . And [I wanted to] bring something to my city that we never had."

Ramos enlisted the help of his original pit partner, and they began to map out a plan. Ramos would take on all of the cooking and back of house duties, while Melig handled the business side of the restaurant. Melig's wife, Selah, a CPA, could tend to the finances and Ramos's wife, Grecia, a pastry chef, would create standout desserts. They were ready to take a huge leap of faith by bringing craft barbecue to San Antonio—but Ramos said some people were skeptical that the city was ready.

"Some of the restaurateurs I talked to laughed in my face," says Ramos. "They were like, 'You can't do that like San Antonio!' They didn't think we could use better ingredients, charge more, have people stand in line, sell out. They said we would be closed within under a year. And I knew it was going to be an uphill battle, because San Antonio's not like the rest of the cities. It's just different here."

Ramos and Melig embarked on a months-long search for a space, and found the WW White Street building while scouring Craigslist. It was previously a gas station, law office, insurance agency, and three different restaurants. The owner was hoping to sell the property and retire, but Ramos proposed leasing it to start because that's all he could afford.

"He was a great landlord," remembers Ramos. "I told him what I wanted to do, and he was just like, 'You know what? I'll give you a shot. I love your story, and you remind me a lot of myself.' And I was like, 'I'll tell you what—you have my word that if, in a year, I can purchase this place from you, I will.'"

The building needed a lot of work, so Ramos and Melig chipped away at a complete renovation, often figuring out how to do things they'd never done before. They built all the countertops and fence post tables, redid all the plumbing, customized the kitchen and rewired electricity. They built a screened-in pit room to house El Mexicano, the Austin Smoke Works offset pit built for him by John Lewis's dad. They created

plenty of outdoor seating and painted the interior of the screened-in porch dining area with vivid turquoise, red and purple accents. They also developed a logo—a fierce looking cattle head flanked by cleavers—which is both painted on the front of the building and tattooed on Ramos's left hand.

Meanwhile, Ramos was perfecting and standardizing procedures and recipes for the meats and sides they would offer. He sources richly marbled HeartBrand Akaushi brisket and rubs it with salt, pepper, garlic, cumin, onion powder, and Lawry's seasoning salt. A low-and-slow cook with post oak transforms that spice blend into an exquisite mahogany bark. All the other meats are rubbed only with salt and pepper, and the pork ribs are finished with a sweet glaze of hot sauce, honey, molasses, and maple syrup. The turkey gets dunked in a bath of clarified butter spiked with rosemary and thyme after it is smoked, and the pork butt is pulled and then tossed in 2M's fresh green salsa (made from tomatillos, serranos, garlic, and lime). Ramos also developed two types of house-made sausage: a more traditional Akaushi beef link, and a pork link made with cilantro, spicy serranos, and the melty Oaxacan cheese he grew up eating.

There was no doubt about the beans Ramos wanted to serve. Maria's Beans are his mother's recipe for ranchero-style pinto beans, simmered with pork bones and housemade bacon, then enhanced with caramelized onions, chopped serranos, tomatoes, and serrano juice. After he developed a creamed corn, Ramos turned it into esquites by topping it with crumbled queso fresco and tajín. His dreams of an exceptional mac and cheese were realized in the Chicharoni Macaroni, topping the classic side with crumbled pork rinds. And for the coleslaw, Melig challenged Ramos to make a version he didn't hate—and the result is a vibrant, sweet red cabbage slaw that brightens up the tray with both acid and color. Ramos also developed a pickle program, fermenting his own serranos, nopales, bell peppers, and onions.

Ramos and Melig decided to name their place 2M Smokehouse, in honor of their grandfathers, Ignacio Márquez and Joe J. Melig Jr. ("But everybody thinks it stands for two Mexicans!" laughs Ramos). Despite any initial doubts, the partners opened the restaurant in December 2016 with tremendous success—and proved that San Antonians are willing to wait in line (and pay a premium) for exceptional barbecue.

"Being able to marry two cultures together and then bring in a different style of barbecue to this city was very cool," Ramos reflects.

In the beginning, it was just Ramos, Melig, and their partners—not even a dishwasher. Ramos's mother, Maria, insisted on coming to help with the dishes, but as Ramos built up a bigger team, he promoted her to tortilla maker. They started off with 500 to 800 flour tortillas a week, and soon needed 300-500 tortillas a day (especially after Ramos began smoking beef cheeks for barbacoa each Sunday). Since

San Antonio has plenty of great tortillerias, Ramos decided to start sourcing from local Alamo Molina to keep up with the demand.

Grecia bakes brioche rolls brushed with smoked tallow for 2M's sandwiches, and her desserts have become another draw, as she routinely surprises guests with dreamy new creations each week like banana pudding tres leches, ube cheesecake, fresh fruit galettes, lemon squares, and buttery pop-tarts filled with flavors like Nutella, chocolate-covered strawberry, PB&J, and piña colada.

A year in, Ramos was able to make good on his promise and buy the building from his landlord—who replied by asking if he wanted to purchase the entire eight-acre property! The former RV park is hooked up with electricity and plumbing, and Ramos has big plans to build a commissary kitchen and a general store, and revive the space as an Airbnb RV park catered to barbecue pilgrims.

"I think Texas is the only place in the United States where people devote their whole trip to barbecue!" he says incredulously.

2M Smokehouse continued to grow in popularity, attracting the attention of national media like *Bon Appetit, Food & Wine,* and the *New York Times.* The restaurant was named a *Texas Monthly* Top 50 pick in 2017 and again in 2021 (the list is refreshed every four years). And then Ramos received the honor of a James Beard Foundation nomination for Best Chef in 2020 and again in 2022. And in 2024, 2M was awarded with a Recommendation by the prestigious Michelin Guide.

All these well-deserved distinctions gave Ramos and Melig the momentum to keep growing. They spent the last half of 2022 and first half of 2023 on a $3 million renovation of a historic meat market in the quaint town of Castroville, "The Little Alsace of

Texas," located 30 miles west of San Antonio. (The duo didn't have to wear carpenter, plumber, and electrician hats for this project!) They opened the spacious 7,423-square-foot smokehouse in the fall of 2023, and Melig has gone on to take the reins there while Ramos continues to grow 2M.

Castroville Barbecue Company offers classic Texas barbecue, but with a twist. Utilizing Cen-Tex offsets and a striking blue M&M BBQ Co. rotisserie pit, they smoke a variety of dishes including cowboy steaks, chicken thighs, wings, pork ribeye, and pork belly. Melig aims to shift the focus away from brisket and highlight the pork and chicken that the town's Alsatian settlers favored. The sides also blend Southern comfort with Alsatian roots, featuring fried potatoes with onions, corn casserole, potato salad, pickled onions, mac and cheese, ranch beans, pasta salad, coleslaw, hand-cut fries, and green beans.

While Grecia doesn't make desserts for Castroville Barbecue Company, her pastry expertise is just a step away—right next door, in fact, at her bakery, aptly named Baked. This is where she crafts fruit-topped laminated pastries, seasonal kolaches, perfect miniature tarts, and sweet and savory croissants filled with everything from pistachio cream to mole. After enjoying a meal at Castroville Barbecue Company, stop at Baked for a sweet treat that's every bit as unforgettable as the meat.

THE SAUSAGE SENSEI

Sausage is experiencing a renaissance in Texas—and at the heart of it is Bill Dumas, known more commonly by his alias, The Sausage Sensei. Dumas has crafted an educational sausage-making program popular with both industry pros and passionate backyard cooks alike. Stepping into one of Dumas's classes is like entering the world of a modern-day meat philosopher: a man whose passion for encased meats is matched only by his encyclopedic knowledge, zany musings, and frequent pop culture references.

"Sausage is, in fact, the oldest food discipline science on this globe," Dumas begins dramatically, as we peer over rows of glistening sausages lined up on an offset Moberg smoker. "Well, beer and bread were probably the first, but you'd have to argue with an ancient Egyptian to figure that out, right? There's ancient archaeological evidence of sausage being made and consumed in Mesopotamia, 5000 BC. The word sausage itself is derived from the Latin term salsus, which means heavily salted. There's a type of sausage described in Homer's *Odyssey*. There's archaeological evidence of sausage within the remnants of Pompeii." He pauses to check the temp on the sausages at hand. "I'm looking for an internal temp of 150°F. If it's more than that—sorry to say, but you've got yourself shriveled old man pecker."

Dumas was raised in Whitesboro, Texas—a tiny speck of a town between Sherman and Gainesville, just

South of Lake Texoma. "Growing up there, in the 1970s, was like living in a mixture of *Leave it to Beaver* and *To Kill a Mockingbird*," he muses. He spent a lot of time with his grandfather, Curtis Dumas Sr., a larger-than-life bull rider turned shoe salesman in the Fort Worth stockyards. Upon retiring, Curtis started a new venture, and became locally known for his split chickens cooked over direct coals and mopped with his signature molasses and coffee-based barbecue sauce.

"I was incredibly close to my grandfather," remembers Dumas. "But children were also free labor, so I was shoveling coal and carrying wood at age five or six. This imprinted itself on me: the sights, the sounds, the smells. My barbecue journey started there, in 1973." When his grandfather passed away, Dumas says he lost his way, becoming a self-described juvenile delinquent and enlisting in the Marines by age 18. After returning home, he worked in a variety of different jobs: retail, commercial truck driving, industrial refrigeration tech.

"But this always kept me centered," says Dumas, motioning toward the pit. His love affair with sausage didn't start until 2014, when he began managing and operating a new food truck opened by Smokey Denmark, a long-standing, family-owned sausage manufacturer in Austin. In 2015, Dumas joined the team at Stiles Switch BBQ and Brew, which joined *Texas Monthly*'s Top 50 list that very same year. At the very end of 2019, he connected with John Brotherton, who wanted to develop an in-house sausage production program for Brotherton's Black Iron Barbecue. The two joined forces, and Brotherton gave Dumas the liberty to create the sausage-making program of his dreams in a kitchen adjacent to the restaurant. There, Dumas began crafting 700 pounds of sausage a week and teaching classes when he wasn't traveling the world for festivals and collaborations.

He's collaborated in Southern California with Smoke Queen BBQ to create Sichuan noodle, chicken satay, and Singapore sambal sausages, plus red mooncake sausage for dessert. In Monterrey, Mexico, he collaborated with NÓMADA XXI to create a tres moles sausage with housemade adobo, Gota-Santa mezcal, guajillo and ancho chiles, toasted pepitas, and Oaxacan cheese, followed by a pan de elote dessert sausage. He's created an Italian beef sausage— bursting with Portillo's Italian beef, gravy, bread, and giardiniera—and sent it to the Chicago Cubs. And on any given weekend, Brotherton's was featuring Dumas's one-off creations stuffed with everything from Philly cheesesteak and mac and cheese to bulgogi with kimchi and broken jasmine rice. For Thanksgiving, he fit an entire turkey feast inside sausage casing, and he's become known for dessert sausages made up of apple pie and peach cobbler components, which he's served backstage to musicians like Willie Nelson and Tyler Childers.

"There's only so much that I can do with a cut of meat," explains Dumas. "But once you crack the code on how sausage is put together, it can become anything. It's like music: you know your notes, chords, scales and you can create anything." His eyes light up behind his trademark dark-rimmed glasses, and he adds, with a salt-and-ginger-bearded smirk, "This is just a way for me to be weird. Salvador Dalí himself said that exceptional artists must be able to take the most mundane objects and create something truly exceptional. Well, this is my medium."

Dumas's sausage-making program is based off a three-day process, starting with trimming the briskets and separating the meat and fat into different buckets. They will then be weighed out to the industry-accepted standard ratio of 70/30, lean meat to fat. (Some of the sausages he makes are 100 percent beef, while some are a beef-pork blend). The average loss on every brisket is about 50 percent from trim to shrink, so using every possible scrap is not only sustainable, but lucrative.

"Sausage is commonly referred to as a meat emulsion. In layman's terms, that means we are going to make a measured amount of proteins to fats, and apply the measured amount of salt," Dumas narrates. He uses 12-mesh black pepper and two types of salts —kosher and pink curing salt—applied at 1.8 to 2.2 percent of the meat weight and rested overnight to penetrate the mixture.

"And that creates the cure," he says, followed by one of his signature Sensei-isms. "And no, we're not talking about the band that was formed in the

Midlands of England by one Robert Smith. If it were, then we might be depressed, we might smoke clove cigarettes, and we might wear dark eyeliner."

Day Two is all about assembling the links. We start off by grinding the meat mixture in his 1979 Hobart, which can process 50 pounds of products in a minute. ("This is my baby! You hear it sing?" Dumas proclaims gleefully.) He primarily uses dry spices as the vehicle for the base flavor, first awakening them by toasting them in a saucepan. ("If you think you've seasoned it enough, season more," is his advice. "We want to bitch-slap it with enough garlic to kill a vampire!").

"When we apply both ambient and frictional heat to it—through this grinder and through physically mixing it—we are going to extract and stretch out the protein strands. When we do that, it sticks together and creates the emulsion."

Dry milk powder is then added as a binder, along with an ice slush to keep everything cold, before we stuff the emulsion into 30-32 millimeter natural casings. Dumas's sausages often feature visual and textural elements suspended within them, and he achieves this by layering the stuffer like a trifle. We soak the casings in water several times to remove the salt before he demonstrates how to shimmy them onto the horn of the stuffer and apply just the right amount of pressure as the meat emulsion is extruded—all while working quickly to keep everything cold.

“Now this process requires a shit-ton of finesse,” says Dumas. “Most people can replicate everything else but this right here is what separates folks—splits the herd. *Now* can you smell what The Rock is cooking?”

He shows us how to pinch and spin the coil into half-pound links, alternating directions. They’ll go into the refrigerator to rest overnight until the next day, when they’ll be smoked. But first we take the opportunity for a WWE-style photo shoot, holding up our links like heavyweight championship belts while Dumas hollers, “I’ve had it with you, Jake the Snake!”

Next, we tend to a batch of sausages that were processed the day before. Dumas slows the fire down to maintain a pit temperature of 150°F, and we line the links up neatly across the grill, where they’ll smoke for just over an hour. These days, though, Dumas is smoking his sausage vertically, using a special offset smoker he designed with Brazilian pit builders True Bomb, who unveiled the prototype at Churrascada, a huge annual meatfest that takes place in São Paolo.

“Sausage operates best when it’s hung in long chains and ropes because you get better air circulation,” he explains. “As the casing contracts and internal mix sets, the weight of that sausage pulling on one another on that chain is going to create better color retention, better mouthfeel, and better snap on the casing.”

Snap open one of Dumas’ sausages, fresh off the grill, and the thin, tight casing creates a satisfying pop, followed by succulent juices flowing freely. (While many pitmasters rely on “restricted melt” cheese to create an aesthetically pleasing cross section, Dumas doesn’t touch the stuff—only naturally melting cheese here.) And his jalapeño-cheese links—an essential offering in Texas barbecue joints—are enhanced with guajillo, ancho, and chipotle morita chiles *plus* jalapeños. Dumas passes around an oak barrel–aged mustard made by a tiny meat market named Fischer’s in Munster, instructing us to slather it on our white bread–wrapped sausage and add some pickle and onion.

“Best mustard on God’s green earth!” he declares after taking a snappy bite and admiring the link’s interior, “Good color retention. The casings are damn near invisible on the cross section. Nice and compact and tight, good moisture—in my view, this is what sausage should be!”

And he would know. After all, he is the Sensei.

BURNT BEAN CO.

SEGUIN

At its essence, barbecue begins with the single spark of a flame—and that's exactly how Ernest Servantes's journey began, in his family's backyard in Uvalde.

"My dad is a phenomenal cook, and he's legitimately old school," says Servantes. "He had these big fires going and he shoveled coals. My dad was doing it before it was cool. So that's how I learned how to really cook with coals and understand what they look like, in the daytime and at night, the way they glimmer."

Servantes also spent hours alongside his grandmother in the tamale shop she owned, then began working in restaurants at a young age, working his way up from washing dishes and bussing tables to cooking. He worked for over 15 years as a corporate chef for the hospitality company Sodexo, ending up as executive chef at Texas Lutheran University in Seguin. During that time, he requested time off to enter his first barbecue competition. When a co-worker joked that he was probably going to burn the beans, Servantes had the perfect name for his passion project—and Burnt Bean Co. was born.

"When you're in a controlled environment, like a kitchen, your creativity can only go so far," explains Servantes. "But when you're using old-school methods of dealing with fires and flames, taming the smoke and bringing out the beauty of the protein with the accompaniment of smoke, it's a lot different flavor profile than just putting it on a grill. And it's a challenge. That's why I like it—every day is different."

Over the next 13 years, Servantes developed his concept on the weekend while working out of his competition trailer, which he painted with Aztec warriors and

Day of the Dead murals. After sweeping up just about every local award he could, he began to compete nationally and appeared on Food Network, Travel Channel, and Destination America, winning both *Chopped* and *Chopped: Grill Masters*.

"My dream was always to open my own barbecue joint, but I had no accolades, I had no vision," remembers Servantes. "I wanted to make sure this is what I wanted to do, and I also didn't have the capital. So I became a competition cook because I figured I could market my name and market Burnt Bean."

When Servantes met David Kirkland on the competition circuit, the two became fast friends. Kirkland, who had a history of competing in cook-offs with his brother Robby, joined forces with Servantes.

"I quickly grew interested in what Ernest had to offer in advice," remembers Kirkland. "Finally someone to have a conversation with who unknowingly satisfied my hunger for direction. I didn't want him to think I was just a guy trying to copy him but merely passionate about the process of cooking meat. The sincerity of my interest in cooking I believe is one of the reasons we work well together."

Before long, the two were competing together and winning cook-offs across the state. In October 2019, Servantes asked Kirkland if he wanted to help with a barbecue pop-up at a bar in Seguin—Kirkland's hometown. It was an immediate success, so the duo started doing it every two weeks, drawing a bigger crowd each time—until the pandemic brought everything to a screeching halt.

"If COVID didn't make you work harder, then the hustle's not in you," says Servantes. "I wanted it, and I got stronger because I honed my skills . . . and David's a workaholic as much as I am. He loves what he does, and he takes pride in everything he does."

After a couple of dormant months, the two picked themselves up and brainstormed how they could regain their momentum. They started running pop-ups out of Servantes's yard and, when they found out the bar they'd been popping up at had shut down, they pooled their money to take over the lease and begin renovations. Servantes sold just about everything he owned to purchase two offset smokers from Mill Scale Metalworks, and he named them after his grandmothers, Amelia and Belia.

"They're my inspiration to cook," he says. "So whenever I wanted to give up, I'd stare at these pits and see their names. I know they have my back, and I can't fail."

The two opened Burnt Bean Co. in October 2020 to a line out the door, and it's grown longer each year. To say they've taken the sleepy town of Seguin by storm is an understatement. Each Thursday through Sunday, a massive queue forms down Austin Street, and on weekends it will wrap around and stretch two blocks west, all the way to the county clerk's office. On Sundays, folks will start lining up at 5 a.m. for the next-level Sunday brunch that starts at 8 a.m., starring dishes like brisket huevos rancheros, bourbon peach cobbler buñuelo tacos, and Hangover Combos featuring barbacoa, menudo, and flour tortillas.

The historic space Burnt Bean occupies opened as a hardware store in the 1800s, and was a bakery for several decades in the 1970s until a fire destroyed it in the 1990s. You can still see some burn marks on the limestone walls, and select bricks are painted white to serve as a canvas for black-and-white portraits of a pig and a longhorn. Light fixtures made from Edison bulbs and antique wheels add to the new-meets-old aesthetic and the words "Viva BBQ" scrawled on the wall are much more than just a cute tagline.

The Burnt Bean menu is a love letter to Servantes's upbringing. He uses his dad's method for smoking barbacoa, using beef cheeks, a process known as "tatema" in Uvalde. The potato salad and coleslaw recipes are his mother's, and the menudo comes as close as possible to his grandmother's.

"You've got to realize one thing about Mexicans," says Servantes. "Why do grandmas and grandpas cook for their families? Because we were poor. We couldn't take any trips, so grandma expressed her love through her cooking. Love is food. And with the Hispanic culture, every food tells a story about our heritage, every food tells a story about our livelihood, and every food tells a story about a certain time of our life."

Beyond dishes directly inspired by family members, there are plenty more that are Servantes's own creation, but with a distinct South Texas twist. A decadent queso mac and cheese is topped with crumbled Hot Cheetos. The street corn pudding is "like Mexican corn in a cup and cornbread had a baby," with waves of salty and sweet accented by pops of tang and spice. A halved sweet potato gets stuffed with marshmallows and torched à la minute for a sweet little homage to Thanksgiving.

These playful sides are served alongside proteins Kirkland and Servantes have perfected smoking on the two Mill Scale Metalworks pits, an M&M rotisserie pit, and a white Cen-Tex showpit that can be made direct or indirect (used mostly for special events). Their brisket is smoked for an average of 14 hours, resulting in a melt-in-your-mouth marbling held together with a sturdy bark made only of salt and pepper—the same rub used for the beef ribs, turkey, and pork chops. The pork ribs get a slightly different house seasoning, with two different meshes of pepper, and the fat is caramelized to a lovely sweetness that I mistook for brown sugar. A snap of the jalapeño cheese sausage reveals Sausage Sensei (see page 431)–approved perfection: a generous ratio of cheese is held together in a moist emulsion and balanced with the perfect amount of heat.

"Ernest is an incredible chef and needs to be able to focus on that," says Kirkland. "I am the one person who was trained and molded to understand the passion and process of preparing proteins the way he himself would. This combo allows us to put up the best variety of not only proteins but every menu item we decide to add."

Servantes's wife, Belinda, developed the Burnt Bean Co.'s first two dessert recipes back in their pop-up days: classic banana pudding swaps out vanilla wafers for pecan sandies in an undeniably delicious upgrade, and the Big Red tres leches is a surprisingly light homage to the beloved, Texas-born cherry cream soda. But now the dessert offerings have grown to include a daily selection of homemade cakes (in flavors like red velvet, Italian cream cake, and turtle pecan), all served by the massive slice. (There's no way you'll have room for cake after a Burnt Bean Co. feast, but I suggest you take a slice home and spend the next couple of days stealing bites of it in front of your fridge, as I did.)

Because the Burnt Bean Co. gets so many regulars, Servantes has created a robust program of specials to give them a reason to keep coming back. Pork steaks and prime rib are served on Fridays and their now-famous smoked red burgers, made from brisket and short rib ground in-house, are only available on Thursdays and Fridays. When annual Fiesta celebrations started up in nearby San Antonio, Servantes created a sandwich called La Babe: pulled pork with chamoy BBQ sauce, chicharron, and pineapple slaw on a pink concha. And any given weekend, they'll offer specials ranging from smoked duck Hoppin' John with charred bourbon peaches to Moroccan-spiced smoked lamb ribs with batbout. These wildly creative—and limited-edition—dishes have earned both Burnt Bean Co. (@burntbeanco) and Servantes (@popeofbbq) quite an Instagram following, outlets that undoubtedly help pull the masses to the small town between Austin and San Antonio.

While some barbecue spots might work for years toward landing a coveted spot on *Texas Monthly's* Top 50 list, Burnt Bean Co. placed number four in the 2021 edition. In 2022, Kirkland and Servantes were named semifinalists for the James Beard Foundation's prestigious award for Best Chef: Texas. In 2023, they were honored as finalists for the award and they were semifinalists again the next year. And at the end of 2024, the restaurant was presented with a prestigious Michelin Bib Gourmand award.

"What made it more special is we're in a small town," says Servantes. "We don't have publicists and we don't have big foodies like the cities do. We just work off word of mouth, so to bring that kind of notoriety to small town USA was pretty humbling. We're butcher paper and brisket, we're not fancy linen or fancy dishes. We just put a lot of love in what we do. We cook from our souls."

MATTI BILLS

Mattison ("Matti") Bills went a year without eating meat for the same reasons she ended up focusing on it. She was studying environmental science at St. Edward's University in Austin and learning about the importance of local food production. But Bills found it was nearly impossible to source all-natural, local meat. She worked for some small farms—like Sand Holler Farm, Green Gate Farm, and Johnson's Backyard Garden—but one of her most influential jobs was catering events at Springdale Farm with Chef Sonya Cote, where Bills gained experience and helped create some of the very first (and most literal) farm-to-table cuisine in Austin.

"It was an integral introduction for me," remembers Bills, "and I started my market business out of the same kitchen just a few months later. It meant a lot to be able to offer what I thought to be the first local, all-natural smoked brisket available at the time. It's important for people to be able to access these types of resources without needing to know the producer themselves."

Bills learned butchery by reading books by Adam Danforth, doing research online, and practicing on local hogs. In 2014, she began sourcing ethically and sustainably raised meat from Texas producers like Strube Ranch, 44 Farms, Peaceful Pork, HeartBrand Akaushi, and R-C Ranch. She then started butchering and smoking brisket, pastrami, ribs, chicken bacon, and sausage to sell at Austin-area farmers markets under the name Mum Foods.

"I wish people understood how much goes into production from start to finish," she explains. "It's an incredible amount of work and resources. The closer you can get to the source, the better. From birthing and raising the animal, transporting it to the processor, butchering it into its many parts, vacuum sealing it, transporting it to a distributor, then to someone like us who [in the case of pastrami] spend hours injecting it with brine, let it sit in that brine for a week, rub it with coriander and black pepper, smoke it for eight hours, let it rest for many more hours, then transport it to a location near you where we hope someone shows up to buy it."

Interestingly enough, barbecue runs in this eighth-generation Texan's blood. Bills's late grandparents used to run a butcher shop, smokehouse, and deli (and Bills only found this out after she'd already started pursuing this career path).

"I think their influence naturally trickled down to me in the form of our family smoker," says Bills. "I grew up cooking on an offset that my dad built before I was born. He eventually gave it to me, and I used it to start [Mum]."

Mum Foods quickly became known for its melt-in-your-mouth Wagyu pastrami, attracting lines at three different farmer's market locations around Austin. In 2017, *Texas Monthly* barbecue editor Daniel Vaughn declared the black pepper and coriander–rubbed and brined brisket the "best in the state," and something he'd been seeking for five years.

In 2019, Bills sold her share of Mum Foods to her previous business partner Geoffrey Ellis (see page 371) to launch Three Six General, named after the San

Marcos zip code, 78666. This deli concept also featured sandwiches and meats sold by the pound, with an even more extensive menu of housemade market offerings like pickles, ferments (from hot sauce to sauerkraut), sides, and condiments. Business was booming at several different farmers markets across Central Texas—until the pandemic forced the markets to shut down.

With takeout and to-go food more in-demand than ever, Bills sought out kitchen space to expand her wholesale operations and open a retail butcher shop featuring Texas products. In 2020, she ended up signing a lease on a building in San Marcos with enough space to turn Three Six General into a brick-and-mortar general store featuring goods made by her farmers' market colleagues: flour from Barton Springs Mill, produce from Fruitful Hill, Mother Culture yogurt, SRSLY Chocolate, and Two Hives Honey, plus local craft beer and cider and low-intervention wine.

Bills also began selling even more food made in-house using meat trimmings (like sauces, chilis, and soups), as well as more pickles and ferments to avoid wasting any locally grown produce. She also crafts rice bowls inspired by the way she eats at home. ("It's a great vessel for utilizing any protein, and can be lightened up with greens and herbs," she describes.)

Some of her best-selling items can be ordered through Farmhouse Delivery and, in addition to the San Marcos shop, Three Six General continues to operate at three different farmers markets (Austin's Mueller market, San Marcos' market and New Braunfels' market). In the summer of 2023, Bills opened a barbecue counter called Howdy Child in the Pearl Food Hall. There, she sells brisket, pastrami, Wagyu beef sausage, and turkey by the pound and plate, plus sandwiches (like her famous Reuben), salads made with local veggies, and sides like beef tallow fries and decadent shells and cheese.

These days, Bills spends most of her time in San Antonio, running Howdy Child and tending to the urban farm plot she started to grow food for the business. Manager Brooke Dinsmore oversees operations at Three Six General, where she acts as lead butcher, barbecuer, and meat buyer. The Texas barbecue industry may still be dominated by men, but Bills is changing the narrative by leading a hard-working, female-dominant staff.

"I did break my finger once using a smoker that didn't have counterweights, but I sold the barbecue like a champ that weekend," she remembers. "There are certainly advantages to being a man, but making good barbecue isn't one of them. Being detail-oriented and resilient is what matters the most."

VERA'S BACKYARD BAR-B-QUE

BROWNSVILLE

Vera's Backyard Bar-B-Que is more than just a charming name. When second-generation pitmaster Armando ("Mando") Vera started cooking here just over 50 years ago, he and his family called this place home.

"This was the business and our living and dining room," says Vera, gesturing within the small restaurant. "That over there was a kitchen, and then me and my three siblings slept in the back on the floor."

In 1955, Amando's parents, Alberto and Carmen, opened Vera's in Brownsville, a border city just across the Rio Grande from Matamoros, Mexico. The specialty here is barbacoa de cabeza de res en pozo a la leña: whole beef head cooked in a wood-fired pit. And Vera's Backyard Bar-B-Que is the only place in the state—and likely the whole country—cooking it the traditional way: buried underground and smoked over wood coals.

"I was 13 when I started doing it on my own," says Vera. "It wasn't by choice, but I started doing it. Something that you do when you're that young, it's instilled in you—it's in the blood. So you keep going and going."

Vera learned how to pit smoke from watching his father, and when his parents separated in 1972 and his older brothers left home to marry, he took over the cooking responsibilities and ran the place with his mother. The process begins by burning mesquite, which is indigenous to the region, for about six hours until it turns to coals. After the beef heads are cleaned, they are lowered into a brick-lined pit, then covered with stainless-steel sheet metal and sealed in with dirt. Once the pit is closed, its contents will smoke for eight to 12 hours.

"We don't use seasoning, not even salt," Vera emphasizes. "The flavor comes from the pit, the coals, the meat."

Pit cooking can be traced back to the pre-Columbian era, and is believed to be introduced by the Taíno people indigenous to the Caribbean. The technique eventually migrated west to Mexico, where it has taken many forms. In Hidalgo, lamb is famously cooked in the ground over agave leaves, while pork wrapped in banana leaves produces the famed cochinita pibil found in the Yucatán. In Guanajuato, goat spiced with cascabel chiles is typically buried with fire, and Veracruz has a dish made from red chile–rubbed chicken wrapped in hoja santa and avocado leaves.

But it was the vaqueros of the Northern Mexican states who began pit roasting beef head barbacoa in Nuevo León, Sonora, and Chihuahua. That method made its way up into South Texas by the nineteenth century, where Mexican ranch hands made resourceful use of the unwanted heads of cattle butchered by Anglo ranchers. While this method of cooking can still be found all over Mexico, tightened health regulations in the 1970s led to its ban in the United States. Luckily, Vera's Backyard Bar-B-Que, now in its seventh decade of operation, has been grandfathered into keeping their underground pits going.

Vera has made very few changes to the restaurant in the last 50 years. Vera's was originally a take-out operation but, after his mother's passing in 1989, he turned it into a dine-in restaurant with seating. The six-foot long, six-foot deep, and three-and-a-half foot wide pit built by his dad was originally lined with adobe brick, but Vera switched to the better-insulating firebrick around 30 years ago. And just five years ago, he implemented a basket with a boom lift and winch to lift the beef heads out of the pit with greater ease. Before that, he would just remove the smoking hot heads by his own heavily gloved hand.

After the cook, which happens just behind the building, the whole heads are brought into the kitchen where they are unwrapped and deboned by Vera and his staff. The meat is separated into cachete (cheek), lengua (tongue), cachete entero (lips), paladar (palate), jeta (jawline), and mollejas (sweetbreads). The rest is chopped up and sold as mixta, a blend Vera compares to chopped barbecued beef.

"There's people who buy the cachete and the mixta and they mix it together because they like the flavor (of the mixta), but they want something leaner," he says. Cachete is certainly the most popular selection, similar to pot roast in flavor and texture. "Lengua is similar to brisket. With the brisket, if you want moist, you get the back part. With the lengua, it's the same thing. If you want something dry, you get the lean at the tip of the tongue."

Paladar has a very fatty, gelatinous texture from the collagen in the palate (this separates the oral cavity from the nasal cavity)—and this is the one part Vera himself has never eaten because he doesn't like the texture. Mollejas can be found at taquerias and some barbecue joints in this area of the Rio Grande Valley, and they are typically firm to crispy. The sweetbreads at Vera's are instead soft and supple ("You're not going to find mollejas like this anywhere else," says Vera), and can be ordered mixed with the jeta for a more robust flavor.

"That part of the head, from the side of the jaw, has the most smoke flavor, so it's tender, juicy, and a little smokier," explains Vera.

There are a couple of offerings that are more rare, and considered delicacies: sesos (brains) and ojos (the eyes). Ever since the mad cow disease scare, the packers removed the brains from the heads. However, Vera says they are sometimes delivered in a separate container after inspection, to the delight of regulars who love their creamy texture. Similarly, the eyes don't always arrive with the heads, but when they do, they are in such high demand that Vera refers to them as "Mexican caviar."

"You have to be royalty to get an eye," he says. There's even a bright green square of posterboard taped to the front door with the message "No hay sesos/ojos, sorry!" handwritten in marker. That doesn't stop some customers from inquiring once they enter and Vera greets them with a "Buenos dias!"

Vera also smokes lamb (for birria) and menudo (tripe stew), adding both to the pit with the cow heads. He smokes a minimal amount of brisket, using an offset smoker, and carnitas get fried on the stovetop. But the barbacoa is by far the most popular offering; he smokes between 50 and 65 cow heads Friday through Sunday, which is when they're open—and was making 250 a weekend during the pandemic, when there was a surge in takeout orders.

Meat is ordered by the pound at the counter, as well as warm flour or corn tortillas from nearby Capistran Tortilla Factory. This is also where you can add on cups of chopped white onion and cilantro, slices of lime, chile pequín (tiny spicy red chiles that grow in Texas), avocado, and a rainbow of housemade salsas. There's pico de gallo, a mild red casera salsa, a creamy green aguacate salsa, a bright tomatillo salsa verde, and a vivid orange habanero salsa that keeps building in spice long after you think it's over.

"I also make a red one I call the American salsa because it's not spicy at all," says Vera. "I thought that white people didn't like spicy at all, but I was wrong!"

It's incredible what flavors are drawn out from the meat by the wood and smoke alone. But fold that barbacoa into fresh corn tortillas, drizzle it with vibrant salsa, and sprinkle it with onion and cilantro for a true transcendental taco experience.

In 2020, the James Beard Foundation granted Vera's an American Classics Award, an honor given to "locally owned restaurants that have timeless appeal and are beloved regionally." When Vera first got the call with the Beard Foundation, he hung up on them—twice—because he thought it was a scam. The foundation eventually contacted the mayor of Brownsville to get the message through to him. In 2022, Vera's was designated a Texas Treasure Business by the Texas Historical Commission. The recognition has helped diversify Vera's customer base, drawing people from other states and countries to try the pit-smoked barbacoa that can only be experienced here.

Until the last couple of years, Vera says the dining room walls were just sheetrock. Now they sport wood paneling, a brick facade, and framed photos of some of his favorite cultural icons: Lucille Ball, John Wayne, Pedro Infante, and Flaco Jimenez. There's also a wall dedicated to veterans, in honor of his dad, who served in World War II. In the window, a neon sign blinks the words: "This Must Be the Place." One line in particular from that Talking Heads song couldn't be more appropriate for this richly historied restaurant: "Home is where I want to be, but I guess I'm already there."

TEDDY'S BARBECUE

WESLACO

Growing up in South Texas, Joel Garcia says cooking with fire was a way of life. However, he never imagined he would pursue it as a career path.

"We grew up along the border, so a lot of the barbecue that we knew was cooking over fire—fajitas, chicken leg quarters," says Garcia. "You know, things that are just grilled, not cooked indirectly, which is still considered barbecue in some parts."

But when Garcia moved to College Station to study at Texas A&M University, his eyes were opened to meat smoked low and slow using indirect heat. He became a regular at places like Fargo's and C&J, then got a small pit and began practicing at home. After graduating with a degree in environmental science in 2013, he moved to Austin for a policy internship at the Capitol with a state representative.

"I didn't really like working in office, but it was when the 2013 Top 50 list came out," says Garcia. "So that's when I started seeing all these different barbecue places, all these different styles of barbecue. And I started traveling a little bit outside of Austin to Lockhart, Snow's, Louie Mueller. Growing up, I was always in the kitchen, always cooking in some way. I just didn't fall in love with barbecue until I started going around tasting the different styles and figuring out that this takes a lot of time and a lot of

patience and a lot of skill. You know, managing a fire isn't easy."

When Garcia and his wife bought a house in Manor, she surprised him with a pit big enough to smoke brisket, which accelerated his education. While still working at the Capitol, he decided to try his hand working in barbecue. At the time, beloved Texas grocery store H-E-B was testing its True Texas Barbecue concept at the Mueller location before it launched at stores across the state. So Garcia's very first job in barbecue was at a very high-volume operation, where he mastered smoking all natural Prime briskets, 20 to 30 at a time. After about a year at H-E-B, Garcia emailed Evan LeRoy, who brought him onto his team at Freedmen's Bar.

"I didn't refine those [pit] skills until I went to Freedmen's, where there was much more attention to detail—how we trim, how we season, how you make sausage, cooking ribs," remembers Garcia. "That was really the first experience I had cooking ribs, because at Café Mueller, we were cooking St. Louis–cut ribs that we just seasoned with a sugar rub and threw in for a certain amount of time, then took them out and wrapped them. That was it—we weren't checking them, feeling them, making sure they were cooking right, and turning them."

At Freedmen's, Garcia worked alongside Lane Milne, who went on to open Goldee's Barbecue (see page 16) along with his friends, Chris McGhee, who now owns Briscuits, Brad Robinson of Chuds BBQ (see page 267), and others. When Garcia's younger brother Jesse graduated high school, he brought him onto the Freedmen's team too; Jesse started in the dish pit, but then moved up to lead prep while attending the Escoffier School of Culinary Arts.

"There were a bunch of great cooks that worked at Freedmen's back in the day," says Joel. "And you would cook everything, you would do it all. So working at Freedmen's really taught me the craft—how to cook craft barbecue."

After LeRoy left Freedmen's to open LeRoy and Lewis Barbecue (see page 258), Joel stayed on, and saw the restaurant land on the *Texas Monthly* Top 50 list in 2017. But he was really feeling the weight of working at the Senate office each day, then heading straight to a barbecue job until late at night—and his wife was expecting. When his son was born that summer, Joel took paternity leave to spend time at home with them. But he couldn't stay away from the pit for long, so he started to smoke meat in the driveway of their Manor home, selling sandwiches under the name Teddy's Barbecue, named after his son.

When his paternity leave was up, Joel decided to leave government work for good. He took on a full-time job working the nighttime rib shift at Terry Black's Barbecue in Austin, where he would fill up five or six smokers with upwards of 150 racks of ribs.

"I mean, talk about cooking in volume!" says Joel. "It's insane how much food they make every single day, and the owners were there, almost every day, making sure everything's turning out great. Everyone that was working there was passionate about producing good barbecue. They really just taught me the efficiency of an operation—everybody has a role, everybody has a job to do, and just don't get out of your lane, basically. It was a crazy operation to see and a really good experience for me in how to stay organized in a kitchen."

Meanwhile, Jesse had moved back home to the Valley, where he was getting experience working in the kitchens of fine-dining restaurants, like Salomé on Main in McAllen. Joel also wanted to be closer to family and was dreaming about opening his own place. He even started making the nearly 300-mile drive back to Weslaco each week to participate in a culinary pop-up before turning around and driving back to work at Terry Black's each weekend. He again found himself fatigued from burning the candle at both ends. So when he was offered the opportunity to open a new barbecue joint called Smokin' Moon in Pharr (just 15 miles west of Weslaco), he took it.

"But I told them I'm not doing it without my brother," recalls Joel. "I didn't want to do it with a bunch of inexperienced guys. I wanted somebody to be there with me to show these guys, to lead them."

So Jesse joined forces with Joel to help open Smokin' Moon in October 2018 and, under Joel's lead, the restaurant landed on *Texas Monthly*'s list of 25 Best New BBQ Joints in early 2019, But when Joel announced that he and Jesse had closed on a building in their hometown of Weslaco to open Teddy's Barbecue as a brick and mortar, the owners of Smokin' Moon promptly fired him. Joel had planned on slowly renovating the former Mesquite Pete's space, but instead he opened two months later, in September 2019, after giving the small dining room a fresh coat of paint and covering the tables with red-and-white checkered oilcloth.

"When we first started, all we had was like a little 250-gallon smoker," remembers Joel. "We would fit maybe six briskets and a few racks of ribs on there. We've obviously built onto it and added things as we went along, and I think we've done a good job of turning that place around."

By 2020, the brothers added a 1,000-gallon offset smoker crafted by Primitive Pits out of Georgia, and in 2021 they acquired one more. In 2022, they bought a trailer so they could haul one of the pits around for events. And more recently, they added a Chud Box designed by Robinson at Chuds BBQ, which they use to cook chicken, and an M&M rotisserie smoker, which they use to cook ribs, turkey, and pork belly. Since Joel is intent on using post oak, which is not native to the Rio Grande Valley, he used to spend his one day off driving up to Luling to pick up post oak. But these days, he is able to get it delivered monthly.

Abiding by the tenets of traditional Central Texas barbecue followed by both LeRoy and Mark and Mike Black, Joel sticks to using just salt and pepper on his brisket: specifically, three parts of 16-mesh Fiesta pepper to one part Morton's kosher salt.

"We have like a tub of rub that we just throw them in and toss them in," says Joel. "We season them the day before they go on the pit, so the salt permeates the meat and brings out some of the water from the fat."

He starts his Creekstone Farms Premium Black Angus brisket off at a lower heat, then slowly builds the fire and the heat. After about nine or 10 hours, the briskets get wrapped in butcher paper, and he finishes them off at a high heat.

"The total cooking time really depends on the ambient temperature," explains Joel. "So if it's cold outside, our brisket sometimes takes up to 14 hours. If it's a summer day, sometimes they're done in like 10 hours of cooking. So it just depends. It gets really hot down here during the summer. When it's over 100 degrees for 90-plus days, it doesn't take much to cook a brisket."

Teddy's brisket has been hailed as the best in South Texas, and it lives up to the hype. A magenta smoke ring is framed by a thick, peppery bark, while a thick vein of expertly rendered fat winds its way through the meat. The barbecue sauce, a blend of ketchup, mustard, vinegar, sugar, Worcestershire sauce, salt, pepper, cayenne, cumin, garlic, and chile powder that Joel and Jesse developed, perfectly accompanies the brisket, supplying a nice balance of sweet, tangy, and a little bit of spice.

The rest of Teddy's proteins all get rubbed with 16-mesh black pepper, followed by Fiesta Season-All, a seasoning similar to Lawry's. The turkey is wrapped with buttered foil for an exceedingly moist mouthfeel and flavorful finish. The chicken is juicy, with a crispy skin and nice color thanks to cooking over direct heat. And the Prairie Fresh All Natural pork ribs have a good chew and a rich, porky flavor with a hint of gloss and tang from a gastrique glaze. Another standout item on the menu at Teddy's is the crispy pork belly, which is hugged by a thick, crunchy, and perfectly seasoned skin.

"The crispy belly—I'm not gonna take credit for it because I've seen other people do it," says Joel humbly. "It's just the way that they prepare it is different from our method. Crispy belly is something that, in our culture, people have been eating forever. They make chicharrónes and carnitas down in Mexico, and they've been cooking bellies and making it crispy for years and years. . . . One place in particular that inspired me was Hoodoo Brown BBQ in Connecticut. They smoke the bellies and then they throw them in the oven for a crispy skin. But I think the skin takes on a whole other

flavor when you throw it over the [direct] heat, because it releases that fat and it drops into those coals and it just takes on more smoke and color."

Joel prepares his by smoking the belly with indirect heat, then crisping it over direct heat in the Chud Box until it puffs up into a chicharrón-like layer. He then slices and serves it.

"Early on, it was kind of a hard sell just because some people didn't want to try it," he says. "And now we can't cook enough of it."

The sausages Joel and Jesse make at Teddy's are all based on the recipes they learned while at the now-shuttered Freedmen's. The ratios of fat, beef, and pork are the same but, while the seasonings at Freedmen's were mostly fresh garlic, jalapeño, salt, and pepper, Joel developed his sausages to have more of a South Texas flavor.

"There's a lot of cumin, there's cayenne, there's paprika—just spices that we grew up eating," he says. "My mom would use a lot of those in stews and rice and different dishes that she always cooked for us. So that was kind of the thought process behind that—how to make a sausage that everyone down here likes, and that's how we came up with it."

In addition to a regular sausage, they craft a jalapeño cheese sausage using fresh jalapeños and two kinds of cheddar, one of which is a high-temp variety. ("So you get like some cubes in there that are still kind of solid, but then get some melty cheese," explains Joel.) They also offer a chile pequin cheddar sausage, a familiar regional offering made with small, fiery local chiles.

"Almost every meat market that you go to down here in the Valley has their own chile pequin sausage, so we needed to put one on the menu," says Joel.

The sides at Teddy's result from a mix of inspirations, but Jesse's experience in fine dining has certainly played a role in engineering them to perfection. The Bernie Mac, in particular, took a lot of work, as Jesse was looking to develop a mac and cheese that would stay creamy throughout service without developing a skin or drying out. (That dish is named after Joel's wife, who loves it.) The creamed corn is an adaptation of a dish Joel started making for Thanksgiving when he was in college. The potato salad is inspired by Aaron Franklin's, and Joel says it's dressed with just mayo, mustard, pickles, salt, and pepper—but whipped into a cloudlike texture. The vibrant Brussels sprouts, a newer addition, are lightly fried, tossed in a gastrique, then served with sautéed peppers and onions.

"I think somebody would start a riot if I took them off the menu because it's ridiculous how many Brussels sprouts we sell," says Joel.

The brothers grew up eating their mother's smoky pinto beans and rice, and Ana Maria continues to make those for the restaurant, as well as the potato salad. Another highlight of Teddy's is the tortillas she makes daily using rendered beef fat. She kneads, presses, and stacks about 120 to 130 of the flour tortillas, then cooks them to order on a comal in the back. Those who know will order these in lieu of sliced bread, and use the tender, pillowy wrap as a superior vehicle for barbecue.

Each weekend, the Garcia family serves brunch starting at 9 a.m., featuring Ana Maria's menudo and Joel's barbacoa made from beef cheeks smoked on the offset, then confited in its own fat and seasoned with salt and bay leaf. They also craft barbecue tacos and sandwiches on massive, buttery biscuits and sling both smashburgers and fried chicken.

"It's more so for us, because we like barbecue for breakfast," says Joel.

For dessert, they keep things simple with homemade banana pudding and occasional beef fat chocolate chip cookies made by their sister, who also manages their events and catering. Joel's wife, Bernardina, is a teacher, but spends her summers helping out, and they have some cousins on staff too. And with all their recent accolades and continued success, the Garcia family needs all the help they can get.

Considering Joel's record, it should come as no surprise that Teddy's Barbecue landed on the *Texas Monthly* Top 50 list in 2021. Then Joel went on to launch a Teddy's truck, mostly used for festivals and events, followed by a second concept inside the Mercado District food hall in nearby McAllen. Joelene's, named after his daughter, serves a more Southern-leaning menu with some barbecue staples. Next, Joel has his sights set on opening a third concept called Bernie Mac's, which will feature customizable mac and cheese bowls with a variety of different noodles, base sauces, cheeses, and toppings.

For the average person, juggling this many different concepts (plus raising two young kids) might seem impractical. But Joel is, and has always been, powerfully driven. In the backyard of Teddy's, colorful papel picado is strung across bright red picnic tables and the outdoor bar and stage. And written across the fence in black paint are these words: "I hope you live a life you're proud of and if not, I hope you have the courage to start over."

Joel's success is inspirational proof of someone who has managed to pull off both.

REESE BROS BARBECUE

SAN ANTONIO

Reese Bros Barbecue reflects Nick and Elliott Reese's love for San Antonio's rich culinary heritage while honoring Central Texas barbecue traditions. The brothers were born in San Antonio, and after their dad's work brought them to Austin, they bounced between the two cities, always returning to the Alamo City to visit their extended family. While attending the University of Texas in Austin, they landed their first barbecue jobs at the highly rated la Barbecue (see page 249) through a mutual friend of the owners.

"We weren't really actively seeking work in barbecue at the time," says Nick. "We just wanted a fun job!"

During their time at la Barbecue, the brothers never set foot near the pits. Still, the experience was enough to ignite their passion for barbecue, and they started to practice smoking in their own backyard and catered small events for friends and family.

"We cut hundreds and hundreds of very well-cooked briskets [at la Barbecue], so we kind of learned backwards," says Elliott. "It was like we knew what we were trying to emulate or how the meat should be cooked from [working with] the finished product."

After they both graduated from college in 2017, a family friend with a West Texas ranch had a lead on a new brewery and barbecue restaurant that had unexpectedly lost their pit hand shortly before launching. After chatting with the manager, the brothers traveled down to remote Marathon, Texas, to cook for him.

"We showed up and they had this funky direct-heat pit, with the fire directly under the brisket, which was totally new to us," remembers Nick. "But we somehow got the job."

The brothers ended up learning how to cook on that direct-heat pit, but they also brought in a 1,000-gallon offset Primitive pit. They spent the next three years perfecting their brisket, spare ribs, pulled pork, and turkey, and pitmaster Phillip Moellering taught them how to craft his family's recipe for German-style sausage.

While they were in West Texas, Nick and Elliott's parents reunited after being separated for 10 years, a *Parent Trap*–esque happy ending. The brothers then decided to return to Central Texas and branch out on their own in barbecue. Now armed with Lynyrd and Skynard, their double 500-gallon Moberg offset pits—secured after a three-year waitlist—they started by doing pop-ups at Austin breweries. However, their long-term vision led them to San Antonio, where they could find more space and be closer to family. The search for a permanent location soon followed, marking the beginning of their next chapter.

The Reese family closed on a property just two blocks south of the Alamodome and the brothers parked their trailer on it in January 2022 while they began remodeling the kitchen of the nearly 900-square-foot building that had been several different restaurants. Nick and Elliott hosted pop-ups on location and created covered patios filled with colorful picnic tables and strung with vivid papel picado flags and miniature piñatas.

"Our attempt was to make it feel very much like San Antonio, with fun Fiesta colors," says Elliott, referencing the citywide festival that happens annually each spring.

By that April, they were serving out of the remodeled kitchen, where guests line up to place their order at the window and then find a seat on the expansive patio, with capacity for nearly 180 guests. There's plenty of fans to counter the lingering heat of South Texas summers, TV screens for Spurs games, and an outdoor bar serving craft beer, frozen agua fresca, and margaritas. And while their staple proteins are simply seasoned and smoked with post oak, per Central Texas tradition, they've crafted a menu of sides and fixings that celebrate their upbringing and love of San Antonio.

"Growing up influenced our menu more than a particular person or family member," Elliott reflects. "Being from San Antonio, we ate lots of Mexican food growing up. It's just our favorite food so, when it came to barbecue, we said let's not do the traditional Texas style—we want to add a little bit of a twist."

"You don't need white bread and pickles to eat barbecue," adds Nick, though they offer both for barbecue purists. "It's really good in a flour tortilla. And barbecue sauce exists for a reason, but it doesn't always have to be tomatoey and sweet—salsa cuts the fattiness of it too."

While in West Texas, Elliott set out to master the art of making flour tortillas—a goal that proved far from easy to attain. Joe Rodriguez, who has since opened Black Board Bar B Q (see page 402), shared his recipe, but Elliott spent months trying to get it right. He tweaked the ratios of flour and water, experimented with water temperature, and adjusted resting times, all to no avail. The breakthrough came during a brisket cook, when a change in his kneading technique finally did the trick. Overcome with excitement, Elliott raced home at 5 a.m. and triumphantly tossed the freshly made tortilla onto his sleeping brother.

"Once that was down, the rest of the menu evolved around the idea that it's all meant to be eaten in a really good flour tortilla," says Nick.

Tortillas, which are made fresh each morning, can be ordered on the side at Reese Bros, or meats can be ordered as tacos, topped with onions, cilantro, and a salsa doña (made from jalapeños, serranos, and tomatillos) created by head chef Gabriel Perez. Reese Bros house sausage is a red chile–spiced chorizo link filled with Oaxacan cheese and serrano peppers. The pork ribs are kissed with garlic and chili powder.

And in lieu of regular pulled pork, they offer carnitas made from bone-in pork shoulder that is smoked and then confited in a seasoned lard. Instead of traditional barbecue sandwiches, they offer the tortas they grew up eating, made with brisket, turkey, or carnitas on a bed of housemade refried beans and fresh avocado spread, then piled with shredded cabbage, lime-pickled onions, and salsa doña. Right now, they locally source their bolillo rolls, but plan on upgrading their ovens and perfecting their own soon.

The sides at Reese Bros Barbecue exude that same South Texas flair, a testament to the creativity of their small but mighty kitchen team, which includes Perez and Jorge Flores.

Uniquely, all the sides are vegetarian—a rarity in Texas barbecue—which has helped attract a loyal following among those who follow a plant-based diet. The okra beans are more like gumbo than any pinto beans you'll find in town, stewed with onions, poblanos, tomatoes, and okra. The coleslaw offers a bright, palate-cleansing contrast to the protein, thanks to a zesty mix of cilantro and lime juice. The mustard-based potato salad is elevated with the smoky flavors of roasted poblanos and onions. And they've become known for their poblano mac and cheese, a nod to the South Texas classic "green spaghetti." Reese Bros' version swaps spaghetti for shells and keeps the spice at bay, ensuring it's a crowd-pleaser

Reese Bros Barbecue is open Thursday through Sunday during the day, and they also open for Thursday night service featuring specials not available on their regular menu, like smoked and fried wings or brisket burgers. In addition to a classic burger (with special sauce and pickles), they craft a Verde Burger inspired by San Antonio's iconic bean burger (a 1952 creation topped with refried beans, Fritos, and Cheez Whiz). Their elevated version is made from a smoked brisket patty topped with white American cheese, a corn tostada, refried borracho beans, and salsa doña on a brioche bun.

These Thursday night events are often made even more lively with bands playing on a stage in the backyard. The brothers envision even more for the space, including transforming another small house on the property into additional seating and retail space, along with plans for natural wine and mezcal programs.

More than just a barbecue joint, Reese Bros Barbecue has become a community hub, blending great food, music, and the vibrant energy of San Antonio. It's a place where friends and neighbors can gather to celebrate the rich cultural tapestry that makes the Alamo City so unique.

GW'S BBQ CATERING CO.

SAN JUAN

Cooking was always a big part of the Watts family's lifestyle, long before Central Texas–style barbecue entered their lives.

"Like most people, it starts in the backyard," says George Watts III (whose friends and family call him "G"). "In the Mexican culture, we eat barbecue all the time, fajitas and chicken and sausage—always grilling, two or three times a week."

G's dad, George Watts Jr., became interested in cooking with indirect heat from his uncle, who was the first in the family to start using an offset smoker. Each Christmas, his uncle would gift whole smoked briskets to family members. G didn't really pay them much attention until he was in high school, when he tried one for the first time.

"I was like, 'This is amazing!'" he remembers. "I probably ate the whole brisket myself!"

After high school, G completed a culinary arts program at South Texas College, but found limited opportunities in the McAllen area. He tried various kitchen jobs and even worked as a waiter before eventually enrolling in the police academy, leading to a law enforcement career in nearby Edinburg. Meanwhile, he and his dad dove deeper into barbecue on weekends, perfecting their skills with an

offset smoker. George Jr. sought guidance from his uncle, while G immersed himself in barbecue books, YouTube tutorials, and the competitive barbecue circuit.

In 2015, George Jr. got a barbecue trailer and the two started to take on weekend catering jobs for friends and family, starting small but working up to weddings and other large events. G and his wife Lisa made a trip to Franklin Barbecue in 2018, where he had his first taste of Central Texas barbecue.

"I'd never had brisket with post oak," he says. "I was used to mesquite. So that was mind-blowing—a very different flavor. . . . That's what we loved and we wanted to bring here because there really wasn't anything like that."

Back in McAllen, the father and son started getting post oak delivered every couple of weeks for their weekend hobby, which was escalating to new levels. They were now parking their barbecue trailer at different hotels and then, in 2019, they parked in downtown McAllen at a place called The Yard—a bar with food trucks around it—and that's where they started to get noticed. At this point, they started to think seriously about opening a restaurant.

They began eyeing a former Mexican restaurant in nearby San Juan that had been vacant for a couple of years, and eventually pulled the trigger on it during the pandemic, signing a lease. George Jr. quit his job as safety officer at a hospital, and G followed suit, resigning from the police force to open GW's BBQ as a brick and mortar with his dad. They revamped the interior of the restaurant—with red stucco walls, corrugated metal trim, and plenty of Texas flags and stars—and opened their doors in August 2020.

"We just went all in basically," says G. "If it works, it works. If it doesn't, at least we tried it. I figured even if we don't make it, for whatever reason, I can go work somewhere else. This is what I want to do."

Though there were a couple of Central Texas–style barbecue places in the region by then, including Teddy's Barbecue (see page 447), locals who visited GW's still weren't accustomed to the style, so George Jr. and G found themselves doing a bit of educating when they first opened.

"Brisket here [in the Rio Grande Valley] was mesquite-smoked for maybe an hour, and then they just wrap it and finish in the oven and put barbecue sauce all over it—that's what the people know here," says G. "People would ask us to take off the 'black stuff' because they thought it was burnt. We'd have to tell them, 'That's not burnt, that's the bark!'"

The Wattses only use salt and pepper to season their Prime brisket, which they smoke with post oak for up to 13 hours. G tried Evan LeRoy's "foil boat" method but prefers to use "foil caps" instead, just to cover the edges, and then they slather each brisket with tallow and wrap it with butcher paper for the last couple of hours of the cook to seal in moisture.

Galindo Smokers (based in Channelview, outside Houston) built their 500-gallon and 1,000-gallon offsets, and local AP Smokers (based in nearby Alton) is building another 1,000-gallon for them. They also have a direct heat Chud Box, which they use to cook cabrito (whole goat), a Sunday special.

Though they've tried different seasonings through the years, G has found that simple salt and pepper is really best for all the meats. ("I really just learned that less is more," he says.) The pork ribs do get glazed with a mustard-based barbecue sauce for the end of the cook, and they're finished with a brown sugar syrup for gloss and a hint of sweetness.

GW's menu is both rooted in simplicity and marked by innovation. G trained with Bill Dumas, the Sausage Sensei (see page 431), and then developed a juicy sausage with a perfectly cohesive grind and taut snap. They offer a peppery beef link and a jalapeño cheese link—plus super inventive specials, like brisket lasagna, stuffed with a beef base plus lasagna noodles, mozzarella, Italian herbs, and a marinara barbecue sauce for dipping.

"That's been a little hard because [our customers] don't like change, they don't like to try different stuff—they fight that a lot," says G regarding the innovations, though that doesn't stop him from pushing the boundaries. He also offers lots of samples, which usually helps ease folks into new territory.

The sides at GW's lean into soulful American comfort food with some subtle South Texas accents.

"Some people will ask why I don't do Spanish rice or charro beans," says G. "But I try not to do too much of what we're used to eating because I want to be different, I want to stand out. I don't want to be like everybody else!"

So instead of using pinto beans, the Wattses offer sweet barbecued beans, and the collards also come with a hint of sweetness. Cilantro lime slaw achieves a nice balance of creamy and bright, and dill Dijonnaise gives the potato salad more personality. Indulgent jalapeño creamed corn is a bestseller, and fresh green beans are stewed with tomatoes for a lighter, but no less flavorful, veggie side. And GW's classic, creamy mashed potatoes are a must alongside pitmaster specials like brisket meatloaf and chicken-fried brisket with tallow gravy.

Any of the meats can be made into a sandwich, but there's one particularly special sandwich that has been getting a lot of attention, and deservedly so. The Peacemaker features tender slices of smoked pork loin, topped with housemade bacon, pimento cheese, candied jalapeños, and barbecue sauce, all on a Martin's potato roll. It was chosen as one of the Top 20 Best Bites by *Texas Monthly* in 2022, and that same year, the restaurant started winning local accolades as well. Then in 2023, *Texas Monthly* ranked GW's as one of the Top 23 Best New BBQ Joints in the state.

Thanks to all their success, GW's is busier than ever, both as a restaurant and as a catering operation, which they run out of the same kitchen. George Jr. handles the business side of things, and G's wife, Lisa, often works the register. G's younger brother Gavin is a meat cutter and creates rotating desserts like seasonal fruit crumbles and creative takes on puddings, in flavors like s'mores and key lime pie. And now G has a bigger kitchen team than ever before, for which he is grateful.

"We knew it was going to be hard work and a lot of labor, but it was way more than I even expected," he says, recalling the early sleepless days of figuring out a cook schedule and squeezing in quick naps in the back. "I have a lot of respect for barbecue people now. Especially if you're small, doing everything on your own—it's a *lot* of work."

Texas
Texas
LaVaca
BBQ
Christine
MAGELLAN

LAVACA BBQ

PORT LAVACA & VICTORIA

What began as casual family barbecues in Lupe and Christine Nevarez's Blessing backyard grew into a shared passion for competition and hospitality. The duo first entered local cook-offs, then joined the International Barbecue Cook-off Association (IBCA), traveling across Texas to compete. Their daughter Kelli grew up immersed in these culinary traditions, learning from her parents and refining her skills even further when she moved away from the Gulf Coast for college.

"Growing up with foodie parents and living in a small town 30 minutes away from a H-E-B or Walmart causes you to learn how to make your favorite foods that you would not be able to easily get," explains Kelli. "Watching my family cook all our traditional favorite dishes also helped me when I moved to college six hours away in Denton. I took some of our dishes and rolling pins with me so I would still be able to make things like tortillas or guacamole whenever I was feeling homesick."

Christine was a teacher for over 30 years, teaching ESL and bilingual education at every level from kindergarten to college. As she approached retirement, she envisioned a small barbecue business, calculating that selling just eight barbecue-stuffed potatoes a day from a food truck would provide the supplemental income she needed while Lupe continued working as a mechanical designer.

But when Lupe stumbled upon an abandoned gas station in Port Lavaca (130 miles southwest of Houston) while searching for a food truck, the family saw the potential for a more permanent home for their culinary dreams. They poured their savings into renovating the space, completing every part of the buildout themselves, then painting the exterior yellow and placing an eye-catching electric turquoise cow right out front, with the words "Jesus. Texas. Brisket." (They named the business LaVaca BBQ, a play on words referencing both the town of Port Lavaca and the Spanish word "la vaca," or "the cow.")

Lupe cleverly outfitted the kitchen inside a shipping container, ensuring that if their lease ever ends, they can simply move their fully equipped kitchen—along with a trailer-mounted smoker—to a new location. With the help of a retired welder friend, he crafted the custom smoker from a decommissioned 1,000-gallon propane tank to handle the demands of a larger crowd. He had always admired the Jambo smokers used by many of the pitmasters on the competition circuit, so he designed "La Blanca" to mimic them, with a raised firebox centered within the larger cooking chamber (rather than hanging lower, as is customary for offsets), which he says helps create a better bark on his briskets.

Kelli was teaching first grade across the street from the restaurant, so once it opened in November 2019, she (as well as her younger brother and sister, who were finishing up college at the time) would come over and help their parents after school and on weekends. Then in March 2020, when the pandemic shut down Kelli's school and classes were all being held online, she began to help out even more at the restaurant, and started learning how to smoke on the pit from her dad.

"I watched my dad grill and smoke at home and in competitions my whole life, so seeing him work with the meat from start to finish really helped me learn the technique later on," says Kelli, who soon fell in love with cooking with smoke and fire. "To me, it's the visual beauty of barbecue. The cook itself is a whole day's work at a slow pace, so you have the time to see all these colors and transformations the meats go through. I love seeing all the different stages and the physical changes, like colors and textures, you see as the meat is cooking."

By the end of that year, Kelli decided to leave teaching to come on full-time and assume most of the pit duties, with the help of her pit hand, Hunter. They smoke melt-in-your-mouth brisket, flavorful turkey, peppery dino beef ribs (on Saturdays), tender slices of pork belly, and quarter chickens finished with a sweet glaze. Kelli also crafts signature items like Big Red Pork Ribs, brushed with a syrup centered around the beloved South Texas soda, and Cubano Pulled Pork, which is given character and punch with a sour orange sauce, plus two types of beef-and-pork sausage: a traditional Central Texas link and another with spicy serrano and Oaxacan cheese. Lupe still smokes the succulent cochinito pork steak, which is marinated with orange and achiote, and salmon (certainly a unique offering in a Texas barbecue joint), which is given a kick with their house pork spice.

With Kelli handling proteins, Christine has more time to work on sides like spicy jalapeño creamed corn and creamy jalapeño coleslaw, savory green beans with bacon, brisket-enriched beans, and a traditional, zingy potato salad. Another signature item is their Mac Belly, made from lush mac and cheese topped

with crispy pork belly, and a potato casserole Christine developed one day while searching for a home for some leftover potatoes. The craveable, homestyle bake is made from layers of shredded potatoes, mushrooms, cream, cheese, butter, and sour cream, then topped with crunchy French-fried onions. LaVaca also makes a brisket sausage gumbo, a rich and savory solution for brisket trim, and it comes topped with a scoop of potato salad, per Cajun tradition.

"A love for gumbo inspired us to make this," says Christine. "Since we are close to the bay in Port Lavaca, we wanted to bring something close to seafood, without the seafood."

LaVaca BBQ has also become known for their smoked tamales, a family recipe Christine adapted for the pit. She spreads the masa on butcher paper in lieu of a corn husk, then adds chopped brisket, pulled pork, and their top-secret tamale sauce before rolling it up. Bathing the tamales in post oak smoke infuses them with a robust flavor and crisps up the edges for a texture you don't get with steamed tamales. The family also recently added a second tamale: the Pollo Verde is filled with chicken and spicy green salsa.

Lupe makes both their blue corn and flour tortillas fresh daily, and those can be ordered alongside a tray of barbecue, or enjoyed as tacos like the Blue Belly, made from sliced pork belly and mango-habanero slaw tucked into a blue corn tortilla. Christine makes both white bread and cornbread fresh daily.

Both Christine and Lupe are on dessert duty, which spans from traditional options like peach cobbler and banana pudding to more unexpected offerings like chocolate sheet cake with chocolate pecan icing and a Cookie Monster sundae made from Oreos, chocolate chip cookies, and brownies, all topped with a scoop of vanilla ice cream. A friend of the family also developed the uniquely decadent smoked pork belly maple bourbon cheesecake.

In 2021, as LaVaca BBQ placed on the *Texas Monthly* Top 50 list and continued to build momentum, Lupe found an old tire shop in Victoria (about 30 miles northwest of Port Lavaca) and the family renovated it to open a second location in 2022. Lupe built another pit, this one called "El Segundo," and they are working on transitioning all of the kitchen operations to this more spacious location. For now, Christine is running it, with the help of a manager, and Kelli comes up to help on their busy Sundays, since the Port Lavaca location is closed.

The bustling operation the family has created is a far cry from the laidback retirement project Christine had originally envisioned. Still, she says making the transition to barbecue from teaching was easy.

"It is *hard* to be a teacher," she says. "Teaching is a different story every day, and you have to plan differently for every day. Running a restaurant deals with consistency. That is what keeps people coming back for more."

BUTTER'S BBQ

SINTON

Andrew Soto grew up in the coastal region of South Texas, immersed in the restaurant business. For 20 years, his father, Marcelo, and his uncle ran Soto's Drive Through Taqueria, a bustling spot known for fresh, hand-pressed tortillas and tacos that kept a constant line of cars wrapped around the building.

Andrew grew up running bags of tacos to customers, and those formative years instilled in him a strong work ethic and an appreciation for quality food. On weekends, his parents would cater events together, his mom making the flour tortillas while his dad smoked brisket and grilled fajitas. They'd prepare for these events in the backyard smoke shack at their house, where young Andrew learned to tend fires under his father's guidance.

"It was up to me as a nine, 10 year old to go check the fires while he slept so he could wake up early and prepare the side dishes," remembers Andrew. "He would just tell me what to look for with the fires, how to stoke them and what to check for—if it's too hot, do this, if it's too cold, do that. Then he would get up the next morning and I would sleep in a little bit, and we'd meet somewhere around like 10 or 11, load everything up in our truck and go serve."

As Andrew reached his teenage years and Marcelo was diagnosed with diabetes, Andrew took on the bulk of the physical work—but then he went to school for a technical degree and got a job in a refinery, processing oil into diesel fuel. But before long, he felt called back to the pit. He read all of Aaron Franklin's books and watched every YouTube video he could find, and started cooking each weekend, selling briskets to friends and neighbors. Then, after much discussion with Marcelo, he decided to take a leap of faith and strike out on his own.

"So I liquidated everything I had in my 401k—it wasn't much, like $16,000," says Andrew. "We had someone build us a smoker and then we found a little shack in Mathis that we rented out for 700 bucks a month."

In late 2017, Andrew launched Butter's BBQ, in reference to his childhood nickname, Butterball (a nod to his 10-pound birth weight despite being born prematurely). Initially, he tried to juggle his full-time job while starting the new business, but soon found that wasn't possible. So Andrew put in his notice to go all-in on barbecue, and quickly made a name for himself in the community for his brisket.

"I know my way around a brisket really well because I've been doing it a really long time," he says. "I already knew the basics of how to maintain fires in smokers, and that's really important because you have to maintain certain temperatures and know how to work with the wood."

However, he is quick to point out that his dad always embraced a South Texas style of meat smoking—hot and fast, fueled by mesquite, and relying on feel over temperature gauges—while Andrew is dedicated to the Central Texas principle of cooking low and slow over post oak.

"We still butt heads about this," Andrew laughs. "But he's an old head. I like to call him a Boomer. He's always telling me I should do mesquite and I'm like, 'Love you to death, Pop, but this is mine, and I'm gonna do it my way. And if I screw it up, all mine.' And over time, he finally got to understanding why we do it and that mesquite can be a little strong. Post oak, to me, just burns better. It's cleaner and more mild, and lets the meat really do the talking rather than the smoke. It's very subtle, and that's what I like."

Also, per Central Texas tradition, Andrew uses very simple seasonings on his meat. The brisket is rubbed with salt and pepper, and he wraps them in butcher paper when they are about 90 percent cooked, which preserves the crunchiness and deep flavor of the bark. And after 14 to 16 hours of smoking, he lets them rest for another 10 to 12 hours.

"Longer rest and you get to go home!" emphasizes Andrew. "That's what these warmers are for!"

The moist, flavorful turkey also gets a simple salt-and-pepper rub, while the pork ribs are packed with salt, pepper, garlic, onion, paprika, chili powder, and brown sugar, then glazed with a thinned-down version of their barbecue sauce (ketchup, Worcestershire, brown sugar, vinegar, salt, and pepper), resulting in tender meat held by a tangy, caramelized crust. And the juicy sausage links, made mostly from brisket trim with a bit of rib trim, have a deep peppery umami, with an option for mild jalapeño cheese too.

Though his meats remain traditional, the sides at Butter's show South Texas flair, a development that owes much to Andrew's mother, Frances Guzman, stepping into the kitchen and quickly making herself

indispensable. In addition to working full-time at Pizza Hut, Guzman proved herself a tireless cornerstone of the business. She rolled out homemade flour tortillas daily, and contributed her recipes, from creamy mustard-mayo potato salad, cheesy elotes, savory pinto beans, and a seasonal summer pasta salad made with rigatoni, tomatoes, olives, and cucumbers.

"She was our rock," says Andrew. "She was the first one there, last one to go. She loved it. She'd get there early and get all the sides going, call me and wake me up—'Get over here, we've got people waiting!' If it wasn't for her, we wouldn't have made it."

Marcelo, drawing from his years of experience, insisted Andrew include a drive-through with the restaurant, and that was what ended up keeping Butter's afloat through the pandemic. Customers were able to efficiently pick up their food to go—or eat outside at one of four tables. The business continued to build momentum and, by the time the lease was up, Butter's had more than outgrown the tiny space they'd begun in. Andrew found a bigger space in nearby Sinton and they launched a bigger, better Butter's BBQ in 2022.

Unfortunately, Guzman was hospitalized for early onset dementia and osteoporosis right before the move. Still, even in sickness, she proved to be her son's biggest supporter—just weeks before her untimely passing at the age of 69, she presented Andrew with a shoebox of money she'd been saving.

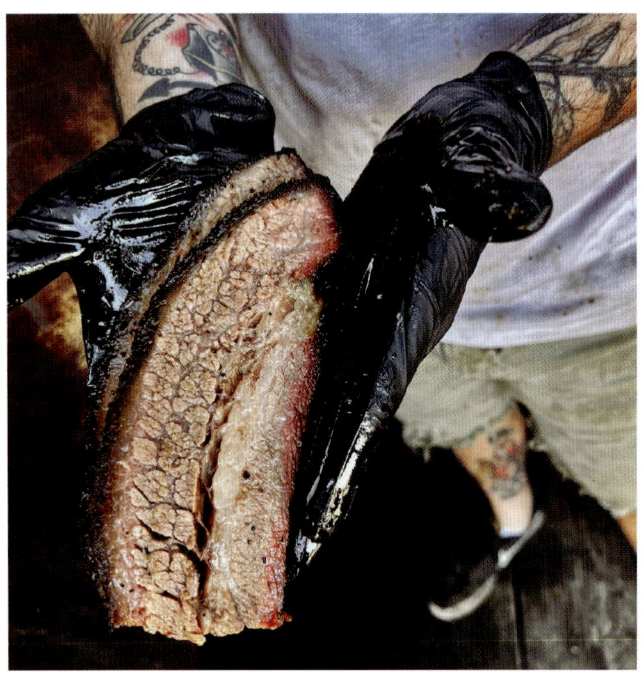

"It turns out, she didn't have life insurance, but she saved every bit of the money that I'd paid her in five years," says Andrew, eyes glistening. "She was the hardest-working woman I've ever met in my life. She was extremely prepared—with an eighth-grade education and all work ethic. We were able to buy kitchen equipment—things that we really needed and help pay labor. I can't say enough about her. Even in the afterlife, she still manages to help us out. She paid taxes on the houses for the next two years."

Andrew proudly carries forward Guzman's legacy, not only by serving her cherished recipes, but by embodying her wisdom and remarkable work ethic in every aspect of the restaurant. The family spirit is alive and well at Butter's, with Marcelo lending his expertise, and Andrew's brother, sister, brother-in-law, and nephew playing vital roles in the day-to-day operations. Andrew's 10-year-old twins even pitch in—by choice.

With more space and better equipment, Andrew has been able to expand the menu, adding sides like tater tot casserole, inspired by Truth BBQ (see page 121), and a brisket chili in the winters. He often runs massive beef rib specials on the weekends and, at Marcelo's urging, he started smoking beef cheeks to offer barbacoa on Sundays. He serves it each weekend, along with menudo, corn tortillas, and his parents' recipes for salsa and pico de gallo.

"I'll never forget, I had some customers ask what it was, and when I told them barbacoa, they said 'Tastes smoky though.'" says Andrew, shaking his head. "We've gotten so far away from the fact that barbacoa *means* barbecue that they were questioning why I was smoking it! So I said—'You know what, as a way to pay homage to my Hispanic heritage, I'm going to keep this on the menu.'"

Lately, Andrew has been rediscovering Tejano music, a favorite of his parents, and often plays it while he cooks. And, much to Marcelo's satisfaction, he even throws a few mesquite logs on the fire, infusing the barbacoa with a distinct flavor that honors their family's tradition.

WEST TEXAS

THE KING OF COWBOY COOKING

The rustic style of campfire cooking that sustained cowboys during the post–Civil War cattle drive boom is one of many influences that shaped Texas barbecue. And few embody the spirit of this tradition as faithfully as Tom Perini, a true steward of cowboy cooking.

While Tom was growing up in Abilene in 1952, his parents, V. C. and Maxine Perini, purchased a ranch in nearby Buffalo Gap, where he spent much of his youth riding horses. Named for the bison that once thundered through the saddle of the Callahan Divide, the town is situated where the northwestern edge of the Hill Country meets the high plains of the Llano Estacado. It was out on this scenic ranch that Tom discovered his love of cooking.

"In the old days, you could drive when you were 14," recalls Tom. "And so I'd get some of my friends, and we would drive out here [from Abilene]. They'd probably get some beer and play poker. I never got involved in playing cards, so I ended up being the cook. I would fix simple things like hamburgers. But from that point on, I've enjoyed cooking."

Tom was 21, selling real estate in Dallas, when he received a fateful call from his mother in 1965. His father had unexpectedly died at age 70 from complications during a surgery. With his brothers away at college, it only made sense for Tom to return to operate Perini Ranch. He didn't know much about ranching, but quickly learned that the 640-acre section (the equivalent of one square mile) was too small to profitably raise cattle, so he started leasing additional land. It was during this time that he really started getting into cooking with fire.

"Of course, we had gas ovens, but cooking with fire is romantic, it's different, it's fun, and it just has more flavor," says Tom. "I just love to cook on wood, period . . . People ask me why I use mesquite. And the answer is—I'm surrounded by it on the ranch, and that's just what you use. So we get the mesquite when it's cut down, we let it dry and the bark will slip, and that's what we use to cook with. And mesquite makes a very hot fire, so you've got to be a little careful with it, but it's a wonderful cooking wood."

In his early days of cooking brisket, Tom recalls digging a hole about three feet wide, 10 feet long, and four feet deep, then filling it with mesquite chunks and lighting a fire to burn them down. The next day, he'd return to smoldering coals, install a two-inch pipe over the ditch, and stretch net wire across its span to create a cooking surface.

"When we were working cattle, after we did the first hour and a half, I'd go back in and start cooking for lunch, and I enjoyed that more than I did working the cattle," says Tom.

It was while ranching that this Texas history buff started to become interested in chuckwagons. Charles Goodnight, Texas cattleman and founder of the Goodnight-Loving Trail (one of the big trails used to drive cattle out of Texas), is credited for inventing the chuckwagon in 1866 by converting a surplus Army wagon into a mule-drawn mobile kitchen used to feed cowboys on long cattle drives. At the back of the box was the "chuck box," used to store spices, utensils, canisters, and other small items. A table would unfold below the chuck box, creating a prep area. Heavier items, such as water barrels that would be filled in creeks and rivers encountered along the way, were stored in the bottom of the wagon, and a white tarp provided protection from the elements.

"The chuckwagon was the first mobile kitchen," explains Tom. "And on cattle drives—it might take three months to drive cattle from here to Abilene, Kansas—they might have 12 to 16 cowboys to feed."

During these drives, the cowboys would harvest wood along the trail—typically mesquite—which they would use to keep warm, cook meals, and boil water for coffee. Meats (typically venison, and occasionally beef from cattle injured during the drive) would be cooked over open fire. They would also burn the mesquite down into coals, then use those coals both underneath and atop cast-iron Dutch ovens, which they would use to cook beans, sourdough biscuits, and gravy.

"It was not gourmet food by any means, but it sustained them to work very hard and go long distances," says Tom. When the cattle drive boom died down in the 1880s, chuckwagons continued to play a vital role in ranching, providing food, equipment, and supplies for cowboys on trail drives and cattle round-ups.

"But after the pickup was developed, [ranchers] got rid of their chuckwagons as fast as they could, because they could now drive out to where they're working cattle and have a nice chest with food and all that," explains Tom, who was leasing an 8,000-acre ranch in Stamford when he started coming across old chuckwagon parts and pieces. "So I started picking up some of these old ones and putting them together and making it work."

Tom began using a chuckwagon to feed his own ranch hands, and soon he found himself catering for famous operations like Swenson Land & Cattle and The Pitchfork Ranch, who invited him to come out to cook for special events. They would provide the beef and the mesquite, and Tom would bring his chuckwagon and cowboy cooks. By the start of the 1980s, Tom was taking home prizes from chuckwagon cook-offs when cattle prices began to tank. After an 18-year run in ranching, he was frustrated and burnt out by the unpredictability of the industry. Long-time family friend Watt Matthews offered him this valuable piece of advice: "Tom, you can do more for the beef industry by cooking beef than by raising beef."

Tom took this advice to heart, and in 1983, he converted an old hay barn into Perini Ranch Steakhouse. He designed flat, lidded steel pits, about 10 feet wide and 4 feet long, which he uses to cook steak and chicken over live fire. He converted 55-gallon drums into burn barrels, where the mesquite burns down into coals. Those coals are then shoveled into the bottom of the pit for slow cooking heritage pork ribs and Certified Angus brisket and prime rib, seasoned simply with salt, pepper, and garlic.

"When we cook briskets, we'll go early in the morning to trim and season the briskets, and then put them on the pit and start putting coals underneath—it's about three feet from the coal to the meat," explains Tom. "Every hour, we would put in more coals, and we'd normally turn the briskets every hour, and use a mop sauce made from the rendered fat. That was just the old time way . . . t's a 12-hour process or, as I like to say, 12 hours and two six-packs!"

Tom added some cowboy classics to the Perini Ranch Steakhouse menu, like biscuits and beans cooked in Dutch ovens, and he also developed unique sides inspired by family and friends. Zucchini Perini, a dish made from squash coins baked in an Italian-seasoned meat sauce, was created by a relative who sang opera in Italy. The Green Chile Hominy was a collaboration between Tom and his late friend Louise Matthews. She wanted an alternative to pinto beans when he was catering for her, so they baked hominy with bacon, New Mexican green chiles, pickled jalapeños, and cheddar cheese. The strawberry shortcake is Tom's great-grandmother Becky Blake's recipe, and involves sweet biscuits cut in half, topped with hot strawberries, and drizzled with cream. And the now-iconic jalapeño glazed cheesecake topped with a whole pickled jalapeño?

"I did it as a joke," laughs Tom, "And it turned out everybody loved it!"

As thoughtful and well-executed as Tom's offerings were, the steakhouse's early years were rocky. Running a restaurant on a private ranch, with little visibility, was not easy, and he remembers staying afloat by borrowing money from his mother for several years. Slowly but surely, though, word started to spread organically—and the full bar with a menu of cocktail offerings from margaritas to martinis was certainly a draw in the practically dry Abilene region. Customers started traveling from farther away to experience the steakhouse built in an old hay barn. Perini Ranch had become a destination restaurant, and the accolades started rolling in.

In 1995, Tom was invited to cook at the James Beard House. To mitigate the expense of the trip, he came up with the idea to generate a little publicity by shipping his mesquite-smoked peppered beef tenderloin to key New York media outlets ahead of the dinner. The tenderloin was then selected by the *New York Times* as the year's best mail-order gift. Next, Governor George W. Bush invited Tom to cater a tailgate party at the Texas Governor's Mansion in Austin for a University of Texas football game. During this time, Tom also met and married his wife, Lisa, who brought her own experience in the marketing and restaurant industries.

In 2001, Perini Ranch Steakhouse was invited to cook for the annual Congressional Picnic at The White House, a celebration which was upended by the events of September 11th, but they returned the next year to follow through and continued to cater for President Bush after that. Over the years, Tom and Lisa were invited to appear on *The TODAY Show*, *The Early Show*, *Good Morning America*, and the Food Network. The restaurant was featured in publications like *Saveur*, *Forbes*, and *People,* and appeared on the cover of *Texas Monthly* in 2011. And then, in 2014, Perini Ranch was awarded a prestigious America's

Classic Award from the James Beard Foundation, drawing even more worldwide attention to the little restaurant on the ranch.

Though brisket has come off the restaurant's daily menu to focus more on cuts of steak, Perini Ranch still smokes plenty of it for caterings. And Tom still gets requests for his chuckwagon, which he brings around the state for various events.

"People love the chuckwagon, so I stand there and talk about it and tell them stories," he says. "The chuckwagon is the center of any kind of event. And for Texans, the word 'chuckwagon' is very, very endearing to a lot of people."

The Perinis have added guest quarters to the ranch, including a restored 1885 ranch house, and they now run two more businesses in the small town of Buffalo Gap: Perini Ranch Country Market, a beautifully curated home goods store, and a homestyle breakfast concept called The Gap Café. But Perini Ranch Steakhouse has not changed at all in over 40 years. It's still housed in the same corrugated metal and weathered wood building with a scratched-up screen door entrance and neon signage. Inside the dining room, a longhorn skull is mounted on a red brick fireplace and hung with strings of dried red chiles.

But don't be fooled by the charmingly rustic atmosphere; you can also enjoy a bottle of vintage Napa Cabernet or Veuve Clicquot with your meal. The Perinis love wine, and Lisa has built up a thoughtful list, which features notable Texas producers like McPherson Cellars and Becker Vineyards, and selections picked to pair with mesquite-smoked meats. Savor a glass at a picnic table overlooking the pasture and the Perini Ranch longhorn cattle will likely make an appearance. These aren't beef cattle (Tom has always purchased the restaurant's meat from suppliers), but rather cherished pets who live on the ranch, and even have names like Griffin and Thunder and Tiger.

"People love to see them because they were the first longhorns that were brought in by the Spanish and ended up in this part of Texas," says Tom. "We buy them from the state of Texas, which is supposed to be the purest longhorn herd. We buy a couple of them a year, and it's just fun. It's Texas history."

EVIE MAE'S PIT BARBEQUE

WOLFFORTH

Unlike a lot of Texas pitmasters, Arnis Robbins didn't grow up around barbecue. In fact, he didn't even grow up in the state. He and his wife, Mallory, were raised on the eastern edge of New Mexico—she in Clovis, and he in Portales, where his family had a peanut farm.

"If we had steak when I was growing up, it would have been a sirloin cooked 'til it was gray all the way through and then divvied up at the table for everybody," Arnis laughs. "You couldn't even source really high-quality steaks or anything back then if you weren't in a larger city."

In 2006, Arnis moved to Tucson, Arizona, to get into the landscaping industry, and by 2010 he'd launched his own landscaping business. But the real turning point in his career didn't start with a passion or a hobby, but rather a diagnosis. In 2011, Arnis found out he had celiac disease.

"Me being diagnosed with celiac has a whole lot to do with the whole trajectory of our lives," he remembers. "I tried to eat out a couple of times, eating gluten-free, and would get cross-contaminated. [Mallory and I] realized that we weren't going to be able to eat out as often as we had before, so we started spending our dining-out budget money on better groceries."

Arnis began grilling a lot, and then bought an electric smoker off Craigslist, with the intent of expanding his home menu. He began smoking racks of ribs and soon cracked the code on pulled pork.

"Eventually, I think I just fell in love with the ritual, too, and experimenting with flavor profiles," he says. "Then I realized that I wasn't going to be able to cook a good brisket unless I had a real wood-burning smoker. And having grown up on a farm, I was resourceful enough that I could do a little bit of welding, and decided that I was going to build a smoker."

Arnis found a 750-gallon propane tank on Craigslist and built his first offset reverse flow smoker in his backyard in Tucson, naming it "The Black Pearl." He wasted no time experimenting with his new toy, hosting gatherings and offering to cook meat for neighbors. ("We were in Arizona, so the neighbors didn't have any concept of cooking on an offset smoker like that," he says.) In early 2014, Arnis took his pit to Albuquerque for a friend's bachelor weekend, and he spent Saturday afternoon cooking a whole hog with his friends.

"None of us really knew what we were doing, but it was just a wonderful time together, spending time with high school buddies that I hadn't seen in a long time," he remembers. "Driving home from Tucson after that, I remember thinking, 'Man, that was cool, I want to figure out a way to sell barbecue. I want to figure out a way to monetize it such that I can afford to just pursue it more.'"

Back in Tucson, Arnis got right to work researching roadside vending, and discovered that the easiest way to start selling barbecue would be to find a trailer that had already been permitted with the county. He found a "real beater of a party wagon" for $2,500, changed the name (to Evie Mae's Barbeque, named after the couple's young daughter), and was set up on the side of a road outside of Tucson by April 2014. Then he found a golf club that had gone out of business, and got permission to park in the empty lot. Arnis would work his landscaping job all week long, then begin prepping on Thursday at 9 p.m. He'd cook all night, open the truck at 11 a.m. on Friday, and sell barbecue all afternoon and into the evening before going home.

"I was always exhausted, but there was never any resentment or hard feelings about having just worked 36 hours straight to sell barbecue," says Arnis. "I would go home and I'd be on such a rush, such a high—and I'd just be so excited about doing it again the next week. The more I did it, the more I wanted to do it. And it was always worth the loss of sleep and the crazy, long hours and the tedious, hard, sweaty, smelly work. Just to cook barbecue."

Due to limited space, Arnis and Mallory only offered a few different side options out of the gate. Their neighbor's mother made a creamy potato salad, and Mallory—who had grown up cooking with her grandmother—developed recipes for a classic coleslaw, as well as baked beans that Arnis cooked in the smoker.

After operating in their original trailer all summer, they decided to upgrade to a larger one. Arnis had already been toying with the notion of leaving the landscaping business to focus on barbecue when they took a trip to visit his parents in Lubbock, the remote city in northwest Texas where they'd recently relocated.

"If we were gonna pursue barbecue [I wanted to] come to a Texas market, where we could see if we're capable of hanging in there," remembers Arnis. "And Lubbock was really starving for a craft barbecue restaurant."

So over the course of a month, the Robbinses sold their house and their landscaping business, and moved to Lubbock in February 2015. The original plan was for Arnis to help his parents manage and maintain rental properties while selling barbecue a couple of days a week. But getting the business up and running proved more time-consuming than he had anticipated.

For one, Arnis discovered that mobile food vending was only permitted in industrial-zoned areas of Lubbock, but the neighboring town of Wolfforth only required a health department license and sales use tax ID. So he found a storage unit in Wolfforth that he thought would be a good place to stage and receive goods, and figured he could set up the trailer in front. Dave Neufeld, their landlord at the storage building, took a personal interest in the Robbinses and their budding business venture.

"He thought I was nuts the first day that I looked at the storage unit and told him what we were trying to do," laughs Arnis. "But he kind of took us under his wing and really went out of his way to help us out. The first winter that we were there in the trailer, he even built an enclosed awning structure over the trailer so that our customers could be out of snow or wind."

Meanwhile, Mallory had developed a few gluten-free desserts for Arnis to enjoy at home, starting with a rich, creamy cheesecake with a homemade graham cracker crust. She also adapted Arnis's aunt's pecan pie and chocolate pecan pie to gluten-free versions. They started selling these from the trailer, and they were an immediate hit.

There is no native wood in the Lubbock area that's good for smoking, so Arnis began sourcing live oak and having it delivered from Central and South Texas. He also keeps a bit of cherrywood around and uses it for special dinners (because it's too expensive to use regularly).

"Oak is the vanilla of hardwoods, so if you're going to cook a brisket for 14 or 15 hours, you're not going to put an offensive creosote-y or acrid flavor on what you're cooking if you stick to oak," explains Arnis. "The cherry adds a little bit of a floral flavor, as well as a ton of color. It's crazy how much of a burgundy color you'll get from cherry smoke."

When Daniel Vaughn (see page 26) visited in May 2015, his rave review for *Texas Monthly* described tender, well-balanced ribs, succulent pulled pork, and slices of moist, peppered turkey and "the best brisket I've had this side of Abilene." He had no doubt that Arnis knew his way around a fire and how to manage it, and he highlighted Mallory's desserts as well.

"When he wrote his review, it was like a light switch that just powered our business on," says Arnis. Vaughn also mentioned something they already recognized as their main hurdle: a lack of visibility or foot traffic. And right around that same time, their landlord Neufeld came to them with an offer they couldn't refuse. As the owner of a metal building construction company and supply house, he owned a lot of properties and storage spaces. One was a nearby piece of land he'd had for seven years, but never knew what to develop on it.

"Mallory and I didn't have the financial resources to build a restaurant," says Arnis. "But Dave told us, 'If you will pay an architect to design the building, we'll build it as you guys design it, and I'll charge you $2,500 a month.' So we got a brand new restaurant on the corner of the highway for $2,500 a month. What are the odds of that happening? But he cared about us and he really saw something in us. *We* knew that we had the drive and the hustle to get it done, but the fact that *he* took note—and was willing to really financially leverage himself to help us out—really meant a lot."

So by 2016, the Robbinses had a restaurant of their own and, now with much more space and a full kitchen, they were able to greatly expand upon their menu.

"When we moved into the brick and mortar, we turned into Cracker Barrel," says Arnis. "I think we have like eight or 10 different side options."

Mallory developed a buttery jalapeño cornbread and rich green chile cheese grits (which served as a gluten-free substitute for mac and cheese), inspired by their New Mexican background, plus a baked potato casserole filled with bacon, cheese, and sour cream. When they tried to remove their jalapeño creamed corn from the menu, a disgruntled customer made about 20 campaign signs for the dish and staked them in front of the restaurant until they brought it back.

Arnis built more reverse flow offset smokers, bringing his total to four. He also became a Certified Angus Beef ambassador licensed partner and still exclusively uses their USDA Prime brisket, a product he loves for its high quality and consistency. He uses just salt and pepper for almost all of his meats, as he's done from the beginning. (Chicken gets a little paprika for color, turkey only gets pepper, and both are brined before smoking.) In the brick and mortar, he began making sausage in-house using brisket trim: a traditional German variety and a green chile cheese link. But once he started moving through much more brisket, he still had leftover trim to utilize.

"We've got brisket trim running out our ears, because we've all realized that the more aggressively we trim our brisket, the happier and more consistent product we're going to have," says Arnis.

So he started adding specials like smoked brisket chili (which can also be made into Frito pie) to the menu as well as brisket burgers, which he makes by grinding salt into the brisket trim, adding a slight cure to the meat. Then he par-smokes the patties to about 99°F and holds them in tallow until they're ordered, at which point they're griddled on the flat top just long enough to melt cheese.

By the next summer, Evie Mae's landed on the 2017 *Texas Monthly* Top 50 list, and customers poured in from all over the state to stand in a long line that snaked from the exterior brick facade, past the wooden picnic tables placed throughout the dining room, and up to the counter. The Robbinses started handing out free beer to alleviate the wait, and realized they'd need to expand even more to accommodate the masses.

"We basically doubled the size of the restaurant in the first 18 months," says Arnis, who expanded the pit room and prep spaces before adding two 1,000-gallon reverse flow pits and an Oyler rotisserie to his lineup. He also built an additional kitchen so Mallory could continue to expand on her baked goods, which were getting just as much attention as the smoked meat.

On any given day, Evie Mae's carries a wide variety of gluten-free offerings: s'mores pie topped with torched marshmallow, salted peanut butter cup pie, seasonal fruit cobblers, Texas sheet cake, and take-and-bake cookie dough. While they don't make their own gluten-free buns, they have gone to great trouble to find a brand with the perfect flavor and chew, and the buns are available by request at no extra charge.

"I'll be honest—Lubbock's not a great locale to cater to a gluten-free lifestyle, but we have probably 50 to 100 customers [who] can come in, order anything off the menu, get dessert, and not feel like they're missing out on going out to eat," says Arnis. "And that's really special for them, so it's very important to us."

In 2019, the opportunity arose for Arnis and Mallory to buy the restaurant space from their landlord, so they did that, closing on the property in February. They had one more year of continuous upward growth before COVID-19 stopped the world in its tracks. But, as usual, the Robbinses did the best they could with what they had. They taped the restaurant menu to one of their tables and hoisted it in the air with a forklift, and converted Evie Mae's parking lot into a three-lane drive-through for an optimized takeout system.

"COVID sucked, but that challenge was the ultimate team building experience," remembers Arnis. "Nobody knew what tomorrow was going to be like . . . so we were all just kind of having fun with it and doing what we could. And man, it's weird to think back on, but we did a really, really good job. I think that we did the best we could with the resources available to us to help serve our community and work with other businesses during COVID."

Though they returned to regular service as quickly as possible, Arnis says the lines at Evie Mae's have never quite gotten back to what they were pre-COVID.

"A lot of that is just the economy at this point," he says. "Our consumer is getting crushed, we know that. And we're getting crushed. Barbecue is not as affordable. Where we see our biggest drop is just in the frequency of our customers. People who used to come twice a month are coming once a month. They say it's actually gonna get worse because of droughts and the shortage in cattle. You know, at this point, I don't even look at food costs because there's nothing we can do. We don't have any other options—we're not getting out of the barbecue business."

Arnis has gotten creative by turning leftovers and scraps into barbecue-centric weekday meal specials for just $6.99. Business at Evie Mae's also tends to ebb and flow with the happenings at Texas Tech University in Lubbock, with sales being very dependent on whether school is in session and the football, baseball, and basketball game schedules. So after years of talking about how they'd love to have a barbecue place in a beach town some day, the Robbinses took their next big leap and opened an Evie Mae's Barbeque in Miramar Beach, Florida, in the summer of 2024.

The Robbins family had been vacationing in the Florida Panhandle for years and, through a series of serendipitous connections and coincidences, they acquired a beautiful building on a lake for the new restaurant. Arnis welded all the pits and crafted ironwork for the restaurant in Wolfforth, and backfilled some positions and trained staff in Texas to bring out to Florida. The idea is that, when the Wolfforth restaurant is slow during school breaks—and both Evie Mae and her younger brother Jack are out of school—the Robbinses will spend their time at the Florida restaurant.

"We have a wonderful staff and very little turnover [in Wolfforth]," says Arnis. "And I think that there's a lot of service industry kind of nomad gypsies down there in Florida that could come into this environment, and it'd be so different from anything that they've done, that they might actually fall in love with it and want to stay there. At least, that's my hope, but I try not to sweat that stuff. At the end of the day, we're not going to be held hostage by a labor crisis. And it just comes down to how much me and Mallory are willing to do if we can't find somebody else to help us. But we're not going to let that stand in the way of our dreams and our passion."

BRANTLEY CREEK BARBECUE

ODESSA

Great barbecue joints are few and far between in the sprawling expanse of West Texas. So it's safe to say Brantley Creek Barbecue took Odessa by storm when Brandon and Ashley McPherson opened it in 2019.

Brandon, like most of his high school classmates in Odessa, started working in the oil fields straight out of school. Barbecue was a hobby of his, and one he honed through trial and error in his backyard. Though he didn't grow up eating too much barbecue in the Odessa area, the smell of burning wood still brings back fond memories of his late grandfather smoking meats in his own backyard. Brandon began competing in International Barbeque Cookers Association events around West Texas in San Angelo and Lubbock, and always dreamed of opening his own place one day.

When Flint Energy Services closed in 2019, he lost his job on a pipeline crew, where he was working long hours as a field mechanic, and suddenly he had a very real opportunity to pursue a new path. He already owned a competition barbecue food trailer, and had some winning recipes up his sleeve, so he set things in motion quickly. Just two weeks later, he and Ashley opened Brantley Creek Barbecue, naming it after their son (and adding "Creek" as a joke because there are so few creeks in this part of Texas).

"I enjoyed competition barbecue, but I was longing for so much more, so I started chasing my dream," says Brandon. "The barbecue I cook now is completely different than competition barbecue. Keeping it simple is best for me!"

Competitive barbecue is known for its over-the-top flavors, gleaned from injections and layers of rub, and incredibly rich and decadent sides. Since judges only take one bite of each dish, it's important to stand out and make that bite memorable. But since branching off his own, Brandon was able to focus on high-quality meats seasoned simply and smoked with post oak he trucks in from the Abilene region.

Before word had gotten out about Brantley Creek, sales were slow, so Brandon bottled a line of seasonings and sauces (one original and a sweeter version) he'd developed while competing and began selling them in local grocery stores. But then, as dining rooms shut down during COVID-19, his sales at the truck started to skyrocket. He added more smokers and kept increasing production, but he was still selling out each week, as customers drove from up to several hours away to visit.

The tender smoked meats drawing such attention are a testament to Brandon's fire management skills, because his preparations couldn't be simpler. Using just kosher salt and 16-mesh black pepper as a rub, he produces moist and flavorful turkey, tender and perfectly porky spare ribs, and juicy Prime brisket with a dark, sturdy bark. His chicken has a few more ingredients ("We use my personal blend," says Brandon cryptically) that render the skin super crispy and the meat exquisitely juicy. Brandon started off sourcing his sausage from Miiller's Meat Market and Smokehouse in Llano, and then he took a class from Bill Dumas, the Sausage Sensei (see page 431), to learn how to make his own, eventually developing both an original and a jalapeño link using brisket trim and a little pork.

Ashley, who grew up cooking with her family, developed all the sides. Standouts include an ultra-creamy mac and cheese, robust pinto beans, jalapeño creamed corn, fluffy potato salad, and a crisp tomato-and-cucumber salad. For dessert, Brandon created a banana pudding, and a bread pudding sold only on Saturdays, and they used Ashley's grandpa's recipe to make cake-like apple cobbler, which was such a huge hit they started to make cherry and peach verisions too.

At this point, the McPhersons had more than outgrown their trailer (and become far too familiar with the challenges of operating a food truck in windy West Texas). They began scouting out locations where they could expand into a brick and mortar, and Brandon found the perfect acre of land in east Odessa.

"This spot was bare land, and I came across a deal I could not refuse and built new," he says. "I drew the design on notebook paper."

CANNON
PITS

For those first four years, Brandon had a staff of just four on the trailer (himself, Ashley, and their nephew and niece, Colby and Kylea Johnson). Once they launched the brick and mortar in July 2023, Brantley Creek grew to a staff of 38, with employees working the smokehouse, kitchen, and bar, plus managing their steady stream of catering business. Brandon opened with four 1,000-gallon offset smokers (cheekily named "The Gambler," "High Hopes," "Hard Times," and "Just in Case") built by Cannon Pits and Fabrication out of Granbury, and he has two more currently being built.

"We went from struggling to sell one brisket to selling 60-plus briskets a day!" he says.

More brisket sold means more trim for smashburgers, and Brantley Creek has become a destination for theirs, which come with American or pepper jack cheese, and can be gussied up with bacon and grilled hatch green chiles, onions, or jalapeños. When they sell out of barbecue each day, their smashburgers and sides are available until closing. There's also Texas twinkies (cream cheese–stuffed jalapeños wrapped in bacon and fried), barbecue topped spuds, and loaded nachos piled high on a tray with layers of tortilla chips, smoked brisket, jalapeño sausage, white queso, beans, pickled jalapeños, and drizzles of sweet barbecue sauce. Brantley Creek also offers a few of their own variations of the Frito pie they originally created for a local fair and kept on the menu. The OG BBQ pie can be made with Fritos or hot Cheetos topped with beans, brisket, and barbecue sauce—add a scoop of macaroni and cheese to make it a Mac Daddy.

Brantley Creek's brick and mortar also affords plenty of indoor and outdoor dining space with long glossy picnic tables (and seating for up to 200), big screens to catch the game, Astroturf with cornhole, and a playscape for kids. They host live music just about every weekend, feature a daily happy hour and drink specials, and have hosted outdoor movies, pop-ups, and vendor markets.

"We grew into more than just a place to eat," says Brandon. "Families gather around tables for more than just a meal; they share stories and meet complete strangers. It's become a space where everyone feels like family, [and] our barbecue matches the warmth of the welcoming feel, making us a cornerstone of the neighborhood."

HALLELUJAH! BBQ

There's a lot of incredible talent, and delicious food, represented throughout this book, but only one place is on a mission to change people's lives through barbecue.

Hallelujah! BBQ is a ministry of the Rescue Mission of El Paso, a nonprofit organization founded in 1952. In addition to offering shelter for people experiencing homelessness, Rescue Mission offers a number of other services for those in need, including street outreach for nonresidents, permanent housing for the disabled, a drug and alcohol relapse prevention program, counseling, a temporary shelter for migrants, and job search services and vocational training for those ready to return to the workforce.

Blake Barrow was born and raised in Houston, then attended Baylor University for his undergraduate studies before earning his master of theological studies at Emory University's Candler School of Theology. He returned to Baylor to complete his law degree, and then a job offer at ScottHulse Law Firm brought him out to El Paso in 1988. He was there until 1995, when he opened his own firm. But two years later, he was talking with a fellow lawyer who was on the board of the Rescue Mission. In need of a new CEO, the board had brainstormed 10 attributes they wanted in that candidate, and Barrow's colleague didn't know how they'd ever find such a person. When Barrow realized he checked all the boxes, he decided to quit his successful career as a civil trial lawyer and devote his life to helping people experiencing homelessness.

"It was divine intervention and God's calling," says Barrow. "The voice of the Lord spoke, and I've been at it 27 years now!"

The Rescue Mission created its first vocational rehabilitation program in 1986 with Rescue Industries, a furniture factory that employed people who were homeless. Over 500 people received employment training from Rescue Industries before it closed in 2015, when the buildings were purchased by the Texas Department of Transportation and torn down for the completion of Loop 375.

Barrow considered restarting the program, but decided to take the opportunity to establish an entirely different type of vocational program. A student of backyard barbecue for the last 50 years ("I went to the Culinary School of Hunger," he says), he first started Hallelujah! BBQ as a catering business in 2016, with plans to develop it into a restaurant if it was successful. Over the next several years, he continued to hone his barbecue skills, cooking and serving hundreds of people through catering jobs for the Coronado Baptist Church community.

"A huge advantage of a homeless shelter being the owner of a barbecue restaurant is there is zero waste," says Barrow. Any leftovers from the

restaurant or catered events go to the Rescue Mission Kitchen, which feeds 500 people a day—200 that are housed in the shelter and others who are still living on the streets and served through their Corner of Hope outreach program.

In 2019, Barrow brought on Candace Blanchard, a graduate of El Paso County Behavior and Health Residential Treatment, as manager, and she has been there ever since. In 2020, Rescue Mission began work on a 100-year-old building that would become the future home of Hallelujah! BBQ. The brick structure was used during the early 1900s as a Buffalo Soldier camp, and then served as a shelter for refugees after the Mormon exodus from Mexico, but it had fallen into disrepair for some years before the Rescue Mission purchased it in 2015. With the help of people being served by the organization, Barrow and Blanchard renovated the building and built out the interior, doing everything from repairing the roof to constructing dining room tables. In April 2023, Hallelujah! BBQ opened its doors to the public.

All the employees of Hallelujah! BBQ must have been homeless or lived in the Rescue Mission shelter, and a preference is given to graduates of their drug and alcohol relapse prevention program. Hallelujah! BBQ provides a great source of job training and experience for those who might have difficulty securing employment due to felony records or a lack of documents like Social Security cards or birth certificates. All employees learn proper handling and safety techniques, then procedures for front-of-house service, which Blanchard oversees, or cooking skills to be used in the back of house. Barrow is the pitmaster, which finds him jetting between his office and the kitchen on a Yamaha scooter throughout the day. But now that he's trained a few team members, he no longer needs to show up at 4 a.m. to get the fires going.

Barrow started Hallelujah! BBQ with a reverse flow offset smoker made by Johnson Fabrication. When the business outgrew that, he ordered a vertical smoker from Johnson, followed by another customized vertical smoker. Then he learned about the rotisserie smokers being crafted by M&M BBQ Company (see page 76). He called to inquire about them, but the $30,000 price tag and one-year waiting list were both too much for the nonprofit. So instead Barrow gathered his troops and resources with the idea to build their own. Someone on staff with a passion for welding taught a crew of residents to weld, and together they converted the original vertical smoker into a rotisserie for less than $2,000. Now they can cook briskets that would normally take 11 to 12 hours in just six to seven, which generates dramatic savings in both labor and wood costs (which is especially important, considering Barrow drives 430 miles each way to Menard to pick up five cords of oak every two months). Right now, the crew is in the process of converting the second vertical smoker into a rotisserie that can hold 36 briskets at a time.

Barrow has developed a pepper-forward spice blend, made with cayenne and Anaheim chile peppers, that he uses to rub all the meats (brisket, turkey, bone-in pork loin, pork ribs, and pork butt for pulled pork). The baby back ribs also get some Vermont maple sugar in their rub, and the turkey is injected with a blend of olive oil and maple syrup before it is smoked. The 13 Habaneros sausage is so named because 13 raw habaneros and 18 jalapeños go into every 30-pound batch of ground pork butt, along with red onion, garlic, red bell pepper, fennel, oregano, and mustard seeds.

Fred Johnson, a graduate of Rescue Mission's relapse prevention program who has now been on the kitchen staff for close to a decade, developed the barbecue sauce. Fred's Habanero Sauce, a barbecue sauce with sweet heat, gets mixed into the pulled pork, and is also bottled and sold. Hallelujah! also makes a milder variation as their standard sauce, though El Pasoans are no strangers to spice. Green chiles, which are beloved in this region, appear in several of the homestyle sides: mac and cheese, potatoes au gratin, and tater tot casserole (which is a variation of the recipe from Truth BBQ, see page 121). Blake's Potato Salad gets added zing from red wine vinegar and dill pickle relish, and the coleslaw is studded with fresh pineapple. Both Granny's Green Beans (green beans enhanced with portobello mushrooms, tomatoes, and an unexpected inclusion: Granny Smith apples) and the uniquely complex Brussels sprouts, which are enriched with bacon, cherry tomatoes, and melted pepperjack, and came to Barrow in a dream.

"I was sound asleep, dreaming about food, and I wake up and I can taste it," Barrow remembers. "So I went to the kitchen and made a batch and everybody loved it. So here we are."

David's Beans are named after David Myers, another graduate of the relapse prevention program who is now an employee. Halleljuah's brisket trim finds a home in these pinto beans, which have a kick from red chile and cumin. Myers also developed their cheesecake recipe, and has made variations like blueberry, raspberry, strawberry, pumpkin pecan, key lime, caramel, Death by Chocolate, Oreo cookie, tres leches, and cinnamon bun. Hallelujah! offers two flavors at a time, but Barrow says the next project will involve a bakery program, so they can offer even more desserts, plus bake their own rolls for the restaurant.

"David is exceedingly creative and comes up with new ideas," says Barrow. "We've probably made 20 different cheesecake flavors, and it's the best cheesecake I've ever tasted."

Hallelujah! BBQ's interior remains simple to let the beauty of the historic building shine through. The exposed brick walls display a few simple Texas-centric design elements (a Texas star, a Texas flag, an outline of the state made from license plates). Golden wood floors contrast darker wood tables, each brightened with vintage glass bottles holding fresh flowers and table tents sharing the employees' recovery stories.

There's a dining patio and event space behind the restaurant, brightened by blooming roses and 20-foot storage containers that have been stacked and painted red and blue. Not only do the vivid structures draw attention to Hallelujah! BBQ, but they also serve as outdoor restrooms for customers, another impressive DIY project completed by a Rescue Mission crew. The restaurant continues to create work opportunities, even for those who don't want to go into hospitality. And still others are gaining industry experience while trying a new career on for size.

"This is my first restaurant job that I've had in my whole life, because I used to work construction," says Kenneth Keeder, who has now been on staff at Hallelujah! BBQ for five months. "It has opened my mind to a new experience and it's pretty educational, I would say, because I need to find myself and focus on something. And I work pretty good under pressure, so it's been helping me a lot to maintain myself and stay focused on what I need to do at work."

"We're in the business of rebuilding people," says Barrow. "We love to cook and we love to eat, but it's not about the food—it's about the people. We use the food as a tool to give people like Kenny the opportunity to succeed in life."

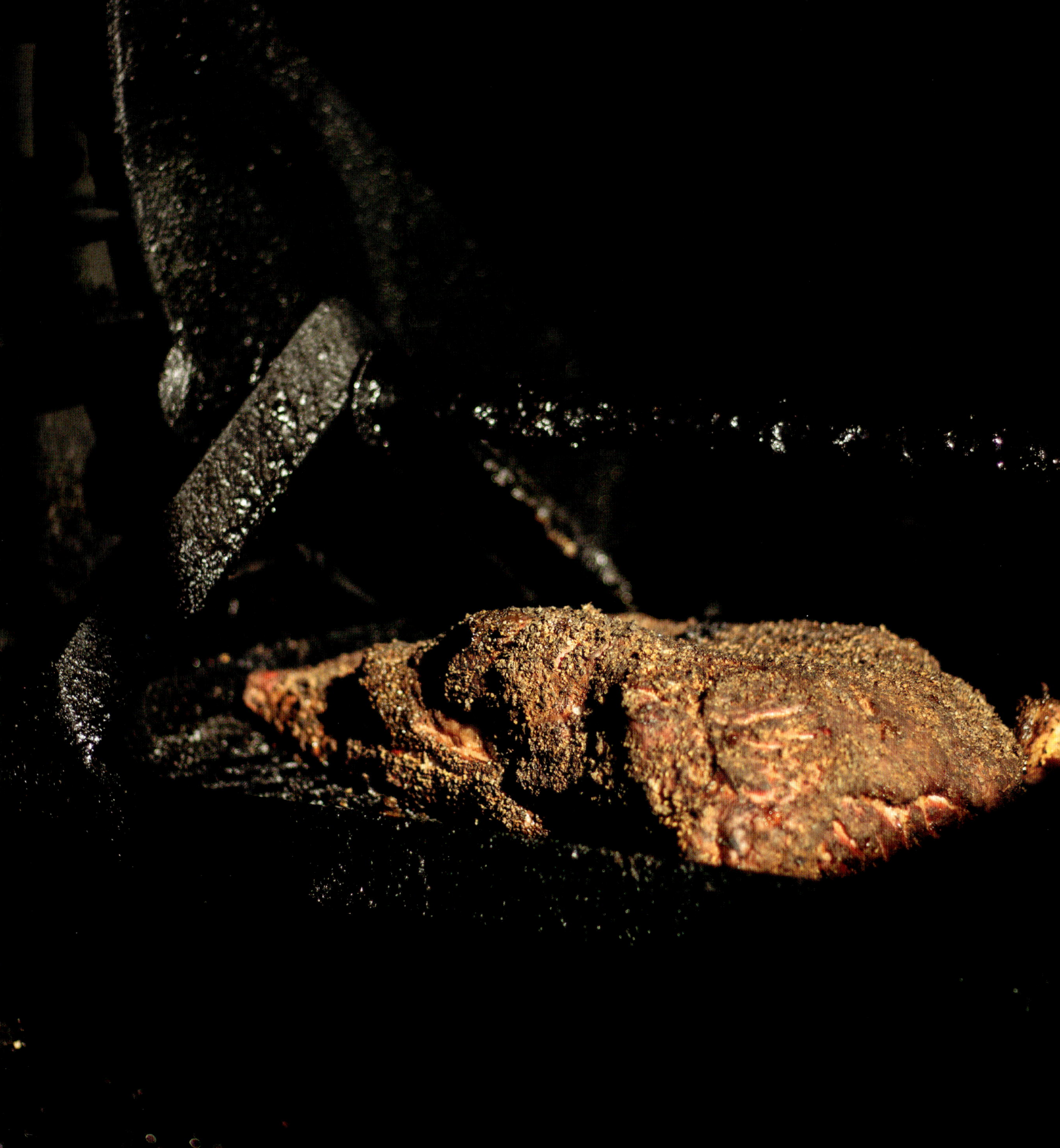

DESERT OAK BARBECUE

EL PASO

As a young boy growing up in Sardinia, Italy, Richard Funk was fascinated by cowboys and all things Western, and he also possessed an innate love for cooking. He grew up watching his mom craft homestyle Italian food, while his dad and uncles cooked over open fires outside. He spent his teenage years in New York before joining the Navy. That brought him to San Diego, which is where he began cooking ("because I needed something a little bit better than Uncle Sam had to offer," he notes). And when Rich finally made it to Texas for the first time—El Paso, to be exact—he knew he'd found his home.

That's where he met Suzanne, a native El Pasoan with a similar passion for food and cooking, who would go on to become his wife. Suzanne began cooking as a teenager, after growing up watching her grandmother prepare things like homemade flour tortillas, tamales, and red enchilada sauce. Richard and Suzanne would often cook together and, when she gifted him with a grill, he became obsessed with cooking over fire. Thus began a years-long study of backyard grilling, smoking, experimentation, and taste-testing, and a seemingly endless quest to achieve the perfect brisket.

When Richard did crack the code on brisket in 2014, he and Suzanne took a barbecue road trip across Texas, stopping at places like Pody's BBQ, Louie

DesertOak
BARBECUE EPTX

Mueller Barbecue (see page 240), and Franklin Barbecue (see page 233 for a profile on founder Aaron Franklin). It was then that they decided they needed to open a place of their own. Richard befriended pitmaster John Lewis, now of Lewis Barbecue, who helped him piece together a 250-gallon offset smoker (appropriately named "Patches") with parts Richard had been collecting from junkyards.

Suzanne and Richard launched their food truck in July 2015, with the help of Suzanne's kids, Steven Ortiz and Alyssa Ruiz. With no telling what the future held, Suzanne continued teaching and Rich kept working as a dental supplies technician and salesman. At first, the truck just featured two meats (brisket and spare ribs) and two sides (pinto beans and coleslaw). And since food trucks hadn't quite taken off yet in El Paso, there were days when it was hard to find a place to park.

Then the owner of El Paso Western outlet Cowtown Boots invited them to park on his event property next door to the store—a breakthrough that could almost be perceived as divine intervention for Richard, the lifelong lover of Western wear. (The owners even gifted him a custom pair of alligator boots with the Desert Oak Barbecue logo on them!) In 2017, they moved into a 7,500-square-foot space that used to house the boot factory. Locals started discovering what soon came to be known as the best barbecue in El Paso—Central Texas–style barbecue, to be exact. Since post oak is not native to the El Paso area, Richard pays a premium for 12 cords every eight weeks, and he keeps a forklift on-site to transport the pallets off the semi.

That wood is key to the gentle smoke flavors infusing Richard's Certified Angus Beef Prime brisket which, also in line with Central Texas tradition, is rubbed with just kosher salt and 16-mesh black pepper. His beef ribs, a popular weekend special, get granulated garlic in addition to the salt and pepper, and a red wine vinegar spritz helps maintain moisture once they are wrapped in butcher paper. Pork shoulder, which becomes pulled pork, and spare ribs receive a more complex rub of salt, pepper, granulated onion, granulated garlic, and chili powder. Turkey soaks in a house brine for 24 hours before it is rubbed with extra-virgin olive oil and 16-mesh black pepper and smoked.

Richard and his brother-in-law Caleb created the housemade sausage using brisket and pork shoulder trimmings, plus beef fat. It is packed with layers of flavor and heat, thanks to 10 ingredients, including red pepper, turmeric, and granulated garlic. Desert Oak also became known for their "stuffed" potatoes—massive baked potatoes they open, smash, and stuff with smoked meats and accouterments. The El Paso Potato is the signature item, layered with butter, salt and pepper, cheese, your choice of meat, sour cream, chives, beans, and a toreado (blistered jalapeño).

Desert Oak serves pretty traditional takes on their pinto beans, creamy mac and cheese, and mustardy potato salad, but puts an El Paso–inspired spin on a few of the other sides. Suzanne was so impressed with the green chile cheese pozole they had at Pody's BBQ, she created a green chile cheese rice in its honor.

"[When Suzanne] suggested green chile cheese rice and I said, 'Absolutely not! We are not going to serve rice out of our barbecue trailer.'" remembers Richard. "But when she made the rice and had me taste it, it blew my mind. She won that argument, and it has been our top-selling side ever since."

Green chiles also dot the creamed corn as well, and the coleslaw is very unique: El Pasoans prefer theirs creamy and sweet, with chunks of pineapple in it.

"The folks out here won't touch coleslaw if it doesn't have pineapple in it," says Richard. "I thought it was strange the first time I ate it, but I decided to keep an open mind and it grew on me. I really enjoy it now."

In addition to meats by the pound, plate, or sandwich, Desert Oak offers a build-your-own-bowl option more barbecue joints should employ. They also make smoked chicken wings, nachos, and a brisket double smashburger with a cult following. And there's a green salad on the menu, which is always refreshing to see on offer. The Cobb salad is a delightful medley of contrasting flavors: smoked turkey, ricotta, bacon crumbles, diced tomato, pickled peppers, and housemade Green Goddess dressing.

Positive reviews in *Texas Monthly* and their local paper helped Desert Oak to continue to grow, and soon they were being featured on shows like *America's Test Kitchen* and the Food Network's *Diners, Drive-ins and Dives*. And landing on *Texas Monthly's* Top 50 list in 2021 really sealed the deal. These days, Richard fills four 1,000-gallon offset smokers each day (his original, Patches, two from Circle T Smokers, and a fourth from Austin Smoke Works.) He also built a bigger food trailer, currently parked at the NEEP (Northeast El Paso) Collective, where he serves a version of the Desert Oak Barbecue menu, with a focus on stuffed potatoes, brunch specials, and locally roasted coffee.

Desert Oak has more plans in the pipeline, and Richard thanks the entire family for their continued growth. Suzanne provides oversight for the original recipes and works with the chef and kitchen manager on quality control. Alyssa, a trained barista, launched Desert Oak's coffee and brunch operations, and handles social media and a heavy load of administrative responsibilities, like payroll and point of sale. And Richard says it is thanks to Stephen, a fastidious number cruncher, that management is organized like it never has been before.

"[He] put systems in place that make our restaurant run like a real business," says Richard. "He runs the operation now, but he has turned it into something that practically runs itself."

BRICK VAULT BREWERY & BARBECUE

MARATHON

Phillip Moellering's passion for barbecue developed at a young age, and he started honing his craft by spending time watching his grandfather, father, and uncles at the pits. He first learned how to cook using direct heat, and mastered his family's sausage recipe, passed down through five generations. After graduating from Texas A&M with a degree in Business Administration, he moved to the tiny West Texas town of Marathon, (which currently has a population of 427) to work at the historic Gage Hotel, making his way from manager to food & beverage director to operations director over the course of a decade.

In April 2018, Moellering channeled his years of barbecue know-how into a new Gage concept, located in a building just across the street from the hotel. The building was constructed in 1886 as an old mercantile, then turned into a Gulf filling station in 1939, and had most recently been a bar called the Famous Burro until Gage Hotel owner J. P. Bryan purchased it. Brick Vault Brewery & Barbecue got its name from the old brick vault still in place from the building's mercantile days. Now, Moellering uses it to smoke house-cured bacon and charcuterie in, while two 1,000-gallon Mill Scale Metalworks offset smokers transform the rest of the meat he sources from 44 Farms and 1855 Black Angus Beef. Post oak and live oak (which Moellering says has a similar flavor profile to post oak, but a cleaner burn), both harvested from his family's Fredericksburg land, provide the smoke.

Gulf Oil signage pays homage to Brick Vault's run as a filling station, and a wall of bright blue-paned windows (in place of the former garage door) welcomes in plenty of sunlight. The brewpub, where brewer Amy Oxenham dreams up and produces her latest creations, is visible through glass windows in the back. Oxenham collaborates often with other brewers and growers, and crafts brews using local herbs, fruits, and even hops, which are very tough to find in Texas. Since everything's a hit, opt for a flight so you can try pairing different beers (from the aromatic Golden West Belgian Witbier to the nutty, malty Captain Shepherd's Pecan Porter) with the barbecue.

Smoked proteins can be ordered by the pound, sandwich, or as one-, two- or three-meat plates with sides. The CPO is one of their more composed sandwiches, a perfect balance of succulent and touch-sweet pulled pork topped with bright, herby cabbage-kale slaw, and crispy onion strings on a pillowy potato bun. Their thick-cut slices of brisket have a rosy smoke ring, well rendered fat, and a pleasantly sturdy bark. The turkey, which was sliced a bit thinner than the brisket, also has a dark, well-defined bark, a quality which seemed to lock in moisture and flavor. Brick Vault offers two types of barbecue sauce: one darker iteration, which is sweeter and molasses-based, and another reddish and more piquant mustard-based sauce. The pinto-based borracho beans are jazzed up with bacon, jalapeños, and spices, and the creamy, comforting mac and cheese had a very subtle hint of spice from green chiles—and can easily be made spicier with the addition of pickled jalapeños. Pickled red onions and a housemade sweet-and-spicy habanero pickle are also at the ready.

If you think you don't have room for dessert . . . think again. Brick Vault's exceptional banana pudding is composed of thick, vanilla-flecked, banana-infused custard, housemade vanilla wafers, a drizzle of salted caramel, and a cloud of whipped cream that is also speckled with vanilla. You might even want to get an extra one for the road; it makes for an excellent breakfast before a hike in nearby Big Bend National Park.

ACKNOWLEDGMENTS

This book has been a labor of love, and I couldn't have done it without a number of incredible people.

I'd like to thank the many pitmasters and professionals who generously shared their time and knowledge with me as I traversed the state of Texas researching this book. It has been truly humbling and awe-inspiring to see firsthand how much grit and devotion goes into perfecting this craft, and to witness the deep-rooted traditions that fuel the barbecue culture in Texas. Their willingness to open their pits, share their stories, and offer invaluable insight has made this book possible.

I'm so grateful for the loved ones who have been so supportive as I embarked on an all-consuming barbecue journey for the last couple years. In particular, I'd like to thank Eric Scott, whose encouragement and understanding (not to mention willingness to eat an unreasonable amount of barbecue leftovers!) has been a constant source of relief and motivation for me throughout this project.

I'd also like to extend my gratitude to the team at HarperCollins, particularly my editor Matthew Doucet, for giving me the time and space needed for this ambitious undertaking. Your patience and support allowed this book to take shape in ways I never could have imagined. I am also deeply grateful to the photographers and designers who brought the pages of this book to life, ensuring that the heart and soul of Texas barbecue are fully captured.

Finally, to the barbecue lovers, both seasoned and new, who continue to keep this tradition alive and thriving—I hope this book does justice to the individuals, flavors, and stories that make Texas barbecue a true cultural treasure.

IMAGE CREDITS

Pages 4, 8, 116, 118, 119, 166, 243, 267, 308–309, 508 Ben Sassani; Pages 6–7, 11, 291, 326, 329, 331, 402–403, 404, 405, 406, 407, 454, and 456 Ben Yanto; Pages 9, 12, 232, 234, and 237 Franklin Barbecue and Wyatt McSpadden; Pages 14, 68, 70–71, 72, 73, 74–75, 80–81, 83, and 84–85 Kathy Tran; Pages 16–17 and 19 Goldee's Barbecue; Pages 22 and 25 Panther City BBQ; Pages 26, 29, and 145 Daniel Vaughn; Pages 30, 310, 444, and 509 Veronica Meewes; Pages 36, 38–39, and 41 Zavala's Barbecue; Page 43 Sean Welch; Page 44 Jeremy Brand; Pages 46 and 48 Smoke-A-Holics BBQ; Pages 51, 52, and 55 Heim Barbecue; Pages 56–57 Brix Barbecue; Pages 60–61, 62, and 63 Sabar BBQ; Pages 64, 66, and 67 Dayne's Craft Barbecue; Page 74 Hutchins Barbeque; Pages 76, 138, and 141 Bar-A-BBQ; Pages 86, 88, and 89 Smoke'n Ash BBQ; Pages 92–93 and 96–97 Stanley's Famous Pit Barbecue and Nick Pencis; Page 98 Chief Firewood; Pages 90, 104, 105, 106, 108, and 109 1701 Barbecue; Pages 110, 115, and 297 Joseph McGregor; Page 112 Blood Bros BBQ; Pages 120–121, 122, 124, and 125 Truth BBQ; Pages 130 and 132 Houston Edge Works; Pages 134 and 137 Tejas Chocolate + Barbecue and Scott Moore Jr.; Pages 142–143 Bodacious Bar-B-Q; Page 144 Nancy Lindsey; Pages 147 and 148 Sunbird Barbecue; Pages 152–153 and 154 (top and bottom) Mimsy's Craft Barbecue & Steak-house; Page 154 (middle) Vyvy Nguyen; Pages 155, 156, 157, 158, and 159 Martin's Place; Pages 160, 162, 163, and 164 Khói Barbecue; Page 169 Harlem Road Texas BBQ; Page 171 Gatlin's BBQ; Page 172 Conor Moran; Pages 178, 180, and 182–183 Pizzitola's Bar-B-Cue; Pages 185, 186–187, 189, and 190–191 Feges BBQ; Pages 194–195 Ally Hardgrave; Pages 196, 198, and 200–201 Killen's Barbecue; Pages 204–205, 207, 208, 209, and 210–211 Redbird BBQ; Pages 213, 214, and 215 Patillo's Barbeque; Page 221 Robert Jacob Lerma; Pages 224, 227, and 229 Corkscrew BBQ; Page 239 Franklin Barbecue; Pages 241, 244, and 246 Louie Mueller Barbecue; Pages 248, 251, 252, 254, 255, and 256 (top) la Barbecue; Page 256 (bottom) John Pingry; Pages 259 and 262–263 Leroy and Lewis Barbecue and Taylor Gorman; Pages 230, 270–271, 275 (top), and 277 Micklethwait Craft Meats; Pages 272 and 275 (middle and bottom) Michael Easthope-Cates; Page 276 Nicole McCrary; Pages 278, 280, 281, 283, 284, and 285 InterStellar BBQ; Page 286 Jay Baltiera; Page 287 David Back; Pages 294, 296, 298, and 301 Kreuz Market; Pages 300, 303, and 352–353 John Whalen Jr.; Page 304 Scott Slusher; Page 313 Snow's BBQ; Pages 322 and 324 Brisket Country and M. Brady Clark; Pages 334 and 337 Cooper's Old Time Pit Bar-B-Que; Pages 338–339, 340, 342–343, and 345 Miller's Smokehouse; Pages 347, 348, and 351 Southside Market & Barbeque; Pages 354 and 357 The Original Black's Barbecue; Pages 361 and 362–363 Terry Black's Barbecue; Pages 366, 367, and 368 Rollin Smoke BBQ; Pages 370–371 and 374 Mum Foods Smokehouse & Delicatessen; Pages 376–377 Geoff Duncan; Pages 378, 382, and 383 KG BBQ; Pages 384–385, 386, and 388–389 Stiles Switch BBQ and Brew; Pages 390–391, 392, and 394–395 Smitty's Market; Pages 396, 398, 399, and 400 City Market; Pages 410, 411, and 412 Victorian's Barbecue; Page 414 Guess Family Barbecue; Pages 418–419, 420, and 423 Helberg Barbecue; Pages 424, 458–459, 460, and 463 GW's BBQ Catering Co.; Pages 426, 428, and 430 2M Smokehouse; Pages 432, 434, and 435 Bill Dumas; Pages 436 and 439 Burnt Bean Co.; Pages 441 and 442 Matt Dixon; Pages 448, 451, and 483 Mark Champion; Pages 464 and 466 Lupe Nevarez and LaVaca BBQ; Pages 468, 469, 470, 471, 472, and 473 Butter's BBQ; Pag-es 474, 502–503, 504, and 507 Desert Oak Barbecue; Pages 476, 477, 478, and 481 Tom Perini and Perini Ranch Steakhouse; Pages 488–489, 491, and 492 Brantley Creek Barbecue; Pages 495, 496, 499, 500, and 501 Hallelujah! BBQ.

About Cider Mill Press Book Publishers

Good ideas ripen with time. From seed to harvest, Cider Mill Press brings fine reading, information, and entertainment together between the covers of its creatively crafted books. Our Cider Mill bears fruit twice a year, publishing a new crop of titles each spring and fall.

"Where Good Books Are Ready for Press"

501 Nelson Place
Nashville, Tennessee 37214

cidermillpress.com